RURAL VERMONT

A Program for the Future

By

Two Hundred Vermonters

The Vermont Commission on Country Life
Burlington, 1931

FREE PRESS PRINTING CO., BURLINGTON, VT.

PREFACE

THIS volume on Rural Vermont has been prepared by Vermonters for Vermonters. Its chapters have been submitted to the Commission by sixteen committees and two individuals, all of whom during the past three years have worked faithfully in studying our resources and our problems. Their reports taken together constitute the starting point for further thinking as the basis for future action. It is confidently believed that specific projects will result, vitally related to the welfare of the state. In behalf of the Vermont Commission on Country Life we accept these reports, and desire to express our keen appreciation of the self-sacrificing service which these men and women have rendered to our state. We desire also to join them in thanking the various cooperating agencies and the many people throughout the state who have helped by giving first-hand information and seasoned opinions. They have played an invaluable part in the preparation of this volume. We hope this will be only the beginning of their cooperation in a constructive program for Vermont. We accept these reports with thanks to everyone who has in any way helped in their preparation. We present them in this volume to the people of Vermont and recommend that they be read and meditated upon in the interest of a sanely progressive future for our beloved state.

The Executive Committee:

JOHN E. WEEKS,
Chairman,
WILLIAM H. DYER,
Vice-Chairman,
GUY W. BAILEY,
Treasurer,
H. F. PERKINS,
Secretary,
MRS. RICHARD AVERILL,
THOMAS BRADLEE,
MRS. H. K. BROOKS,
C. F. DALTON,
C. H. DEMPSEY,
H. E. LUCE.

TABLE OF CONTENTS

I

INTRODUCTION

For more than a century, Vermont has been one of the most reliable seedbeds of our national life. In the present generation an extraordinary number of her sons and daughters have risen to positions of distinguished service. How may the fertility of this seedbed be maintained and how may the quality of the human stock be conserved are questions which rightfully command the attention of the leaders of today in the Green Mountain State. The Vermont Commission on Country Life is a manifestation of statesman-like interest in these questions.

The plan to organize the Vermont Commission on Country Life was brought forward by Prof. H. F. Perkins of the University of Vermont in the summer of 1927. Two years earlier he had organized the Eugenics Survey. The work in Eugenics led to the conviction that a comprehensive survey of the factors influencing life in Vermont was essential to the understanding of the human forces which make for progress in the state. Thus, the center of interest from the beginning was in the people. The interest in land utilization, agriculture, forestry, and summer residence was in the background. This interest in the people was not centered primarily upon their economic welfare but upon the preservation and further development of those qualities which have made the Green Mountain State so powerful a factor in the life of the nation. The health, the education, the religion, and the recreation of rural people were to be studied from the standpoint of their influence upon the quality of the life in the farm and village homes, their outlook and their ideals.

The sources of income were studied in the belief that possession of the basic necessities and comforts of life is essential if people are to develop the best that is in them. But while income is of very great importance, major attention is here focused upon the values which cannot be measured in gold. The deepest yearnings of the Vermonter are for things which money cannot buy. In the work of the Vermont Commission on Country Life, "the starting point and the objective point is man."

1

The fear had been expressed by certain Vermonters that the people were becoming complacent, that there was danger of their drifting unawares into channels which in future years would be recognized as below the level expected of Vermonters. In this regard, Vermont may have been in less danger than many other states, not to mention the nation as a whole, but it is significant that the Green Mountain State is conscious of this danger and has been the first to use the methods of scientific planning exemplified in the following pages as a means of insuring progress. Whatever may have been the misgivings when the work of planning for the Vermont Commission began, they have since been dispelled. The great flood of November, 1927, and the magnificent response to the call for concerted effort awakened in Vermonters a fuller sense of their power and gave them a new impulse which will be felt through the years. Fortunate it was that the development of the work of the Vermont Commission on Country Life synchronized with this new impulse.

The Vermont Commission on Country Life was organized in April, 1928. It was made up of about three hundred progressive citizens of the state. The chairman, ex-Governor John E. Weeks, has defined progressives as those who strive for "the furtherance of present ideals in life and the ideals which may grow out of our activities." This is a dynamic concept. It gives recognition to the process of evolution; it gives warning that the goals toward which we are now striving will not satisfy us when attained; it promises the challenge of new ideals.

The immediate purpose of the Commission is that of scientific planning for action leading towards higher goals. Scientific planning consists in gathering facts, sifting them, and meditating upon them until their significance is clearly seen in their true relation to the everyday life of a forward-looking people. The clarified mental pictures which result from this deeper study of the facts of life in their varied and complex relations make possible the setting up of useful plans. A vision of the possibilities gives new courage. The execution of well-laid plans makes that courage fruitful.

A score of committees have worked for more than two years. Some of these committees have been administrative in function, but sixteen committees and two individuals have prepared statements of fact and recommendation which make up the content of this volume on Rural Vermont. The men and women on these committees have worked without compensation, often at great personal sacrifice, in order to make contributions to the common cause of the coming Vermont.

They have raised and attempted to answer many questions. What are the facts, pleasant and unpleasant, about Vermont people? In what measure can the shifts and substitutions of the population be interpreted as progressive steps and in what measure do these changes raise serious questions regarding the future of Vermont? How may the best elements and qualities in the basic human stocks be conserved and improved? How do topography, soil and climate affect their development? What do fundamental economic conditions indicate as to the trend of future development in agriculture and the rural people? How can farmers secure a better market for their products? What further contributions can the forests and the woodworking industries make to life in rural Vermont? Are there areas where it is hopeless to try to support a rural community?

What bearing does the change in home conditions have on the development of Vermonters? Has community activity declined, and, if so, what has been the effect on the people? How have different family stocks differed in their support of community activities? What of rural government? In what ways has it been a help or a hindrance in rural life? What are desirable developments in this line? Do the people of Vermont use their citizenship with a due sense of responsibility or has there been an ebbing of interest in public affairs? If so, what has been the cause? Does the opportunity for occupation in village and city industries draw people undesirably from the land? How does it change the character of the rural population? Are summer visitors an economic asset? If so, are they a social and moral asset as well? What is the effect of their presence on the quality of the life of Vermonters? Is the answer to these questions the same for all classes of summer visitors? If not, which classes should be encouraged to come?

Have inadequate or poor facilities for promoting the well-being of the people been responsible for changes in the nature and distribution of our population? How has the shortage of doctors in the country affected population shifts? Do people leave because the doctors aren't there or do the doctors leave because of lack of demand for their services? How can medical care best be provided for those who remain scattered over the hills? Have schools been a leading force or a drag on life in the rural areas? How can they be made to contribute

most effectively their share to the richness of the life of the people?
Are there "pockets of degeneracy" hidden among our hills? How can
the people of the state perform to best advantage their duty toward
handicapped children? How can the lives of the blind, mentally defective and other handicapped persons be made as cheerful and useful
as possible? How can this portion of the population be kept at a
minimum in the future? What can be planned for the wise administration of gifts and bequests made for the welfare of rural people?
Are rural communities making the most of the recreational possibilities
of their environment? How can recreation be made to add more to
the richness of life? What measures should be taken to conserve the
recreational and æsthetic opportunities offered by the fish, game and
wild life of the state?

Are the churches performing their duty to the people? Are the
people performing their duty to the churches? What are the best
ways of fostering and promoting the spiritual life? What have been
Vermont's contributions to the æsthetic and cultural life of the nation?
Are Vermonters awake to the finer values in our traditions and ideals?
How may these traditions and ideals be conserved and passed on to
future generations?

Such are the questions for which the committees of the Vermont
Commission on Country Life have been seeking answers. In approaching these problems they have recognized that times have changed and
that the conditions of life are ever changing, that these changes have
wrought countless links which connect Vermont with the rest of the
world, that the achievements of others can give many suggestions and
much inspiration, and that the resources and advantages at hand should
be fully appraised and appreciated as the starting point for further
progress.

While it was recognized that a large share of the facts needed in
answering questions and planning for the future were matters of common knowledge among the leaders in the various fields of thought and
action, it was also recognized that research work by trained workers
was essential in securing the more obscure facts which supplemented
this knowledge. Much of this detailed material does not appear in the
present volume. Some of this will be published by cooperating
agencies, the remainder will be in the custody of the University of
Vermont and available under proper safeguards to students of the
problems to which the facts relate. The committees have drawn from

the reports of research workers the facts essential to verify or correct their general impressions, but their conclusions are based upon the old as well as the new information, and are the product of the group thinking of Vermonters.

While Vermonters are strongly individualistic—independent in thought and action—yet, as a people, they are coherent and capable of working together. They live their own lives, knowing that others prize and choose a different course. They are a spirited people. They meet the challenge when obstacles stand in their pathway, but they do not let others mark the goals toward which they strive. The motto of the state, *Freedom and Unity,* is exemplified to a marked degree in the life of the people. Freedom and unity are both possible only when the people are of one mind. The ideas evolved by the group thinking of a free people, when based upon a thorough understanding of all the facts and conditions, will be so tempered with common sense that while pointing toward far-reaching changes through the future years, they will not be out of harmony with a moderately progressive present. Under these conditions, freedom leads to unity in thought and harmony in action. Thus have freedom and unity lived on together in Vermont for a century and a half. They stand apart as the arms of the balances, yet in the life of Vermont they have stood together in equilibrium like the symbol of justice. May the people of Vermont ever conserve that which is best in freedom and that which is best in unity while continuing "the furtherance of present ideals in life and the ideals which may grow out of our activities!" This is the aspiration of the Vermont Commission on Country Life.

HENRY C. TAYLOR,
Director.

II

VERMONT

A Comment[1]

By WENDELL PHILLIPS STAFFORD

Vermonters have always had a way of cutting their garment according to their cloth. It has never been their habit to build their chimneys by laying the top brick first. Their corner stones have often been laid with prayer and grim determination, but it is only the capstone that is put on with shoutings. So now. In this effort to which you have pledged yourselves you have adopted a method in perfect keeping with such traits and habits. You have a serious business before you, and you have gone about it in a business-like way, first making as sure as possible of your facts. Your aim being to build up a greater and better Vermont, you have patiently and thoroughly examined the condition of things as they are, seeking to find wherein improvement is most needed, and the chance of success most promising.

In the next place, you are taking up the task in the right spirit. Between a saint and a sinner the chief difference has been said to be this, that a saint knows and feels that he is a sinner. Socrates said that if the oracle had picked him out for the wisest of men, it must have been because he, Socrates, knew that he knew nothing. Michelangelo, when he was well on towards ninety, was seen hurrying along a street in Florence, one day, and was asked: "Where are you going so fast this morning, Master?" And he answered without stopping: "Going to school to see if I can't learn something." A conceited young man may make us smile, but a conceited old man must make the angels weep. Now Vermont is an old state, as states in this country go. At any rate, it is old enough to have acquired a character of its own, and a character that has come to be recognized of all men. The traditions and ideals of Vermont turn our attention to the past, and also to the future. Our traditions come out of our past. Our ideals are manifested by our past, but they also beckon us to the future. A President of the United States, when he was urged to appoint a certain

[1]This comment is a part of an address prepared by Justice Stafford to be delivered at the general session of the Commission, June 17, 1931.

6

man to a high judicial office, asked: "Does he look this way?" (to the front) "or this way?" (back, over his shoulders). Well, a good judge looks both ways, and so does a statesman. He looks to the past for the lessons of experience, and for the inspiration of great examples. He looks to the future as the field where his work must be done, and where his hopes may be fulfilled. I speak in this way because the work to which you have set your hand is really a work of statesmanship. That may seem at first too ambitious a name, but I believe the statement will bear analysis. When representative men and women come together from almost every community in the state, to consider seriously the most practical matters affecting the welfare of their own neighborhoods and of the whole commonwealth, when they are listening to the reports of competent committees that have made a first-hand study of present conditions, when they are asking themselves and one another, what can be done to improve the health of the people, to repair the waste places, to give the most remote inhabitants better means of communication, information, opportunities for recreation and self-improvement, when they are studying out ways of making the most beautiful scenery in New England known to all men, when they are looking into all the resources of the state, physical, mental and spiritual, with the purpose of fuller use and higher development, and finally when they are pledging themselves to unselfish cooperation for the common good, they really are, whether they call it so or not, dealing with problems of statesmanship. It is not always by being elected to office, nor even by making new laws, that such problems are best to be solved. After all, laws and institutions are only the expression of the supposed beliefs and sentiments of the people, and they are feeble and ineffective unless they are charged with the dynamic power of purpose and conviction. A great orator of a former generation was wont to say that we are not governed by statutes and institutions, we are governed by men and penny newspapers, and the office holder, he said, may be like the manikin in the show-window—he seems to be turning the coffee-mill, whereas in fact the mill is turning him.

What Vermont has already contributed to the upbuilding of the nation has been a favorite theme, and it has not been overlooked by your committees. Figures have been arrayed to prove that, out of all proportions to her size and wealth, she has had her hand in business, in war, in studies and professions, in the making and execution of the laws. Her vigorous blood has made its pulse felt through all

the arteries of the Republic; and it is there you must look to find the
greater Vermont in our first century and a half of existence. We
would not have had it otherwise. And yet we cannot help wondering
what Vermont would have been like if all this energy and intelligence
had been kept at home. Some loss there would have been. Some
never would have come to their full stature here for lack of opportunities; and here at home the struggle for survival, Yankee against
Yankee, would have been fierce indeed. But when all allowances have
been made, who can doubt that there would have been seen here a development to challenge the attention of the world? Something like that
is what we dream of for the future. The cry is no longer, westward ho!
but *Vermont* for the Vermonters. Earnest men and women are saying
now: "Here between the Bay State and the Province, between the
long bright river and the azure lake, we will build that Greater
Vermont." Greater in what? Greater, for one thing, in a fuller development of her natural resources. We mean that every mine shall
give up its treasure, every quarry shall open its primeval corridors to
the sun, every sleeping giant in our unused water courses shall be
wakened and put to work; our forests shall be fended, our fields shall
be fed, that they, in turn, may feed the "hungry generations." We
mean to be husbands and not ravishers of the land, that her fruitful
womb may never know sterility. And we mean to make this labor so
attractive that the children shall not be lured away as the fathers were,
but turn with eager eyes and hands to the realm around their doors.
We mean to knit and lace the state together with the best roadways
in the world—roads that feel like velvet, and stand like adamant, and
stretch away like a satin ribbon in the shade and sun. And over these
shall come seekers of health and beauty, drinking in from many land-
scapes the enchanted draught that leaves the gazer restless and unsatis-
fied until he can return. And so we mean to guard with jealous care
the nobility and freshness of our scenery. Here is that wealth that
never can be exhausted but by our own stupidity.

Of Vermont have many books been written, many pictures painted,
many songs sung. Yet who shall say that he has ever really seen
Vermont. She cannot be seen or described. She can only be suggested. The history of a hundred and fifty years is in the name.
When you hear it you see the pioneer pushing his way through the
interminable forest. You see his cabin in the clearing, and his wife
sitting on the door-stone as the night comes down, listening to the baying

of the wolves, or the long, quavering wail of the catamount. Vermont is Allen at Fort Ti, and Warner at Bennington, and Stannard at Gettysburg. It is Proctor rising in the Senate and speaking the quiet word, which, as a whisper may dislodge an avalanche, launches war and drives Spain from her last American possession. It is the Oregon ploughing her way up through the world of waters, ready to fight a whole navy at a minute's notice. It is the boys of a later day, only yesterday it seems, fighting the new battle of freedom in a land beyond the sea. Oh, yes, there is plenty of grit and iron in the name, but there is infinite tenderness in it, too—the delicate beauty of unnumbered springtimes, the flaming glory of unnumberd autumns. The straggling gray stone wall, the hillside orchard, the red schoolhouse by the busy-grown road, the slender white steeple among the clustering elms—all these swim up before us when we hear the name, Vermont.

It is always a perilous thing to let a Vermonter get started on the subject of Vermont. A lover is never so happy as when he is praising his mistress, or listening to her praises on the lips of others. We who were born and reared in her own haunts drew in this love with our mothers' milk and those of us who knew her at first only from our fathers, through tradition, history, poetry, romance, or who came to her in later years, we too pay her the homage that belongs to her. There is something noble and elevating in a love like this because it is unselfish through and through.

> "The love that no return doth crave
> To knightly level lifts the slave."

We do not look to her for honors or rewards. Many who love her best will never see her face again except in dreams; but that can make no difference. We know she still is there, and *will* be there, "far on in summers that we shall not see." We know that each returning spring will dress her in the same wild robe of loveliness and make the same glad music round her feet. She will be looking out upon the same bright rushing rivers and blue, limpid lakes. Mansfield and Camel's Hump and Killington will still be shouldering up against the sky, and Champlain will catch the sunset in his bosom and hold it for one golden hour that turns the valley into fairyland. We have no quarrel with the children of other states, and yet we always feel there is no other quite like HER.

III

THE PEOPLE OF VERMONT

What is happening to the old Vermont stock? While the population of the state increased from 314,120 in 1850 to 359,611 in 1930 or about 14 percent, more than 176 Vermont towns had significantly smaller population in 1930 than in 1850. Most of these show a continuous decline, and many have lost well over half their former population. In 1850, more than 60 percent of our towns contained more than 1,000 people; in 1930 fewer than 40 percent of them were of that size.

There is no wonder that concern has been expressed for the future of the state and its hardy pioneer stock. This concern led to the organization in 1925 of the Eugenics Survey of Vermont under the auspices of the University of Vermont. It was supported by funds contributed by Vermonters who believe in the state and its possibilities for developing a higher type of citizens. Its purpose was to gather information, as full and accurate as possible, that can be used for social betterment in the state.

The first study was made with a view to securing as expeditiously and economically as possible significant facts in regard to hereditary trends in Vermont families. Because the records of institutions and welfare groups were the only ones available, the early investigations had to do exclusively with individuals whose misfortunes had brought them in contact with these bodies. The second year's work saw this material supplemented by the contribution of the National Committee for Mental Hygiene, which made thorough psychological studies in sample rural schools. The third year of the Survey brought a very great growth in the scope of the work. The study of defectives was extended into the better branches of their families, a study of "key families" was begun, and the Vermont Commission on Country Life was organized.

Besides a continuation of most of this work in 1929-30, two new studies were made. One was an investigation of the relation between delinquency and mental deficiency in the people of the Rutland Reformatory. The other was a study of the "waiting list" of the Brandon State School, with the purpose of finding out how these young people were adjusting themselves in their communities. The major enterprise of the Eugenics Survey in its fifth year was a study of emigration from the rural communities of Vermont, with a view to ascertaining its effect upon the quality of the stock of those remaining.

In all of its work since the beginning of the comprehensive survey by the Vermont Commission on Country Life the Eugenics Survey has operated as an integral part of that Commission. Its detailed findings have been published in the form of annual reports and its main conclusions are embodied in the present volume—in this chapter and in the chapter on the Care of the Handicapped. In addition to the findings of the Eugenics Survey the Committee has had at its disposal the material secured by special field studies of population shifts, made by trained investigators under its supervision. Publications of the United States Census Bureau have also been used.

Early Vermonters

The people who first settled Vermont, in the middle and latter part of the eighteenth century, were chiefly of English origin. Coming largely from Massachusetts, Connecticut and New Hampshire where their families had already for two or three generations been accustomed to the rigors of pioneer life, they were admirably fitted to make homes for themselves in the dense wilderness which then covered this state. By 1790, the population numbered 85,425 of which the English element constituted about 81,200 and the Scotch element about 2,600. The growth of the state since that time is indicated by the following table:

TABLE 1. GROWTH OF POPULATION IN VERMONT

Year	Population	Percent increase
1790	85,425	....
1800	154,465	80.8
1810	217,895	41.1
1820	235,981	8.3
1830	280,652	18.9
1840	291,948	4.0
1850	314,120	7.6
1860	315,098	0.3
1870	330,551	4.9
1880	332,286	0.5
1890	332,422	less than 0.1
1900	343,641	3.4
1910	355,956	3.6
1920	352,428	—1.0
1930	359,611	2.0

It will be noted that the early decades show rapid growth in the population of the state, while since 1850 only in one decade has a gain of more than 4 percent been made.

Most of the early settlers brought with them a few head of live-stock and started farming. Each family was very nearly self-sufficing but soon, of course, local industries and trades connected with farming sprang up. There were blacksmith shops and gristmills, sawmills and tanneries. Almost every village had its general store. With improved communication and the development of machines, creameries, cheese factories, and butter-tub factories were established. Schools and churches were also important elements in community life. Already villages were becoming small industrial and trade centers for the regions surrounding them. In the period from 1830 to 1850 most Vermont towns reached the peak of their development.

One town now having a population of less than 1,000 is thus described in the report for 1930 of the Eugenics Survey:

Between 1812 and 1830 the town grew rapidly so that even before 1850 it had reached the highest period of development with a population of nearly 1,700 At this time, besides the four sawmills, there were several distilleries and two tanneries. In the one village in the town were two general stores. There were four active church societies. An academy for secondary education flourished and drew its students from long distances. Though every farm family was self-sufficient there was a strong sense of community life and members of the old families took keen interest in politics, religion and education.

The same source describes the present life in the town as follows:

Instead of keeping up the old local activities the interest of the people has centered more in the nearby city so that the town has become something like a suburb to that city. Most of its people go there for amusements and for shopping. Those wanting higher education go to the city, for the famous academy has long since died. Instead of the four Protestant churches, which we may assume to have been well supported in the early days, only one now draws to it any congregation.

These changes and corresponding changes in the open country, characteristic of many towns of Vermont, have not been accidents. They have been caused by a variety of more fundamental changes. Partial exhaustion of natural resources, particularly forests, the coming of the railroads, the lure of new lands in the West and broader opportunities in the metropolitan centers have all been felt by Vermont towns for three-quarters of a century. Changes in farm economy and the influence of summer visitors have been operating for a shorter period.

Reduction in the birthrate has been no small factor in the shrinkage of our towns. This is shown clearly in the age distribution of the population of different years.

TABLE 2. PERCENT OF POPULATION IN VARIOUS AGE GROUPS

Ages	1920	1900	1850
Under 1 year	1.9	2.0	2.1
1 to 4 years	7.9	7.6	9.9
5 to 49 years	67.6	69.1	73.9
50 and over	22.4	21.1	14.1

We thus see that young children make up a distinctly smaller proportion of our population now than in 1850, and that the proportion of persons over fifty years of age has increased from one-seventh of the total population to over one-fifth.

Some of these changes and some others of equal importance are beyond the control of Vermonters. To such, the people must adapt themselves, and have in many cases. Still others can be controlled to a greater or less extent and shaped to suit our ends if we will but look and plan together far enough into the future.

Distribution of Population

The facts mentioned previously concerning the decline of our towns are abundantly confirmed by further study of census reports. Though the aggregate population of ten towns has increased 197 percent since 1850, the population of the rest of the state has actually decreased 8.3 percent. In spite of this tendency of the population to become concentrated in a few towns, Vermont remains dominantly rural if "rural" be defined according to the usage of the Census Bureau as applying to populations living outside of incorporated places having a population of 2,500 or more. In this respect it is unique among the New England states. A comparison of the trend of rural population in Vermont with that for the United States is shown in the following table:

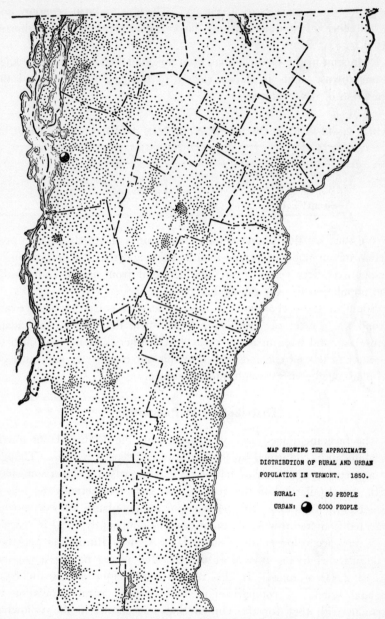

MAP SHOWING THE APPROXIMATE
DISTRIBUTION OF RURAL AND URBAN
POPULATION IN VERMONT. 1850.

RURAL: · 50 PEOPLE
URBAN: ● 6000 PEOPLE

FIG. 1. This map shows the approximate distribution of the 314,120 people who lived in Vermont in 1850. Comparison with Fig. 2 shows the thinning of population in the rural areas and its concentration in the cities and larger villages.

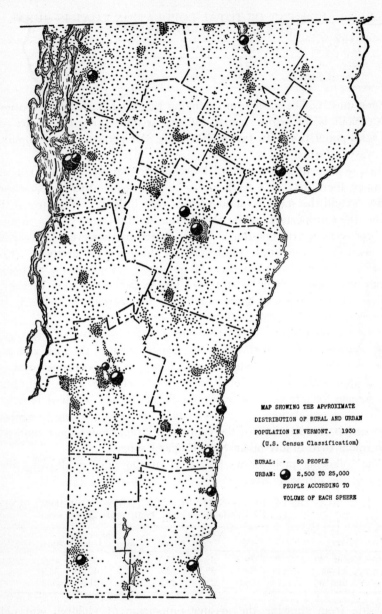

Fig. 2. This map shows the approximate distribution of the 359,611 people who lived in Vermont in 1930. Though rural population has decreased materially since 1850, the population of the state as a whole has increased more than 14 percent.

TABLE 3. PERCENT OF TOTAL POPULATION THAT IS RURAL, VERMONT AND UNITED STATES

	1930	1920	1910	1900	1890
Vermont	67.0	68.8	72.2	77.9	84.8
United States ..	43.8	48.6	54.2	60.0	64.6

One must not be misled into thinking that over half the population of Vermont is on farms. Small villages account for a large part of our rural population. In fact in 1930 only 31.1 percent of our population was on farms.

In the face of this substantial decline in the rural population of Vermont, there may be a tendency to be consoled by the fact that the decline within the state has amounted to very little more than one-fifth of the 1890 proportion, while the decline in the country as a whole has been very nearly one-third. It is dangerous, however, to assume that decrease in the rural population is a thing to be regretted. This committee does not try to answer the question: How can the decrease of our rural population be stopped? but rather: Does this decrease produce better or worse living conditions for Vermont's people? Is it desirable that it should continue or be checked?

This tendency of the cities and larger towns to draw in the rural population has a greater effect on the women than on the men and, as might be expected, its greatest effect on people in the prime of life. The United States Census for 1930 shows nearly 118 males per hundred females in our farm population and only 94 per hundred females in our urban population. The discrepancy has been growing in recent years, and is characteristic of the country at large, though more marked in Vermont than in any other New England state.

The following table shows the effect of the cities in drawing the people in the prime of life:

TABLE 4. AGE DISTRIBUTION IN PERCENTAGES, VERMONT AND UNITED STATES, 1920

Age	All	Vermont Urban	Rural	All	United States Urban	Rural
Under 20	36.9	35.4	37.5	40.7	35.8	45.9
20 to 44	34.4	38.5	32.6	38.4	42.7	33.8
45 and up	28.6	25.9	29.7	20.8	21.3	20.2

Aside from showing the greater proportion of children and old people on our farms it shows that Vermont is not raising its proportion of children as compared with the country as a whole.

In spite of the decrease in the number of farmers and farm families there is a marked stability in the residence tendency of the farming population. In seven towns whose agricultural populations were studied intensively[1] the average length of residence of the farm families on their present farms ranged from 10.4 years in one town to 15.7 years in another. For the whole number of families (1,140) in the seven towns, the average length of residence was 13.65 years. Since these towns as a group are not thoroughly typical of Vermont, having an unusually high proportion of foreign born, it seems safe to conclude that the average farm tenure for the state as a whole is somewhat longer.

When farmers move they tend to move short distances. The majority of those investigated had moved to another location in the same town, a goodly number had moved to a neighboring town and fewer to more remote towns. Of those coming in from other states, the majority came from New York and New Hampshire, many having previously lived in Vermont. An attempt was made to find out why the few families which previously lived in Kansas, Minnesota or Illinois had come to Vermont, and it was found that almost without exception a parent or husband or wife had been a Vermonter, and family associations and visits to the old home had drawn some members back to become residents. Familiarity with a region and associations with friends and relatives appear to be the most effective of all motives leading to a change of farm homes.

The practice of renting farms rather than owning them makes for less stability of the population than would otherwise prevail. In the seven towns slightly less than one-seventh of the farmers were tenants. Their length of residence on their present farms averages 7.6 years—a bit over half as long as the length for the group as a whole.

Summer residents are in some towns tending to cause shifts of the farming population.[2] Where hotels take many summer guests or where any significant number of city families occupy summer residences a considerable movement of the farming population often results. The land sometimes becomes so valuable for these purposes that farmers cannot afford to hold it for farming. In these cases it is sold

[1] Population shifts in the seven towns mentioned here and elsewhere in this chapter were studied by Miss Genieve Lamson. Her report is entitled "A Study of Agricultural Populations in Selected Vermont Towns." Since the towns were selected with particular reference to population shifts, they have a higher proportion of foreign born in their populations than has the state as a whole.

[2] Material on the influence of summer residents was gathered by H. D. Pearl.

and the people either move away or change the nature of their work.

Some farms, not particularly desirable for summer residences, lose their value as agricultural plants through changes in the nature of the community. Because of scarcity of farmers it becomes impossible to exchange machines and labor. The school enrollment dwindles and winter activity is reduced to almost nothing. The community thus becomes unattractive for farmers and they move away.

Composition of the Population

Additions from other states. The population of Vermont has been continually augmented by immigration from other states. In 1850, this immigration was almost entirely from New England and New York, over 80 percent of the total number coming from the former. As years went on fewer people came from New England, more from New York and more from other states farther west. All during the present century more natives of New York than of any other state have come to live in Vermont. At present, however, the New York proportion seems to be declining slightly and that from Massachusetts and Maine to be gaining. In 1920, 18.4 percent of the natives of the United States resident in Vermont had been born outside of the state. Neighboring states sent most of these people as follows:

New York ....36.6 percent
Massachusetts ....20.0 percent
New Hampshire ....18.5 percent
Maine .... 4.5 percent

Foreign born. As would be expected in an inland agricultural state, the proportion of foreign born residents of Vermont has always been low compared to that in the neighboring industrialized coastal states. Only twice has this figure been as high as 14 percent. Of late years it has been declining slightly, and in 1930 it reached 12 percent. In the United States as a whole the proportion of foreign born persons is somewhat greater and in all New England it amounts to over one-fourth of the total population.

There has been a marked change in the origin of our foreign population. Of those in the state in 1850, according to Rossiter,[3] "approximately half were born in Ireland, and most of the remainder was con-

    [3] W. S. Rossiter. "Vermont. An Historical and Statistical Study of the Progress of the State." From this article we have also taken certain statistical material as well as suggestions for arrangement.

tributed by what was probably the English-Canadian element." Since that time there has been a strong swing toward a diversity of nationalities. The British immigration has waned decidedly, while the French-Canadians now make up over 40 percent of our foreign born, and the Italian, Swedish, Polish, Russian and Spanish elements have made marked gains.

In the seven towns intensively studied the percentages of foreign-born parents of native-born farmers show a shift in the proportions of immigrants from different sources. Of these foreign-born parents, 50 percent came from the British Isles, compared with 13 percent of the present generation of foreign born; and 41 percent from Canada, compared with 71 percent at present. Other nationalities make up 8 percent of the foreign-born parents as against 15 percent of the present generation. Thus foreign born of the last generation served to strengthen the elements of the original settlers, while those of the present generation are in the main from Canada and of French extraction.

Until recently the various foreign-born elements have tended to swell our urban population more than the farm population. The result is that at present they compose 15 percent of the former, but only slightly more than 10 percent of the latter. In recent years the trend seems to have been changing. In the past decade (1920-30) though the percentage of foreign born in the state as a whole has decreased, the proportion on farms has increased from 9.9 percent to 10.8 percent. This change is due, no doubt, to the present large proportion of French-Canadian immigrants and their marked tendency to take up farms rather than to live in the larger centers. While they form 55.7 percent of the foreign-born farm population they make up only one-third of the foreign population in villages and but slightly more in the cities. Along with the increase of the foreign-born population on farms there has been an increase of foreign stock. According to the census of 1930, foreign-born persons and persons one or both of whose parents were foreign born make up nearly 30 percent of our farm population.

In the seven towns where the farm population was completely canvassed, it was found that less than three children made up the average family of native parents while nearly five children were born on the average to each foreign-born couple. This indicates a relatively more rapid increase in our foreign stock than in our native stock. Such

relative increase seems to be becoming less rapid, however, if we judge
by the age distribution in the following table:

TABLE 5. CHANGES IN AGE DISTRIBUTION BY NATIVITY
CLASSES IN PERCENTAGES

Age	All classes		Native white Native parents		Native white foreign and mixed parents		Foreign born white	
	1930	1920	1930	1920	1930	1920	1930	1920
0 to 19 years.......	37.0	36.9	40.2	39.2	41.0	43.6	11.9	13.0
20 to 44 years.......	33.7	34.4	32.6	33.1	32.9	32.0	41.8	45.9
45 and up	29.2	28.6	27.1	27.7	26.2	24.4	46.3	41.0

There has been a decrease in the proportion of recent foreign stock
in the lower age groups, meaning fewer children and people in the
prime of life.   On the other hand there has been a slight but perceptible
increase in the proportion of children of native stock.   It must be remembered, though, that the third generation of foreign stock is classified in this table with the native whites of native parentage, leaving it
impossible to distinguish between the original Vermont stock and the
descendants of the immigrants of sixty to eighty years ago.   The only
definite conclusion which we can draw, then, is that our recent foreign
stock seems to be increasing less rapidly than was formerly the case.
This points to assimilation of a kind.

The foreign-born farmers in the seven towns studied have not
stayed on their farms so long as the natives.   The averages are 9.9
years for farmers of foreign stock (including those of foreign or
mixed parentage) and 15.1 years for those of native stock.   This
difference can be only partly due to shortness of time in this country,
because less than a quarter of these families of foreign stock are
occupying their first Vermont farms.

There is evidence of a gradual shift southward on the part of the
Canadians in Vermont.   Those in the northern part of the state have
moved but once or twice, while those in the central part have moved
several times before reaching their present positions.   More temperate
climate and greater opportunity for diversity of crops seem to be the
chief influences drawing them southward.

Contributions of the foreign born. Members of forty-five farm
families in Barre work in the stone sheds, of these thirty-six belong to
the foreign-born group.   In this way our foreign-born farmers furnish
a part of the labor for specialized industries.   They also constitute a

large part of the supply of farm laborers and by taking up farms that would otherwise be abandoned, keep the land active and enlarge the market for local merchants.

The other side of their contribution is more often overlooked. Most immigrant farmers bring with them a musical and artistic heritage far richer than that in possession of our native stock. Many a shy and unappreciated French woman could "show up" the Vermont housewives in needlework. Folk songs, dances and other forms of artistic expression are in the blood of these people. If they could but be given a suitable outlet and receive the appreciation they deserve they could add greatly to the enrichment of our rural life.

Assimilation of foreign born. The immigrants of British stock are on the whole quickly assimilated because they find themselves among people of similar origin. The French-Canadian and natives of central Europe, however, are much more slowly absorbed into their communities if at all. Some of their customs, their language, and usually their religion are different from those of the people among whom they settle.

The chief agencies which could help these people to become a part of the communities in which they live are the church, the school and business contacts. Except in regions in which there is already a nucleus of native or Irish Catholics, the church more often keeps the foreign born separate from the rest of the community rather than merging them with it. In church contacts they often speak their native language and meet people of similar origin rather than native Vermonters. There are numerous cases where they must in fact go to another town for worship, thus having their interest definitely drawn away from the community in which they live.

The school is probably the most effective agency of assimilation. Here the children meet on an equal footing and grow up with common experiences and aspirations. The parents are also included to some extent in meetings, socials and entertainments. The possibilities of the school in developing community spirit are unlimited.

The business contacts of the men, such as creamery and store, the exchange of labor and machines, road work and other enterprises give them an opportunity to meet their neighbors and to learn the language. The women, confined by many household duties, often remain practically isolated from the community throughout their lives.

It is to be regretted that the town meeting is not more fully used to initiate the newcomers into the privileges of citizenship. In one town, thirty-eight out of 110 farmers are not registered as voters. The majority of these, like the majority of non-voting farmers in all towns studied, are foreign born. The expense and inconvenience of naturalization is probably the most important reason why these people do not take up the advantages of citizenship. Many have taken out first papers so as to be able to obtain hunting and fishing licenses, but have gone no further.

Clearly the burden of bringing our foreign-born neighbors into community activities lies with the established residents. There is much that they can contribute. Neighborliness and willingness to meet them a little more than half way will do much toward turning their interest and support to community activities.

Emigrants

Vermont has always sent a large proportion of her sons and daughters to live in other states. In fact every census since 1850 has

FIG. 3. Where emigrant Vermonters lived in 1850. Each dot represents 1,000 natives of Vermont living in other states. Each state and territory had some Vermonters but no dots are shown for less than 500. New York, Pennsylvania and Ohio were at this time receiving their greatest numbers.

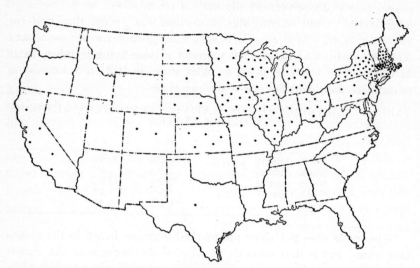

FIG. 4. Where emigrant Vermonters lived in 1880. Each dot represents 1,000 natives of Vermont living in other states. Each state and territory had some Vermonters but no dots are shown for less than 500. Note the large numbers which had evidently been attracted by new lands in the Middle West.

FIG. 5. Where emigrant Vermonters lived in 1920. Each dot represents 1,000 natives of Vermont living in other states. Each state had some Vermonters but no dots are shown for less than 500. The Middle West has lost, the Pacific Coast and the New England urban centers have gained since 1880. There are forty-six dots in Massachusetts.

shown nearly 40 percent of the natives of this state to be living in other states. Until recently this proportion was greater than that for any other state. At present it is somewhat greater for Wyoming and Nevada. With 40.5 percent of Vermont natives living in other states in 1900 and 38.5 percent living in other states in 1920, it is interesting to compare their distributions at the two dates.

TABLE 6. DISTRIBUTION OF NATIVE VERMONTERS RESIDENT IN OTHER STATES

Division	1900	1920
North Atlantic	58.2%	70.4%
South Atlantic	1.3%	2.4%
North Central	31.0%	15.9%
South Central	1.3%	1.4%
Western	8.1%	9.9%

This table does not show the marked decrease found in the mountain states, and it thus conceals the size of the increase in the Pacific states. In fact California has moved up from ninth place to fifth place as a home for native Vermonters. The decrease in the proportion of

Fig. 6. Where native Vermonters lived whose names appear in "Who's Who in America, 1930-31." Numbers beside the dots for Vermont, New Hampshire, Massachusetts, Rhode Island, Connecticut and Maryland, represent the numbers of these Vermonters in those states. Numbers beside the dots for New York City, Washington, Chicago and San Francisco, represent the numbers of these Vermonters who lived in those cities. Five other natives of Vermont whose names appear in the volume resided in outlying possessions or foreign countries.

MAP SHOWING BIRTHPLACES OF
NATIVE VERMONTERS WHOSE NAMES
APPEAR IN "WHO'S WHO" FOR 1930-31.

● BIRTHPLACES OF PERSONS WHO
HAVE LEFT THE STATE

+ BIRTHPLACES OF PERSONS NOW
LIVING IN THE STATE

FIG. 7. Each dot on this map represents one native of Vermont now residing in another state whose name appears in "Who's Who." Each cross represents one such native of Vermont who now lives in the state. The locations of the dots and crosses on this map indicate the birthplaces of these people.

Vermonters going to the central states is due very largely to the passing of the era of free land. Formerly they went west to take up new land, now they go largely to the cities, chiefly to those nearer home.

What have these departed sons and daughters done? A study of the names in "Who's Who" shows that Vermont has, in proportion to its size, produced a very large proportion of leaders. The names of 309 natives of Vermont appear in "Who's Who" for 1930-31. If this same proportion held for the United States as a whole the size of the volume would have to be increased approximately fourfold.

The following table shows the fields of achievement of natives of Vermont according to "Who's Who."

Field of achievement	Resident natives	Non-resident natives	Total
Artistic	1	9	10
Business	8	44	52
Educational	12	76	88
Governmental	20	26	46
Legal	11	22	33
Literary	5	23	28
Medical	3	9	12
Religious	4	15	19
Miscellaneous	2	19	21
Total	66	243	309

Counted here in other fields, according to their present activities, are three ex-congressmen and four ex-governors of other states. When we consider further the large proportion of educators, we begin to grasp the influence which Vermont has upon the nation, and especially on its future.

The birthplaces of these people are scattered widely over the state. It is apparent that rural Vermont is contributing its share, because approximately three-quarters of the native Vermonters whose names appear in "Who's Who" were born on farms or in rural villages. Truly, Vermont can be said to be a seed bed of the nation, and it is a matter of deep concern to the country as a whole that this seed bed be kept in good condition.

The Heritage

What of the seedlings? How can Vermont stock best be conserved and made to continue to provide its share of leaders for the nation and builders for the state?

The remaining stock.[4] Emigration from the state and migration from the country to the larger centers within the state have had a definite effect on the general make-up of the population remaining. This effect was studied intensively in three carefully chosen towns. One represented a progressive rural community, one an average one, and the third a community which seemed to be declining. The serious aspect of emigration from the rural communities is not in the number but in the kind of people who leave. Agricultural conditions are such that it is to the best interest of farming that many people leave the farms. But if the farming communities are drained of their outstanding members who are needed to produce the future leaders of the state, the loss can never be made up.

The members of the communities studied by the Eugenics Survey were little aware of any migration from their towns. The best informed citizens insisted that practically no one leaves town nowadays. It is true that a large proportion of those leaving had lived in the town in question for only a short time before they proceeded in their search for better opportunities. They may thus have made but little impression in the minds of the long-standing residents. But they gathered into their number a surprising proportion of people who are either children or near relatives of the present residents. Between the transients and the scions of old stock, the emigration from each of these towns within the past twenty years has amounted to almost twice as many people as the present population of each town.

All types of people leave these towns. But more hired men, laborers and their families move than do tenants, their children or the children of farm owners. Farm owners themselves move least of all. More than 65 percent of this migrating body moves hesitantly from one town to the next until the majority locate in the larger towns within the state or in neighboring states. There, by far the larger number engage in other than agricultural pursuits.

But there is within this migrating army a small group which differs from the average. It is composed almost entirely of the children of the present members of the community, and particularly of those who have descended from the early settlers of the town. This small group has received education far above that received by either the average resident or the average emigrant, and when they have emigrated there

[4] This section is a condensation of the Fifth Annual Report of the Eugenics Survey of Vermont, 1931.

has been little hesitation in their movements. They have almost invariably gone direct to the largest cities of the country and there in competition with thousands have won positions of important responsibility. It is when this unnoticed but persistent drain of such people from the rural towns of the state impairs the social life and the quality of the stock that it is to be deplored.

There are, however, counteractive trends at work which may partially if not wholly compensate for this loss. In these towns the immigration of people who take up more or less permanent residence, though very small compared to the emigration, partially counterbalances it. The age, education and training of the average immigrant is similar to that of the average emigrant. In social background he is little different from the average resident of each town. Eighty-nine percent of the immigrants in the three towns studied are of American stock— 76 percent consisting of native Vermonters, 13 percent of natives of other states—while only 11 percent are foreign born—mostly French-Canadians. (The figures are nearly the same for the state as a whole.) Most of these immigrants fit into the work and the social life of the community and are therefore fair substitutes for the emigrants. But among them are very few who have an education and training comparable to the choice group of emigrants, and few of them seem to have that stability which is characteristic of the older residents.

One of the most obvious effects of the migration is that it has drained the countryside of its young people. By far the greater number of those remaining are old—older than the average for Vermont, which according to the census has more old people anyway than almost any other state in the Union. Because the proportion of old people is high the birthrate is very low. A comparison of the excess of births over deaths per thousand in these towns with the excess for Vermont and for the United States shows the following: For rural United States the excess is 10.0; for Vermont it is 6.0; and for the three towns studied it is 3.1. There is little hope therefore that the people of these towns will reproduce their kind in any great numbers.

However, in two of the three towns studied there seems to be no very obvious deterioration in the quality of the stock of those remaining. There may be a lack of that energy and venturesomeness which marked the early pioneers. But there are found fine substantial qualities which show the people to be responsible citizens of upright character. The greater number in two of the towns show an earning capacity and an ability in making of their farms "going concerns" comparable to the success of the small business man.

But there are communities in which the effects of emigration are more serious. In a town which represented the poorer rural sections of the state, it would seem that the most enterprising stock had emigrated long since, and left a residue of poorer stock to which has been added the immigration of people who frequently have been failures elsewhere. Though most of the residents live on farms, few cultivate more than an acre of land. They prefer to earn their living at road work and odd jobs. The young people do not express any of that healthy discontent that is heard among the young people of the other towns. The whole philosophy of life in the town is not "to get on" but "to be content." Its charm is expressed in the words of one of its citizens, "There is no hurry here. It is always afternoon." But this very atmosphere is not conducive to bringing out the dormant capacities of the people. Even though they would probably not be happy anywhere else, one is compelled to suggest that for their own good and for the future well-being of their children it would be advisable for them to move to more progressive communities in the state where in the competitive atmosphere of "getting on" they would have to make use of any latent capacities.

The outstanding conclusion of the study in these three towns is that the migratory movement tends to drain from the rural communities of the state two types of persons, first, the "potentially distinguished" who can best express their capacities in the responsible positions which exist in the complex environment of cities, and second, unsettled farming people whose abilities are often as well if not better adapted to the supervised routine of industry than to the independent responsibility of agriculture.

There remain in the rural sections where farming is still the chief industry, people of fine average talent who, judged by their ability to make of their farms "going concerns," are capable of carrying out constructive programs for the state. Furthermore, there is little reason to doubt that they will continue to produce many dependable future citizens and a few exceptionally talented ones, whose services belong to the country as a whole. At the same time there are sections in the state where the effects of emigration are more seriously felt in the social life of the community and in the quality of the stock of those remaining.

The chief recommendations of this study are two. First, that in the productive rural areas of the state all the relevant recommendations made by the other committees of the Country Life Commission be carried out. This is essential to the finest upbringing of the future generation in the state, and to encouraging those people to remain in farming communities who really "love the land" and are potential rural leaders. Second, that in the less productive rural areas of the state the recommendations made for the utilization of the land for whatever purposes it is most suited—usually forests—be carried out. This would encourage the people living in these sections to move both for their own good and for the well-being of their children to more progressive communities in the state.

The prospect. From the foregoing studies it appears that though the old stock may be holding its own in quality for the most part, it shows a slow decrease in quantity. This decrease is not always apparent because in almost all communities the influence of the old families still predominates.

When we look at the prospect for the future—whether Vermont stock will continue to furnish leaders in the state and nation—two factors need attention. The first of these is the birthrate. It has been determined by students of eugenics that for a given group of people to maintain their numbers through several generations, allowing for celibacy, childless marriages and early death, most of the married couples must have four children and the rest must have three. With 40 percent of native Vermonters leaving the state, nearer six children to a family would be necessary to keep the quantity of old stock from decreasing in the state. Under present customs and economic conditions, families of this size are the exception rather than the rule. Unless in future the birthrate shows a marked increase it appears that the volume of the old Vermont stock is bound to dwindle.

The second factor needing attention is the quality of the rising generation of Vermonters. Perhaps we can make up in quality what we have to lose in quantity. It must be remembered that the natives of Vermont who have made their mark were growing up at a time when the amount and kind of activity in this state were similar to the amount and kind of activity throughout the country. They are at most one generation removed from the time when rural Vermont was rising to its greatest development. These conditions, besides furnishing an ideal environment for the development of youth, stimulated their ambition and imbued them with a tradition of achievement. In 1880, according to the Ayres Index, Vermont ranked sixth among the states in school rating; in 1920 it ranked twenty-fourth. With this difference in send-off, will the present generation of young Vermonters be able to accomplish what their uncles have?

It is clear that if the valuable characteristics of our old Vermont stock are to be conserved and passed on to future generations for the good of the state and the nation, conditions must be brought about which will favor the maintenance of that stock as far as possible. As farmers are the backbone of the state, ways must be found in which farming can be made to pay, so that desirable families will remain on the farms. Not only farming and other economic conditions must be made favorable, but community activities should be made to enrich rural life as much as possible, and our educational facilities must be of the best, that our youth may be given as good a start as those of any other state. In short all the potential resources of the state must be examined, and plans must be made for their fullest development.

Summary and Recommendations

The study of the people of Vermont has revealed a sturdy British stock, augmented in recent years by a slow inflow of French-Canadians and small numbers of other nationalities. This influx has been slow enough to be better assimilated in Vermont than in the rest of New England and there is prospect of its decreasing. Vermont families have a strong tendency to stay on the farm, and even a stronger one to stay in the same locality. In spite of this, there has been a persistent flow of young people in the prime of life into the larger towns and to other states. Many of these have found their way to positions of far more than ordinary importance.

To promote the best future citizenry in the state, this Committee makes the following recommendations:

1. That Vermonters be encouraged to keep and study their own family records with a view to arousing their pride in the achievements and high qualities of their ancestral stock so that this pride may in turn stimulate their better efforts and guide them in their choice of mates.

2. That the doctrine be spread that it is the patriotic duty of every normal couple to have children in sufficient number to keep up to par the "good old Vermont stock."

3. That public opinion be strengthened in regard to the importance of heeding those laws of nature which affect human inheritance. This can be done only by educating that public opinion. The circulation of the best library books on eugenics, population and heredity, public discussions, debates and study classes, lectures and newspaper letters are among the means to this end. The Eugenics Survey will gladly furnish reading lists and suggestions to organizations wishing help.

4. That the natural leaders of rural Vermont, individually and through their organizations, assume the responsibility for making general the best mental and moral attitudes, hopes and aspirations which they themselves now possess, with a view to increasing the appreciation of our people for their environment as it now is and their appreciation for it as their determined efforts to improve it can make it to be. Let every organization take up these opportunities to serve coming Vermont.

―――――――

Prepared for the Commission by its Committee on the Human Factor.

PAUL D. MOODY,
Chairman,
E. A. STANLEY,
Vice-chairman,
H. F. PERKINS,
Executive Secretary,
RUSSELL G. SHOLES.
Advisory Committee of Eugenics Survey:
H. F. PERKINS,
Director,
T. J. ALLEN,
GUY W. BAILEY,
CHARLES F. DALTON,
W. H. DYER,

SHIRLEY FARR,

K. R. B. FLINT,

A. R. GIFFORD,

HOWARD N. HANSON,

HORACE G. RIPLEY,

LENA C. ROSS,

E. A. STANLEY,

L. JOSEPHINE WEBSTER.

Sub-committee on Population Changes:

RUSSELL G. SHOLES,

Chairman,

HENRY BRANCHAUD.

Research Material on Which Committees' Findings are Based

A Study of Agricultural Populations in Selected Vermont Towns, 1929-1930. A Manuscript by GENIEVE LAMSON.

A Study of the Effects of Summer Residents, 1930. A Manuscript by H. D. PEARL.

Eugenics Survey of Vermont. Annual Reports, 1927-1931, published by the Eugenics Survey, 138 Church Street, Burlington, Vt.

United States Census Reports.

Vermont, An Historical and Statistical Study of the Progress of the State. W. S. ROSSITER. Quarterly publications of the American Statistical Association, New Series, No. 93, Vol. XII, March, 1911.

IV

THE TOPOGRAPHY AND CLIMATE OF VERMONT

"Know'st thou this country?"

To present the chief physical features of Vermont in miniature, to show the mountains that rise in majesty and the "complaining brooks (and lakes) that make the valleys green," to portray in their proper perspective the uplands, the deep, quiet valleys, and the broad rolling country of the Champlain Lowland, to locate the lines of communication, the centres of population, and the most striking scenic features of the state; furthermore, to tell the truth about the climate of our commonwealth, neither stressing nor hiding its extremes, and to indicate the possibilities of the service of the United States Weather Bureau—such have been the aims of the Committee on Basic Geographical Features of the Vermont Commission on Country Life.

The Relief Model

Of all the methods of presenting a region comprehensively to the eye none, the Committee feels, equals that of the relief model. For here can be depicted so that, without training in interpretation or much stretch of the imagination, "he who runs may read" the topography of a region in its true areal relationships, the trends of the mountains and valleys, the relative positions of uplands and lowlands, the courses of the streams, the positions of the lakes, and many minor features. The vertical distances are of necessity exaggerated but even this can be done in such moderation that no undue distortion is produced.

The relief model of Vermont (Figure 1) was made at Rochester, New York, by Ward's Natural Science Establishment, Inc. The data has been taken from the topographical sheets of the United States Geological Survey. The state covers forty-five whole sheets and parts of twenty others, of which eight whole quadrangles and parts of five others have not yet been surveyed. Data for these missing areas have been obtained from other Government preliminary mappings and from field studies made by the committee. The model is eighty-five inches long by fifty-four inches maximum width. Areally, it is made

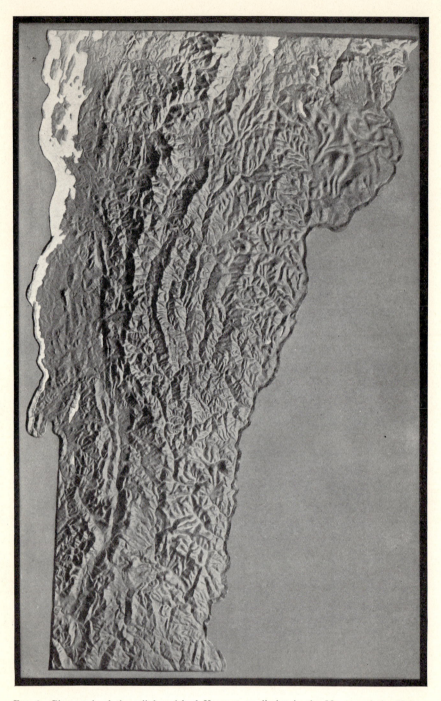

Fig. 1. Photograph of the relief model of Vermont on display in the Museum of the University of Vermont.

on the scale of one inch to two miles which is approximately half that of the scale of the topographical sheets; while vertically, the exaggeration is four to one, which makes the loftiest summit, Mt. Mansfield, one and two-thirds inches high.

On the model the chief relief features stand out clearly. In the southwest portion are seen the Taconic Mountains which enter the state from Massachusetts. One sees lying east of these the Vermont Valley trending to the north and debouching upon the Champlain Lowland with its low ridges and shallow valleys. Then comes the backbone of the state, the Green Mountain system, which extends northwards from Massachusetts as a great massif almost uncut by passes to the latitude of Rutland whence trending somewhat towards the northeast, it spreads out, fanlike, into many parallel ranges, of which the highest range contains Jay Peak, Mansfield, Camel's Hump, Ellen, Killington and many lesser eminences. East of the mountain backbone lies a plateau region with a general elevation of 1,000 to 1,500 feet above sea level, very much dissected into hills and low ridges and shallow valleys. This is the Vermont piedmont. Many cross valleys or passes are to be noted, through the largest of which flow the Winooski and Lamoille, "antecedent" rivers of vast antiquity which, having their sources in the piedmont region, were able to maintain their courses to the northwest in the face of the rising mountain mass. The Otter is seen draining the west slopes of the mountains in Addison and Rutland Counties, while many smaller streams are shown east of the mountains and tributary to the Connecticut. Vermont contains within her borders hundreds of lakes, large and small, which are due to a ponding action of the glacial débris scattered over the state during the Great Ice Age of the long ago. The largest of these bodies of water are shown upon the model: Willoughby with its wild beauty, Dunmore and its mountain background, Bomoseen and St. Catherine among the hills of the Taconics, and many smaller but no less lovely lakes and ponds dotting the landscape.

The trunk highways are shown in red, as are also some of the secondary roads when they extend through places of great scenic beauty, such for instance as Smugglers Notch, Hazens Notch, Caspian Lake, etc.

The county lines are shown in black, and the counties are named. The township boundaries are shown in fainter lining but the names are omitted, in order not to clutter the model. The accompanying key map will enable one easily to find them.

The first copy will be housed in the Geological Department of the new University Museum where it will be open daily to public inspection.

The original model will of course be kept on hand in order that copies may be obtained. It is hoped that the demand will be considerable—that the colleges of the state will want them, that the various departments of the state government will call for them and that towns and hotels may find them of use. Arrangements have been made with the makers of the model by which copies may be had for $100 each, these copies to show the rivers and not to exceed ten cities or towns. Of course additional "culture" can be added to any extent desired. It is hoped that with a copy of this model available, the beginning of a modern geological map of the state may soon be undertaken and ultimately carried to completion.

Arrangements have been made with the National Survey Company of Chester, Vermont, whereby photographic reproductions of the model and its "culture" will be obtainable at moderate prices. It is hoped that every school in the state may have one or more of these maps displayed and that, in addition, the maps may have a wide distribution. The accompanying print from a photograph of the model, gives a very imperfect notion of the attractiveness of the large photographs and the model itself.

The Climate of Vermont

The climate of Vermont is controlled by the following factors: the state's geographical position in the northern hemisphere, location in or near recognized storm tracks passing from west to east across the country, diversity of physical features, and Lake Champlain on the western boundary.

Unfortunately, all records are lacking which would give definite information of actual conditions at Vermont's higher elevations. From observation and general meteorological knowledge, we know that the mountain ridges have lower annual temperatures, much more snow, shorter growing seasons, and more wind than is experienced at lower levels.

The following climatic data, charts, and deductions are a result of extensive search through Weather Bureau records covering a long

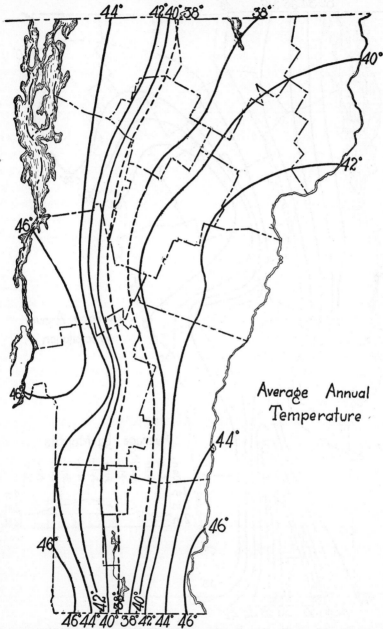

Average Annual
Temperature

FIG. 2. The lines on this map are drawn through points having approximately the same average annual temperature as indicated at the ends of each line. The general course of such lines for the United States is east and west. The fact that they run north and south on this map shows that altitude is more important than latitude in determining the variations in average temperature in Vermont, and explains why Vermont has good summer resort areas from one end of the state to the other.

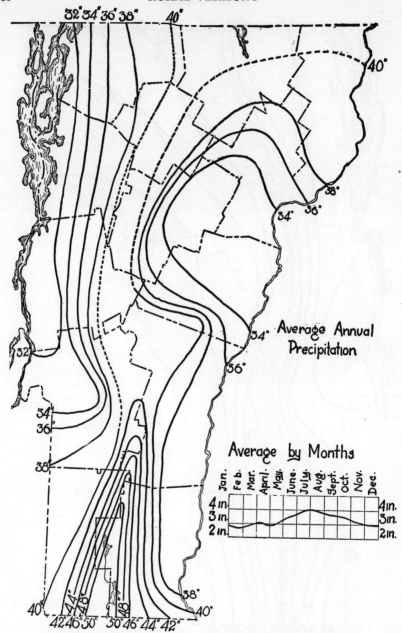

FIG. 3. The lines on this map are drawn through points having approximately the same
average annual precipitation as indicated at the ends of each line. Precipitation includes
the rain equivalent of snow as well as the rainfall.

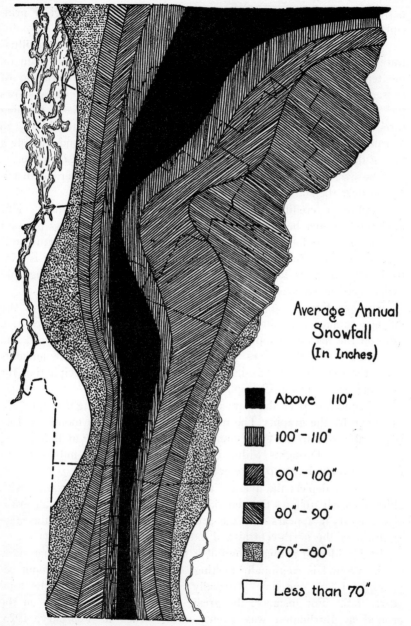

Average Annual
Snowfall
(In Inches)

■ Above 110"

▥ 100" - 110"

▨ 90" - 100"

▧ 80" - 90"

▦ 70" - 80"

□ Less than 70"

FIG. 4. This map shows the average annual snowfall in the different parts of the state. Note that the areas of heavy snowfall, suitable for winter sports, extend the whole length of the state.

period of years with general meteorological and climatological principles applied.

Temperature. Figure 2 (Average Annual Temperature) illustrates the influence of the Green Mountains and Lake Champlain on the temperatures of the various sections of Vermont. Variation of average temperatures down either slope of the mountains clearly shows the relation of temperature to elevation. Lake Champlain, forming three-fourths of the state's western boundary, contributes locally to Vermont's climate. Along the lake and some distance inland we note a toning down of extreme temperatures both in summer and in winter.

The average temperature chart for July shows the thermal distribution over the state at the warmest period of the year.

Vermont is credited with having delightful summer weather. This moderate summer heat gives way to a cooler but none the less pleasant fall period, usually extending into October. In winter, fortunately, atmospheric conditions are such that on the coldest days the air is relatively dry, there is little or no wind, and the damp penetrating cold experienced at seacoast stations is noticeably lacking.

Precipitation. Figure 3, with accompanying graph, shows the average annual precipitation. The greatest amount of precipitation falls on the mountain tops with a lessening both to the eastward and westward down the slopes. In general, somewhat greater amounts cover the east than the west sides, and the minimum precipitation for the state occurs in the Champlain Valley.

Precipitation over the state is well distributed throughout the year as shown by the graph. The maximum amount in the month of July is probably due to the extra number of thundershowers at that period of the year. Droughts within the state are practically unknown and floods, fortunately, are of rare occurrence.

Figure 4 depicts the average annual snowfall. The variation with altitude closely follows the general precipitation chart. From all available records it appears that the greatest annual snowfall of the state occurs over the north-central and extreme northeastern sections.

In considering annual snowfall it should be remembered that snow on the ground is continually melting or evaporating. The amount remaining at any one time is usually a small percentage of the total yearly fall. For instance, the greatest amount ever recorded on the ground at Burlington was twenty-seven inches in February, 1925. One week later only six inches remained. Abundant snow is of value in this latitude. It prevents excessive freezing of the ground and thereby protects dormant vegetation, water supply, sewer pipes, and the sub-surfaces of transportation lines.

Even heavy snowstorms no longer block Vermont roads for weeks as in "ye olden days." During the past winter, with the heaviest snowfall in many years, the main highways were kept open for automobile traffic, and general travel over the state was maintained.

Vermont's dependable supply of water from rain and melted snow is used to advantage by power companies which are constantly expanding within the state.

Sunshine. From available records kept at the Burlington and Northfield weather bureau stations we find that Vermont receives about 45 percent of possible sunshine. This compares favorably with the same latitude in other northeastern states. At Burlington the highest monthly average is 59 percent, in July, and the lowest is 22 percent, in December.

Wind. In general, winds over most of the state are relatively moderate and destructive gales of large extent are not on record. The average hourly velocity at Burlington with a twenty-five-year record is 10.8 miles per hour. At Northfield, on the east side of the Green Mountains, the records show approximately one-third less. The highest velocity ever recorded at Burlington, with instruments in a well-exposed position, was at the rate of fifty-seven miles per hour from the south on March 26, 1908. This record was for a five-minute period.

The prevailing wind direction for the year at both Burlington and Northfield is south. Reports from cooperative stations over the state vary considerably. It would be a fairly accurate estimate to say that the prevailing wind direction is between northwest and north in winter and southerly in summer.

Humidity. As would be expected, humidity over Vermont, an inland and mostly upland state, is not excessive. Too few figures are available, however, to give an average. Humidity is a most varying phenomenon. It ranges greatly from day to day and even from hour to hour when expressed as a percentage of total saturation. There is also a wide local range varying with location. From the Burlington records we find the lowest humidity from April to June, inclusive, with little choice between the other months.

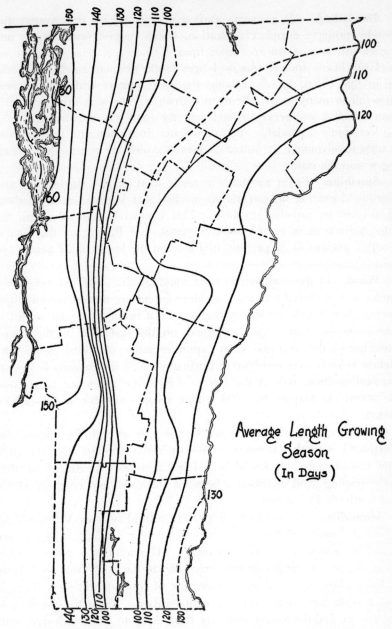

Average Length Growing Season (In Days)

F<small>IG.</small> 5. The lines on this map are drawn through points having approximately the same average number of days between the last killing frost in the spring and the first killing frost in the fall as indicated at the ends of each line.

Dense fog. The average number of days with fog at Burlington is only eight per year. This does not mean that fog lasts all day, but rather that fog occurs at some period of the day. Many times these periods are of short duration and an all-day fog is rare indeed. The river valleys of the state experience more fog than the uplands. These valley fogs are advantageous from an agricultural point of view as in many cases they prevent late frosts in the spring and early frosts in the fall.

Thunderstorms. Thunderstorms have been reported in Vermont during every month of the year. The average annual number at Burlington is thirty. Grouped by months, March, April, and October average one each, September three, May four, June and August six each, and July eight. Each of the other months averages less than one per year.

The growing season. Figure 5 gives the length of the average growing season in the different sections of the state. By growing season we mean the number of days from the last killing frost in the spring to the first killing frost in the fall. Killing frosts have been reported in Vermont during every one of the summer months. This is not as serious as it sounds for the same fact applies to practically all northern border states of the Union. High elevation in this case accounts for the unseasonable frosts occasionally experienced.

Flying weather. From a weather standpoint, modern aviation is hindered or stopped by lack of visibility, destructive storms, and ice freezing to the planes when aloft. Lack of visibility may be caused by snow in the air, heavy rain, fog, dense haze or smoke, and low clouds. Destructive storms are usually thundershowers where excessive winds, lightning and hail all threaten. As a flying lane for airplane traffic, Vermont compares favorably with most of her sister states. The New York-Montreal mail has been flown through the Champlain Valley for the past three years, comparatively few trips have been missed, and no serious accidents have been reported in the vicinity of Vermont.

Weather Service for Vermont Residents

The United States Weather Bureau maintains two fully-equipped stations in Vermont, located at Burlington and at Northfield. Through these stations daily forecasts of the weather, or related information, is furnished to interested parties who apply for such. Weather forecasts are published in the daily newspapers, and several radio stations within and adjacent to the state include Vermont forecasts in their everyday programs.

At the present time thirty or more cooperative observers who are distributed over the state are keeping daily records of Vermont weather and submitting monthly reports to the New England section center at Boston, Mass. These reports are compiled and printed and are the basic climatological data for the state. The work of these cooperative observers is without pay, and both the state and the nation are indebted to them for this scientific labor conscientiously performed.

For the past two years the Weather Bureau at Burlington in cooperation with the county agents has rendered special service to the farmers of the state during fruit-spraying and haying seasons. This service has consisted of making and distributing weather forecasts for as many days in advance as conditions justified, in order that the agriculturists might make their plans accordingly.

Any individual within the state is entitled to all weather information available from his nearest weather bureau station. It would seem that even more advantage of this free service could be taken for both personal and state profit.

Prepared for the Commission by its Committee on Basic Geographical Features.

ELBRIDGE C. JACOBS,
Chairman,
F. E. HARTWELL,
Meteorologist (1919-1930),
PHELPS N. SWETT,
Geographer.

The charts and the text of the report on the Climate of Vermont presented in this report were prepared by Mr. Charles N. Bemis of the United States Weather Bureau of Burlington.

V

SOILS OF VERMONT

Soil Origins

The soils of Vermont have been developed under a humid climate and in their native state were covered with a heavy forest growth. The cold winters have prevented leaching and weathering through a long period of the year. At higher elevations, above 1,000 or 1,200 feet, which prevail over a large area of the state, the conditions are favorable to the accumulation, under forest cover, of a fairly thick (one or two inches) layer of organic matter on the surface. Under this is a layer from which the iron and soluble salts have been removed by the organic acids, and below this is a brown zone of accumulation of these materials. At lower elevations, under normal rainfalls for this region, the soils are brown with a well-defined organic layer upon the surface. These areas are covered with deciduous trees, while conifers predominate upon the higher elevations.

At low elevations, below 400 or 500 feet, and where the rainfall is thirty inches or less the gray-brown soils are developed which have a thin surface organic layer mixed with mineral soil. A large area of Vermont was cleared during the early settlement and since that time much of this area has been in grass. As grass has a tendency to combat the influence of leaching of the fertility from the surface soil, and to build up a condition under which it thrives, the surface soil has been considerably altered and improved under this influence. The development of the surface soil varies considerably with the texture of the soil material, the lighter textured soils being more easily leached than the heavy ones.

The parent material from which the soils have been weathered, has been accumulated, at least in the upland, by glacial action and upon the terraces by outwash or water-deposited material of glacial origin. The stream bottom or alluvial soils are derived from weathered material. All of these soils are comparatively young when contrasted with the soils of the unglaciated region. Weathering has taken place to only fifteen to thirty inches, depending upon the character of the parent ma-

terial. Even within the weathered zone disintegration is far from being
completed as much raw material is found in the surface soil. This
mineral matter becomes available slowly as weathering progresses.
Under these conditions the lithological character of the parent rock material has exerted a strong influence upon the soils. The subsoils are
usually yellowish brown, yellow or greenish yellow, fading off below to
the color of the unweathered deposit which is some shade of gray,
ranging from greenish gray to gray.

The soils of Vermont are best suited to grass. Although they are
not inherently as fertile as the Prairie Region or the Great Plains of
the West, the humid climate of Vermont prevents serious checks to
grass growth from droughts and fosters a luxuriant grass cover
throughout the season. The soils of Vermont, as grasslands, are better
than most of the soils of New England and compare favorably with
those of any section of the Eastern United States.

Soil Groups

The relation of the soil groups to the crops that are grown upon
them depends upon a wide range of factors that are expressed in the
individual types of the group. These factors are also used in differ-
entiating the soils. They consist of color; texture, which includes the
quantities of gravel and stone; the structure, particularly the looseness
or compactness of the substratum as this affects the moisture-holding
capacity; the depth to and quantity of calcareous material; topography
and drainage; all of which factors were considered.

SOIL TYPES COMPOSING SOIL GROUPS
(Legend shown on soil map)

Group	Major Soils	Minor Soils
Worthington	Worthington loam+ Marshfield loam+ Marshfield stony loam+ Worthington stony loam Reading loam+	Calais loam+ Calais stony loam+ Worthington fine sandy loam+ Worthington stony fine sandy loam+ Shelburne loam and stony loam
Calais	Calais loam and stony loam+ Marshfield loam+ and stony loam	Worthington loam and stony loam Shelburne loam and stony loam
Vergennes	Vergennes clay loam Vergennes silty clay loam	Addison clay loam Sheldon fine sandy loam+

Group	Major Soils	Minor Soils
Addison	Addison clay loam+ Addison loam+	Addison gravelly loam+ Vergennes clay loam Suffield silt loam Sheldon fine sandy loam+
Pittsfield	Pittsfield loam Pittsfield stony loam Madrid loam Madrid stony loam	Stockbridge loam Lenox loam Lenox stony loam
Pittsfield Stony	Farmington stony loam	Addison stony loam+ Pittsfield stony loams
Mohawk	Mohawk shale loam St. Albans shale loam+	Mohawk silt loam Mohawk stony loam

Colrain	Colrain fine sandy loam and
	  Colrain stony fine sandy
	  loam
		Colrain loam and stony loam
		Shelburne loam and stony
		  loam

Blandford	Blandford loam
	Blandford stony loam
		Berkshire loam and stony
		  loam
		Woodbridge loam and stony
		  loam

Woodbridge	Woodbridge loam Woodbridge stony loam	Berkshire loam Berkshire stony loam Berkshire loam, shallow phase
Dutchess	Dutchess loam Dutchess stony loam	Dutchess shale loam Dutchess, shallow phases
Hollis	Hollis fine sandy loam Hollis stony fine sandy loam	Hollis loam and stony loam Bernardston loam
Berkshire	Berkshire loam and stony loam Becket loam and stony loam	Blandford loam Woodbridge loam
	(Some stony areas of all four)	
Berkshire stony	Berkshire stony loam Becket stony loam	Berkshire loam Becket loam

Hermon	Hermon fine sandy loam and
	Hermon stony fine sandy
	  loam
		Gloucester fine sandy loam
		  and stony fine sandy loam

Hermon stony	Hermon stony fine sandy loam	Hermon fine sandy loam

Merrimac	Merrimac fine sandy loam
	Merrimac sandy loam
	Merrimac gravelly loam
	Colton fine sandy loam and
	  gravelly fine sandy loam
		Copake fine sandy loam and
		  gravelly fine sandy loam
		Bristol loamy fine sand+
		Agawam fine sandy loam

Ondawa	Ondawa fine sandy loam+ Meadow Muck	Podunk fine sandy loam Hadley very fine sandy loam
Rough stony land		

Other small series and types occur that are not listed. These are not of sufficient area to affect the groups as a whole.

Note: A complete description of the soils unmarked can be found in publications of the Bureau of Chemistry and Soils.

Soil Survey of Berkshire County, Massachusetts.
Soil Survey of Worcester County, Massachusetts.
Soil Survey of Franklin County, Massachusetts (not yet published).
Soil Survey of Columbia County, New York.
Soil Survey of Clinton County, New York.
Soil Survey of Herkimer County, New York.
Soil Survey of Windsor County, Vermont.
Soil Survey of St. Lawrence County, New York.

Soil types marked ($+$) have been encountered for the first time in the Survey of Vermont and their complete description will not be available until the report on the state is published.

Vergennes. The soils of the Vergennes group are potentially the most fertile of this region although from the standpoint of usage the Addison soils are the most used and most productive. The Vergennes soils, due to the general level surface and heavy subsoil, have imperfect drainage and owing to the heavy nature of the surface soil they are difficult to handle. They have gray clay loam surface soils and dark gray rather heavy clay substratum, which is highly calcareous below fifteen to twenty inches. Alfalfa and clover succeed exceptionally well in the better drained positions.

The Vergennes covers about 5 percent of the state and is not used to anything like its full capacity. The difficulty of handling is probably the principal drawback to its use. On some of the extensive flats of the clay loam there is brownish or reddish-brown compact horizon developed at about six to eight inches below the surface. This is not more than an inch or two thick, but where this occurs, little success seems to be had with alfalfa, or any deep-rooted crop. Over the remainder of the type, especially where it is undulating or cut by drainageways, alfalfa succeeds to a marked degree. The Vergennes soils are admirably suited to grass and only the better grasses should be seeded. The roads in this section are all but impassable in wet seasons and place it at a disadvantage as a milk-producing section. Most of this land is relatively cheap.

Addison. The Addison soils occur on smooth low hills and ridges and have better drainage conditions. The soils range from a loam to clay loam in texture and are somewhat browner in color, and weathering is slightly deeper than in the Vergennes. The dark gray calcareous clay is encountered at thirty to thirty-six inches below the surface. These factors make this soil easier to cultivate, and being

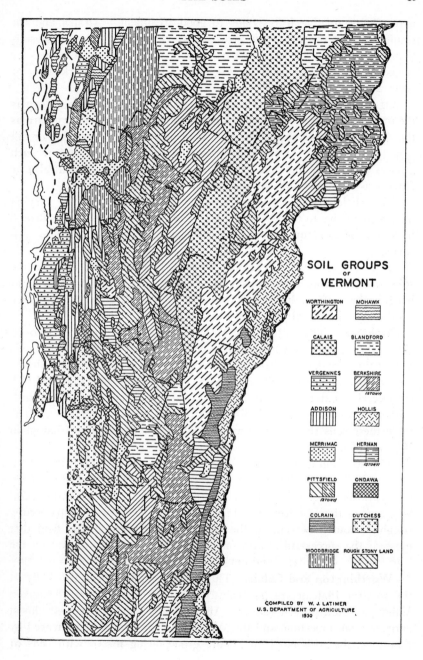

SOIL GROUPS
of
VERMONT

WORTHINGTON   MOHAWK

CALAIS   BLANDFORD

VERGENNES   BERKSHIRE
(STONY)

ADDISON   HOLLIS

MERRIMAC   HERMAN
(STONY)

PITTSFIELD   ONDAWA
(STONY)

COLRAIN   DUTCHESS

WOODBRIDGE   ROUGH STONY LAND

COMPILED BY W. J. LATIMER
U.S. DEPARTMENT OF AGRICULTURE
1930

naturally productive it responds to good treatment. Alfalfa and the staple crops of the valley are grown more extensively upon these soils than any other. The loam in particular is well suited to a variety of crops. The Addison loam is closely related to the Dunkirk soils of New York State.

Of the minor soils of the Addison group the Suffield silt loam is the most important. This soil has much the same color and structure as the Addison but is non-calcareous. It occurs on the outer edge or hill edge of the valley. It is highly adapted to the production of such grasses as timothy and red top, but is not as well suited to alfalfa or clovers as the other soils of this group.

The Sheldon soils represent a smear of sand over clay, at varying depths of twelve to thirty-six inches. They respond well to fertilizers, have a good moisture-holding capacity, and produce well where well farmed.

The Livingston soils represent the low, poorly-drained areas in the soils derived from calcareous clay. They range from dark gray to black in the surface, due to organic matter. When drained they produce good crops of corn, alfalfa, beans and vegetables.

Mohawk. The soils of the Mohawk group occur on low smooth ridges throughout the Champlain Valley, but differ from the other soils in that they are derived from glaciated calcareous shales and are calcareous at shallow depths. They are good general-crop soils and used to a considerable extent for alfalfa, oats, barley, silage corn and beans. Although productive these soils unfortunately are not extensive. It is upon these soils that the agriculture of the islands of Lake Champlain is developed.

The Addison and Mohawk groups of soils are already utilized, not to their full extent, but nearer to their capacity than the other soils. They are the most valued farm soils of the state. More alfalfa might be grown as they are well suited to this crop. These two groups occupy roughly about 7 percent of the state. It was noted in the field that most of the successful alfalfa on the Addison soils was found on the loam and gravelly areas, and not upon the clay loam.

Worthington and Calais. The Calais and Worthington soils of the Central Plateau are less calcareous than those of the Champlain Valley or southwestern valleys. Although the Calais is derived almost entirely from limestone and the Worthington is strangely influenced by limestone, the rock is of an impure grade, being mixed with beds of schist and phyllite. These soils will not effervesce at any depth unless a piece of raw limestone is encountered but are neutral to alkaline in the substratum. The region covered by these soils is highly suited to grass and even the stony areas are in pasture. Although these soils are less broken and less stony than most of Vermont, they are decidedly more stony and rougher than the soils of the Champlain Valley. The Calais-Worthington region has extensive areas in hay and while the acreage in cultivated crops is not high it is greater than in any section outside the Champlain Valley. Corn (silage) and apples are not as extensively grown as in other lower sections.

The Calais soils are loams as are most of the soils of this region. The fine sandy loam soils occupy a relatively small belt, mainly in the region northwest from St. Johnsbury. The Calais loam has a brown surface soil which passes quickly at eight to ten inches into a greenish yellow, partially weathered till which changes at an average depth of twenty inches into a greenish gray unweathered till, rather firm to compact in place.

The Worthington loam is slightly more undulating although it occupies mainly ridge tops. The surface soil is browner, extending to twelve or fifteen inches before passing into the greenish yellow till, which at twenty-four inches grades into the characteristic raw till of this region. The Worthington is not quite such good grassland as the Calais, but it is equally well suited to other crops.

The Marshfield soils occupy the hillsides of the Calais-Worthington country. They are derived from shallower till and contain more stone, but the brown soil is deeper. It is more extensively used for pasture than the other soils.

The Shelburne soils occupy the rather small areas of deep till or drumlins. They have excellent moisture-holding capacity due to the rather compact nature of the substratum, and are highly suited to grass and the other staple crops. They are better suited to orcharding than most of the other soils of the region as their position is usually lower and more protected.

The Reading is a light textured fluffy soil, brown to three feet. It is developed in the region around Woodstock, and occurs on rather steep hillsides. It is excellent grassland and is used mainly for pasture.

The Worthington and Calais soils are primarily grass soils and their full use for dairying should be fostered. They are not as well adapted to the production of some of the other crops needed in conjunction

with dairying as the soils of the Champlain Valley. As a grass country
it is without equal in the Eastern United States. The Worthington is
used successfully for potatoes in Massachusetts and in a few towns in
Vermont. The Calais soils probably contain too much lime for the best
results with potatoes.

Blandford and Woodbridge. The portion of the North Central
Plateau dominated by the Blandford and Woodbridge soil groups is
located on both sides of the northern end of the Green Mountain Range.
It does not support quite as good an agriculture as the Calais-Worthington region due mainly to the fact that the soils are derived from non-
calcareous material. The Blandford soils, which are invariably loams
in texture, occupy the smooth portions of the plateau, while the Woodbridge is along the lower slopes and at the base of the hills. The inter-
vening hillside is more broken and is occupied by the Berkshire soils.
While the materials from which these soils are derived carry slightly
more stone than the Calais or Worthington group, they are not nearly
so stony as the Berkshire and Becket soils of the southern part of the
Central Plateau.

The Blandford loam is a young soil which has not been leached of
its mineral plant food and is a productive soil especially for grass. The
stony areas are comparatively small and most of this soil can be plowed
without difficulty.

The Woodbridge loam is marked by an intense compactness of the
substratum. Water moves along the top of this stratum especially if
there is higher ground from which to drain and this is usually the case
in Vermont. This soil is also comparatively free from stone and is
well suited to meadow and pasture. It contains extensive sugar maple
groves.

The Berkshire soils are more variable in texture, both loam and
fine sandy loam occurring. They are more stony than the soils previously described and contain more shallow spots. The soil is brown in
cultivated fields and the yellowish brown color of the subsoil extends to
twenty or twenty-four inches. The substratum is variable, rarely being
as compact as the Woodbridge and often only firm in place. The
topography is broken to hilly. This land although containing a considerable acreage in hay and other crops is used more extensively for
pasture than for crops. Large areas are in forest.

Berkshire. The Berkshire soils extend south along the Central
Plateau and form most of the soils in the southern part of the plateau

where the stony phase of this group is formed mainly by the Becket soils. These soils, unlike those in the northern part, which are derived from schist, come from gneiss. This rock being more resistant to glacial action is left in quantities upon the soil as bowlders. This region lies at a relatively high altitude of about 1,500 to 1,800 feet above sea level. Most of the stony areas are forested. The smooth and less stony ground is in hay and pasture with a small acreage in other crops. Much of the pasture that at one time was used for cattle and sheep has been abandoned to brush. In this region most of the abandoned farms are found. This region is much the same as the Berkshire Highlands of western Massachusetts. The rugged relief, the stone, and its isolated position are all responsible for the abandoned condition of this region.

Pittsfield. West of the southern extension of the Green Mountain range lies the Southwest Valley and the Taconic range and foothills. In the valley the Pittsfield group of soils is dominant. This group is composed of good farm land and lacks area only to make it the most important soil group of the state. These soils are derived from limestone till, the various members differing mainly in the amount of adulterants of non-calcareous materials. They possess an excellent structure and are very productive, especially for lime-loving crops. The agriculture consists of growing grass for hay (timothy and clover), oats, buckwheat and apples. The soils contain little stone and permit of easy cultivation.

The Pittsfield loam is the highest in lime of any in the group, being highly calcareous at fifteen to twenty inches. The Madrid soils contain some quartzite and are less productive than the Pittsfield soils. The Madrid present few abandoned farms but contain much idle land. The stony areas of this belt are composed mainly of Farmington stony loam. This is a shallow soil and entirely unfit for cultivated crops. Being derived from limestone it is highly suited to pasture.

The Stockbridge and Lenox soils contain much slate and schist admixture, the former heavy and derived from deep till, rather compact in the substratum and the latter darker and having a more friable substratum. Both are good agricultural soils of the same productive power as the Pittsfield but much smaller in area. West from the limestone valleys lies the Taconic range upon which the Dutchess soils are developed. They are derived from non-calcareous shales that have been thinly glaciated. Most of the soils are shallow and filled with small

slate fragments. The region is broken and hilly. The steeper sections are used for pasture and the smoother slopes are used for hay crops, apple orchards, oats and buckwheat. The yields are low.

Most of the soils of the Pittsfield group are used to fair advantage. There are considerable areas of pasture grown up to hardhack (Potentilla fruticosa) which furnishes only fair grass under present conditions. Much of the cultivated land is used for hay (timothy and clover), oats and buckwheat with good results. Most of the recently idle land is on the Madrid, which is a grade poorer than the other members of the Pittsfield group. Soils of the Lenox and Stockbridge series, while not extensive, are highly valued for farming. The dark color of the Lenox, due to a dark graphitic schist from which it originated, might lead to the assumption that it is a better soil than the productive facts warrant. The Farmington soils, composed of shallow stony soil, occur in small areas surrounded by cultivable land, and their use as pasture is unquestioned although their value for other crops is negative.

Colrain. The Eastern Hill region is occupied by two main soil groups, Colrain and Hollis, both hilly and comparatively thin soils. The Colrain soils are derived from schist and impure limestone. They are brown fine sandy loams and carry a noticeable amount of stone. They are used for pasture, hay (timothy and clover) and to a limited extent for other crops, and for apple orcharding. The limestone content enables these soils to maintain a better agriculture than the other soils of this section. These soils make possible the apple orchard belt of Franklin County, Massachusetts.

Hollis. The Hollis soils are derived from schist and quite an area is very shallow and stony, although the loam type is deeper and contains very little stone. They are used to a limited extent for crops and orcharding and are only fairly productive. Much of the area is in forest or used for pasture.

The Bernardston soils are found in small areas in the southeastern part of the state. They are derived from argillite and are dark in color, heavy and fairly deep and although non-calcareous they are productive.

Hermon. The Hermon soil groups are developed in Essex County and other small scattered areas over the eastern part of the state. Most of the soils are stony, being derived from granite. Forest covers most of the land. The cleared areas are used mainly for pasture. Small areas of the Gloucester soils are located southwest of Ascutney

Mountain. They have browner soils than the Hermon and, occurring at lower elevations, are somewhat better adapted to crop production although they contain much stone.

Merrimac. The terrace soils, represented by the Merrimac group, scattered over the entire state along the larger streams, bring the average of some sections up where otherwise their agricultural rating would be very low. These soils are grouped under the Merrimac. They are derived from a wide variety of materials, but all have gravelly or sandy substratum which furnishes excellent drainage. The fine sandy loam texture predominates. They are free from stone and have a level surface. The excellent texture makes a good medium in which to grow crops where the fertility is added. Most of the potatoes produced in the state are grown on these soils.

The true Merrimac soils are developed in the terraces in the southeastern part and are derived from granite, gneiss and schist of the state. These soils also are the leading terrace soils in Massachusetts and are responsible for a great deal of the tobacco and market crops grown in that state. In Vermont this group of soils maintains a substantial agriculture. These soils are highly adapted to such crops as potatoes, tobacco and vegetables but are not particularly well suited to grass.

The Colton soils (of the Merrimac group) are derived from the same material, but are found at higher elevations where the surface soil has developed a gray layer under the forest drift. They occur mainly in the northeastern part of the state, and are adapted to the same crops as the Merrimac with the exception of tobacco.

The Agawam is found on the terraces of the Connecticut River. It is highly productive when supplied with fertilizer. It possesses the best structure of any soil of this region.

The Copake soils are found in the southwestern part and are derived from a mixture of limestone and slate. They have calcareous substrata below two and one-half feet. These soils are adapted to the same range of crops as the Merrimac and, in addition, to clover and alfalfa.

The Bristol soils are derived from quartz and a small admixture of other materials. They reach their greatest development on the sand plains of Chittenden County. They are sandier and less productive than the other terrace soils.

The terrace soils grouped under the Merrimac are all-round soils and highly desirable for small farms, for house sites and for crops which require intensive cultivation. Although fertility must be supplied, the structure is such that crops respond readily to good cultivation. These are the best potato and vegetable soils of this region. These soils are widely distributed and they are held at the highest acreage price of any soils in the state.

Ondawa. The bottom land widely distributed over the state is listed under the Ondawa group. It is composed of fine sandy loam. These soils are only fairly productive. The overflow soils along the Connecticut River are in the Hadley series, which contain darker and decidedly more productive soils which are used for corn, hay and vegetables.

The Podunk and Meadow soils occur on imperfectly to poorly drained overflow land and are used for hay and pasture. Muck areas which also include peat deposits are of little importance under the present agriculture. The bottom land or overflow soils are not as valuable as they were at one time. Disastrous floods in recent years have damaged them in many places by overwash and cutting, and in addition there is the threat of recurrence of floods. In the larger stream bottoms these soils represent the best corn land in the state while the smaller streams contain much good meadow land.

Dutchess. The Dutchess soils are not productive for general crops, but are suited to apple orcharding, and it is upon this land in the western hill region that this industry should be extended. Other soils of the lower belts are highly suited to orchards, but these soils are relatively low in price compared with some of the other soils.

Rough stony land. Rough stony land occupies about 20 percent of the area of the state. It is almost entirely in forest and should remain so for it has little or no agricultural value. There are also extensive areas, approximately 20 percent, covered by the stony types of the Berkshire, Becket, Hermon and Hollis groups that should remain in forest unless there is a far greater demand for pasture than at present. The stony areas of such soils as the Worthington, Calais, Blandford, Woodbridge and Colrain can be successfully used for pasture, under present conditions. The stony areas of the Pittsfield, Madrid and Addison group are highly adapted to and are used for pasture. The Berkshire and Becket stony loam types are used for hay and pasture. In the abandoned districts where most of these soils are found, the pastures have grown up in brush or forest and the meadows have degenerated into pasture, or are fast approaching that stage.

On areas of stony soils, adapted to grass, where they occur in conjunction with smooth cultivable land, the value of the stony land for pasture is enhanced. Where the stony areas are too extensive they can only be utilized for forest.

———

Prepared for the Commission by W. J. Latimer of the United States Bureau of Chemistry and Soils. Mr. Latimer was in charge of the Soil Survey of Vermont, conducted under the joint auspices of the United States Department of Agriculture, the Vermont Agricultural Experiment Station and the Vermont Commission on Country Life. The detailed results of the Vermont Soil Survey will appear in the publications of the United States Department of Agriculture.

VI

AGRICULTURE

The Committees whose findings are epitomized in this chapter have attempted to set forth existing conditions, to state current problems and to point out the needs for development. Topography, soils, temperature, rainfall and markets have influenced Vermont's agricultural evolution. Her people could do little to change these fundamental conditions, but have done much by way of adapting themselves to them. Hence it is that her agriculture has had an active, illustrious past. It certainly is enjoying a vigorous present. It looks forward to a prosperous future.

Vermont may be roughly divided into four agricultural sections: the Champlain Valley on the west, the broad rolling plateau to the north, the river valleys on the east and throughout the central part, and the rough, hilly Green Mountains running north and south.

The Champlain Valley is a glaciated limestone section ranging in elevation from 100 feet above sea level on the west to 600-800 feet on the east. It extends from northern Rutland County through Addison, Chittenden, Grand Isle and part of Franklin counties. It contains much nearly level land and is well adapted to livestock farming.

The plateau areas of eastern Franklin and Orleans counties are more rolling than is the Champlain Valley and their soils are more easily worked than the heavy Champlain clays. This is a well-developed farming section.

The river valley soils are excellent farming lands and some of Vermont's best dairy farms are located thereon. Silage corn does well. However, many valley farms are either short of pasture or depend on adjacent, rough hill pasturage.

The Green Mountains' hill areas are too rough and too inaccessible to sustain a prosperous agriculture, although narrow valleys form small areas of good land. Most of this great area seems best fitted to timber production or, in a more limited way, to recreational purposes.

Climatic conditions are well suited to the production of grass, oats, potatoes and dairy cattle but are less well suited to the growth of corn. The Weather Bureau maps set forth the average length of growing season, temperatures and rainfalls throughout the state. Along Lake Champlain the average frostless season is 160 days, in the mountains 110 days or less. Precipitation is usually ample. Droughts causing crop failure rarely occur. However, the rainfall is less abundant in the Champlain Valley than elsewhere and its heavy clay pasture lands occasionally suffer.

Vermont's abundant rainfall, cool climate, somewhat irregular topography and inherently fertile soils fix the type of her agriculture. She can produce hay and pasture to better advantage than other farm crops. Her success in the past has depended on, and still depends on, turning the grass which grows on her meadows and pastures into the highest priced salable product. This means that livestock farming must remain her main agricultural industry, although its exact nature may change. The feeding of cattle, horses and sheep has been important in the past, but now grass can most profitably be turned into fluid milk.

History

The first settlers in Vermont came from nearby colonies. The conditions that confronted them were hard. Their courage and resourcefulness command our admiration. There were no cleared lands, no houses, no barns, few neighbors, no good basis for judgment in choosing a farm location and no accepted code of agricultural practice.

As a rule the more elevated areas were first cleared and settled and gradually a farming procedure, based on the environment at that time, became established. No sooner, however, had these new practices become settled habits than changing economic conditions necessitated their revision. Even unto this day continual readjustment to changing conditions has been necessary; and who shall say that our present-day agriculture has become static?

The early agriculture was largely self-sufficing. Cattle were kept to supply butter, cheese, milk and beef for the family larder and leather for shoes and other farm purposes. Sheep were kept to supply mutton for the table and wool for family clothing. Swine, turkeys, geese and other poultry were kept for family use. Maple products were used in place of imported sugar. Wheat, corn, oats and other crops were grown to supply the family needs or to feed livestock. The small amounts of cash needed were first secured from the sale of potash and pearlash and, later from the sale of surplus farm products not needed for family use. Gradually a commercial agriculture was established.

Prior to 1850 general livestock farming was common in the central and eastern sections. Sales of sheep, lambs and wool early became a main source of cash income. In 1850 one-half of the farms in a typical Orange County town carried upwards of fifty sheep and one-fourth from 50 to 500 sheep, the average for all sheep farms being fifty-three. While wool was the main product, some fat sheep and lambs were butchered and were hauled in the sled loads of produce from this area to Boston and other cities. Even after Merinos had become the current breed elsewhere in Vermont, mutton sheep were still the prevailing type in some sections.

Horses were raised for sale in the early days to a greater extent than is generally realized, especially in regions too remote from cities to engage in grain raising. For example, Randolph and Royalton furnished many to the export and to the driving-horse trade during the first part of the last century. These sales continued to be an important source of income up to 1860, the cheaper grades being sold as street-car horses. Mule colts were also raised from 1840 to 1860 for the West Indies sugar trade. In 1789 a Randolph farmer brought into Vermont from West Springfield, Mass., a stallion which came to be called the "Justin Morgan" horse and became the foundation animal of the Morgan breed.

The 1850 census data show that in Randolph there were 4.4 milch cows and 7.3 other cattle one year old and over per farm. Apparently cattle raising was then of more importance than dairying. The average 1850 production per cow was 66.6 pounds of butter and fifty-eight pounds of cheese. Only two Randolph farmers produced 1,000 or more pounds of butter, only thirteen, 100 or more pounds of cheese. No material development of dairying occurred prior to the advent of the railroad in 1848.

Pork brought in a tidy sum each year, but after 1840 the eastern markets apparently were supplied largely from New York, Ohio and the West. At any rate, in 1840 the average Randolph farm carried eleven swine, and in 1850 only five.

Farming in western Vermont became specialized earlier than in eastern sections of the state. Grain growing became an important industry before 1820. The grain was distilled locally or hauled to markets as such and sold. Wheat early became the staple crop grown on the level and heavy Champlain soils, being sold in Troy and Albany. Wheat, wheat and more wheat was the goal, as it has been of late in Kansas and North Dakota. However, disease, insect ravages and Western New York competition ruined Vermont's grain business about 1820, and nearly ruined the farmers themselves before they could reorganize their practices and install a new type of farming. This, however, was eventually accomplished. Between 1820 and 1850 Western Vermont became a prosperous livestock producing section, the Champlain Valley became a noted, pure-bred Merino sheep producing area. It furnished breeding stock to the wide world, especially to Ohio and adjoining states and, in later years, to the range country of the great West, to Australia and to South Africa. But the sheep that produced the golden fleece was thus killed; for Western, Australian and African wool could be, and was, sold in New England markets at such low prices that Vermont could not compete.

Cattle in large numbers were driven to Boston, Montreal, New York and other markets in these early days. However, the railroads upset things. The livestock grown on the (then) cheap grazing and crop lands in the Middle West began to reach eastern markets; and Vermont's horse, wool and meat producing industries started on the downward path. Her farmers turned then to the cow.

Butter production developed rapidly from about 1850, reaching its peak about 1900. Sales of Vermont butter in Boston and New York were first reported about 1840, and, some years later, St. Albans became one of the greatest of butter producing centers in the world. For thirty years most of the butter was farm made, but creameries developed rapidly after 1880. During the last half of the past century Vermont butter was the acme of perfection in New England markets, but from 1890 on, competition with western butter became increasingly acute. There were apparently made in Vermont in 1899, 1917 and 1927 approximately 35,000,000, 11,000,000 and 4,000,000 pounds of butter. These figures are more or less guess work—except the last one—but they serve to indicate the trend.

The production of sheep, wool, horses, pork and butter having become unprofitable because of the competition of lower-cost areas, Vermont farmers and farming faced a difficult situation. However, the large eastern city milk sheds were continually expanding and, after 1900, sweet cream and fluid milk sales began to afford more profitable outlets for dairy products than did butter. The modern development of Vermont's fluid milk business began about fifteen years ago.

A decision of the Interstate Commerce Commission in 1916 which placed the freight rates on milk from Vermont points to Boston on a favorable basis gave great impetus to dairying in Vermont. In the ten years from 1917 to 1927 the total deliveries of milk and cream to dairy plants, expressed in milk equivalents on a 3.7 percent basis, increased from 691 to 1,056 million pounds. During this period there was a marked change in the disposition made of the product. In 1917, 22 percent was shipped as milk, 29 percent as cream, 38 percent as butter and 11 percent in other forms. In 1927, 45 percent was shipped as milk, 37 percent as cream, 14 percent as butter and 4 percent in other forms.

TABLE 1. UTILIZATION OF MILK EQUIVALENTS IN VERMONT PLANTS

| Year | Total pounds 3.7 percent milk equivalents | Pounds shipped | | Pounds made into butter | Pounds manufactured otherwise |
		As milk	As cream		
	(thousands)	(thousands)	(thousands)	(thousands)	(thousands)
1917	690,838	153,395	197,633	263,084	76,726
1918	693,115	184,437	180,511	249,710	78,457
1919	786,606	222,754	189,611	262,009	112,232
1920	865,990	239,196	243,351	301,478	81,965
1921	948,695	242,780	294,793	343,983	67,139
1922	957,572	290,333	324,754	307,355	35,130
1923	988,466	327,547	334,493	272,994	53,432
1924	988,693	335,463	339,886	251,585	61,759
1925	975,286	398,046	330,274	198,705	48,261
1926	1,030,334	415,947	391,839	152,060	70,388
1927	1,055,564	477,072	389,415	150,494	38,583
1928		Not available			
1929	914,438	474,299	310,498	93,159	36,482

As the production of market milk became greater after 1916, coincidently most other production lines declined in importance. A study of the trends clearly indicates that fluid milk production is increasingly engrossing the energies and attention of Vermont farmers.

The total numbers of all cattle and of dairy cows have varied up and down from 1910 to 1930, while the numbers of sheep have steadily declined, only one-third as many being fed now as in 1910. Swine were formerly, and until quite recently, used as a ready means of converting skim- and butter-milks into money, being a side line to the butter industry; but there was less than one hog left on the average Vermont farm in 1930. Horses have shrunk in numbers and fewer colts have been raised. There are now fewer farms than of old and less field work done per farm, and the voice of the tractor is heard in the land. Chickens have varied in numbers from thirty to forty per farm. Poultry keeping is a minor enterprise on most farms and has maintained this status for many years.

The records of trends in numbers of farms, acreages in farms and acreages of crops grown show that Vermont farmers have abandoned crop land to woods and pasture, and that they have profoundly decreased the total acreages of most crops other than hay. Farms have been abandoned more rapidly than farm land, and hence the average size of Vermont farms has increased. Furthermore, as has been already indicated, despite farm abandonment there has been an impressive increase in the amount of milk produced. The data show how greatly the emphasis has changed. Market milk production has replaced almost every other line, and less attention is being paid to the growth of livestock other than cows.

TABLE 2. NUMBER OF FARM ANIMALS IN VERMONT

	1910[1]	1916[2]	1920[1]	1925[1]	1930[1]
All cattle	430,314	443,000	435,480	393,274	421,242
Dairy cows	222,838	273,000	290,122	279,448	251,940
Sheep	118,551	100,000	62,756	34,670	41,000[3]
Swine	94,821	113,000	72,761	43,864	19,551
Horses and mules	81,213	89,000	77,832	63,504	52,661
Chickens	911,730	......	799,797	941,014	748,704

Crop acreages decreased rapidly from 1910 to 1930. Corn grown for grain occupied only 5,712 acres in 1930 as compared to 21,186 in 1920. Although previous reports probably confuse corn for grain with corn for silage, apparently the drop in acreage of corn for grain from 1910 has been continuous. The 1930 acreages of threshed oats and barley, as compared with those of 1910, were respectively 43 and 31 percents. The 1930 potato acreage was but half that of 1910.

The reversion to forest and to non-agricultural uses and the retention of crop lands and pastures have not occurred evenly all over the state. The larger percentages of lands passing into non-farm uses since 1900 pertain to the three southern counties, Windham, Windsor and Bennington, and to Essex County in the northeast. The larger percentages of land retained in farms pertain to five northern counties,

[1] Current United States Census Reports.
[2] Yearbook United States Department of Agriculture 1916.
[3] Crops and Markets February, 1931.

Grand Isle, Franklin, Chittenden, Lamoille and Orleans. Every county except Franklin shows some decrease. The first named group of counties has lost more than one-fourth of its farms since 1930; the northern group less than one-tenth. In the other five counties the farm areas have decreased between one-tenth and one-fifth.

Yields per acre, particularly of hay and potatoes, seem to have increased over the period of years from 1910 to 1929, the average per acre yields for 1910-1919 as compared with those for 1920-1929 being for potatoes 122 and 158 bushels, for hay 1.33 and 1.56 tons.

TABLE 3. FARMS AND USE OF FARM LAND IN VERMONT

Census years	1910	1916	1920	1925	1930
Number of farms	32,709	......	29,075	27,786	24,898
Acreage in farm land	4,663,577	......	4,235,811	3,925,683	3,896,097
Acres corn for grain	42,887[1]	45,000[1]	21,186	8,046	5,712
Acres of corn for silage	.....	.....	49,872	59,639	44,472
Acres potatoes	26,859	23,000	24,182	18,507	13,874
Acres of oats threshed	71,510	80,000	83,097	51,368	33,127
Acres of barley threshed	10,586	15,000	8,594	4,619	3,239
Acres hay cut	975,177	980,000	926,366	930,180	918,946

TABLE 4. CHANGES IN FARM AREA

County	Land in Farms 1900	Land in Farms 1930	Decrease	%
	Acres	Acres	Acres	
Franklin	361,000	361,000	.....	..
Grand Isle	47,000	46,000	1,000	2
Chittenden	291,000	277,500	14,000	5
Orleans	385,000	360,000	25,000	7
Lamoille	220,000	200,000	20,000	10
Addison	404,000	355,000	49,000	12
Caledonia	349,000	301,000	48,000	13
Rutland	458,000	382,000	76,000	17
Orange	426,000	351,000	75,000	18
Washington	378,000	304,000	74,000	19
Windsor	548,000	400,000	148,000	27
Essex	159,000	115,000	44,000	28
Windham	429,000	282,000	147,000	35
Bennington	279,000	162,000	117,000	41

The major 1931 agricultural enterprises on Vermont farms are: The production of such crops as can be produced most economically to feed the dairy cow; fluid milk production. Certain relatively minor enterprises are to be noted: Maple products, poultry products, apples, potatoes, beans, and truck crops. Many agricultural problems center about

[1] Probably includes some corn for silage.

these major and minor enterprises and are discussed in the following pages.

Feed Crops

The all important problem confronting Vermont farmers has been to utilize feed crops, turning them into cash or into marketable livestock and livestock products. Before rapid transportation obtained, a market existed for some crops used for human consumption and grain feed crops were raised in amounts sufficient to supply livestock needs. But as railway and motor transportation has developed, Vermont farmers have found it increasingly advantageous to purchase grain

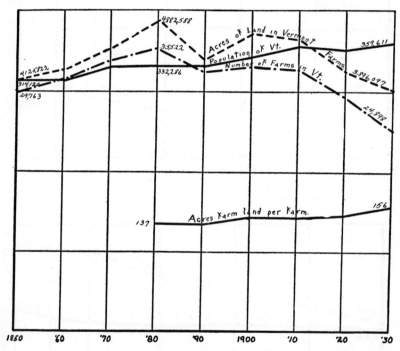

FIG. 1. Population, farms and farm land in Vermont (U. S. Census Reports).

grown on areas of more easily worked and more fertile farm land, to utilize more of home lands for the growth of hay and other roughages and to cease cultivating much of the rough and stony land, turning it, in so far as possible, into pasture. And in proportion as it becomes necessary or economical to produce more pasture feed of high quality, these rough and hilly pasture lands will find their way back into the forests from which originally they were converted.

During the last fifty years the tendency has been towards more rather than less intensive agriculture, while at the same time, the acreage per farm has increased. These tendencies are shown graphically in figures 1 to 3.

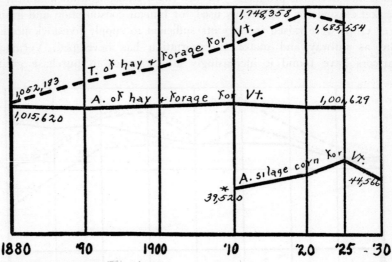

FIG. 2. Tons of hay and forage, acres of hay and forage, and acres of silage corn in Vermont (U. S. Census Reports).
*Silage and fodder corn for 1910.

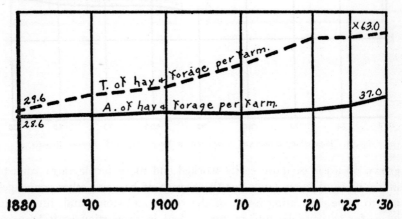

FIG. 3. Tons of hay and forage per farm and acres of hay and forage per farm in Vermont (U. S. Census Reports).
xHay and silage only for 1930.

Figure 1 illustrates the fact that while population has increased since 1850, both farm land and numbers of farms have decreased since 1880 at the same time that acres per farm have increased. Farms have shrunk in numbers but grown in size.

Figure 2 shows an increase of 60 percent in hay and forage yields on a decreased acreage of hay and silage corn combined, while figure 3 shows a much greater increase in hay and forage production per farm than in acreage of hay, the principal forage crop.

The growth of grain crops may prove profitable on large areas of easily tilled land. However, it usually costs more to raise than to buy grain in Vermont. Whenever and wherever more high quality hay can be grown than can be fed locally, grain growing is much more likely to prove profitable than under other circumstances. Trends in grain crop and oat production during the last fifty years are shown graphically in figure 4.

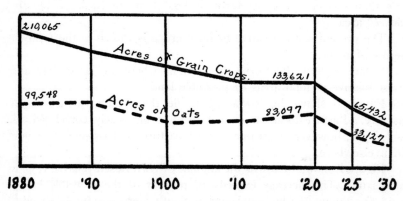

Fig. 4. Acres of all grain crops and of oats in Vermont (U. S. Census Reports).

TABLE 5.   GRAIN CROPS—ACREAGES AND ACRE YIELDS

	Corn		Oats		Rye		Buckwheat		Barley		Wheat	
	Acres	Acre yield	Acres	Acre yield	Acres	Acre yield	Acres	Acre yield	Acres	Acre yield	Acres	Acre yield
1880	...55,249	36.5	99,548	37.6	6,319	11.4	17,649	20.2	10,552	25.4	20,748	16.3
1890	...41,790	40.7	101,582	32.6	3,379	12.8	13,429	20.2	16,427	25.6	8,397	19.6
1900	...60,633	38.3	73,372	37.4	2,264	14.1	9,910	19.8	12,152	31.3	1,796	19.3
1910	...42,887	40.0	71,510	29.9	1,115	15.0	7,659	22.7	10,586	26.9	678	20.8
1920	...21,186	44.2	83,097	28.8	527	13.2	4,330	18.6	8,594	22.9	11,276	15.6
1925	... 8,046	45.2	51,368	34.1	221	25.5	2,310	21.6	4,619	28.5	1,307	21.0
1930	... 5,712	46.5	33,127	30.5	...	..	...	..	3,239	36.6	...	..

Table 6 presents the average situation per farm in relation to crop acreages and animals.

TABLE 6. CROP ACREAGES AND ANIMALS PER FARM
(U. S. Census for 1930)

Number of farms 24,898	Acres plowable pasture 11
Acres 156	Acres silage corn 1.8
Acres of cleared land 96	Acres of oats, barley and corn (for grain) 1.7
Acres of hay 37	Animal units 19.6
Acres of open pasture 47	Horses 2.1

Hay lands comprised 37 and hay and pasture 84 of the ninety-six acres of cleared land per farm, or 39 and 89 percents, respectively, of the totals. Farm buildings, yards and uncropped land occupy several acres on every farm. Hence when dealing with yield and quality increments of all other crops, consideration is being given to an average of less than sixteen acres per farm or less than one-sixth of the total cleared area.

The present status relative to farm crops is shown in the following series of maps.

Figure 5 shows by towns the sections where the larger hay areas exist relative to total areas of plowable land.

Figure 6 shows by towns where lie the greatest areas of open pasture. Pasture locations do not seem to be closely correlated with soil types; however, a greater area of pasture land exists in the north than elsewhere.

Figure 7 shows by towns the amount of corn raised relative to plowable land. This acreage exceeds 10 percent of the plowable land in only five towns, the highest being in South Hero, Grand Isle County, where 14 percent of the plowable area is thus occupied.

Figure 8 shows by towns the amount of small grains raised relative to plowable land. Only in limited areas does the small grain acreage reach 10 percent of the plowable land.

Figure 9 shows by towns the small grain acreage per farm. This is a significant showing. In only ten towns is there an average of ten acres grown per farm and in many good farming towns the average is less than one acre.

Dairying seems likely to continue to be the main Vermont farm enterprise and horses to continue to be used for power purposes on most dairy farms. Hence the question naturally arises what are likely

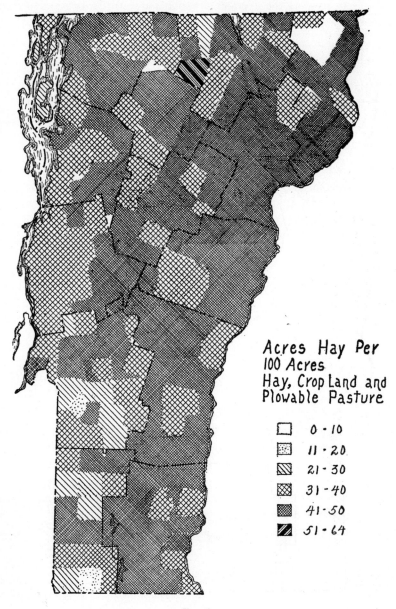

Acres Hay Per
100 Acres
Hay, Crop Land and
Plowable Pasture

☐	0 - 10
▨	11 - 20
▧	21 - 30
▨	31 - 40
▨	41 - 50
▨	51 - 64

Fig. 5.

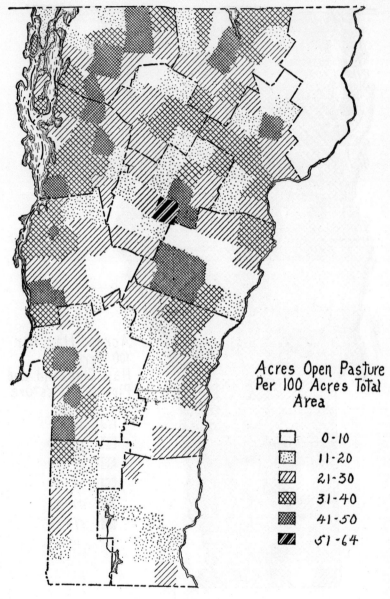

Acres Open Pasture
Per 100 Acres Total
Area

☐   0 - 10
▦   11 - 20
▨   21 - 30
▩   31 - 40
▦   41 - 50
▧   51 - 64

Fig. 6.

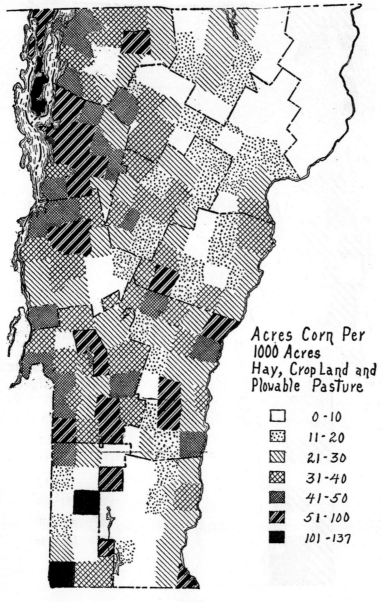

Acres Corn Per
1000 Acres
Hay, Crop Land and
Plowable Pasture

☐	0 - 10
▨	11 - 20
▨	21 - 30
▨	31 - 40
▨	41 - 50
▨	51 - 100
■	101 - 137

Fig. 7.

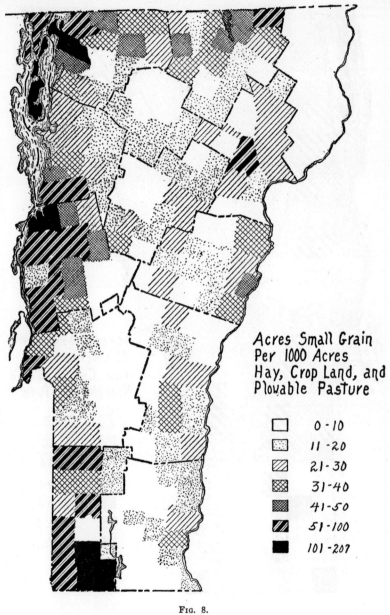

Acres Small Grain
Per 1000 Acres
Hay, Crop Land, and
Plovable Pasture

☐	0 - 10
▦	11 - 20
▨	21 - 30
▨	31 - 40
▨	41 - 50
▨	51 - 100
■	101 - 207

Fig. 8.

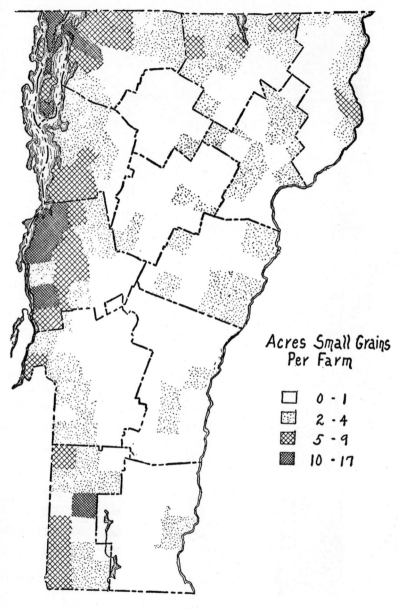

FIG. 9.

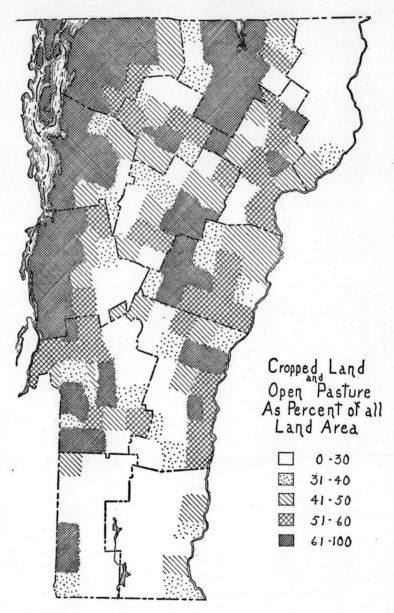

Cropped Land
and
Open Pasture
As Percent of all
Land Area

☐   0 - 30
▦   31 - 40
▨   41 - 50
▩   51 - 60
▦   61 - 100

Fig. 10. This map not only shows where the farm land is located, but by reading it inversely, it shows the woodland areas.

to be the most important livestock feeds grown for these animals. If past trends are indicative of the future, it may be expected that home-grown grains and rough open and wooded pasture will furnish a decreasing amount of feed. The future source of home-grown feeds will be the better hay and pasture lands.

Expansion of the dairy industry has been made possible in part by selling less and feeding more hay. Relatively little hay is now being sold. Yet further expansion may be made possible if hay yields on the better meadows are increased and some of the rougher or poorer meadows are turned into pasture. A large share of Vermont's hay land and pasture areas produce low yields of poor quality. Effort should be directed first toward putting the soil into such condition that heavier yields and more legumes can be raised. This implies better farming, greater lime usage, more liberal fertilization, better care and better use of manure, supplemented with phosphatic fertilizers.

Table 7 indicates the number of farmers using limestone and the tonnages applied, as shown by county agents' yearly reports.

TABLE 7. GROUND LIMESTONE USAGE

Year	Number farmers	Tons used	Year	Number farmers	Tons used
1924	532	2,337	1928	917	6,446
1925	526	2,740	1929	966	8,601
1926	828	3,705	1930	898	7,268
1927	1,061	6,746			

There seems reason to believe that the 1928-1930 figures and perhaps some others are too low. While some advance is being made, the total amount used is far below the estimated yearly requirement of 500,000 tons if the Vermont farm soils are to be maintained in a neutral condition.

Table 8 shows present acreages and yields of the various hay crops (1930 U. S. Census).

TABLE 8. ACREAGES AND YIELDS OF HAY CROPS

	Tons per acre	Acres	Percent of total acreage
Timothy or timothy and clover mixed	1.30	680,707	74.5
Other tame grasses	.94	183,665	20.1
Small grains	1.86	20,692	2.3
Clovers	1.73	14,582	1.6
Wild hay and annual legumes	.93	7,460	.8
Alfalfa	2.00	6,805	.7
All hay	1.25	913,911	100.0

The trend towards better quality is shown below by the increase in acreages of clover and alfalfa. Increased acreages of the legumes result not only in better quality but also, since they are high yielding hay crops, in better yields.

TABLE 9. INCREASES IN THE ACREAGE OF LEGUME HAY CROPS

Year	Clovers	Alfalfa
	Acres	Acres
1900	3,692	38
1910	4,136	252
1920	5,580	1,765
1930	14,582	6,805

Vermont pastures have received less attention than have the meadows and their condition is less favorable for feed production. There are 284,000 acres of open plowable pasture and nearly 890,000 acres of open pasture that is not plowable in the state, or one and one-fourth times the total number of acres of meadow. The average (1929) acre yield of nine Rutland County pastures was 1,596 pounds of well-cured grass. Possibilities of improvement were shown by the fact that the average yield of these same nine pastures was economically increased 123 percent during the same season by the spring application of lime and fertilizer as a topdressing.

Opportunities along this line are many, but as yet little work has been done to determine what pasture treatment will be most effective over a period of years. Research along this line should greatly benefit the dairying industry. Of equal importance is the question of fencing and controlled grazing. No information is available on this point.

The 1930 United States Census report is the first one to list sweet clover pasture in Vermont. Two hundred twenty-six farmers reported 708 acres. If less than one-tenth of the acreage of open plowable pasture were sown to sweet clover it would be equivalent to three acres on each farm. This would add 25,000 acres of sweet clover pasture to our feed resources. Coming as it does into use the first season after seeding and at a time when grass pastures are relatively unproductive, this would be likely to increase the available food by an equivalent of the needs of 20,000 or more animal units.

The Committee makes the following recommendations with respect to feed crops:

1. Much Vermont farm land, especially hay land, should be limed often enough to produce approximate neutrality An appli-

lication of at least 500,000 tons yearly would be needed if this end is to be accomplished.

2. Effort should be made to decrease the cost of lime and to lessen the labor of delivery at the farm through bulk handling and regular trucking service.

3. Superphosphate should be used as a supplement to all stable manure used. An application of 200 pounds per acre per year is usually sufficient.

4. The alfalfa acreage should be increased as rapidly as hay land can be fitted for its growth; and until land is fitted to grow alfalfa in pure culture, some seed should be included in meadow seeding mixtures wherever the land is well drained and has been limed.

5. Sufficient acreage of sweet clover pasture to replace soiling crops should be grown on every dairy farm where late summer and early fall pasture is apt to be short, so be it the land is made fit for its growth.

6. Information is needed on:

   (a) The minimum hay yield below which, under various farming conditions, the crop is likely to become unprofitable.

   (b) The merits of different methods of increasing or maintaining hay yields: *e.g.,* plowing and reseeding; plowing, fertilizing and reseeding; plowing, liming, fertilizing and reseeding; the use of stable manure, commercial fertilizer and lime as topdressing without plowing.

   (c) The optimum acreage of pasture relative to that of other roughages; the number of animal units pastured.

   (d) The factors determining whether or not land should be retained as pasture.

   (e) The economic conditions which make intensive pasture land farming practicable (fencing, fertilizing, liming, controlled grazing, growing sweet clover).

   Pending the answer to these questions, pasture fertilization seems advisable on most of the better pasture lands.

7. A general survey of needs for and the economy of using the different kinds of farm machinery would be helpful. Information is needed as to the kinds of farm tools needed in order that Vermont farmers may successfully compete with

other sections of the country in the production of dairy-farm crops and as to the acreage necessary to the profitable use of each farm tool.

Dairy Products

The major dairy problems confronting Vermont farmers are low cost of production to meet competition, adjustment of supply to demand and efficient marketing. Low cost of production can be secured only with well bred, well fed, well stabled and healthy cows. Supply can be adjusted to demand by producing a more nearly even year-round supply of a safe, clean milk product. Efficient marketing can be secured only by eliminating inefficient marketing practices and by better producer organization for marketing purposes.

As heretofore has been set forth, fluid milk and sweet cream now constitute the principal sources of farm income. About 65 percent of the total Vermont farm income is derived from the sale of dairy products—mostly fluid milk and sweet cream—and surplus dairy cattle. On many farms over 90 percent of the total income is thus derived. Vermont is unique in that for a long time her bovine population has outnumbered her human population (421,000 cattle, 359,000 people in 1930).

The numbers of milk cows per county, per farm and per 100 crop acres by counties appear in table 10.

TABLE 10. DISTRIBUTION OF COWS DENSITY OF COW POPULATION, JANUARY 1, 1930

Counties	Total number of milch cows	Cows per farm	Cows per 100 crop acres
Franklin	34,274	14.9	27.2
Rutland	28,685	13.3	25.0
Orleans	28,402	12.2	27.8
Chittenden	24,226	13.1	24.6
Addison	23,805	11.8	17.1
Caledonia	20,193	9.7	25.6
Washington	19,030	8.7	23.8
Windsor	17,793	6.8	18.6
Orange	16,920	7.4	19.1
Lamoille	13,701	9.6	25.7
Windham	9,826	5.6	15.6
Bennington	6,865	7.2	15.1
Essex	5,216	9.1	20.2
Grand Isle	3,544	8.1	15.7
Total and average	251,940	10.1	22.3

The outstanding dairy counties are located in the Champlain Valley and in the broad northern plateau region, and tend to be located on the following soil types: Mohawk, Calais, Vergennes, Addison, Blandford, Merrimac, Woodbridge, Dutchess, Pittsfield and Worthington. The state soil map (p. 49) indicates that the better dairy towns roughly follow the location of these soils.

Two Champlain Valley counties, especially adapted to dairying, are relatively undeveloped, namely, Addison and Grand Isle. Addison was the center of the sheep and horse development of the middle of the nineteenth century and started late in the dairying game. Furthermore her broad areas of heavy soils are ideal grass lands and hay was grown and sold for years. But there is now little market for hay to be sold as such. Then again the sheep and horse barns of the fifties and sixties are not well fitted to house dairy cattle. And, finally, her heavy clay roads are almost impassable in spring and fall. Grand Isle was, and to some extent still is, given over to orcharding and to bean growing. It was an isolated area until in 1899 the Rutland Railroad reached and traversed its length. It, too, lacks modern dairy barns. When Addison and Grand Isle farmers become fluid milk minded, build cow barns, grow alfalfa, improve pastures and build year-round roads, a great expansion of the dairy business in these areas may be expected.

Low cost of production. Milk production per cow is relatively low. According to the 1925 United States Census, Massachusetts cows averaged 5,280 pounds per year, New Jersey cows 5,600 and Vermont cows 4,100. While these figures are considerably below the United States Department of Agriculture figures they seem relatively comparable. Vermont farmers raise their stock. Massachusetts and New Jersey farmers are apt to buy rather than to raise replacements. Many Vermont farmers have surplus stock to sell at attractive figures. This means a low average age of cows kept at home and milked and a low average production due to their relative immaturity. Then, too, Vermont milk as a whole tests higher in butter fat than that of southern New England where the sale of whole milk rather than of butter fat has long prevailed. In short many Vermont farmers are still breeding as if they were butter makers instead of market milk makers. Furthermore our dairymen feed less heavily than do their southern neighbors, relying more on the use of home grown hay and pasture and less on the use of purchased grain.

Changes taking place in average production per cow in Vermont dairy herd improvement associations are illustrated by the following 1910 to 1930 averages:

TABLE 11. AVERAGE PRODUCTION PER COW, 1910-1930

Year	Pounds	Year	Pounds
1910	5,120	1920	5,320
1911	5,470	1921	5,340
1912	5,932	1922	5,820
1913	5,550	1923	6,030
1914	5,450	1924	6,060
1915	5,680	1925	5,940
1916	5,710	1926	6,450
1917	5,720	1927	6,700
1918	5,040	1928	6,632
		1929	6,628
1919	5,060	1930	6,450

Of course the dairymen, members of such associations, naturally are among the intelligentsia of the dairying world. They are likely to be better informed, to own better cows and to feed better than do the dairying hoi polloi. These figures are unquestionably much higher than the state average. However, the increases are heartening, in round figures being: 1910-14, 5,500 pounds; 1915-19, 5,450 pounds; 1920-24, 5,700 pounds; 1925-30, 6,450 pounds.

If association record data be compared with successive census figures, it becomes manifest that the tested herds are making greater progress than the average herds.

There were thirty associations in Vermont in January 1930, with several hundred dairymen members. What these everyday dairymen and everyday cows have done, other humans and bovines can do—to increase the surplus. If, however, a less number of cows, eating as a whole less for maintenance and more for milk making, give the same yields, the milk surplus is not increased and the surplus of money in the dairyman's pocket is increased.

It is well understood that the herd sire is vitally important in the future of any herd which is raising its replacements. Registration *per se* affords no guaranty that an animal is prepotent for characteristics of production or type. However, since purebred stock breeders as a class pay more attention to care and productivity than do breeders of stock of unknown ancestry, and since the several dairy breeds have been developed through selection and long years of continuous breeding for certain characteristics, including production, other things being equal the registered is advantaged over the non-registrable sire. The 1930 listers' figures show that there were 2,480 registered and 10,565 unregistered sires in use, 19 percent of the total being registered.

Individual cow and parentage records enable one, with some degree of assurance, to select herd sires able to transmit high production capacity. Studies of dairy herd improvement association data indicate that when a herd sire consistently raises the production of five or more unselected daughters over that of their dams, he may be expected to induce similar increases under similar conditions throughout his life. Thus is afforded a method of herd improvement which can be followed by owners of grade cattle as well as of purebred stock. Such production and parentage records in hand for 136 Vermont bulls indicate that seventy-two increased and sixty-four decreased production. Now it obviously takes some years to "prove" a bull. Unfortunately only twenty-one of these seventy-two sires of high producing animals were alive when "proved." In order to stimulate the proving of dairy sires while living, the Vermont Extension Service is putting into operation a proved sire program. Cooperators agree, so far as possible, to follow a system of proving sires with production records on the progeny of living animals and, with the assistance of a central committee, are trying to place with other breeders those sires proven worthy of further use in order that they may continue to do good work.

Vermont is ideally fitted to be a dairy stock raising area. Southern New England looks to it for replacements. Yet Vermont, which now has become a milk shipping state, is not as likely to have surplus stock to sell as in the past. According to the 1930 census, Vermont as a whole had one yearling heifer for each seven cows, and three-fourths of her farms had such heifers on them. Speaking in general terms, the counties at the north end and on the west side of the state, most largely given over to market milk making, averaged thirteen yearling heifers to 100 cows; on the east side and south end, seventeen to 100.

There would appear to be a buyers' market for surplus stock in Vermont in certain sections and a sellers' market in other sections. Neither Vermont farmers nor southern New England farmers who sell only whole milk care as a rule to raise their own replacements. However, Vermont farmers having surplus stock are reasonably sure of a market provided high quality animals are made available. Buyers claim that Vermont cattle are apt to be undersized and that too many culls are offered; yet Vermont cattle are usually preferred to western stuff because they are more accessible, are persistent producers and are raised under climatic conditions analagous to those of southern New England. Jersey blood is somewhat predominant in the surplus stock sections. Jerseys are well adapted to their home conditions and to butter or cream making, but the intensive dairying industry of southern New England as a rule prefers larger animals.

It is well known that a cow's capacity to make milk depends on her inherent ability to convert food and on the amount and kind of food she eats. A definite amount is required for maintenance and on this low plane of feeding she gives little more than enough to enable her to care for her calf. If more milk is called for, more food must be supplied. The cheapest food she eats is roughage and all that she can advantageously consume should be fed to her. The suggestions dealing with feed crops are of vital importance in this connection. The types of roughage now commonly fed, apart from the summer pasture, are used largely to maintain the cow, to keep her alive, to run the living machine. If plenty of a good quality of roughage is fed, it contributes more or less to the maintenance of the milk flow; however, the amounts and kinds of grain fed determine the milk flow to a considerable, and probably to a larger, extent. Unless grain is fed, a cow will rarely make more than 2,500 to 3,000 pounds of milk during a year.

The well-informed dairyman under normal conditions feeds about a pound of grain for each three and one-half pounds of 4 percent milk, a bit more in winter, a bit less in summer. He is quite apt to feed, with the general run of Vermont roughages, a 20 percent protein grain ration. When his cows are fed a high protein roughage or are on summer pasture, a 16 percent protein grain ration suffices. For growing young stuff and for dry cows a 12 percent protein grain ration is used.

Vermont farmers buy upwards of $10,000,000 worth of feed annually, largely and increasingly in the form of proprietary or ready-mixed rations. The grist mills of former days have become feed stores, and the newer ones which have been established are located near railroad sidings rather than by the old water power. These stores formerly carried ingredients and the farmers did their own mixing; they still do so but to a less extent. Ready mixed dairy feeds first appeared in 1905 but did not bulk large in the trade until about 1915. They are now sold in vast amounts and brands are rapidly multiplying in numbers. They are quite generally what they are said to be, since the Experiment Station is constantly on the lookout as to their quality. It takes upward of 4,000 samples of feeds found on sale in Vermont markets yearly, of ingredients and mixed goods alike, examines them chemically and microscopically and reports its findings.

Time was when cow stables were dark, damp and dirty. Sunshine, window glass, fresh air, and whitewash have wrought great changes. These have been brought about in the main by inspection, by decree of state and local boards of health. The extra price paid for extra quality (cleanliness) has also proved an incentive. There are still many poor barns; manure is still pitched out of some windows; but increasingly milk is being made under relatively sanitary conditions.

Diseases. The bovine race, as is the human, is prone to disease of many sorts. Three in particular need mention here, two of which have long been a burden, one of which seems recently to have become a menace.

Bovine tuberculosis has been with us for generations. Pointed attention was first drawn in 1894 to the situation in Vermont. The Experiment Station "spilled the beans." From that date onwards for twenty-five years, the state made half-hearted efforts to cope with the malady. These encountered the bitter antagonism of the less well informed and prejudiced dairymen. Beginning with 1919, when the work was placed in the hands of the state Commissioner of Agriculture, and continuing to date, more consistent and effective work has been done, especially since the adoption of the so-called "area test" plan. Yet these advances also evoked intense opposition which culminated in a concerted attack on the state Department in 1923, which failed of its immediate end but hampered the work for some time. Gradually public sentiment has swung around to favor as nearly as may be complete eradication. Whereas proposed "T. B." legislation in bygone sessions of the General Assembly has often aroused passionate resistance, the most advanced program ever proposed evoked enthusiastic and unanimous support in the General Assembly of 1931. On June 30, 1930, the State Commissioner of Agriculture, in charge of this eradication work, reported that 12,523 herds were under supervision, including 56 percent of Vermont's bovine population. Since the last General Assembly appropriated $600,000 for the biennium 1931-33—a larger sum than heretofore has been made available—it is predicted that by January, 1933, all the cattle in the state will be under supervision and the control, if not the end, of this devastating disease will be in sight.

Contagious abortion (Bang's abortion disease) is widespread and causes serious financial loss. A questionnaire sent out in 1930 elicited replies from 688 herd owners in 155 towns. In approximately one-half of these herds abortion had occurred within ten years, in two-fifths within the last three years, 10 percent of all cows reported were said to be active aborters and about 100 herds of the 688 were said to be unaffected. Doubtless most, if not all, of these cases were due to Bang bacillus infection. The financial loss incident to this disease in several experiment station herds has been fixed at $40 to $50 per cow. The Vermont station reports a decrease in milk production approximating 20 percent of a normal yield. Aborting cows often manifest sterility following their misfortune and other diseases are more apt to attack an animal whose system has thus become weakened. Some informed dairymen claim that the losses incident to this disease are more serious than those caused by tuberculosis. And, unfortunately, it is an infinitely more difficult malady to combat.

The use of the so-called agglutination test which, with a fair degree of certainty, diagnoses the presence of the disease in a given animal will enable herd owners to tell where they now stand. The poultry disease laboratory of the Vermont Extension Service at Burlington is prepared to make, and is making, many tests for anxious dairymen. But the job of getting rid of the disease is a heartbreaking and sometimes a purse-breaking task. Some day the state must grapple with this problem with a view of protecting herds already clean and encouraging dairymen who wish to free their herds of this incubus.

Certain udder troubles, known as mastitis, which appear to be of a chronic and infectious nature have become somewhat prevalent of late. Since mastitis not only causes great financial loss to the dairyman but also bears possible relation to milk-borne epidemics of septic sore throat, its control seems of great importance. To date, the only effective method is elimination of the diseased animals. No survey has as yet been made as to the extent of the malady in Vermont herds, but buyers should be on the lookout for it.

Tuberculosis is well in hand, and there is little need of further research; but abortion and mastitis are not under control and there is much that we do not know about them. Federal and state investigators long have been and are busy on these problems, but they are exceedingly baffling and not much advance has been made. Information is needed along lines of more accurate advance diagnosis, adequate control methods, advisable methods of eradication, following which there is needed a practicable and vigorous program looking toward eradication.

Adjusting supply to demand. The market demands a safe and clean milk product and if Vermont dairymen are to enjoy the market they must produce accordingly. Time was when relatively little care was exercised in handling the milk on its route from the udder to the milk plant. Utensils were not well cleaned, the cows' flanks were encrusted, the barn floor filthy, the air in the stable full of dust, the milker's clothes untidy and his hands grimy. Just as the Babcock test cleaned up the prevalent milk watering practice of the eighties and early nineties, the sediment test, the methylene blue test and the bacterial count have been potent factors in clarifying not only the milk but also undesirable situations. Vermont milkmakers of the present generation know, as their forefathers did not, why milk should be kept clean and cool and covered. Those who do not know, or, knowing, do not conform to the rules laid down by state and local boards of health, are out of luck and out of a favored market. Farms, farmsteads, dairy houses, barns, cows, utensils are inspected; the cows—more of them every year—are tested for "T. B."; the product is tested for cleanliness and quality. Vermont milk is "day by day in every way becoming better and better."

November is the month of lowest milk production not only in Vermont but in the entire New York and Boston milk sheds of which Vermont is a part. Production begins to increase in December, reaching by the following June a point at least double that of November and then rapidly decreases again. On the other hand demand for fluid milk is relatively constant throughout all seasons of the year. Hence the milk shed which has a sufficient November supply for fluid purposes has more than enough during the rest of the year. This "more than enough" is known as "surplus" and sells at a price far below that sold in fluid form.

As market demand increases, and it has increased rapidly and steadily for several years until the 1930 economic depression caused a temporary lull, more milk will be needed. This will call for an extension of the milk shed unless the demand at all times of the year is met within its present borders. Meantime there is plenty of milk produced within the present borders were its production more evenly distributed throughout the year. Furthermore, studies show that those dairymen who produce more nearly in adjustment to demand do so at a lower cost. In view of this increasing demand, obviously the trend should be toward more nearly even or adjusted production, especially since a higher price without increased production costs is likely to result.

The Extension Service has stressed these facts with the milk producers and an appreciable movement toward adjustment appears to have been started. Further study and more information are needed so that the farmers individually and through their organizations may rapidly and economically bring about this change.

Efficient marketing. A generation ago small butter and cheese factories were located throughout Vermont. Today these small plants are being replaced by relatively large milk plants located at strategic rail points. Cream is no longer brought in twice or thrice weekly but milk is trucked daily over improved roads—kept open the year round— thirty to fifty miles from farm to milk plant. In olden days a few carloads of butter were shipped weekly. Nowadays sixty-five or more cars of milk and cream in great milk trains daily enter the great consuming centers. Indeed milk constitutes the main source of freight revenue of Vermont origin to our main rail lines. The milk is sold largely by representatives of farmers' organizations, either located in the market or making frequent trips to it, directly to dealers, whereas formerly the butter was sold largely through commission merchants.

These changes in the methods of disposing of the dairy product are the result of the shift from the business of producing butter to the business of producing market milk. A whole new system of marketing has grown rapidly and, as is to be expected in such a rapid, unplanned development, many inefficiencies and undesirable practices have obtained; for example: (1) Inefficient collection; (2) inefficient plant handling; (3) duplication of plants; (4) inefficient transportation; (5) price instability; (6) lack of farmer bargaining power. On 150 miles of one of Vermont's railroads twenty different shippers—that is to say, milk dealers and cooperatives—send milk to many different distributors in twenty-three cities or consuming centers. There is more than one shipper, often several, at each station; the lots picked up for the various destinations are small, almost always less than car lots. For example, the milk train one day picked up at a station located in the center of a heavy producing area: one car of 130 cans (much less than a minimum carload) for the city of A; one car with fifteen cans for B, and three cans for C; two other cars from two dealers owning milk plants at the station; and five other cars were spotted to load 102, 50, 41, 11 and 10 cans, respectively, for destination D, E, F, G and H. This example is far from being an unusual one but is quite typical of the situation now existing in several parts of the state.

An organized industry would tend to eliminate duplicate plants or those located so closely together as to reduce the volume handled to so low an amount as to make plant handling costs exorbitantly high. It would tend to do away with duplicate collection routes and to lessen collection costs. It would tend to eliminate railroad transportation in less than carload lots and to lower freight charges.

It has already been said that consumers in the markets available to Vermont use about 60 percent of her present total yearly production in its fluid form. The remaining 40 percent must be sold in the so-called surplus class, which is consumed as table cream, ice cream and other milk products. The price for fluid milk averages nearly double that at which surplus can be sold. Obviously there is a price advantage in selling one's entire product for consumption in fluid form, even though it is sold at a considerable discount from the fluid price. It is this situation which lies at the root of the marketing difficulties so commonly recurring in this trade, which is the cause of destructive competition between producer groups, tending to depress fluid prices to the level of those paid for manufactured products.

The obvious remedy for this situation is a single sales agency which, in so far as it is possible to do so, will maintain stable and uniform prices to all groups of producers and which will pool the sales so that each producer participates in the sale of milk and surplus on terms of essential equality with other producers. A cohesive organization of producers dealing with a cohesive organization of city dealers should make for practical equality of bargaining power between the two groups. When the dealers made individual contracts with the individual producers, the bargaining power was all on the side of the dealers. Farmers' organizations have helped to increase the producers' bargaining power. This is still limited, first by the fact that the various farmer groups are wasting energy competing with each other and leaving each uncertain as to what to expect from the others; and secondly, because complete information relative to supply and demand is practically unobtainable without a more unified organization. The facilities in these small groups for assembling such information are of course greatly limited. The strongest factor in bargaining power is

correct and adequate supply and demand information, and its secure-
ment is one of the best lines of economic work in which a united
farmers' organization can engage.

The committee believes that the outlook for Vermont's dairy industry is promising, providing the problems herein outlined are solved.
Dairymen, their organizations and the public institutions closely related
to the farming industry, should further develop and maintain a strong
program: 1, To keep down the cost of production; 2, to bring about
close adjustment to demand, both in respect to the quality of the
product and the seasonal distribution of production; 3, to develop a
more efficient marketing procedure.

Apples

Apples are a minor crop in Vermont but they furnish an important
source of income in certain communities and to certain individuals.
Some 5,000 acres are given over to commercial orchards of five or
more acres, which contain about 325,000 trees. This acreage is small
as compared with that in the more prominent apple regions, indeed as
compared with other sections of New England and the Middle Atlantic
States. About as many more trees are located in home orchards and in
the smaller commercial plantings.

There is one nine-acre commercial orchard located in the northeastern part of the state. Five-sixths of the orcharding expressed in
terms of acres and trees, is located in the two southern and three
western counties (Windham, Bennington, Rutland, Addison, Grand
Isle). There are 230 acres located in the relatively hilly counties of
Orange, Lamoille and Washington of Central Vermont, as many in
Windsor County in Eastern Vermont, also a hilly region, and 350 in
the upper Champlain Valley counties of Chittenden and Franklin.

The present commercial industry is in the main a growth of the
last twenty years, although there were far more apple trees in Vermont
thirty years ago than there are today. Thirty-five percent of the trees
in the present commercial orchards in 1928 were less than nine years
old, the age when trees usually begin to bear, and most of the remainder
were between nine and eighteen years of age.

The leading commercial variety in Vermont is the McIntosh which
constitutes 42 percent of the plantings. The percentages represented

by other important varieties are as follows: Northern Spy, 16, Delicious, 7, Wealthy, 7 and Rhode Island Greening, 5.

The following requisites are necessary for successful apple production in Vermont:

1. *Soil.* While some varieties exhibit soil preferences, one may safely generalize on orchard lands. Deep, well drained soils with open, porous sub-soil should be chosen, since trees are deep rooted. Soil fertility, though important, is a less vital matter than favorable physical characteristics.

2. *Air drainage.* Land somewhat, but not unduly, elevated above adjoining lands is desirable and often imperative in order to allow heavy, cold air to flow away.

3. *Slopes and declines.* Much depends, in this connection, upon the particular contour and environment of the orchard. The site should be protected from the prevailing strong winds.

4. *Windbreaks.* Natural windbreaks may be found in many locations. If prevailing winds are severe, a windbreak should be planted on the exposed side.

5. *Transportation.* Plantings should be located within ten miles of and with good roads between the orchard and the shipping station.

The Champlain Valley contains much land meeting these requirements, but windbreaks must be provided and well drained soils chosen. Many of the mountain coves provide suitable apple sites. Several foothills in the Connecticut River Valley have the required characteristics for apple production.

If one is to acquire an orchard by planting and growing his trees, one must look forward to a nine- to fifteen-year undertaking, and an expense of from $300 to $500 per acre. Ten acres is probably the minimum profitable unit, and this, even when in full bearing, will not support a farm family as most farm families should be supported.

The expense per acre involved in successfully operating such an orchard will amount to $250 to $300 per acre per year ($3.50 to $4.50 per barrel). In Vermont or elsewhere, the orchardist has to look forward to an occasional unfavorable year.

The very high quality of Vermont apples particularly of the McIntosh variety makes the sale of the product a simple matter. This factor along with the location of the orchards within easy access of large eastern cities insures sales. Vermont has no acute apple marketing problem.

Maple Products

Maple sugar and syrup production is a material source of income
on many Vermont farms. It is said that fully one-fourth of the
farmers tap trees and that from $2,000,000 to $3,000,000 annually flow
into their pockets. More trees are tapped in Vermont than in any
other state. New York and Canada are the main competitors. New York
production is declining, that of Canada expanding and increasingly
threatening. Other areas formerly prominent are gradually disappearing from the picture. Vermont alone seems so situated as to be able
to continue to make maple goods to advantage.

TABLE 12. NUMBER OF TREES TAPPED (THOUSANDS OF TREES)

Year	Vermont	New York	United States
1909	5,586	4,949	18,484
1917	5,100	5,724	17,301
1918	5,500	6,236	19,119
1919	5,665	6,062	18,785
1920	5,665	6,122	18,831
1921	5,100	4,193	15,106
1922	5,559	4,487	16,264
1923	5,281	4,000	15,282
1924	5,445	4,080	15,407
1925	5,554	3,998	15,313
1926	5,554	3,958	15,245
1927	5,665	3,839	14,603
1928	5,722	3,647	14,388
1929	5,665	3,647	14,130
1930	5,778	3,720	14,421

It is usually held to be more profitable to tap an orchard than to
leave it untapped, even though the theoretical cost of operation exceeds
the receipts. This paradox is readily explainable. Many items of cost
must be borne whether one "sugars" or not; taxes have to be paid, interest charged off and depreciation occurs in either event. The only
direct savings made if the orchard is left untapped are labor costs,
fuel costs, container costs. If the owner of a sugar place can use his
man and horse labor in sugaring time to better advantage elsewhere, it
may not pay him to tap, but usually sugaring occurs at a slack time for
labor. Fuel is a minor item since the wood used is commonly waste
stuff. If extra labor has to be hired especially for sugaring, if the
product is sold at wholesale, if a large surplus is on hand from the
preceding year, the sugar maker may very well consider the advisability
of remaining shut down until the market improves.

The area of greatest production in Vermont is found in the four northern counties, Franklin, Orleans, Caledonia, and Lamoille. Washington County, also, is a heavy producer. In general, production is heaviest in the northern part of the state, and follows the line of the Green Mountains.

Data obtained in 1925 on 457 Vermont farms indicate that the average labor expenditure was forty-two hours per 100 buckets hung, 1.75 hours per gallon of syrup produced, 424 man hours per farm. The most profitable orchards hung about 2,200 buckets. The factors primarily affecting profit were: yield per bucket, size of orchard, percentage of crop sold at retail, percentage of crop grading No. 1. There are those who fear that excessive lumbering operations are likely to endanger the future of this industry. However, there seems reason to believe that the number of trees now being cut does not menace that future, since a sufficiency of young maples is starting to replace them.

The production of maple products has an important place in the future development of Vermont's agricultural program, especially on marginal farms where the land is ill suited to ordinary crop production. The sugar bush is usually located on land not adapted to cultivation, hence the better areas on such marginal farms can be otherwise employed and the total farm income becomes augmented. There are many such farms in Vermont which would hardly be worth cultivating were it not for the sugar money.

The study recently conducted in thirteen Vermont hill towns demonstrated how important a factor therein was the production of maple products. There were sugar bushes on nearly half of the farms. There were many abandoned or partially operated farms in these towns, but those with good sugar bushes were less likely to be deserted in part or wholly than those without this valuable adjunct. Touching abandonment, three assumptions are possible. Either the farms may have been given up because they had no sugar bushes; or the timber (including the sugar bush) may have been cut when abandonment had been determined; or else the sugar bushes tend to lose their identity as such on long deserted farms. Most sugar bushes are reported on farms which are or recently have been operated. While their lack may not be a main cause for farm abandonment, on the other hand since a sugar place greatly helps out the farm income, it is not likely to be sacrificed as long as the farm can be worked. Once a farm in the regions typified by these thirteen towns has been abandoned, it is rarely operated again, a tendency much aggravated by ruthless timber cutting.

Time was when maple products were mostly sold at retail. Now for many years the bulk of the crop has been sold to centralized processers. However, many sugar makers cater to a producer-to-consumer trade. They usually make enough to pay them for their extra trouble. It appeared in the 1925 study above cited that 60 percent of the product went to dealers and 35 percent was sold direct from the farm to the consumer; that the average bulk syrup price was $1.45, that sold to retail stores $1.67 (net), that sold to Vermont consumers $1.87 (net), that sold to out-of-state consumers $1.95 (net). The bulk syrup was doubtless, as a whole, of lower grade than the retailed goods. Allowing ten cents for lowered grade, one has $1.55, $1.67, $1.87, $1.95 for the comparative gallon prices. Clearly it paid the producer to seek the special markets.

Potatoes

Potato growing is a minor enterprise in Vermont. Probably more potatoes are annually moved into than are moved out of the state. Most of the crop is grown for farm family use and such as is grown for sale is usually produced as a side line to dairying. Probably not more than twenty-five growers make potatoes the main source of their farm income. The crop succeeds on most soils other than the heavy clays or very light sands. Since considerable machinery is used, level lands only should be planted, and of course their proximity to market or to rail should be taken into account.

Certified seed growing has become of late the most important phase of commercial production in Vermont. The relative costs of growing certified seed and table stock are continually narrowing. Few methods are used in growing the one which should not be used in growing the other. The inspection fee, the submittal of a seed sample and "roguing" are all that the seed grower ventures in attempting certification, and the roguing of an uncertified field is often a paying proposition.

The certified seed grower must constantly bear in mind the table stock market. His fields may not pass inspection, and more or less his crop always must be sold as table stock. The premium paid for certified over non-certified stock amounts usually to from twenty-five to fifty cents per bushel. The fact that enrollment for certification serves as an incentive to the use of better cultural methods is a valuable feature of the project. Better quality and larger yields usually result and more than repay the extra costs and care that are involved.

Certified seed producers seem to group. This is due partly to the practice spreading among neighbors, partly to the fact that groups of growers supply a large quantity of seed at one shipping point, thus naturally attracting buyers, and partly to the special adaptability of certain sections to the business. Orleans, Washington, Franklin, Orange, Windsor and Windham counties produce considerable quantities; the towns of Greensboro, Waitsfield, Sheldon, Highgate, Randolph, Barnard and Rochester are important centers. About 800 acres represents a normal enrollment.

One hundred twenty-eight growers in 1929 averaged to plant 6.5 acres costing $156 per acre to grow, yielding an average of 240 bushels. This particular crop sold for over $1.50 per bushel and netted its growers a handsome profit over the sixty-five-cent average production costs.

Most Vermont certified seed sells in Suffolk County, Long Island, and in New Jersey. Its quality is based largely upon freedom from disease, more especially mosaic, leaf roll and other virus maladies, and the general appearance and condition of the tubers.

Potatoes grown to meet the demands of the certified seed trade will meet the requirements of table stock trade. Apparently about 400 carloads are annually shipped into Vermont. Some of these imports enter during the summer from the southern states but heavy shipments are made from Maine. If this competition is to be met, better grading, packaging and warehousing seem necessary.

Any one contemplating engaging in a commercial business should carefully consider what acreage will justify the purchase of planting, spraying and harvesting equipment. Five acres is apparently the minimum that will justify ownership of a power sprayer, the planter and digger being hired; and at least ten, and probably fifteen, acres are necessary to justify complete ownership of all equipment. One should also consider whether the enterprise will seriously conflict with other, and perhaps more important, projects, as, for example, market milk making.

The technic of growing potatoes must be learned. This involves: selection of disease-free seed stock, proper fertilization, spraying, disease recognition and elimination, the question of the available labor supply and its effective handling, and other marketing procedures.

Poultry

Poultry keeping has been concerned mainly with supplying the farm family with food. From 1880 to 1930 the average egg production per hen has been that which is typical of the family flock, but during the past ten years it has increased in some sections, more especially in Caledonia, Orange, Washington and Windsor counties and in western Bennington and eastern Windham counties. However, on only a few Vermont farms is poultry husbandry likely to provide a main source of income in the near future. On farms where haylands and pasturage are limited in area, where on this account the size of the dairy can not be increased, the introduction of poultry as a side line is quite common and helps out the family dietary and income. On other farms poultry keeping is, and may well continue to be, an appreciable minor source of cash income. This was evidenced in farm management studies conducted in two towns in eastern Vermont wherein sales of milk products furnished 67 percent, and of poultry and eggs 7 percent of the farm income, the latter being approximately equal to the income derived from potato sales.

Material development is not to be looked for since poultry can make no use of meadows and pastures, which constitute the major part of Vermont's improved acreage of farm lands. However, in certain sections where subsidiary sources of farm income are important, it may expand somewhat despite strong competition from the Middle West and the Pacific Coast. These regions profit by lower feeding costs, but the East is advantaged by lower carriage costs to points of consumption. Only those Vermont poultry husbandmen can meet such competition who produce at low cost through restricted investment per bird, who efficiently manage their flocks, maintain the flocks' health, secure high egg production per hen, preserve original quality and handle a unit of profitable working size. Several such husbandmen now find poultry keeping profitable in Vermont, and there seems reason to believe there is room for more.

Poultry farm management data recently secured from more than fifty Vermont poultrymen indicate that gross returns on investments when the flocks averaged from 100 to 200 birds approximated $700; from 200 to 500 birds, $1,800; for more than 500 birds, $3,900. The investments roughly were distributed: $\frac{1}{3}$ in value of flocks; $\frac{1}{2}$ in value of buildings; $\frac{1}{10}$ in value of equipment; $\frac{1}{20}$ in value of land. The net average cash cost of setting up a 200-pullet enterprise was stated to be approximately a thousand dollars. The same study indicated, under conditions obtaining at the time the survey was made, that eggs on the average cost thirty-eight and one-half cents a dozen to produce, and that the credits to the laying flock averaged 45.6 cents a dozen, a gain of 18 percent. Feed costs averaged 49 percent, labor costs 20 percent, depreciation, 15 percent. Of course, wide variations from these averages occurred in individual cases.

Ninety percent of the eggs and poultry in flocks of 100 or more birds are shipped to New York, Boston and other eastern cities on a commission basis. A few such producers ship directly to hotels and stores. Such poultry products of smaller flocks as are not consumed on the farms are usually sold locally. Little candling and some grading is done—twenty-two men in the state using the state label. There is not enough concentration of product to justify cooperative organization.

At least a 100-bird flock is essential if the enterprise is to be worth while as a farm enterprise. Furthermore, if one is to undertake the enterprise he should realize that success involves a knowledge of the technic of the business and conformance to sound business principles. One cannot make a real success in the poultry business by "just keeping a few hens." For one willing to take the pains poultry as a supplementary source of income or even as a main business offers an opportunity for success in Vermont.

Cooperation

In addition to the cooperation with neighbors in the ownership of machinery and the accomplishment of farm work—rather common practices—Vermont farmers are interested in three types of organized cooperation, namely, cooperation for general improvement of the farmers' lot, cooperation for improvement of some phase of the farming industry and cooperation for strictly commercial purposes.

The Patrons of Husbandry (Grange) and the Farm Bureau are the two outstanding cooperative organizations working for general improvement of the farmers' lot. In respect to their interrelations it may be said that they have taken to heart and put into practice the precept laid down in the first verse of the 133rd Psalm. The former, in the main, is given over to self-educational and social activities; the latter is concerned more with economic problems and has definite and organic relationship to the work of the Agricultural Extension Service.

FIG. 11. Each dot on this map shows the approximate location of one of the 152 subordinate Granges.

The Grange, organized on the community, county and state basis, is a part of a nation-wide movement started in December, 1867. Men, women, boys and girls are comprised in its membership. The locals, or community units, hold semi-monthly meetings at which educational and entertaining programs are conducted. The county or Pomona unit meets much less often and tends to bring representatives of the various local units together to exchange ideas, become acquainted and generally assist in promoting the welfare of the organization. The state unit meets annually in a three-day session to consider problems of the organization from a state-wide standpoint as well as problems of a state-wide nature which intimately relate to farms and farm families.

The Farm Bureau, organized first on a county basis as a local organization to foster county extension work, has since developed state and national organizations. The county unit in Vermont continues to foster county extension work as its primary function, but it also supports the state and national Farm Bureau movements. The Farm Bureau in most counties is organized on the family membership basis, supporting county agent work with rural men, home demonstration work with rural women and 4-H Club work with rural boys and girls. The state unit employs a full-time manager and engages primarily in promoting activities in the interests of agriculture.

There is room and need for both of these organizations in rural Vermont as a means of promoting acquaintance among farm people, encouraging adult education, stimulating the cooperative spirit, mobilizing farmer support for sound legislation. Thanks to good leadership long continued, conflict and duplication of effort have been avoided. Neither of them, as such, should engage in business enterprises— nor have they often; nor should they dabble in politics, nor have they. They should be—and they have been—of distinct service in setting forth the merits or demerits of important issues before the body politic and ascertaining the position of prospective officeholders on such issues. They have long worked in closest harmony with the State Departments of Agriculture and Forestry and with the College of Agriculture of the University of Vermont in its several lines of activity.

Several cooperative organizations promote the interest of certain phases of the farming industry. Their activities are most helpful. These include: a, State dairymen's association. b, State breed associations for the four dairy breeds. c, Several county dairy breed asso-

Fig. 12. Each dot on this map shows the approximate location of one of the 351 4-H Clubs.

ciations. d, Several dairy herd improvement associations. e, State poultry breeders' association. f, State horticultural society. g, State bee keepers' association. h, County fair associations. i, State and local certified potato growers' associations.

Cooperative organization for commercial purposes has had its greatest success in organization for marketing dairy products and purchasing dairy feed, fertilizer and seed. These comprise the largest sources of farm income and outgo and naturally lend themselves to cooperative effort.

There are thirty-three cooperative creameries or dairy plants locally owned and operated which process, manufacture and sell dairy products in various forms. Twenty-one of these are so organized as to conform to the Capper-Volstead Act and the other twelve are stock companies not so conforming. However, they operate in much the same manner as do the twenty-one. These organizations handle from one-fifth to one-fourth of the milk output.

The New England Milk Producers' Association, a New England-wide organization with about 7,500 farmer members in Vermont, is a cooperative bargaining organization which negotiates for its members the sale of their products with large Boston milk dealers. Somewhat over one-third of the milk output is sold through this organization.

The Dairymen's League, a farmers' cooperative milk marketing organization in the New York City milk shed, has a relatively small Vermont membership, which, however, has recently increased considerably by virtue of its purchase of several Whiting Milk Company plants in the Champlain Valley. This organization now probably handles somewhat under one-tenth of the milk output.

The Sheffield Producers' Association is an organization of patrons of the Sheffield Farms Company, a New York milk dealers' organization. This association, fostered by the Sheffield Farms Company, represents the producers at conferences at which the price of milk for the patrons of the company is fixed. This organization represents probably about one-tenth of the milk output.

About 80 percent of the milk produced in Vermont is sold through some type of cooperative organization. The remainder is consumed at home or handled by independent proprietary dealers.

While four-fifths of her milk products are sold through cooperative organizations, the various cooperative groups compete with each other, often destructively, and price instability results. Cooperation

between these various cooperative dairy marketing groups is at present
a very great need. The New England Dairies, Inc., has just been incorporated with the hope of supplying this need. It should be a means
of bringing about greater price stability, closer adjustment of supply to
market demand, increased efficiency in collecting, processing and trans-
porting the product to the market and enhanced producer bargaining
power.

Maple syrup and sugar producers organized a cooperative corporation in 1922 for the purpose of marketing the bulk crop of syrup
and sugar. While this organization assisted in stabilizing the price of
the product, lack of a sufficient volume of business to maintain the
overhead resulted disastrously. At present there exists a maple product cooperative association which functions as a bargaining organization.
If maple producers are to have an effective organization, greater interest
and support are needed than now exist.

For at least a generation various attempts have been made by groups
of farmers to cooperate in purchasing their feed, fertilizer and seed.
For the most part, until about 1914, these were poorly organized
attempts and resulted in indifferent success. Between the years 1914
and 1918 five Vermont county farmers' exchanges were organized
and incorporated for the purpose of buying farm supplies. These
organizations functioned successfully for many years, the transactions
of some of them amounting to nearly $500,000 a year. Later, the
Eastern States Farmers' Exchange, a non-stock, non-profit corporation,
was organized for the purpose of handling feed, fertilizer and seeds for
New England farmers. This organization has grown steadily, has replaced some of the county exchanges previously organized and it bids
fair to replace them all. It has not attempted to furnish supplies at a
price lower than that of the competing dealers, but has continually and
successfully provided high-quality products. It apparently has made
a distinct contribution in improving the quality of supplies used by
the farmers and in its stabilizing effect on the trade.

A farm loan association was organized in each of several counties
in the state following the establishment of the Federal Land Bank
system for providing long-term mortgage loans on farm property.
These constitute the local units through which loans are procured by
farmers throughout the entire state. Since their organization they have
grown steadily and include a large number of farmer members in each
county.

Cooperative effort among farmers of Vermont has often resulted in failure, but on the whole, in a large measure of success. At present it probably plays a more important part in the life of the farm people than ever before. Its continued growth will depend on the wisdom and ability of its leadership in directing its course and on the loyalty and support of the people taking part in it.

Agricultural Education

Education by means of and in the interest of agriculture is of relatively recent origin in Vermont. The late Senator Morrill—then representative from Vermont—was active from 1858 to 1862 in securing the passage of a federal enactment which apportioned public lands to the several states for the purpose of establishing "at least one college where the leading object shall be, without excluding other scientific and classical studies, and including military tactics, to teach such branches of learning as are related to agriculture and the mechanic arts, in such manner as the legislatures of the states may respectively prescribe, in order to promote the liberal and practical education of the industrial classes in the several pursuits and professions in life." The State of Vermont accepted the trust after some years (1865) and united the Land-Grant College with the University of Vermont forming one collegiate institution.

As a matter of fact no agricultural instruction was given at the University or elsewhere for twenty or more years, save that a few itinerant addresses were made at farmers' meetings by its representatives. Short courses were inaugurated in the late eighties which attracted a handful of students. Winter short courses in dairying were begun in 1891 and have been continued with brief interruptions and much success until this date. The first four-year student in agriculture received his diploma in 1892. The College of Agriculture is now and long has been one of the four coordinate colleges in the University system.

The original land-grant Act of 1862 brings into the University treasury an annual income of $8,130. This original Act has been supplemented by other federal enactments in 1890 and 1907—that of 1890 being put through Congress at the instance of Senator Morrill—still further endowing collegiate activities to the extent of $50,000 annually. The usage of these sums is restricted to "instruction in agriculture, the mechanic arts, the English language and the various branches of mathematical, physical, natural, and economical science, with special reference to their applications in the industries of life and to the facilities for such instruction." It will be observed that the $58,130 annually derived from federal sources is not spent solely in agricultural instruction, but along many lines of educational endeavor. However, as a matter of fact, every year for a long series of years a substantial proportion of the total has been spent in furthering resident instruction in agriculture.

The General Assembly of 1886 established at the University an Agricultural Experiment Station, endowing it with the modest sum of $3,500 annually. Its educational function is to conduct research in the field of agriculture with special reference to the conditions obtaining in the state as a whole. In 1888 a, federal appropriation for research became available which was added to in 1906 and 1925. These federal appropriations have continued to this day, the total sum now available for research in agriculture and home economics from federal sources amounting to $90,000 a year. Sundry state enactments have placed certain regulatory and other duties upon the Station and have provided funds approximating $35,000 a year for the maintenance thereof.

The General Assembly of 1913 established the Vermont Agricultural Extension Service and endowed it with the modest sum of $8,000 annually. The next year a federal appropriation for agricultural extension became available, which has been added to from time to time and has continued to this day, the total appropriation available from federal sources for 1930-31 being $89,402.18. Several General Assemblies have supplemented the original state grant and the sum directly and indirectly available from state and town sources for the current year approximate $89,000. The functions of the Extension Service as defined in federal legislation "consist of the giving of instruction and practical demonstrations in agriculture and home economics to persons not attending or resident in said college, in the several communities, and imparting to such persons information on said subjects through the field demonstrations, publications and otherwise." It long has been a vital factor in adult agricultural education in this and other states.

About twenty years ago Vermont embarked upon secondary school teaching of agriculture. A former state superintendent of education was wont to say in those days that if a Vermont lad wished to secure training in agriculture within state borders and was not fitted to enter the College of Agriculture it was necessary for him to commit a crime.

He then would be placed in the Industrial School at Vergennes—then called the Reform School—where secondary school agriculture was being taught, the only place in the state where at that time it was being taught. The General Assembly of 1910 remedied this situation by establishing a State School of Agriculture at Randolph. Coincidentally the late Hon. T. N. Vail established a private school on his home estate at Lyndonville, which was taken over by the state in 1915 and, later, abandoned by it. Beginning about 1910 certain high schools began to set up courses in agriculture. The passage in 1917 by the federal Congress of the Smith-Hughes Bill gave to this movement increased impetus since it supplied to some extent funds wherewith to operate such courses in high schools, provided for the training of teachers of agriculture and for the supervision of their work as teachers.

Thus we have the pyramid: Adult education in the several counties by means of the county agent system under the guidance of the Extension Service and backed up by the research work of the Experiment Stations in this and other states and of the Federal Department of Agriculture; education of boys and girls, all of school age, in agriculture and home economics at the hands of the club agents; secondary school and state school education in agriculture; collegiate education in agriculture.

The situation in Vermont with respect to agricultural education differs in no material respect from that obtaining in other states of the Union, except that, owing to Vermont's small size and limited means certain phases of the work inevitably are less adequately supported than in other and more populous commonwealths.

Farm and Home Life

In farming, as in no other occupation, the place of business and the home are one and the same. The very trees and stones in the pasture are part of the home to the farmer and his family. The adoption of sound policies in respect to crop production, milk making and marketing is of little worth if it does not result in the maintenance of a reasonably good standard of living in the farm home. Farmers' organizations, churches and schools should work to that end—and they are doing so. Better farming should not mean only bigger barns, larger acreages, fatter bank accounts, but also finer and better equipped farm houses, more music, literature, education, travel and more leisure on the part of everybody on the farm to enjoy these good things. And these things can be—as indeed they are—on thousands of Vermont farms that are not in the marginal or submarginal class, and to some extent, at times, some of these benefits may be secured even on these relatively disadvantaged homesteads. To this end, not only have the thoughts of the writers of this chapter been directed but all the energies of the entire Commission been bent, to the upbuilding of happy and successful farm and home life in Vermont's open country.

————

Prepared for the Commission by its Committee on the Farm Production and Marketing Program.

E. S. BRIGHAM, St. Albans,
Chairman,

THOMAS BRADLEE,* Burlington,
Executive Secretary,

L. H. BALL, Randolph Center,

E. H. BANCROFT, Barre,

C. W. FITCH, Montpelier,

J. L. HILLS, Burlington,

E. H. JONES, Montpelier,

A. H. PACKARD, Underhill,

C. H. PALMER, New Haven,

W. F. SINCLAIR, Johnson,

E. H. WEST, Dorset.

Sub-committee on Dairy Problems:

E. H. BANCROFT, Barre,
Chairman,

E. H. LOVELAND, Burlington,
Executive Secretary,

W. C. ARMS, Burlington,

CLARENCE R. CARLTON, East Poultney,

A. A. DUNKLEE, South Vernon,

EARL GREY, Morrisville,

SOLON GREY, Derby,

*Owing to the death of Thomas Bradlee, February 21, 1931, J. L. Hills, J. E. Carrigan and H. P. Young assumed the responsibility formerly carried by the Executive Secretary of this Committee.

J. B. HOAG, Grand Isle,
E. H. PEET, Middlebury,
T. J. REID, South Shaftbury,
D. H. RICKERT, South Royalton,
JOHN E. SOMERS, West Barnet,
GEORGE WEBSTER, Georgia,
GLENN WEBSTER, Randolph.

Sub-committee on Potatoes:
L. H. BALL, Randolph Center,
Chairman,
H. L. BAILEY, Montpelier,
Executive Secretary,
EARL A. JONES, Waitsfield,
H. P. MARSH, Sheldon,
LAWRENCE MARVIN, Essex Junction,
F. C. NELSON, West Pawlet.

Sub-committee on Apples:
E. H. WEST, Dorset,
Chairman,
M. B. CUMMINGS, Burlington,
Executive Secretary,
J. W. COLLINS, Westminster,
S. EVERETT HARWOOD, Bennington,
E. E. HILL, South Hero,
R. R. MACRAE, Castleton,
H. R. STALKER, Shoreham,
ELMER WRIGHT, Weybridge.

Sub-committee on Forage and Pasture:
C. W. FITCH, Montpelier,
Chairman,
E. VAN ALSTINE, Burlington,
Executive Secretary,
ROY BURROUGHS, Vergennes,
R. A. DUTTON, Irasburg,
CHARLES JEWETT, Weybridge,
DONALD LEACH, Wallingford,
J. R. MOOR, East Barnet,
H. H. NYE, Georgia,
A. E. RICKETSON, Stowe.

Sub-committee on Poultry:
C. H. PALMER, New Haven,
A. W. LOHMAN, Burlington,
            Executive Secretary,
T. R. HUMPHREY, Proctor,
GRAY KNAPP, Middletown Springs,
G. S. TALCOTT, Williston,
J. G. UNDERWOOD, Hartland,
R. W. WOOSTER, Randolph Center.
Sub-committee on Farm Forestry and Maple Products:
A. H. PACKARD, Underhill,
            Chairman,
JOHN M. BICKNELL, Tunbridge,
LLOYD CHAFFEE, Enosburg Falls,
HARRY DAVIS, Cambridge,
GEORGE M. JONES, Waitsfield.

VII

FORESTRY AND THE WOODWORKING INDUSTRIES

The forests of Vermont cover three-fifths of the land surface of the commonwealth and constitute one of our three largest natural resources. As such, the forests, together with the activities concerned with their development and use, have always exerted a profound influence upon the economic and social life of the state. In the past, much of Vermont's prosperity has been directly attributable to her forests and wood-using industries. At the present time, there are many disturbing elements in the situation which warrant study.

History

To fully appreciate the place of the forests in the social set-up of the state, it is necessary to examine certain basic information. Historically, the biggest question regarding the influence of Vermont forests on Vermont life is the magnitude of that influence. Vermonters have always had contact with the forest. The state has excellent forest soils, a fine climate for tree growth, and an abundance of desirable native tree species, including such woods of long-recognized value as the white pine, red spruce, sugar maple, white ash, and basswood.

The first settlers found Vermont clad with forests to the tops of her mountains. They not only had to wrest their farms from the grip of this vast, green growth, but also had to maintain a vigilant fight to keep their hard-won clearings from the encroachment of the forest. The forest, however, acted as a friend, for it was a great storehouse of axe-ripe timber of great variety and high quality, easily accessible for use in every phase of the developing colonial life.

With the passing of the pioneer stage, and the establishment of communities, the need for the products of the forests increased tremendously; and each year saw an increasing demand upon the supplies of timber with the result that a separate industry grew up to meet the calls for wood in all its forms. Defebaugh in his History of the Lumber Industry in America, Vol. II, page 155, states: "The first sawmill in Vermont of which there is record was built in Township

No. 1, or Westminster, in 1738, or 1739. . . . The census of 1840 showed Vermont as having 1,081 sawmills. . . . In 1900 the census showed 658 establishments." In 1928 there were 550 going concerns using the products of the forests for raw material. From 1860 to 1890, there was a general growth of the industry; from 1890 to 1906, a marked decline; in 1906 to 1907, production increased to a peak of 374 million board feet, the all-time peak being in 1859, when 901 million board feet were produced. Since 1907, production has declined to a point between 150 and 200 million board feet annually, which production seems to be fairly stable.

With all this cutting, there has been little so-called forest devastation; that is, the major portion of the areas were not clear cut or else they restocked naturally. It has been the practice of many lumbermen to cut selectively, in such a manner that the entire timber stand is not removed. Yet this continuous drain on the forest has had its serious consequences. The cutting policy has always been to take the best. Many areas have been lightly culled, but the process has been repeated with the best always being removed, so that today there is little or no timber land in the state which has not been subject to this culling process. Where cutting was clear, no attention has been paid to the cultivation of new growth. The result is that, while our forests in many cases are æsthetically satisfying, from a utilization standpoint, they are in a deteriorated and degraded condition. The proportion of inferior trees and inferior species has been greatly increased by this logging process. Each year's cut sees a smaller percentage of the higher, profitable grades, and an increase in the loss-bearing low grades. This is true to such an extent, that today many industries cannot compete with those in other regions where timber quality is higher. Industries in the state requiring high-grade lumber in any quantity are forced to migrate, or else to import the requisite grade from other regions.

Our Forest Resources

Accurate statistics regarding the present area of forest land and existing timber supplies are not available. These are sorely needed in order to completely analyze the situation, but can be obtained only by expensive and time-consuming surveys. However, it has been roughly estimated that the forest area of the state, including farm woodlots, is 3,750,000 acres, of which 50,000 acres are so situated (mountain tops, ledges, bogs, etc.) as to be out of the commercial timber-growing class, though it has its value for scenic and watershed protection purposes. About 300,000 acres of the remainder is in stands of pure softwood (spruce, pine, etc.), while the rest is covered with a growth of the several hardwoods in admixture with the softwoods in varying degrees. In addition, there may be about 200,000 acres of non-restocking abandoned hill farmland which should be reforested artificially. It is idle to attempt to estimate the amount of merchantable timber in the state for such estimates must be conditioned to such an extent that they lose significance.

A survey made by the Vermont Forest Service and published in 1928 gives the most accurate picture available of the present status of the forest industries. (Vermont Forest Service Bulletin No. 32; Annual Cut, Consumption and Value of Forest Products in Vermont, 1928, pp. 9-10.)

Our forests supply annually about:

180,000,000 board feet of lumber
 19,250,000 board feet of pulp and excelsior wood (38,500 cords)
225,000,000 board feet of fuel wood (350,000 cords)

424,250,000 total board feet

The lumber cut or manufactured in Vermont gives employment to 8,100 people in nearly 550 industrial establishments and over 2,000 men in the woods. This number does not include those who are employed in the pulp and paper mills.

The annual payroll of the employees in sawmills and wood-using plants amounts to approximately $6,750,000.

Sawmills and wood-using industries represent a taxable investment of about $15,736,000.

The value of the annual cut of saw logs at the mill each year amounts to approximately $3,650,000.

There are about 127,578,000 board feet of logs and lumber manufactured annually into products other than sawn lumber.

Upon the forests depend the industries which manufacture the following products: Agricultural implements, boxes and crates, chair stock, furniture, wooden handles, clothespins, butter tubs, flooring, screens, sash and doors, spools and bobbins, veneers and plywood, wooden utensils, caskets, sporting goods, musical instruments, shade rollers, last blocks, wood heels, refrigerators, toys, wooden novelties and numerous miscellaneous products. For each 1,000 board feet of logs cut in the woods about $52 are paid out in wages before the finished products from these logs are offered for sale.

In addition to the utilization value of the forests of Vermont, there is their value for taxation purposes. Forests are taxed by the towns in which they lie under the *ad valorem* general property tax. Since so much of the land surface of the state is under forest, it is very easy to realize that a large portion of the local governmental revenue is derived each year from forest taxation. The industries dependent upon the forest for raw material, also yield tax revenue. Thus, decreases in forest values have a great and ramifying effect, and while the bulk of the timber land is privately owned, from this angle alone its maintenance is a matter of public concern. Add to this, public benefits accruing from soil and watershed protection, recreational use, and wild life, and the public interest in our forests becomes increasingly apparent.

The annual drain upon the forests is probably not in excess of the gross cubic foot growth, but when it is considered that the cut is from the cream of the existing timber, it may be understood why alarm is felt with regard to deterioration of grade in the remaining timber. In addition, an annual toll is taken from the forest by fire, insects and disease. Public interest in the situation has manifested itself in the creation of state forest areas, cooperation with private owners in fire detection, and disease control, the distribution of cheap nursery stock to encourage planting of waste lands, and the appropriation of moneys for the purposes of research, education, and demonstration. Beyond this point, all development of the industry and its basic resource, the forest, has been in the hands of the forest owners and users.

Forest Policies

With this background in mind, the Committee has endeavored to consider the subject from as broad a viewpoint as possible, in the hope that some entirely new ideas of policies more effective and simple than any heretofore in effect might present themselves. It was at once apparent that, from the practical standpoint of the handling of forests under present economic conditions, the inherent elements of the situation do not lend themselves to the practice of any methods other than those now in use; and that our future policy must be built around the essential features of our present forest practices, modified or refined in such a manner as to work for the building up of our forests, and the maintenance, on a permanent basis, of our forest industries.

Committee discussions developed one specific objective toward which our forest policy must work; namely, the restoration of the depleted and deteriorated forests of the state to full productivity so that they may render maximum service to the state as sources of raw material for our wood-using industries, as protection for our soil and watersheds, as recreational areas, game refuges, and public hunting grounds.

The following five lines of endeavor seem to be the logical and practical channels through which to attain this objective:

1. The creation of more favorable conditions for the private owner of forest land, so that he will be encouraged to conserve and improve existing forests, and to reforest additional lands now idle.
2. The acquisition, by the state, of certain highly scenic forest areas, such as areas along highways, waterfalls, lakes and places of unusual interest, as state forest parks.
3. Increase in the areas of state forest and municipal forests.
4. Continuation and strengthening of the protection of Vermont forests from fire, disease and insect attack.
5. The education, through an organized effort, of all elements of Vermont business, professional, civic, and social life to a true recognition of the overwhelming importance of the forests of Vermont in plans for future prosperity and development.

Private Forest Holdings

Taxation. Of all the obstacles deterring the private owner from investment designed to improve or conserve the forests, the chief one seems to be taxation. A survey of fourteen representative towns, made by the Vermont Forest Service indicates:

1. That the present rate of taxation in many cases is so high as to constitute an unfair and often unbearable financial burden; and
2. That throughout the state there is no uniformity of rate of taxation on lands of similar character.

In order to correct these conditions, revision of forest taxation methods is necessary. At the outset, in considering this question, we are confronted with the rather acute difficulty which arises from the fact that proper taxes for forest lands will not meet the revenue needs of the township. This is particularly true in townships where a large portion of the grand list (and hence, of town revenues) is represented

by forest land. The fallacy of taxing a growing forest, which is cut
but once in a lifetime, annually, under the general property tax is at
once apparent. This method of taxing annually a crop of timber which
matures once in sixty years or more has been compared with taxing
every day a crop of corn which matures in sixty days. Most forest
economists are agreed that during the growing period, forests should
be taxed at only a nominal rate, and that the principal tax should come
at maturity in the form of a yield tax, based on the amount and value
of the produce harvested. One big objection to the application of this
method under the present set-up in Vermont is that towns, as now
organized, require annual revenues. Since, in many towns a large portion of the town income is derived from forest taxation, the change
would be too radical to be made at once. The Committee is thus confronted with the situation which demands that either the town or the
forest be sacrificed. There is no doubt that in certain instances, it is
absolutely essential and would be infinitely better for the town organization to be changed in order to conform to the economic conditions
within the town. It should be expected that if forests are of sufficient
importance, this adjustment would take place naturally. In order to
foster this natural tendency, the Committee does not believe in adopting
the yield tax system at the present time, but does recommend amend-
ing the present laws so that timber land will be taxed as follows:

A graduated maximum-per-acre fee covering all timber land in the
state should be adopted. Land incapable of producing a crop of trees in
several hundred years, such as barren and rocky areas with shallow soil,
would be taxed at a maximum fee of three cents per acre. Timberland
which has a tree growth averaging under 3,000 board feet per acre
would be taxed at a maximum of ten cents per acre. All land with a
stand of timber averaging over 3,000 board feet per acre would be
taxed at not over twenty-five cents per acre. Such a system of taxation
would permit the holding of timber land until maturity without excessive carrying charges during the growing period. In only a comparatively few towns would it require any very considerable alteration
of the grand list. And in those towns timber land is now unquestionably taxed more than an investment of this nature can stand. So
long as the annual tax approximately equals the value of the annual
growth no amount of skillful management will avail to make an investment in growing timber profitable.

Management. The maintenance of the volume and quality of produce in our forests by scientific methods of forest cropping is a factor of first importance in any forestry policy. There are two phases to this problem. One is the handling of young natural stands of timber through proper and timely cultural methods, weeding, thinning and improvement cuttings, so as to eliminate poor trees, inferior species, and to increase yield and growth rate. On cut-over land greater results may be obtained more easily, cheaply and quickly than on any other areas. The other phase has to do with land now clear of tree growth. Here reforestation is in order. There are about 200,000 acres in the state, mainly in hill towns, which are now idle, producing neither tree, farm, nor forage crop, and which are yearly growing poorer and brushier, and financially going further into the red because of the assessment of annual taxes. To allow such land to remain idle is not only a shameful neglect, but also as unbusiness-like as to permit money to lie idle. Optional laws are now in effect, which lighten the burden of taxation on such areas when reforested, and if, in addition, the state should adopt some tax reform, such as the one recommended above, there would seem to be no reason for further permitting this vast acreage of potentially productive timber land to lie idle, or to produce crops of cordwood instead of sawtimber. We have become hardened to the sight of maltreated woodlands and idle hillsides; but if Vermont is to maintain its place among the progressive states of the Union, this form of neglect must cease.

State Forest Parks

The reasons for acquiring these park areas are self-evident. Vermont contains many natural attractions. These can be maintained useful and beautiful only if the forests along the roads and in highly scenic areas are under public ownership with a definite policy for their maintenance in a wild or natural condition. Logging, caused by economic pressures, can ruin forever a beautiful stretch of highway or a waterfall. No amount of money or effort can restore the beauty of a cut-over gulf. Hence, such areas should be in public hands. Supplemental to this, roadsides already ruined should be improved as far as reason allows, either as public projects, or as cooperative projects between private owners, organizations and the state.

State Forests

At present, the state owns nineteen state forests, with a total area of 39,000 acres. These tracts have been purchased for an average sum of $2.83 per acre. They are held with the objects of:

1. Furnishing dependable sources of raw material for local wood-using industries;
2. Protecting areas affecting stream flow, thereby aiding in the control of flood waters;
3. Furnishing public hunting and fishing areas;
4. Serving as sanctuaries for game birds and animals;
5. Serving as recreational areas;
6. Serving as demonstration forests on which to develop and exhibit correct practices in the management of forest lands;
7. Ultimately producing revenue for the state.

At the present time, forest land values are low, and state forests can be developed more economically than when values are higher. The present state appropriation for this purpose is $8,000 per year. The Committee unanimously approves the continuance of the purchase program and strongly recommends the acquiring of a minimum of 100,000 acres by 1940.

Municipal Forests

Municipal forests are a valuable source of practical education. Schools as well as the general public can here secure first-hand information that often is obtainable in no other way. Such a forest area may well be a recreational center for the community, and when properly administered should become a source of revenue. Unemployment may be alleviated by improvement work on public forests. If for no other reason than their educational possibilities, the Committee strongly advocates municipal forests.

Forest Protection

This Committee has in its possession the outline of a forest fire prevention organization which is deemed practical for the proper protection of our forests. It calls for the strengthening of the present lookout and patrol system, for the organization of the state into forestry districts, each of which shall be in charge of a technically trained forester, and for the purchase of certain modern equipment for fighting fires. The annual cost of such an organization would be approximately

$35,000. As further means are available, we recommend the gradual adoption of this plan. More attention should be directed toward the study and control of dangerous forest insect pests and diseases. To *maintain our wood-using industries we must protect our forests from fire, insects and diseases.*

Forestry Education

Before any progressive forest policy can become really effective, an immense amount of educational work must be done. There must be an organized effort to bring all elements of Vermont life to a true recognition of the overwhelming importance of our forests. Agriculture, highways, and other important state assets have gone through the educational periods, each eventually to reap its just reward. Forestry is now entering this stage, and will probably require more time than most other development problems because of the great length of time required for forest growth. Especially should this subject be brought to the attention of school children. We find that most states of the Union are gradually awakening to the great value of their forest land and are acting accordingly. There are few states in which the forests occupy such a large part in the state's economy as in Vermont. Even in these last few years of depression the lumber industry in the state employed over 8,000 men with an annual payroll of over $6,500,000. At present our forests are deteriorating. To restore them to their normal productivity, much educational work is necessary. Their inherent value to the state warrants far greater attention on the part of the Legislature and the public than they now receive.

We are too prone to take our immense wooded areas for granted. If properly protected and administered, their value to the state is incalculable; not only for the timber supply, but as guardians of our watersheds, as the chief source of our scenic attractions, as wild life preserves and recreational areas. It must be remembered, however, that taxes, fires, disease and improper management are mighty and destructive forces. Today our forest lands are of far less value than they were some years ago. In terms of timber, our forests produced 384,000,000 board feet in 1890 and 126,000,000 in 1925. If sufficient deterioration takes place, their reconstruction will seem quite hopeless. Such depletion must not occur. The state has done much to benefit the forests of late but far more must be done.

In this report we have attempted to point out the most vital needs and where possible have made recommendations for improving the situation. All attempts for adequate reconstruction, however, are quite futile unless and until the public appreciates the magnitude of wealth and beneficial influences to be found in this great natural heritage.

———

Prepared for the Commission by its Committee on Forestry and the Woodworking Industries.

MORTIMER R. PROCTOR,
Chairman,
PERRY H. MERRILL,
Executive Secretary,
W. K. BARROWS,
G. H. BOYCE,
CRAIG BURT,
J. J. FRITZ,
BURTON S. WARD.

VIII

SUMMER RESIDENTS AND TOURISTS

Vermont's development as a recreational region affords the most promising opportunity for business growth in the state at the present time, and so far as can be foreseen, for a considerable period in the future. The beauty and variety of our scenery, our proximity to great urban centers of population, our situation in the midst of America's principal vacation region, constitute advantages of great potential value. If industrial growth is retarded, if agricultural problems are difficult of solution, the recreational field offers a wonderful opportunity if we are wise enough to establish and maintain high standards of genuine hospitality and wise and consistent policies of protection of our scenic assets.

Trends of Development

From 1830 to 1880 nearly all the towns in Vermont were prosperous. There were flour mills, tanneries, wheelwright shops, carding mills and other manufacturing establishments which made nearly every locality in the state well nigh sufficient unto itself. When the Middle West began to develop, it drew largely from the younger population of Vermont, also from the savings accounts. Agricultural machinery and highway machinery came into existence about this time in Vermont and population and capital began to shift out of the state or to urban points within the state, with the result that at the present time there are approximately forty towns which have prospered in the last fifty years. There are about two hundred towns that have stood still or have declined in population.

The forty towns which have prospered have done so, in part, at the expense of the two hundred. Not a few of the inhabitants of the rural towns mentioned, who have accumulated sufficient wealth to allow them to move to one of the urban centers, have taken up their residence in one or another of these centers. Lumber has been cashed in and the money has drifted to the forty towns in which are located the banks and 54 percent of the population of the state, including a large proportion of the professional men, the mercantile business, manufacturing, etc. The backward movement in the two hundred towns has been gradual but today a very large percentage of them are carrying debt. The average income for each person in Vermont is four-fifths of that given as the average income of each person in the United States. The forty prosperous towns have been able to install electric plants, water systems, cement streets and municipal buildings, which have made the property in these towns assume a value on which banks could loan money; but in two hundred towns today, with few exceptions, there is no way to establish a value on the real property unless it be on an income basis.

There is an exception to this in 9 percent of the two hundred towns, which within the past few years have prospered to a limited extent through summer guests, tourists and summer residents. The prosperity of these towns is so marked that it seems the one way in which the state can bring back to Vermont some of the capital that has been leaving the state for fifty years.

Recreational Assets and Possibilities

Vermont has nearly 1,000 mountain peaks that equal or exceed 2,000 feet in height. This gives just the right altitude to make Vermont one of the most healthful states in the Union. In addition to these mountains, there are in this state over 300 ponds and lakes and more than 1,000 beautiful mountain streams. It is estimated that if the state could be developed as a summer playground for eastern America, the resultant gain would be equal on an income basis to 74 percent of the land in the state. There are said to be 250,000 cows in the state which under normal conditions bring in an income of about $22,000,000 per year. Now, if 250,000 summer guests could be accommodated in the towns which the 74 percent of the land includes, and these summer guests should leave in the state $100 each during their vacation period, it would bring an income into the state of $25,000,000, which would double the income in these towns. This would soon create a value on the property which would enable the banks to loan money for development. It has been conservatively estimated that 56 percent of the buildings in the rural towns could be made available for summer guests with the use of a very limited amount of capital.

Growth of the Vacation Idea

Recreation in its various phases has developed enormously during the past few years and the business of supplying its varying demands now constitutes one of the three or four major industries of this country. The general use of motor vehicles and the rapid increase in the building of hard-surfaced roads have revolutionized transportation, making possible, within the limits of the ordinary vacation, journeys of hundreds and even thousands of miles. It is reasonable to anticipate during the next decade a very great increase in air navigation, which will shorten materially the time necessary for travel. The greater part of Vermont may now be reached by motor vehicle from the cities of Boston and New York in less than a day, and by aircraft in two or three hours.

Nature has endowed Vermont with a wealth and a variety of natural scenic attractions which constitute one of its chief assets. The recreational business offers probably the most promising field for development to be found in the state, and there is hardly a limit to what may be accomplished in this field. Tourist resorts, large and small, summer homes, camps for boys, girls, and adults, all offer opportunities for investment.

The Value of Summer Resident Property

In making the survey in 1930 of the value of Vermont property used for summer resident and tourist purposes, the procedure was to visit the town or city clerk and from the grand list books secure information as to the listed value and type of property. This was followed by conversation with the town clerk for the purpose of getting additional and more detailed information, including some estimates of the actual value of recreational properties. Local real estate men, insurance agents, chamber of commerce secretaries and other well informed citizens were consulted for estimates of reasonable valuations of such properties. By visiting the properties for a general idea of the state of repair, the possibilities of future development, the prices of shore property and the value of adjacent farm lands, together with a general average of estimates given by citizens in the vicinity, valuations were determined upon.

The total value of this property is estimated at $26,000,000, including private property, valued at $20,713,000 and public property valued at $5,389,000. These estimates do not include one town in Bennington county, one town in Windsor county, and five towns in Windham county. The estimates by counties follow:

VALUE OF PROPERTY USED BY SUMMER RESIDENTS AND TOURISTS

Addison	$ 1,310,350	Lamoille	$ 472,875
Bennington	7,491,750	Orange	1,663,125
Caledonia	507,700	Orleans	2,178,900
Chittenden	2,680,250	Rutland	3,405,350
Essex	461,950	Washington	622,375
Franklin	542,980	Windham	1,058,700
Grand Isle	1,121,450	Windsor	2,684,350

Total $26,102,085

Summer Hotels

The total number of hotels in Vermont where summer visitors are kept is approximately 250. Many of these are all-the-year-round hotels. There are very few strictly summer resort hotels in Vermont because the six or seven months of non-revenue and a twelve-month overhead make this class of business hazardous and in most cases unprofitable. Resort hotels located in towns and able to keep open during the winter through local patronage, also the strictly commercial hotels, are the types best suited for successful operation in our state. Summer visitors who stay at the resort hotels become interested in local affairs and often prove an important aid to the community.

Summer Homes

The establishment of summer homes in Vermont began seventy-five or one hundred years ago, when former Vermonters occasionally came from the cities to spend a few weeks of the summer at the old home. This movement has expanded to include many who are natives of other states and has grown gradually until in the aggregate, several thousand persons spend a part or all of the summer in the state. The property varies from little shacks used as fishing camps, hunting lodges or inexpensive cottages, to extensive and costly estates owned by persons of large wealth. Summer homes in Vermont have been established by a very desirable class of summer residents. These people take a real interest in the communities in which they are located. They help the churches, they take an interest in schools and libraries and all community enterprises. Many of these visitors are teachers in schools and

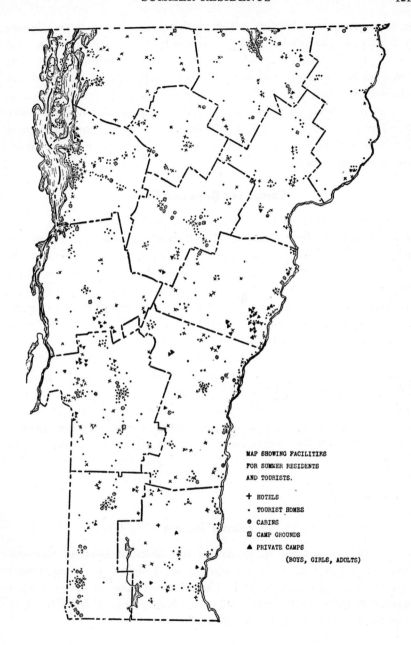

MAP SHOWING FACILITIES
FOR SUMMER RESIDENTS
AND TOURISTS.

+ HOTELS
. TOURIST HOMES
⊙ CABINS
⊡ CAMP GROUNDS
▲ PRIVATE CAMPS
     (BOYS, GIRLS, ADULTS)

colleges, clergymen, lawyers, artists, authors, and other persons who are
a distinct asset to any community.   Not only do they patronize the local
stores and shops, and furnish employment to local residents, but their
influence is wholesome and helpful.   The community is stimulated and
benefited by their presence.   There are hundreds of abandoned farmhouses in various parts of the state that may be purchased by city
dwellers at small cost.   The establishment of summer homes in such
localities would benefit both the purchasers and the community in which
the purchase is made.

Camps for Boys and Girls

Special mention should be made of camps for boys and girls.   Last
year (1930) the State Board of Health listed seventy-seven camps for
boys and girls.   There were reported 2,521 boys, 3,056 girls, 1,328
counselors and 538 attendants, making a total of 7,445 persons in attendance or employed at these camps.   Twelve of the fourteen counties
are represented.   The counties containing the largest number of camps
are: Orange, 17; Rutland, 11; Chittenden, 9; Addison, 8.   The value
of property used for boys' and girls' camps is a little more than
$2,000,000.   A considerable sum is disbursed by the managements and
by the boys and girls, both for land and supplies purchased, and for
incidental expenditures made by the occupants of the camps.   Employment is furnished local residents and the incomes of many Vermonters
are substantially increased by revenue from the camps.   Of even greater
value is the fact that hundreds of boys and girls are learning to love
Vermont and when they become men and women many of them will become summer residents of our state.   The opportunities for increasing
these camps are practically unlimited.

Tourist Homes

A study was made to determine the effect of opening Vermont
homes to tourists upon the homelife, general outlook and contentment
of our farm and village people.   The estimated value of 485 properties
studied in 1929, mostly rural and village homes, was $2,780,850.   This
was distributed by counties as follows:

THE VALUE OF TOURIST HOMES BY COUNTIES

Addison	$110,000	Lamoille	$143,000
Bennington	152,000	Orange	124,000
Caledonia	82,200	Orleans	264,500
Chittenden	547,400	Rutland	340,400
Essex	204,500	Washington	175,750
Franklin	117,500	Windham	142,650
Grand Isle	164,700	Windsor	252,250

The total number of guests which could be lodged at one time in the 485 farm and village places was 6,808. Chittenden county had the largest capacity, 894, and Lamoille county the smallest, 230. The tourist homes visited, arranged by counties, show the following totals:

NUMBER OF TOURIST HOMES BY COUNTIES

Addison	22	Lamoille	16
Bennington	30	Orange	19
Caledonia	25	Orleans	48
Chittenden	75	Rutland	56
Essex	25	Washington	38
Franklin	24	Windham	26
Grand Isle	34	Windsor	47

Total 485

The age of the proprietors of these places varies from twenty-one to eighty-four, but the majority are between the ages of thirty and seventy. The length of time proprietors have been in business varies from one to fifty years, but the period of one to ten years predominates. Stops are mostly for one night with the exception of Grand Isle county, where seasonal or regular vacation business is an important feature in the farm and village homes.

The total number of persons employed in the 485 places, not including members of the families of owners, was 596, and only twenty-four of this number were residents of other states or persons of foreign birth. Orleans county employed the largest number, with eighty-eight, and Addison county the smallest number, with twelve.

Most of the homes visited contained modern improvements, including running water and electric lights. As a rule, tourists patronize more village than farm homes, but Chittenden, Lamoille, and Grand Isle counties are exceptions to this rule.

Why Rural Homes Are Patronized

The reasons advanced for patronizing farm and village homes are a desire for accommodations less expensive than hotels, proximity to fishing privileges, quiet, attractive surroundings, and convenient stopping places on mountain trips. The farmer, the wage earner, and the business man operating on a limited scale, are taking vacations where a few years ago only the more prosperous business and professional men enjoyed an annual outing. Because hundreds of thousands of these families cannot afford to pay the rates charged by summer hotels, they patronize farm and village homes which have been opened for the entertainment of tourists all along the main routes of travel. The business is rapidly becoming an important one in Vermont. Great numbers of neat and comfortable cabins have sprung up to supplement the farm and village homes in meeting this demand. There were in 1929, 110 cabin developments. Rutland county led with fourteen and Addison county had the fewest with two. There were more new tourist homes and cabins in Chittenden, Orleans, Windsor and Washington counties than in other parts of the state.

Effect Upon Families Who Keep Tourists

Almost without exception, in the several hundred homes studied, the result of this development has been beneficial to the families. The following comments, taken at random from individual reports, are fair examples of the general opinions expressed:

We enjoy seeing new faces and hearing stories of travel; we derive benefit irrespective of financial returns.

This business keeps one out of a rut.

The family enjoys meeting cultured people.

We have income enough to live on without taking tourists, but we enjoy meeting new people.

The tourist business is a great help to the community. It is an education for children to come in contact with visitors.

Helpful farm ideas are obtained from visiting farmers from other states.

The tourists are a good thing for the country town, as trade is better in garages and stores, and it is a good thing for people in an out-of-the-way place to see strangers.

Tourists help the children to overcome their "greenness" and shyness, and they learn about different parts of the country from the tourists.

I take great delight in serving the tourists for they are such a fine class of people, refined and very appreciative.

Contacts with tourists make life pleasanter. Guests write in winter, and pleasant friendships are formed.

Tourists help the whole community. Since they began to come, a community club has been organized, street lights have been installed, and a schoolhouse has been built.

We get hints as to clothing and manners from guests and learn how other people live and what they do.

The tourists are as good as a school for the boys and Mr. S.

Taking tourists affords a pleasant break in the monotony of farm work.

A New York woman, a native Vermonter, repaired her old home and established a good summer business. She has employed girls from neighboring farms, and trained them so well that some of the guests have hired them to go back with them to the cities. She has bought and renovated some houses nearby. In several instances women whose husbands are absent a good deal take tourists in order to have something to do. The tourist business enables one woman to keep her own home rather than live with relatives. The tourist business is an important part of the family income for a young woman, whose father is ill and whose sister is in college. The family enjoys the social contacts and the father said he felt he should pay the guests for the pleasure they have brought him instead of charging them for their stay.

The income obtained from the tourist business has made possible the installation of new bathrooms, additional bathrooms, lavatories, running water in rooms, electric lights, electrical equipment, the purchase of more and better refrigerators, furnaces, new furniture and dishes, and new kitchen furnishings. Hardwood floors and new walks have been laid. Verandas, screened porches and sun porches have been added. Houses have been painted and the interiors have been improved. Old farm houses have been rebuilt or renovated. Additional rooms have been built. Grounds have been improved. Wayside stands and cabin developments have been erected. Keen competition for new and profitable business is compelling proprietors to improve their properties, thus adding greatly to the comfort and the beauty of hundreds of Vermont homes.

Effect on the Communities

Nearly every Vermont town has been influenced in some way by out-of-state visitors who come here for varying periods of time in the summer months. A study was made with the view of discovering what these effects are and to determine, if possible, which are desirable and which undesirable.

The towns selected for this study covered three types of summer residents. The *transient or tourist;* the *vacationist* who stays for some definite period of time in property owned by others (cottage, hotel, camp, etc.) ; and the *property owner* who becomes a permanent member and a tax-payer in the town.

The tourist. Typical towns of the tourist type are St. Johnsbury, Waterbury, Westminster and Brattleboro. They are all located on the trunk highways and draw a large tourist trade because of the through travel to Canada and neighboring states. The outstanding effect in this group is economic. Indirectly following and dependent on the economic improvement is an improvement in the homes, living conditions and general tone of the community. This is much more noticeable in the rural centers than in the larger places such as St. Johnsbury or Brattleboro. It is, however, present in those places but because of the small percentage of the total population actively engaged in catering to the tourist and also because life in the large villages is more complex and subject to many more influences, this effect is easily overlooked. The influence on the social life of the community by the tourist group is the least of the three classes. They also do not cause the shifts in population found where the more permanent type of visitor locates.

The economic effect of tourists is altogether the most far reaching. The real estate value of a farm or village home that has developed a good tourist business is increased. It is a "cash crop" and owners of such places consider the tourist business a definite asset and sales point. There are unfortunate cases where tenants have been displaced by owners solely because of the desirability of the summer tourist business which had been worked up. This increase in the sale value of property without any change in capital outlay might be compared to the good-will value of a business, intangible but nevertheless of real value. However, almost without exception the development of a good tourist business has been accompanied by an improvement in the condition of the property. The change in the Vermont homes that have a tourist sign displayed is very marked. The owners have discovered that an attractive exterior is good advertising and the best possible investment. The tourist is very often critical and it is not at all unusual for them to examine the rooms. Comfortable beds, modern conveniences and cleanliness are imperative. These improvements add to the value of the property and also the comfort of the family.

Tourists furnish employment for local people besides the members of those families immediately caring for them, in this way extending the sphere of their economic influence. They must eat and in serving them the help in restaurants or the private homes that give this service must be augmented during the summer months. This work is frequently quite attractive and remunerative and furnishes summer employment for many high school and college students who do not wish to be away from home. The redecorating and modernizing of these places also adds to the work available for painters and plumbers and to the business of the dealers in building materials. More money thus comes to all the local merchants indirectly. Directly the tourist leaves a worthwhile amount. The drug stores receive a large percentage of his business, though the department stores do some business in the staple lines of small articles of clothing, etc., which he is forced to buy enroute. Gasoline sales, tires and automobile accessories bring a good revenue to such dealers. The roadside stands also pick up many dollars for candy, ice cream, soft drinks, fruit, etc.

From an economic standpoint the tourist seems desirable in every way. He leaves cash, increases the value of property, furnishes employment for local people and both directly and indirectly adds to the volume of the business in the local stores.

The effects on the daily lives of the people in these towns is in most ways dependent on the economic effect. The homes catering to these tourists are much more comfortable places to live in now than they were before the improvements were made. Attractive rooms, modern conveniences and habits of cleanliness have improved the standards inside many homes, and well-kept grounds and freshly-painted buildings broadcast the change to the rest of the town. The rest of the town notices, and the improvements spread. The man next door grades his lawn and paints his house, the woman has a new bathroom because she wishes to enjoy the comforts she sees at her neighbor's, and so the improvement spreads through the town. In the small towns this change has been most noticeable and rapid. The last twenty years have seen some of our little run-down villages blossom into clean attractive places due largely to the money and influence brought by the tourist. The larger towns have kept their parks attractive and there have been enough well-to-do people to set a good example. On the farms along the main road outside the village and along the streets where the traffic goes this change can be found.

The vacationist. Typical towns where vacationists spend a period of days or weeks in property owned by others are Middletown Springs and Sudbury. The social effects are not important enough in these small places to have materially affected community life. The church is the only local organization that affords contact between the groups, and its activities are primarily schemes for raising money. The moral influence is good in that the visitors are a good class of people. Population shifts are negligible except where local people have found opportunity for employment elsewhere because of contact with the summer people. The displacement of local residents has not begun.

The property-owning summer resident. While the development of this type remains small so that the summer population is only a small part of the resident population and is not displacing them from their farms, the effects are simple and economic in nature. When they expand as in Fairlee or Manchester, other factors come in. Where the summer people outnumber the native population, the whole town is occupied in direct contact with them in all capacities from laundress, caddy or waitress to local merchant. Employment is furnished for a much longer period of time than the two summer months. During the spring months every one is busy getting ready for their arrival and in the fall there is much to do in caring for and closing the summer places. At best, however, the economic influence is one of spasmodic activity for a few months. Often individuals and businesses make their yearly profits in two months and run along as best they can for the rest of the year.

Real estate has been raised to a level far above the worth of the property for agricultural purposes. Much of the land is no longer used for agricultural purposes. In Manchester, particularly, almost all the farms have been turned into summer properties. Some opportunity is present for the truck farmer, but the small grower is too dependent on weather to be reliable enough to suit the better hotels. The wage scale is raised to a point where it is practically impossible to get farm help during the summer and at other seasons the working men try to get summer pay.

The civic effects are noticeable both in the appearance of the town and in local improvements. A great many summer residents take a real interest and give generously of money and services.

Recommendations

1. There should be a more careful consideration of the possibilities afforded for the development, on a more extensive scale, of the recreational opportunities of this commonwealth, and a keener realization of the responsibilities that are involved. The whole subject should be approached in a broad-minded, intelligent, patriotic spirit. The narrow and petty rivalries between neighbors, between communities and between groups ought to be discouraged and condemned, as this attitude works injury to the welfare of the state at large.

2. As rapidly as possible, the state should extend the scope of the Vermont State Bureau of Publicity, which has been of large service to our people since it was first established nearly twenty years ago. Money spent wisely in advertising and developing Vermont should be considered an investment rather than an expenditure. In order that the development of the state for recreational purposes shall be conducted along economic lines, it seems necessary that educational work be done in establishing standards, policies and a code of ethics that our people may receive and treat summer guests in an equitable and hospitable manner. In this there should be close and harmonious cooperation of the Publicity, Highway and the Fish and Game Departments, and the Agricultural Extension Service of the University of Vermont, with agricultural, commercial and other civic organizations.

3. The improvement of our highways as rapidly as may be possible, is an essential feature of recreational development. Much progress has been made, but much remains to be done, and good roads are a prime requisite of success in developing recreational business. A larger development of our fish and game interests will prove a valuable asset in attracting visitors to our state.

4. The Agricultural Extension Service already has held a few meetings in different parts of the state for the instruction of owners of tourist homes in the fundamentals of the tourist business. It is desirable that this work be continued on a larger scale.

5. It ought to be possible for Vermont farmers, or groups of farmers, to be able to supply to camps, cottages and hotels, vegetables and fruits that may be produced within our borders, so that it will not be necessary to send to metropolitan markets for products that can be raised here. Proprietors of resorts have experienced difficulty in getting the needed supplies in such quantities and at such times as conditions

demanded. This business ought to be profitable and groups of farmers should be able to furnish such products and thus build up a profitable trade. The roadside stands should be limited to products grown by Vermont farmers or groups of farmers, and should not be allowed to become commercialized organizations that do not maintain a close connection with the local farms, and thus compete with the regularly established stores and markets.

6. In considering the attitude of Vermonters toward summer visitors, two extremes should be avoided. There should be no fawning or servility in their relations toward their guests. On the other hand, a narrow, intolerant, suspicious attitude should be avoided. The traditional dignity and independence of Vermonters should be maintained in a friendly way. A genuine, kindly hospitality should be shown, a willingness to make the stay of guests pleasant, and a cordiality that will induce them to come again. Many excellent men and women who have contributed much toward the growth of the state and who have been important benefactors of our institutions, came into Vermont first on vacation trips. They returned to make their homes in Vermont, and have given generously both of time and money, to the betterment of their local communities and the state. We should consider all our visitors as potential residents.

7. Valuable as is the rapidly growing tourist traffic in this state, the most promising feature of recreational development for Vermont probably lies in the extension of the summer homes movement. Everything possible should be done to call the attention of city dwellers to the opportunities Vermont offers for summer residences. With our wealth of lake and mountain scenery, with the large amount of low-priced land in our hill country, with good roads every year growing better, and with proximity to the great industrial cities of the East, we ought to increase, largely and steadily, our summer residential population. This does not mean that we should, as a rule, displace our productive farms with a non-agricultural class of residents, but rather that we should utilize the areas where the scenery is beautiful and the soil is not very productive. It appears to your Committee that a special effort should be made to interest possible purchasers of summer homes in what Vermont has to offer in this respect.

8. The Long Trail extending along the crest of the Green Mountains from the Massachusetts to the Canadian line provides splendid opportunities for hiking where the scenery is at its best. The development

of this trail with its lodges at convenient distances apart is an expression
of unselfish service on the part of Vermont citizens which is highly com-
mendable.   It is recommended that the Long Trail be·further developed
and that the Forestry and Publicity Departments continue to cooperate
with the Green Mountain Club in improving it and promoting its use.

9. The development of trails for horseback riding offers an inducement to persons who love the out-of-doors and prefer to seek their
recreation in ways that are not followed by the great majority of
tourists.   Our hill roads offer beautiful views and the further development of *bridle paths* will bring to portions of Vermont, not hitherto
patronized largely by summer visitors, a share of the recreational
business.

10. Ultimately, after our main trunk lines are hard surfaced, it may
be well to consider the possibility of linking up some of our country
roads far up on the hills, on either side of the Green Mountains, into a
system of scenic highways which afford vastly better outlooks than
the valley roads.   A scenic highway, well up on the slopes of the Green
Mountains, on either side of this range, constructed in semi-permanent
form, would appeal strongly to lovers of beautiful scenery.   A similar
policy might be followed in connecting the roads nearest to Lake Champlain in a system that would extend from the Canadian border to the
southern extremity of the lake, thus affording what might be made one
of the most notable scenic highways of the United States.

11. The Committee would recommend that the state take over, as
rapidly as possible, the summits of the principal mountains for park and
forestry purposes.   Our higher educational institutions already have
some important holdings on the summits of mountains.   The National
Government is establishing a Forest Reservation in southern Vermont
which will probably be enlarged from time to time.   If the towns, the
state, the Federal Government and our educational institutions can
secure control of the mountain summits, and manage them in a co-
ordinated manner, this control may be utilized to advantage, from both
a forestry and a scenic point of view.   It may be possible, under suitable
restrictions, to lease these lands in certain areas, for the erection of
camps and summer homes.   It seems to your Committee, that the possibilities of such development deserve careful consideration.

12. Your Committee would recommend the state supervision and
licensing of farm and village homes used for tourist purposes, of cabin
resorts and wayside stands.   The last Legislature passed a bill provid-

ing for a system of voluntary inspection. Unfortunately, the wording of the act leaves the measure somewhat obscure, but it is hoped that through a liberal interpretation of the law, it may be possible to make a beginning in this direction. Sanitary arrangements should be carefully investigated, and the welfare of the traveling public should be safeguarded.

13. There is much to be said in favor of the establishment of a small but efficient body of state police, the duties of which might be combined, in part, with the motor vehicle inspection force. Property owned and occupied during the summer by persons living without the state, is increasing every year in value. There are many complaints that summer residences and cottages are broken into by lawless elements and it is believed that a state police force, not only would add to the protection of our rural residents, but would aid in the protection of the property of non-residents and would be of assistance in the enforcement of our fish and game laws.

14. It seems to this Committee that there is need of the establishment of more and better equipped information bureaus at gateway points, on main highways of travel entering the state, for the benefit of the traveling public. Other states find such bureaus of service, both to the visitor and to the state, and custom demands that such a service shall be maintained. Every resort should be an information bureau, and each proprietor should familiarize himself with routes of travel and points of interest in his vicinity.

15. It is desirable to emphasize again the importance of extending a cordial and friendly welcome to our visitors. Business interests are sometimes developed by summer visitors who have been well received and have investigated the industrial possibilities of some of our communities. Fruit growing as an important industry may appeal to some of our visitors. Care should be taken, however, by the summer residents, that generosity to a few individuals shall not be allowed to add to the difficulty of the farmer by a serious derangement of the wage scale.

16. In the larger development of our recreational resources, which may be expected, care should be taken to avoid features that disfigure the landscape and are an offense to good taste. Nature has made Vermont a state of great natural beauty. It is not important that Vermont shall be made the greatest tourist state in the Union. It is important that Vermont shall rank with the most beautiful and attractive regions

in our country. There ought to be a united effort to preserve the characteristic features of our old New England architecture, and the best in our community life. So far as possible we should keep our state free from crude and offensive advertising signs, from cheap and vulgar displays along the roadside, and from all that would offend good taste. Our visitors from other states do not expect or seek a standardized commonwealth. They expect something distinctively beautiful in our colonial houses, in the steeples of our churches, in our village greens, in the neat and thrifty appearance of our farms and our homes. If our homes and grounds are well kept and attractive, if our roadsides are made pleasing to the eye, if flowers add to the beauty of our homes, then visitors will spread far and wide the loveliness of Vermont as a vacation state.

Prepared for the Commission by its Committee on Summer Residents and Tourists.

FRANK E. LANGLEY,
Chairman,

WALTER H. CROCKETT,
Executive Secretary,

J. K. HYDE,

W. C. LEONARD,

J. H. LOVELAND,

C. J. PETERSON,

H. P. WHITE.

Research Material on Which Committee's Findings are Based

A Study of the Effects of Summer Developments in Vermont on the Native Population, H. D. PEARL, Principal, Burlington High School.

A Survey of the Effects of the Recreational Industry in the Rural and Village Homes of Vermont and A Survey of the Value of Vermont Properties Used by Summer Residents and Tourists, MRS. PEARL R. BROWN, Special Field Worker.

IX

FISH, GAME AND THE PRESERVATION OF WILD LIFE

The fish, game and wild life resources are one of Vermont's chief assets in connection with the state's development. Your Committee found that very little attention was paid to these resources until about 1892, when John W. Titcomb began some real constructive work in creating a Fish and Game Department. In recent years there has been some very constructive work done by the Fisheries and Biological Department of the United States, and in some of the states which have money to spend fish and game are propagated so that the ratio of wild life to human inhabitants is very much in favor of the fish and game. At the present time the State of Vermont maintains three state hatcheries, a rearing station in Vernon and a game farm at Milton. Owing to lack of sufficient supply of spring water, not one of the three hatcheries can run to full capacity.

The Waters Available for Fish Production

It is recommended that a survey of the state be made with a view of ascertaining available supplies of spring water where hatcheries and nurseries for fish can be established and that a survey be made of the ponds and lakes to ascertain their capacity, natural food supply and possibilities for artificial propagation of fish. A survey of each stream is needed to determine the temperature of water throughout the year, natural fish food supply, nature of stream bed, growth of vegetation, general topography of the land through which the stream passes, names of owners of land through which the stream runs, whether the water has an acid or alkaline reaction, the kind and average quantity of fish that inhabit the waters, and the possibilities for development of natural food, artificial feeding and propagation.

A study of the experiences by the United States Government and some of the states convinces your Committee that Vermont has the natural resources for propagating game fish and that fish can be artificially reared as successfully as chickens, but to do this they must have water of proper temperature and the right kind of food.

The question of how to classify the streams in relation to their capacity for the adequate care of trout involves, first, the temperature of water in summer, freedom from pollution and abundance of food. This is not easy to determine without special training and equipment. The first thing, however, is to recognize the importance of finding out these facts before turning trout, particularly those under six inches in length, loose in the waters.

Wardens ought to be able, if equipped with suitable thermometers, to take temperatures in certain streams methodically and to keep accurate record of the readings. Streams which show a temperature of over seventy degrees Fahrenheit in a large part of their course, should be listed as questionable. No brook trout should be placed in such streams until upon further investigation it is found that there is a sufficient amount of water in sheltered pools which never reaches seventy degrees.

As an example of the results of present methods in stocking streams with trout, one club reports that it has, since the flood of 1927, put in an average yearly planting of 53,916 by actual count. The number of trout in the streams seems very small by comparison. Over the state, enormous numbers of fingerlings are placed in the streams every year and comparatively few ever find their way into the fisherman's creel.

Because of the crowding of trout in the rearing pools and the consequent epidemics of disease, great numbers of trout die during every summer before they can be planted and the tendency is to plant them as early as possible to avoid this trouble, thus exposing too young fish to all the hazards of life in the open. Infected fish are frequently present in the batches that are planted. These carry disease into the newly stocked streams.

In addition to the danger of infecting the native trout by introducing diseased fish into their streams, a still more serious danger is encountered and apparently with very little thought on the part of those who plant the fingerlings. That is the danger of starvation or of death as a result of water that is too warm. There are good trout streams and there are bad trout streams in Vermont as anywhere else, and it is nothing short of wholesale slaughter to dump thousands of fingerlings without finding out whether the stream will support its new inhabitants. The ordinary six-inch wild trout in our streams where there is insufficient food for quick growth is usually three years old. Breeding stock among fish should be selected the same as among animals.

Your Committee believes that hundreds of streams in Vermont are suitable for rearing fish of several species and that the upper waters of these streams should be closed for rearing purposes, allowing fishing in the lower waters which the fish of legal length inhabit. To accomplish this economically it will be necessary to secure the fishing rights on certain desirable streams and prepare or restore the streams with water holes as a refuge for the young fish, that they may protect themselves from the birds and animals that prey upon them. It is also necessary to supply food, and by utilizing the local inhabitants as caretakers, this can be done at a minimum expense.

Fish Foods

It is recommended that experiments be conducted looking toward the artificial propagation in the streams themselves, or in breeding pools, of the minute animal life used by the trout as food.

Your Committee has done some experimenting and investigating regarding fish foods. Fish in the fry stage require very minute particles of food and in their natural state this food includes that cycle of life where the plants develop into animal life. The series is something like this: Single plant cells, fed upon by single animal cells like the Amœba, fed upon by Rotifers and microscopic worms, these serving as food for the smallest Crustacea, like Daphnia; larger Crustacea, like Cyclops eating Daphnia, and, in turn, eaten by the young of insects such as May flies; and finally these aquatic larvae serving as a chief part of the diet of the trout, especially during the winter months. No link can be dropped out of this chain without endangering the entire series and that means starvation to the trout. Without abundance of suitable plant life in the water, the chain is impossible.

A great mass of highly nutritious food material can be speedily produced either in the natural habitat or in suitable breeding pools and the culture of these food animals should run parallel with the hatching of the trout and they should be used as largely as possible in the feeding of the young fish.

Mosquito larvæ, being larger than the Daphnia and its cousins, form a suitable food to use for the larger trout of late summer and fall. These can be taken in great quantities in any stagnant pool with a twenty-mesh wire sieve and, like the Crustacea, they can be artificially bred in tubs, vats, etc., screened to prevent a mosquito nuisance from developing in the neighborhood.

As a test of the practicality of the rearing pool method, a special pool fifty-five feet long by eight feet wide and three feet deep at the deepest point, was excavated at the Bennington hatchery. A truck load of muck, known to be heavy with Daphnia, etc., was spread over this pool and two two-inch streams of brook water were led in. The muck not only supplied abundance of animal life but also nourished a variety of water plants. The overflow was carefully screened. In the trench carrying the overflow were placed boards partitioning it off into small pools and 750 fry from the hatchery were put into these pools. They refused the usual ration of liver and yet thrived, and it was discovered unexpectedly that the minute forms of animal life which could pass through the screen in the outlet of the large pool were furnishing the fish with a diet more acceptable than liver. The trout which enjoyed this natural though limited diet did not grow as large as some others reared at the hatchery, but their appearance was a delight to the eye and the mortality was very low.

Regarding artificial foods, they should comprise first of all food which the fish will eat readily with apparent relish. Customarily liver is fed to very young fish but after they reach the size of two inches other meat can be fed in connection with sour milk and cottonseed meal, on which they will thrive if proper sanitary measures are taken. In this connection it will be necessary to establish demonstrations for educational purposes. There are many fish and game clubs in the state which will be interested in these demonstrations as well as the inhabitants who are not so-called sportsmen.

Stream Pollution

It is recommended that a survey be made of our streams with a view of ascertaining the degree of and remedy for pollution. No one should have a right to pollute a stream any more than he should have a right to deposit garbage, filth, germ carriers or any other waste matter in the public highways, in parks and other public property or on the private premises of his neighbors. Vermont with its rather sparse population is one of the states where further pollution can be prevented and the damage of the past partially overcome.

It is, of course, impossible to remove the pollution from such streams as the Black River, the Winooski including Stevens Branch, the Hoosick, the Passumpsic, the Otter Creek north of Rutland and Proctor, the Walloomsac and possibly a few others which carry the sewage from the larger towns and the acids, dye stuffs, analines, etc., from manufacturing establishments.

There are other streams such as the Lamoille, the Missisquoi, the Ottaquechee, Sleeper's River, the Barton River, the Dog, the West River, the Battenkill, the White River and its splendid tributaries and many others which are somewhat affected already but can be saved from the fate that has befallen the Black River, the Winooski, the Hoosick, the Walloomsac and some others that are polluted to such an extent that it is often offensive to drive along beside them during the season of low water.

Actual accomplishment in Ohio under the leadership of the State University sanitary engineers has proved that it is unnecessary to pollute a stream to any serious extent. Household sewage can be roughly filtered and sterilized, while acids, dye stuffs and other poisons can be kept out of running water through cooperation of industrial establishments and municipal authorities.

The pollution of springs and wells anywhere ought to be a criminal offense and the practice of a city like Burlington pouring its poisons into beautiful Lake Champlain without sterilization is most reprehensible.

It is not agreeable to camp beside a brook or river, and find it to be little better than an open sewer. It is not economic, healthful or creditable for a town or city to scatter its sewage and other poisons along the banks of a stream for many miles when it can be avoided. It is not honorable to camp or throw waste where drainage will contaminate a natural spring and that anyone should carelessly fail to consider this point is unaccountable.

Pertinently related to this issue is also the practice of drawing lakes and ponds to a late summer level so as to expose the banks to an offensive and unhealthful degree. No more natural ponds should be chartered to power companies to be exploited except under strict regulations to protect the shore line.

In considering pollution it is also well to consider the question of dumping ashes, rubbish, tin cans, automobile wreckage and other waste along the banks of streams, at the sides of public highways adjacent to cemeteries, school grounds and other public property as well as in city streets and too often in the back yards of private property. Every municipal body in Vermont should be alive to this issue.

It is not possible to overcome the pollution of streams and lakes that have already been badly damaged except by a carefully worked-out plan covering a term of years, but the further pollution of public waters should be strictly prohibited.

The Planting of Fish

It is recommended:

1. That no fingerlings be planted in streams that are known to be, or suspected of being, insufficiently supplied from springs to take care of the fish in dry, hot spells of weather; or inadequately stocked with natural trout food; or infested with enemies; or subject to pollution.

2. That only as many fingerlings should be planted as can be adequately taken care of by the streams. An eminent authority, G. C. Embody, declares that a stream averaging ten feet wide and showing an abundance of A1 food should be stocked per mile with no more than 1,440 three-inch fingerlings yearly.

3. That spring planting is desirable and necessitates the establishment of an abundance of winter pools at the breeding stations.

4. That only legal size trout should be used in spring planting. Trout should be planted only on streams found by expert examination to be adequately stocked with food materials.

Your Committee finds that the Fish and Game Department have spent about 60 percent of the receipts of the Department in overhead, policing, etc., and that about 40 percent per year has been spent in propagating fish and game. About two-thirds of the fish that are reared to fingerling size before planting in the streams have been reared by fish and game clubs, and these together with the number the state have reared amounts at the present time to about twenty-two fingerling fish for each licensed fisherman. It is estimated that with a proper supply of spring water and the utilization of local energy this ratio could be increased several times, which would in turn increase the number of license holders, but the ratio of increase would be very much in favor of the fish, so that Vermont could furnish one of the best, if not the best, fishing grounds in the country.

Incidental to your Committee's findings regarding Vermont's wild life resources, it is their opinion that the commercial rearing of fish could be made profitable by land owners who have streams running through their land which could be tapped for supplying artificial ponds. The water supply for this purpose should be augmented where possible by springs. Fish thus reared could be marketed or restricted angling privileges could be sold.

It is also suggested that propagation could be promoted in a practical way by legislating the state rights in certain public waters to certain associations with limited rights and privileges as to the propagation and protection of fish within these waters, association members and other licensed fishermen being allowed to take fish under prescribed regulations.

Game and Wild Life

Large game as deer and bear as well as fur-bearing animals propagate extensively in Vermont if adequately protected by closed seasons and from molestation by dogs.

Game birds must be more fully protected by the establishment of additional game sanctuaries and the destruction of their natural enemies known as vermin, or they will soon become practically extinct.

Every possible effort should be made by the inhabitants of our state to cooperate with the Federal Government in protecting our migratory song birds.

Nature Study

Your Committee, recognizing that the right place to begin teaching our people to know and love their state and tell others about it is in our schools, recommends that we urge all who have any connection with our educational system to lay as much emphasis as possible on that part of the recently issued Course of Study for Vermont Schools which deals with Nature Study. We would seek to have the schools which train our teachers endeavor to send them out with a great love for our state and well equipped to teach about its wild life, geological and geographical features and natural resources. We would have members of the local school boards in full sympathy with the program so that they would willingly vote the expenditure of the small necessary funds for books and equipment and authorize the arrangement of schedules to include time for the important occasional field trips as well as the indoor study. We would enlist the cooperation of all superintendents of schools to bring this matter to the attention of their Boards and encourage their teachers in every way to undertake as much work as possible along these lines. We would see that all teachers are supported in their own efforts to teach this subject, would place in their schools helpful books and equipment, and encourage them to take advantage of the help offered by the museums and libraries of the state.

A Comprehensive State Police Department

Your Committee would recommend a State Police Department with a view of organizing the constabulary in the rural towns for the enforcement of traffic, fish and game, sanitary and all other state laws.

Your Committee has found that there is an astonishing waste of money in the duplication of enforcement officers. One well-organized police department, which in turn could organize the constabulary of the rural towns, would administer the law with a great saving to the state, as it would reduce traveling expenses and the local officers could be paid for time spent on duty only.

There is another feature of law enforcement which this system would embrace and that is the trend of public opinion towards local or self-government from inside out instead of from outside in.

———

Prepared for the Commission by its Committee on Fish, Game and the Preservation of Wild Life.

W. C. Leonard,
    Chairman,
Earl L. Flanders,
    Executive Secretary,
Frank E. Howe,
L. D. Mills,
Hortense Quimby,
E. L. Sibley.

X

LAND UTILIZATION

The land utilization problem in Vermont is that of determining the proper use of the hill land which has been in farms. The problems of the plainly agricultural land in the river valleys, on the more nearly level and fertile uplands, and in the Champlain valleys are problems of farm management and marketing. The problems of the plainly forest areas are problems in forestry. This study and the recommendations which follow have to do with the problems of the so-called hill towns where there is a question as to the use to which the land should be put.

The Vermont Experiment Station in cooperation with the United States Bureau of Agricultural Economics and the Vermont Forest Service has made a study in the following Vermont hill towns: Granville, Roxbury, Fayston, Warren, Ripton, Goshen, Stockbridge, Pittsfield, Sherburne, Plymouth, Mt. Holly, Shrewsbury and Wardsboro. This study has furnished the facts used in this report.

The total number of towns in Vermont that constitute this phase of the land utilization problem is upward of 100 and while the conditions vary in these towns, it is believed that the thirteen selected are representative and furnish the basis for analysis of the problem as a whole. The fact that the population in these thirteen towns is rapidly declining and that most of the decline in recent years is in farm population, furnishes convincing proof that farming in these areas is unprofitable.

The total population of these thirteen towns increased from 1791 up to 1840. There was then a period of thirty years when population was nearly constant for the thirteen towns as a whole, yet, during this period, ten towns declined in population while only three gained. This was a period of considerable activity in lumbering. By 1880, the decline in population had begun in all but one of these thirteen towns. Since 1880, the decline of population has been rapid. In 1930, there were less than half as many people in these thirteen towns as in 1880. The decline from 1920 to 1930 was 18.8 percent. Apparently, most of the decrease in population in these towns has been due to a decline in the wood-working industry and to the abandonment of farms and the

POPULATION IN THIRTEEN TOWNS 1791-1930

	1791	1800	1810	1820	1830	1840	1850	1860	1870	1880	1890	1900	1910	1920	1930
Granville	101	185	324	328	403	545	603	720	726	830	637	544	464	393	280
Fayston	...	18	149	253	458	635	684	800	694	638	533	466	452	424	318
Warren	...	59	229	320	766	943	962	1,041	1,008	951	866	826	825	654	485
Roxbury	14	113	361	512	737	784	967	1,060	916	938	768	712	615	609	594
Ripton	...	...	15	42	778	771	567	570	617	672	568	525	421	237	190
Goshen	...	4	86	290	555	621	486	394	330	326	311	286	212	131	84
Stockbridge	100	432	700	964	1,333	1,418	1,327	1,264	1,269	1,124	894	822	737	618	460
Pittsfield	49	164	338	453	505	615	512	493	482	555	468	435	402	343	256
Sherburne	...	90	116	154	432	498	578	525	462	450	451	402	409	336	293
Plymouth	...	497	834	1,112	1,237	1,417	1,226	1,252	1,285	1,075	755	646	482	449	331
Mt. Holly	...	668	922	1,157	1,318	1,356	1,534	1,522	1,582	1,390	1,214	999	871	856	726
Shrewsbury	382	748	990	1,149	1,289	1,218	1,268	1,175	1,145	1,235	974	935	751	620	540
Wardsboro	483	868	1,159	1,016	1,148	1,102	1,125	1,004	866	766	704	637	559	380	355
Total	1,129	3,846	6,223	7,750	10,959	11,923	11,839	11,820	11,382	10,950	9,143	8,235	7,200	6,050	4,912
Increase or decrease	...	+2,717	+2,377	+1,527	+3,209	+964	—84	—19	—438	—432	—1,807	—908	—1,035	—1,150	—1,138

departure of the farm population. The decline of farm population for the five-year period from 1925 to 1930 was 535 or nearly half the decline in total population from 1920 to 1930.

How the Land is Used

The total area of the thirteen towns studied is 344,000 acres. In 1929, 194,072 acres were classified as in farms; 141,540 acres were classified as woodland not in farms; 5,722 acres were classified as recreational land; and 2,666 acres were designated as used for residential, power development and business purposes.

USES OF LAND IN 1,375 FARMS IN THE THIRTEEN TOWNS, 1929

Status of Farms	Crop Lands		Open Pasture		Woods		Farmstead and Waste	
	Acres	Percent-age	Acres	Percent-age	Acres	Percent-age	Acres	Percent-age
Operated	24,500	23.5	23,856	22.1	56,657	53.5	959	0.9
Partially operated.	9,461	19.6	10,040	18.8	30,808	60.6	464	1.0
Abandoned less than 10 years	2,946	18.0	1,591	8.7	12,452	71.8	252	1.5
Abandoned 10 years or more	469	2.3	1,121	5.3	18,218	91.0	278	1.4
Total	37,376		36,608		118,135		1,953	

The woodland in farms and not in farms totals 259,675 acres, or, 75 percent of the entire area of the thirteen towns.

In 1919, there were 944 occupied farms in the thirteen towns. In 1929, there were 735. This represents a decline of 22.1 percent. There were 431 unoccupied farms in 1919. In 1929, there were 640. The increase was 48.5 percent.

LAND IN FARMS 1919 AND 1929

	1929		1919	
	Acres	Percent	Acres	Percent
Operated	105,972	54.6	136,795	70.5
Partially operated	50,773	26.2	36,368	18.7
Abandoned less than 10 years	17,241	8.9	9,660	5.0
Abandoned 10 or more years	20,086	10.3	11,249	5.8
Total	194,072	100.0	194,072	100.0

These figures show the trend of land utilization in the thirteen towns.

Farm Income

Of the 1,375 farms in the thirteen towns, a sample of 162 was selected and studied to determine the economic condition of these farm families, the profitableness of farming and other means used in making a living.

The cash on hand at the beginning of the year, the cash received from all sources, the total expenditures and the cash on hand at the end of the year were obtained for 162 farm families. This shows that 142 farmers made an average of about $5 for savings from the excess of total receipts over total expenses during the year. There were, however, twenty who had an average of $721 for savings from the year's operations.

Most of these farm families lived very frugally and they apparently got ahead on an average of only about $13 for the year ending April 30, 1929. Receipts from strictly agricultural enterprises average $1,232 and the average cash expenditure in operating the farm was $1,172. Income from other sources, such as labor off the farm, sales of wood and lumber, and all other sources, amounted to $784, which, added to the average net return of $60 per farm, gave an average of $844 from which $227 must be subtracted for payment of interest, etc., leaving $598 for family living expenses. This is, of course, in addition to a house to live in and supplies produced on the farm. Farm families are leaving these hill towns in search of more remunerative occupations and a more satisfactory community life.

As in other sections of Vermont, dairying is the type of farming best adapted to these areas. However, not one farm in eight has sufficient size to make dairying a profitable occupation. If people are to continue to live on these smaller farms other than for summer homes, most of the family income must come from some other occupation than agriculture.

The Relation of Agriculture and Industry

The good land is usually in small areas widely scattered. It is not usual to find enough good land within easy reach to make a farm which will give profitable employment for a farm family. The utilization of the small areas of good land for farming purposes is practicable only in case there are mines, quarries, wood working or other industries in the neighborhood which give remunerative employment. Under these conditions, the land and buildings, of what would otherwise be an abandoned farm, are valuable as a residence, and a place to do some part-time farming. These industries are important not only because they provide supplementary employment for the part-time farmer but because they provide taxable property and a grouping of population which make it possible to maintain local government, schools and the voluntary social institutions. Where such centers of life do not exist, it is better that the small, scattered areas of good farm land in the hill towns revert to forests.

NUMBER OF MANUFACTURING PLANTS IN THE THIRTEEN HILL TOWNS, BY TYPES OF PLANTS, 1850-1929

	1850	1860	1870	1880	1890	1900	1910	1920	1929
Starch	4	..	..	..	..	..	..	..	..
Leather	8	6	4	2	1	..	..	..	..
Wood working	..	12	47	73	73	52	46	40	20
Cheese factories	..	..	..	5	10	9	4	9	5
Creameries	..	..	..	..	..	1	3	4	2
Other	4	3	4	7	8	6	3	4	3
Total	16	21	55	87	92	68	56	57	30

The decline in the number of manufacturing plants from ninety-two in 1890 to thirty in 1929 withdrew the source of much of the outside income of the small farmers.

In some towns, mines and quarries will furnish employment. In others, working on roads and for summer residents will supply the need. In the main, however, wood working establishments offer the best possibilities as sources for future employment in the hill towns of Vermont.

Therefore, there should be comprehensive plans for rehabilitating the depleted forestry resources of these towns. This involves:

1. State acquisition of farm lands suited only to forestry;
2. Forest planting and better cultural methods in handling young growth and the application of modern principles of forestry in cutting in order that annual crops of lumber may be insured;
3. Revision of the town organization to reduce the tax burden;
4. Encouragement of lumber companies to acquire large holdings of timber land in these towns.

Summer Residence

There are some very excellent houses on the abandoned farms of Vermont. Many of them are from the standpoint of open spaces, views, healthful surroundings, and delightful climate ideal for summer homes. In 1929, there were in these thirteen towns 171 such summer homes. Of these, sixty-three were on farms and 108 in villages. Ten years earlier, in 1919, the number of summer homes in villages was not ascertained, but there were but sixteen summer homes on these farms.

While the use of abandoned or about to be abandoned farmhouses for summer homes has been increasing especially since 1923, there have been over 200 such farm homes vacated in the ten-year period from 1919 to 1929. Only forty-seven of these have been utilized as summer homes. Thus, there are now in these thirteen towns over 100 abandoned farmhouses that can be purchased at very low prices and that could be made into summer residences with a moderate expenditure for repairs. If there are comparable numbers of such houses in other hill towns of Vermont, some 1,000 idle and unoccupied farmhouses are available for sale for recreational purposes.

Each year sees additional houses abandoned and while some are being acquired by city people, the number abandoned each year is in excess of the number purchased for summer residence purposes. For instance, in the year 1929, in the thirteen towns, forty-four were abandoned and only eight taken for summer homes. There is little or no demand for abandoned farms on which there are no buildings. Splendid examples of what may be done along this line are found in the towns of Wilmington, Dover and Ripton.

Summary and Recommendations

From the study made, several fundamental facts stand out:

1. Most of the land in these hill towns is submarginal from an agricultural production standpoint.

2. The people whose ancestors came into these towns when a very different set of economic conditions existed or when there was a lack of proper appreciation of the limited possibilities, are rapidly leaving, frequently under distressing circumstances.

3. The lands in these towns are well adapted to timber and most of the area is now growing trees.

4. In some towns, there are exceptional opportunities for the development of the land resources for recreational uses and while the number of summer homes in these areas is increasing, the increase is less rapid than the rate of abandonment of farmhouses.

5. The economic difficulties of the hill farmers of Vermont have become more severe with recent trends in agricultural production.

6. High taxes in most of these towns operate to retard the development of forestry, the use for which most of the land is best suited.

7. As abandonment of farms in these hill towns progresses, the tax burden increases for those who remain so long as roads and schools are maintained. After the schools are closed and many roads are abandoned, taxes decline and forestry becomes more profitable as an investment for private funds.

8. Abandonment of farms in hill towns does not mean that the agriculture of the state is on the decline. Agricultural production is being increased on the better lands while the hill farms are being abandoned.

9. The responsibility for the solution of the hill town problem should be assumed by the state.

Further study of the situation in each town is necessary and there should be formulated a program and plan for the economic development in each hill town.

We recommend that a permanent state land utilization commission be set up, composed of the State Forester, the Commissioner of Agriculture, an agricultural economist from the Agricultural College and two other men chosen to represent the lumber, wood working and recreational interests. This commission should work with similar local organizations in problem towns to study the situation and work out a solution for each town.

Prepared for the Commission by its Committee on Land Utilization.

H. P. YOUNG,
Chairman,
G. H. BOYCE,
W. H. CROCKETT,
E. H. JONES.

XI

RURAL HOME AND COMMUNITY LIFE

Ideals of Homemaking

Rural welfare can be measured only by the satisfaction the individual members of the farm family derive from their occupation and their situation on the farm. Is rural life in Vermont satisfying to those who are living it? In order to answer this question, we would need to know, first of all, the aims or goals in life that Vermont farm people hope to attain. The goal is the controlling motive which shapes the homemaker's philosophy. As set forth in recommendations made at the Franklin County, Vt., Farm and Home Economic Conference,[1] "the aim of homemaking should be to produce another generation of farm people that shall be equipped physically, mentally, morally, and financially to cope more successfully with its problems than the present generation." As the dominating spirit of some homes, instead of such a far-seeing, well-defined motive of preparing the younger generation for life, there exists merely the "comfort standard" or a desire to enjoy life *now* and be assured of security in old age. It is possible that in an ideal philosophy of homemaking these and other aims in their proper perspectives, one to another, would be included. This would call for a positive consideration of the subject, which is difficult, because most people have not consciously evolved a life plan.

Family relationship. That most people have a pattern or certain ideals toward which they are striving, is evidenced by their reaction to different situations. One's ideals are determined by his inherited characteristics, as they are affected by his education and environment. The manner in which all phases of living are woven together determines the life pattern of the individual and of the family.

Probably the success of a person's contacts with humans and especially with the members of his family has the most to do with his happiness and fullness of life. His outlook on life is shaped to no small extent by the mutual understanding, loyalty and sympathy existing in the family circle. One has a courageous spirit about his daily task,

[1] Held at St. Albans, December, 1929. Apply to Extension Service for complete report.

V

Vermont Homemakers' Creed

We believe that the family life of the Vermont home has in it all the elements needed for the successful building of character and citizenship.

That there abiding is a sense of permanence and security which makes for stability of character; a feeling of strength; an appreciation of the dignity and rhythm of labor; an awareness of the beauty of our surrounding hills; and high ideals of truth, justice and faith.

That through daily contact in the home with living and growing things comes a spiritual sense of nearness to the Giver of life.

That therein are developed a true hospitality, a kind neighborliness, an appreciation of the value of education, and a fine spirit of community cooperation.

We believe that for the enrichment of life, every home will provide its members with comforts and conveniences; maintain a high standard of health; afford opportunity through reading, recreation, and self-expression for the development of personal tastes.

We believe that groups of homes of this type will form an ideal community providing inspiring surroundings and stimulating contacts.

Thus will the finest traditions of Vermont be preserved.

V

feeling the firm support of a loving family always with him! The urge to be true to one's family gives one a desire to act in such a way that the group will be proud of him and keeps him from doing things which will cause sorrow. If critical advice between members of a family were more sparsely given and then in a considerate polite way, how happy an atmosphere would exist! There should be less effort expended in trying to make many grown and responsible people conform to the wishes of one in matters which do not concern the whole group. In order to have a smoothly running organization, there must be a head, but the head must be governed by tolerance. There must be a responsibility of each person toward the group as a whole and toward each other. The handling of finances often gives rise to difficulties. These will seldom arise if all members of the family share a knowledge of the income and outgo of money. The children should have training in the handling of money and gain a conception of its value by having an opportunity to do some spending without direct supervision. Each member of the family needs some money, if only a very small amount for his own personal use.

On the medium and lower income levels, one of the great advantages of farm homes over urban homes is the feeling of security. One is assured, on a Vermont farm, of fuel, some food and shelter, no matter how adverse the conditions. If insurance is added, the homemakers will approach old age with a feeling of tranquillity. The sense of well-being of which the adults are conscious seeps into the thinking of the children and they are so given a fundamental of their training.

In lives where faith in God and trust in His providing for the ultimate good of human beings have been instilled from childhood, there is the greatest possible feeling of security. People who have known this influence would surely include it in the child's life pattern.

So when we consider the standard of living of Vermont farm families, we include not only the economic goods that satisfy the material needs of the family, shelter, clothing and food, but also the non-material needs for education, health, recreation and religion.

Food. Food as an essential to life must be such that health and vigor are maintained for the strenuous work on the farm and the many other activities of the family. For economic reasons, the family must be adequately fed so that efficient human beings, not gourmands will be the result.

Clothing. Clothing, our second essential element in life, must first of all afford protection from cold and moisture. After these primary needs are met, we may give thought to being beautifully and appropriately dressed. The Clothing Committee at the Windsor County Conference recommended:[2] "That the clothing of our farm families should be such that each member is adequately and appropriately dressed for his activities and associations of work and social life."

Shelter. The third and last material essential to life is shelter. When Vermont farm homes were built, living was more significant than ownership of land. Under modern conditions, in more recently established agricultural areas, competition for possession of the land has made people build houses far less spacious, beautiful and substantial. The present problem Vermont has in this respect is to adapt these houses to modern living ideals as well as they were adapted to the concept of homemaking at the time they were built. We need to make the home a more efficient workshop and a suitable place for all the members of the family to carry on their various activities.

Health. Health is so important as a family asset that it often determines success or failure of the family. The economic situation of the family as well as its even tenor of life are greatly affected by the inroads of doctors' bills, lack of ability to work and the difficulty its members have in being agreeable in ill health.

Education. The education of the children of Vermont homes is the force upon which to a very large degree their future happiness and usefulness depends. Education at home, in school and elsewhere has as its object the imparting of the ability to live and the ability to earn. Since all experiences in life are educative forces, the farm offers an unusually fine chance to supplement the formal training of youth in schools. The child must depend upon his home life to give social training as this branch of education belongs peculiarly to the home. The education of the farm family must not stop with the children, for the adults should seek to increase their education through reading, and by taking advantage of all opportunities for cultural and technical training to keep them abreast of modern developments.

Recreation. Recreation is an essential in personal development and the molding of family spirit. By recreation is meant some activity which brings a person out of his work-a-day personality. Playing

[2] Held at Woodstock, Vt., December, 1930. Apply to Extension Service for full report.

golf is too much like going after the cows to be a compensating recreation in the routine of a farmer. Children like to play "grown up"
and dress in long clothes to bring themselves out of their everyday
personalities. By the very nature of their differences, one member of
a family might not need the same activity as any other member in
order to recreate himself.

Personal. In line with individual recreation comes smoking
and similar habits and desires. Some attention to personal appearance
becomes a near essential. The money spent on tobacco and similar
luxuries should be in scale with the amount allowed for more necessary
articles and this appetite not overemphasized or indulged. From an
unselfish standpoint, good grooming is more to be desired than the
satisfaction of an inordinate desire for smoking. Self-respect in the
family group is affected by the appearance of the various members.

Religion and community welfare. Every person who would
live a happy, calm, full and well-rounded life must have a deep, spiritual
consciousness which will hold him securely through all trials. This
must be instilled from early childhood through religious training and
the development of an interest in other human beings and a desire to
assist all those in need. Religious training should be given the children
both in the home and at some church classes; both consciously, through
study, and unconsciously through the general attitude of the family
and community toward religion. Membership in and active support of
a church seems to strengthen a family by making it an important factor
in community life and through the experience of working closely with
other families for the lofty purpose of maintaining a place of common
worship.

The successful farm family has a great love for fellow men. This
should be expressed through a tolerant, charitable, cooperative attitude
and a willingness to assist in all worthwhile community enterprises,
whether of a welfare, social, educational or business nature.

Development and Financial Demands of Each Element of Homemaking

In olden times the farm was self-sufficing with the land producing
and the members of the family manufacturing the necessities of life.
The efforts of the farm family were concentrated on making the farm
an independent unit. The families were large and a small amount of

paid labor was required. Little produce was sold except in exchange for spices, tea and the comparatively few needs not met by farm production.

Now the order is reversed; farm privileges are fewer and the cash from goods sold satisfy both farm and home needs. When the farmer has a good year, the extra money may well be put into something which will contribute to fuller living or it may be used for more land or more efficient equipment for the farm. So we find that in agriculture, the home and the business are more closely associated than in other industries; and on the understanding of the farm business as well as a knowledge of the demands of the homemaking activities by both husband and wife, depends very largely the standard of living achieved. Because family relationships may become so much involved in deciding between farm and home needs, both sides of the family should be "sold" on this mode of living before farming is entered into.

Greater efficiency in farming must be accompanied by an elevation of the standard of living and the attendant increase in family expenditures if it is to be a permanent benefit to the farmer and his family. If the new increments of income are used to buy more land and inflate land values, increased overhead costs will result. If they are used to develop more intensive farming, the result will be increased production and depressed prices. In either case, this increment will disappear and the farm people will receive no benefit from their increased efficiency. It is important, therefore, that the permanence of the new income be insured by directing it toward the improvement of living standards.

This general principle applies, of course, to the farmers of a whole region such as the Boston milk shed. If some of the dairymen of this region build high living standards upon the basis of new incomes and the neighbors live low, bid up land values and expand production, a part of the new income will disappear for the farmer with the high as well as the farmer with the low standard of living. The building of a higher standard of living will form the basis of holding increases in incomes only when it becomes a common practice among all competing on the same market in the sale of their products. In their Home Economic Conferences the farm women of this state are putting their heads together to make general the improvement of living standards in Vermont homes.

The standard of living set up at the Windsor County Farm and Home Economic Conference shows a minimum of advantages that

farm people are willing to accept. Let us see what things are omitted
by farm folks on lower living levels and what things are added by
people on higher living levels. It is of interest to look back at early
farm life in Vermont in order to guide us in forming a picture of
what we may expect in the future. We will consider, one at a time,
the elements which make up the standard of living, beginning with the
necessities which must be provided before the desirables can be.

Food. Whether or not the farm family is well nourished depends quite as much upon the food produced by the farm as upon the
money available for spending. We think of a supply of dairy products,
maple sugar, eggs, vegetables, and perhaps fruits and meat as part
of the living supplied by the farm. The tendency is to produce less
and less for home consumption. Butter and cheese used to be made on
the farm but now the fluid milk is sold and dairy products, other than
milk and cream, are purchased. The old smoke houses for home-cured
meats are fast disappearing, for since butter is no longer made at home,
the skim milk for hog feed has also gone. Fruit growing is declining,
for the orchard is not being replaced and cared for when its trees are
damaged by storms and disease. Fruit growing is becoming a specialized
business.

There is a study of the food habits of fifty farm families nearing
completion at the Vermont Experiment Station. This study will show
the adequacy of diet as regards calories, protein, calcium, phosphorus,
and iron. At present our only basis for comparison is the money spent
on food. This is scarcely indicative of the adequacy of diet because
faulty food habits may exist on the higher as well as on the lower income levels. There is a strong tendency, however, in a low cost dietary,
not carefully thought out, to omit altogether fresh fruit and vegetables
when they are out of season and comparatively expensive.

Let us compare the amounts allotted for food in the Windsor County
recommendations with amounts actually spent by 225 farm families
having varying amounts of cash available for family living.

EXPENDITURES FOR FOOD

Cash available for all living	No. of families reporting	No. in family	Total for food	Food purchased	Food supplied by farm (figured at retail prices)
Windsor County Conference[3]					
($1,095 average cash available)	..	5	$707.00	$287.00	$420.00
Purnell Project No. 28[4]					
($296 average cash available	6	2.8	391.00	131.00	260.00
($437 average cash available)	7	3.8	522.00	201.00	321.00
($665 average cash available)	21	3.4	593.00	260.00	333.00
($1,210 average cash available)	60	4.4	774.00	371.00	403.00
Peet's Study[5]					
($294 average cash available)	34	3.5	621.00	171.00	450.00
($515 average cash available)	77	3.9	746.00	300.00	446.00
($718 average cash available)	20	3.4	767.00	272.00	495.00

In arriving at the "cash available for family living," the items "Insurance" and "Car Expenses" were deducted from the Purnell Project figures. This makes the study comparable with Peet's study and the Windsor County recommendations where such items were not included under "Household Expenses."

In using the figures from Peet's study, 39 families with $497 and 38 families with $534 cash available for living were combined to give the 77 families with $515. The figures for value of farm produced foods in Peet's study are estimated and an average for 10 records used as a check. These figures as given in his study were changed to 1929 retail prices for purposes of comparison. These 1929 prices are quite naturally higher than the 1930-31 figures of the other two groups.

A study of the above figures would lead one to believe that in the lowest income groups, the food requirements of the family are not fully met. In the groups with medium incomes, the choices of food purchased would need to be carefully made with regard to balancing the diet; and the family meals, if adequate, would in all probability be fairly monotonous. According to the "Family Food Guide," published to assist in planning meals on minimum budgets, it is possible to provide food for a family of five with three young children for $376.00 and for a family of three, two adults and one child for $306.00. This would seem to show that even on the lowest income levels, if the proper choices are made in raising food and purchasing it, there is a fair possibility of adequately feeding such a Vermont farm family. A detailed study of the figures indicate that in the low income group, not enough

[3] Windsor County Farm and Home Economic Conference recommendations.
[4] Tentative figures from Purnell Project 28, dealing with standards of living of Vermont farm owner families.
[5] L. J. Peet's "Study of Land Utilization in 13 Hill Towns in Vermont"—1929.

fat and meat are consumed.   This can be overcome by raising pork and increasing the consumption of home produced cream.   Raising more meat would also liberate some cash for fresh fruits and green vegetables in the winter.   The recommendations made at the Windsor County Farm and Home Economic Conference follow:[2]

In order to supply food most economically and in its most palatable form, we recommend that the following practices be adopted on the farms and in the homes.   The figures are based on the needs of a family of five.

1. That at least four quarts of milk be saved out for family use each day;
2. That more attention be given the vegetable garden;
   a. That it be at least one-half acre in size so as to supply vegetables for summer use and for a winter supply to be canned or stored, and that it be laid out so that it may be horse cultivated;
   b. That it contain more greens and more vegetables which may be eaten raw, as cabbage, carrots and celery;
   c. That special attention be given to planting late varieties of cabbage so it may be available for use in the late winter;
   d. That parsnips, vegetable oysters, asparagus and rhubarb be planted for use in the early spring;
   e. That the vegetable garden include some of the less common varieties as cauliflower, vegetable oysters and brussels sprouts, so as to give added interest and variety to the diet;
   f. That the vegetables planned be of varieties best adapted to Vermont;
3. That special study be given to best methods of planting and raising vegetables;
4. That methods of storage of vegetables be given special study so as to eliminate waste and provide more variety in winter vegetables;
5. That more greens and tomatoes be canned;
6. That whatever fresh and raw vegetables, as lettuce, cabbage and celery, cannot be supplied by the farm during the winter be purchased so that the health and vigor of the family may not suffer during this period of low body resistance;
7. That fresh fruits, especially citrus fruits, be purchased during the winter to supplement the apple supply so that raw fruit may be served each day;
8. That the minimum canning budget for the farm home be 100 quarts of fruits and 100 quarts of vegetables per year;
9. That a flock of twenty-five hens be maintained and seventy-five chickens be raised each year to supply meat and eggs for family use throughout the year;

[2] See reference on page 152.

10. That every family put down eggs during the season when they are cheap and plentiful;

11. That the cash expenditures for food be cut down by raising one hog per year and when possible, supplying beef from the farm or buying it in large quantities as halves or quarters;

12. That the canning and curing of beef, pork and chickens to provide meat during the summer be practiced;

13. That a maximum effort be made to live on home-grown products in view of the fact that it takes $3 worth of products sold from the farm to cover cash expenses of producing that product and provide $1 cash with which to purchase family supplies;

14. In order to provide a family of five with the minimum food which must be purchased, that at least $287 per year be set aside—that if beef and pork are not furnished by the farm, this amount be increased by $100 at least.

15. That according to the food standard stated above, the total amount be divided approximately as follows:

Class of food	Cash expenditure	Credit to farm	Total
Milk	.....	$ 87.36	$ 87.36
Fruit	$ 34.45	51.43	85.88
Vegetables	8.40	104.30	112.70
Meat (cheese, eggs, fish) ..	48.00	149.80	197.80
Sugar	20.50	12.00	32.50
Cereals	86.26	.....	86.26
Fats	72.63	13.57	86.30
Miscellaneous	17.08	2.00	19.08
Totals	$287.32	$420.46	$707.88

The changes in home production methods and modern food preservation and transportation result in more variety and better balance in the diet. It is true that the production of less food for home consumption means a greater expenditure of cash. But this allows for a wider range of choice in the family dietary. Greater variety of foodstuffs purchased, together with refrigeration and preservation of home-raised foods gives a better all-year-round balance to the diet. There is not the tendency to overeat pork at butchering time and go without citrus fruits in winter.

This change in the source of the home-food supply has taken away the opportunity for employment of older children and dependent relatives. It means a higher cash cost for dependents living at home and results in non-producers leaving home at an earlier age.

Clothing. Clothing like food was principally home produced in the early days. Wool and flax were grown, and spinning, weaving, and construction of garments were home activities. Now, clothing the family is a matter of spending money and making selections. This seems like a much simpler process but in reality there are more pitfalls for the unwary housewife. She needs, instead of skill with her hands, a knowledge of the factors entering into the selection of garments. She should know textiles, materials available, wearing quality, appropriateness and treatment in laundering. She should know enough of current fashions to be able to decide between the conservative and the ultra new. She should know markets so that she will not waste time in finding the garment or supplies needed. She must decide whether it is wise to purchase ready-made clothing or whether the garments can more profitably be made at home.

The sewing machine has greatly facilitated the making of garments at home. With fewer articles made at home and those which are requiring a minimum amount of time, we find that another industry has, to a great extent, disappeared from the farm.

In adjusting the clothing budget within a family, we find that the cost varies with the age of the individual. From a study made in 1922-24,[6] it appears from the figures relating to the clothing of the families of the New England States that it costs nearly as much to clothe the man of the family as the woman, sons over twenty-four take less than their fathers while girls of that age take considerably more. Boys and girls of high school age require about the same and both more than their parents; while between the ages of six and fourteen, girls are slightly more expensive to clothe than boys. The women at the Windsor County Farm and Home Economic Conference drew up a clothing budget which allowed $83.70 for clothing for father, $77.41 for mother, $61.25 for sixteen-year-old son, $42.74 for eleven-year-old daughter and $26.98 for three-year-old son.

The following table makes it possible to compare the amount considered a minimum essential for clothing by the Windsor County Farm women with amounts actually spent by Vermont farm people on different income levels:

[6] Dept. Bul. 1466, United States Department of Agriculture, "The Farmer's Standard of Living," by E. L. Kirkpatrick.

EXPENDITURES FOR CLOTHING

Average cash for living	Size of family	Amount spent for clothing	Percent spent for family clothing	Percent spent for clothing each individual
Windsor County Conference ($1,095 average cash available)	5	$315.00	29%	6 %
Purnell Project No. 28 ($296 average cash available)	2.8	35.00	12%	4 %
($437 average cash available)	3.8	80.00	18%	5 %
($665 average cash available)	3.4	108.00	16%	5 %
($1,210 average cash available)	4.4	200.00	16%	4 %
Peet's Study ($294 average cash available)	3.5	38.00	13%	3½%
($515 average cash available)	3.9	73.00	14%	3½%
($718 average cash available)	3.4	130.00	18%	5 %

There is no suggestion as to the number of articles, quality or kinds purchased but it would be safe to assume that if a family of four is to be clothed on forty dollars a year, only protection from the elements can be considered. Working clothing for the man of the family is probably the principal item. Footgear for school children might be the second essential.

Our clothing has increased in quantity and in quality since the early farming days in Vermont. Less labor in the home is required to obtain it but conversely more money must be brought in by the farm business so that clothing may be purchased elsewhere.

Shelter. The passing of food and clothing manufacturing industries from the home somewhat changes the housing needs of the farm family. The large kitchen, pantry, back kitchen and extra rooms for hired help are no longer necessary. Today, due to the ease of transportation we entertain in a different manner. Consequently, such contributions to early times hospitality as second-floor ballrooms and numerous bedrooms may be put to different uses now.

The large number of people in families not only necessitated a large house but helped to supply the labor necessary for building it. Materials for construction had principally a labor cost as they were readily available. This situation explains why, as was reported in the 1930 census for the state as a whole, the farmer's house is more valuable than all other farm buildings and the value of all buildings is 30 percent greater than the value of the land.

One problem is to adapt these beautiful farm houses of an early age of home manufacturing and large hospitality to our present-day needs. Whereas formerly the areas needing protection from animals, such as lawns and gardens, were fenced, we now have the animals confined to a desired place. The farm woman is paying more attention to flowers and shrubbery for she has been released from so many operations within four walls. It is found necessary to rearrange the kitchen to give a compact working area for what is now the main operation in the kitchen, the preparing of meals. A laundry or storage room may take the place of the back kitchen or part of the large kitchen no longer needed for serving meals. The sitting room may be converted into a dining room and the parlor opened up for a living room. A bathroom may be installed where previously was a bedroom for help or a large closet. All these changes are made feasible by a central heating plant which makes it possible to open the whole house for all-year-round use. Many farmers capitalize their large house by using their extra rooms for conducting a tourist business.

Modern living standards demand running hot water and a bathroom. Stoves both for heating and for cooking formerly burned only wood. Supplementing this farm-supplied fuel, some electricity and coal are now used, and oil is a common summer cooking fuel. Again this advancement means less farm-supplied living and necessitates more money for the substituted change. A central heating plant is equipment that the modern housewife expects. Labor-saving devices are gaining ground in farm homes. Churns, separators and sadirons are being replaced by power washing machines, carpet sweepers, electric irons and pressure cookers.

The value of the entire furnishings of the average Vermont farm home is from fifteen hundred to two thousand dollars. From the recommendations of the Committee on Furnishings at the Windsor County Farm and Home Economic Conference, between five and six hundred dollars is necessary to start housekeeping. Between $125 and $150 was deemed necessary for kitchen furnishings, $130-$160 for the living room and $75 to $100 for the furnishings in each of two bedrooms. It was suggested that $80 be set aside each year for the purchase of extra equipment and furnishings so that in twenty years, the following additions may be made to the original equipment; running hot water, bathroom, electricity, power washing machines, electric iron, furnace, oil stove, two additional bedrooms, more and better living-room equipment and some small electrical appliances. The amount necessary for setting up housekeeping as well as the amount required for additional equipment would be modified by household goods inherited and by gifts to the bride. Following is a table showing what was recommended as a minimum and what is actually spent for household expenses:

EXPENDITURES FOR FURNISHINGS AND EQUIPMENT

Cash available for living	Furnishings and equipment
Windsor County Conference	
($1,065 average cash available)	$117.00
Purnell Project No. 28	
($296 average cash available)	19.00
($437 average cash available)	19.00
($665 average cash available)	45.00
($1,210 average cash available)	84.00
Peet's Study	
($294 average cash available)	6.00
($515 average cash available)	31.00
($718 average cash available)	13.00

Where the smallest amounts were spent, no new equipment could have been added, for the replacement of lamp chimneys, brooms, dishes and similar necessities would be primary considerations.

The homes of today are less formal than those of yesterday. The parlor is a living room used not only for state occasions but adapted to the everyday needs of the family. There is space for games, writing, studying and music. We find in the physical set-up of the home more consideration for the varied activities of all members of the family; play space for children, grouped equipment for writing, sewing, laundering and cooking, an office where farm business may be transacted, and bedrooms that are heated so they may be used for other purposes than sleeping.

Health. Better sanitation, comfortably heated homes, clothing adapted to the needs of the wearer, and a wider range in choice of food contribute to more healthful living. Home treatment of illness is being replaced by reliance on doctors, dentists, specialists, hospitals and nurses. A recent survey showed that a large percent of Vermont farm people are within one-half hour's traveling from a doctor in the summer and that in the poorest traveling they would be able to reach him in one hour with a reasonable amount of luck.

The availability of the doctor has made possible his attendance at childbirth in preference to midwives and neighbors. Registered nurses are easily obtained and public health nurses are employed by some towns. The community is taking an interest in health by supporting a nurse and sponsoring regular health examinations of school children. Every means is used to avoid infection; quarantines are respected and vaccination and immunization are familiar to all. The farm home should cooperate in and take advantage of such public supported assistance in health maintenance but in the last analysis the welfare of the family is in the hands of the parents in the home.

The following table compares amounts spent on health by families with different amounts of money available for living:

EXPENDITURES FOR HEALTH

Cash for family living	Health
Windsor County Conference	
($1,095 average cash available	$55.00
Purnell Project No. 28	
($296 average cash available)	17.00
($437 average cash available)	21.00
($665 average cash available)	44.00
($1,210 average cash available)	74.00
Peet's Study	
($294 average cash available)	38.00
($515 average cash available	40.00
($718 average cash available)	93.00

The expenditures for this item by families spending the least would cover only minor illnesses or routine examinations with prevention of illness in mind. A major illness on such a budget would affect the distribution of the entire income and even handicap farm operations.

These are the recommendations set up at the Franklin County Farm and Home Economic Conference: "That each member of the family visit the dentist semi-annually. That older members of the family be given annual physical examinations. That each home have a small but complete medicine cabinet to take care of first-aid emergencies. We recommend that every family make a special effort to use all preventive measures against illness, keeping in mind the ideal of perfect physical health. That each child be given an examination for eyes, tonsils, and adenoids. That when possible, advantage be taken of free clinics and school examinations."

There is a changing concept of the meaning of health. Prevention is becoming more significant than the application of a cure; therefore, health is not an occasional but an everyday consideration.

Education. In earlier days a grade or high school education met the requirements of the average person. Advanced education was looked upon as the privileged training of ministers, lawyers, teachers and doctors. Whether a present-day boy or girl wishes to farm for a life work, or to direct his energies along other channels, he realizes the advantages of specialized training. As fewer people are required to run modern farms, more and more boys and girls are being forced into other lines of work where a clearly defined and high type of training is recognized as an important preparation.

The farmer of today is finding it imperative to have a knowledge of economics, marketing, disease control and agronomy. Brute strength plays a less important part in farming since the advent of machinery, and skill has become correspondingly significant. The homemaker's job grows more complex as the years go by. An increasing amount of skill in management, judgment in making decisions, and knowledge of technical operations are required for this many-sided task. Homemaking is being recognized more and more as a cooperative enterprise and since it is the most important job of most women and men, training for it should be carried on during their whole lives in school and elsewhere.

Homemaking training. a. In all the grades, boys and girls should receive health training and in the upper grades girls should have a survey course of the duties of the homemaker including a study of foods, clothing, and family relationships, which are closely related to their own home experiences and will serve to create an interest in homemaking.

b. In high schools, the course in Home Economics should equip the girl to be an intelligent, alert member of a home—by surveying for her the phases of the homemaker's job, teaching her standards to be attained, giving her a mastery of simple practical processes and instilling in her a sense of the vast importance of her profession. When desirable, similar courses may be arranged for the boys.

c. College courses in Home Economics should provide two varieties of training: (1) Technical training for teachers, dietitians, Extension workers, and others; and (2) advanced training in practical homemaking for the girl who expects to marry at once. Both of these courses should include nutrition, food preparation, parental education, family relationships, clothing, and home management work comprising handling of family finances, time studies, selection and arrangement of equipment and furnishings.

d. Summer school courses in practical homemaking should be provided for teachers and homemakers—these should be intensive courses arranged to rotate so that over a period of years one may secure training in several phases of Home Economics.

e. Teacher-training courses should include health education, nutrition, selection, construction and care of clothing, and elementary work in home management and family relationships.

f. The Extension Service of the State Agricultural College should disseminate information on all phases of homemaking to men, women, boys and girls. This material should make practical application of science to everyday problems of family finances, parental education and child training, home equipment and furnishings, home management and time studies, nutrition and food preparation, clothing, gardening, landscaping and recreation.

g. Short courses giving intensive, practical work on definite phases of homemaking should be made available to the women of the state.

Books, magazines, newspapers and radios are educative agencies which are within the reach of the average person. The following table indicates the expenditures for education including books and magazines:

EXPENDITURES FOR EDUCATION

Cash available for living	Education
Windsor County Conference	
($1,095 average cash available)	$112.00
Purnell Project No. 28	
($296 average cash available)	6.00
($437 average cash available)	10.00
($665 average cash available)	33.00
($1,210 average cash available)	141.00
Peet's Study	
($294 average cash available)	4.00
($515 average cash available)	20.00
($718 average cash available)	35.00

The recommendations of the Windsor County Farm and Home Economic Conference Education Committee call for expenditures exceeding all but the highest group.

They recommend:

1. That as a minimum each farm boy or girl should have a high school education. In order that this may be assured, an educational fund should be accumulated either by means of insurance, taking out bonds, or by setting aside $50 yearly to be compounded for a period of years.
2. That each family take one daily paper, one farm magazine, one home magazine and one children's magazine.
3. That several families club together in magazine subscriptions in order to make more reading matter available and to reduce expense.
4. That at least one good book a year be purchased for a home library, and that $2 be set aside for that purpose.
5. That attention be given to special talent, as music or vocational development, and that $50 yearly be reserved for such.
6. That the family attend educational lectures or concerts whenever possible.

A high school education, which for a farm boy often necessitates living away from home, causes a drain on finances which is not experienced in the urban home. Until it is time for the children to go away to school, many families can maintain a high level of living. Since this expense can be anticipated over a period of from fifteen to twenty years, it should be prepared for and even taken into consideration by homemakers when they select a farm.

People living on a farm sufficiently productive to pay for schooling, who make use of community organizations such as Granges, Women's Clubs and the Extension Service, are able to maintain satisfactory junior and adult education.

Recreation. The auto has given an entirely different radius of activity to the farm family. The young people now go to dances miles distant from home, whereas they were contented, in horse and buggy days, to go to a local barn dance, husking bee or house raising. These events were attended by the older as well as the younger people. Movies have, to a great extent, taken the place of parties at home and community games. Picnics, camping trips, and outdoor sports are now as thoroughly entered into by girls as by boys.

Community groups such as fraternal organizations, outing and recreation clubs, church organizations, women's camps and 4-H camps emphasize and provide wholesome recreation. Surely some provision should be made for recreation in the budget and in the physical set-up of the home. Recreation is not necessarily the playing of games. For some people, it is a creative pursuit or hobby, such as crocheting or cabinet making. Some type of reading is particularly enjoyable to most every person. The followng table shows amounts spent by farm families on recreative material or pursuits.

EXPENDITURES FOR RECREATION

Average cash available for living	Recreation
Windsor County Conference	
($1,095 average cash available)	$55.00
Purnell Project No. 28	
($296 average cash available)	5.00
($437 average cash available)	13.00
($665 average cash available)	21.00
($1,210 average cash available)	60.00
Peet's Study	
($294 average cash available)	3.00
($515 average cash available)	15.00
($718 average cash available)	80.00

Above all, recreation whether it be quiet or active, of a sociable or isolated nature, must answer to the needs of the individual. If home is a place where one can "even up," there must be a chance for recreation or enjoyable activity which gives an opportunity for self-expression.

Personal. Changing styles have brought changes to needs of personal nature. One has a self-conscious feeling if his shoes need shining or his hair needs cutting. The farmer's contacts with a larger community remind him to keep himself groomed in a way which conforms with present-day customs. If he ignores this accepted standard, he may expect to be considered eccentric. In even the most conservative farm woman's scheme of living, there is a need for simple toilet accessories, such as cold cream, manicure materials, etc. These requirements must be weighed against items of a personal nature such as tobacco and candy, and each individual must decide how to apportion the money allocated for this purpose.

The following table shows what was spent by ninety-four farm families and the amount recommended by farm women in conference for personal expenses:

PERSONAL EXPENDITURES

Average cash available for living	Personal expenditures
Windsor County Conference	
($1,095 average cash available	$51.00
Purnell Project No. 28	
($296 average cash available)	8.00
($437 average cash available)	14.00
($665 average cash available)	24.00
($1,210 average cash available)	53.00

Church and charities. Vermont villages were established around churches and the picture of childhood surroundings which many of our illustrious sons and daughters carry in their hearts is comprised of a village street of comfortable modest homes, shaded by graceful elm trees, with the white steepled church in a prominent position.

The activities of the church held a similarly prominent position in the life of our pioneer ancestor. He contributed to it generously both in time and material things—furnishing the logs and the labor when it was built and giving money and donations of produce and wood toward its upkeep yearly. He supported it staunchly by attending all meetings and taking an active part in determining its policies—sometimes even too active a part in this! The church provided much of the social and intellectual life of the village and the minister was a person much respected and feared or beloved intensely. His salary was never large but he lived abundantly on the food and in the house provided by his parish. Much of the pioneer spirit of debating exhausted itself in hair-splitting arguments over creeds and dogmas which often led to schisms and the establishment of several churches in even small communities. This resulted in smaller congregations and smaller budgets and finally in gradual reduction of the influence of the church program in the community.

The church is not at present the well-supported organization in rural communities that it once was. First, there are so many sources of recreation today that the church no longer is as significant as a social or an emotional outlet as it was fifty years ago. Second, there is an added load on a community with a decreasing population in supporting a church. People living in urban communities have the advantage of being able to contribute smaller sums and receive superior service. Nearness to church and size of community should enter into the choice of a farm, if one has a chance of selection.

So, as we review in our minds the changes which have taken place in farm homemaking in the past fifty years, we are convinced that here is no static occupation of small interest. Instead, we find that homemaking is ever changing and has a dynamic effect on the welfare of the country.

Family Contacts Outside the Home

In these days of quick and easy transportation the life experienced by a family and the various members of a family is increasingly influenced by the world outside of the home. To a large degree this can be controlled, especially in a small neighborhood where each family has such a large influence over the social life of the other families. The type of community or neighborhood is more or less established and in selecting a farm, on which to rear a family, people should consider just what its neighborhood stands for.

Selecting the farm home. Since an adequate family life is dependent in a large measure upon adequate income it is necessary first to select a farm, as has been stipulated in the foregoing, from which a family may expect to derive that income, and second, to be sure that it is located near a sufficient number of other farms which will also support families of high standards. For example, a church will require the contributions and effort of a large group of families if it is to be adequately housed and retain the services of a valuable community worker.

1. *Neighbors.* The ideal way to select a farm would be to spend some time there and observe the type of people living on the surrounding farms. Are they living there permanently or only transiently, which will determine to a large measure the real interest that they take in the community? Whether or not they are of American or foreign blood is somewhat important but their standards of living are of more concern. It is also well to observe whether or not a large number of the farms are inhabited by people past middle age with no children who will naturally take the farms over.

Much can be learned about the type of people from a casual survey of the community. Do the people take pride in their homes? Are their porches, lawns, and yards neat? Is time and thought given to flowers, shrubbery, and trees and are the buildings kept painted? Are the parkways, road-triangles and the grounds around the community buildings planted and cared for? Are the lakes and other natural beauty spots appreciated?

That intangible something called community spirit or community consciousness has a great deal to do with the community as a place to live. Are the people cooperative? Do they respond quickly to drives for the Red Cross and other charities? Are they open to new ideas and organizations such as Business Men's Clubs, Extension Groups for boys and girls and adults? Is there a feeling of wholesome competition and good-natured independence of thought as regards local and state politics? Are there distinct cliques or factions among the adults or boys and girls?

2. *Health facilities.* Health has been discussed previously as a matter of concern both from the home and community points of view. In selecting a home it would be natural to inquire as to whether a doctor was available within a reasonable time both in the summer and winter? Is there a public health or school nurse; are pre-school child clinics conducted in that community? Is it possible to get to a hospital easily at all times of the year? Are the local health authorities vigilant as regards quarantine and enforcement of public sanitary measures? Is there a hot lunch served in the school? Is the school healthful as regards sanitation, ventilation, and lighting, and are the seats adapted to the size of the children?

3. *Schools.* The schools of a town reflect the type of people who are supporting them and a community soon gets a reputation for being liberal and progressive or niggardly and backward in its school policy. To assure the proper sort of training for the young people a family moving into a community could well question the schools as to their equipment, supervision, and type of teacher generally employed. Does the community maintain a critical or cooperative attitude toward the school and the teacher? Is it tolerant with new departures in the curriculum which strive to broaden the training for life given to the boys and girls?

4. *Churches.* Since connection with a church seems to be a strong factor in the development of successful family life, it should be of prime concern that there be a church within easy driving distance of the farm home.

Whether to affiliate with a local church and thereby become more definitely tied up with the community and give the young people the chance of leadership training which is more easily found in a small church, or to go to a church in a larger center where more stimulating sermons can be enjoyed, is the question which must be settled by many families.

5. *Library.* The fact that there is a library within reach of the family does not always mean that it is of the sort which will be used. It is well to inquire if there is a good assortment of books for children and adults and up-to-date reference books, if any special attempt is made to interest children by story hours, exhibits of pictures, charts of wild flowers, and if the furniture is intended to make small readers

comfortable? It is also of importance whether the library is open frequently and at times convenient for farm people.

6. *Recreational activities.* It is recognized that the ordinary family of today has an ever increasing area for all sorts of recreational activities. It still seems important, however, that neighborhoods or communities retain some recreational events as safeguards for community good-will. Facilities and leadership for recreation should, therefore, be considered. The number of organizations, such as Granges, lodges, outing clubs, women's clubs, church organizations, scouts and 4-H clubs, which offer opportunities for wholesome social contacts should be ascertained and, of course, their personnel and programs checked as far as possible. The type of movies, dances and other commercial amusements which are within the family range should be considered. Is there any activity which is particularly popular such as dancing, games, cards, or outdoor sports? Is there any provision for baseball, tennis, swimming and skating, and is there a chance for some indoor sports such as basketball during the winter? Is there someone with adequate training to coach dramatics and teach music within the reach of the young people? Can they expect to play in an orchestra or a band at some time and take part in pageants and other similar events?

The most important influence in recreation perhaps is the community attitude toward it. Are the people sympathetic with the need for recreation and anxious to share in it?

Community development plan needed. Many of our Vermont farm families are not choosing a place in which to live but are looking out upon the surroundings of their present home with an eye which should be both critical and constructive—critical to both the good and bad influences to which the family is exposed and constructive to seek methods for their removal or improvement.

The area which may be properly classed as the community or the radius of the contacts of any one farm is changing rapidly with more autos and better roads. During the next few years the size of the community unit will probably increase considerably and many small centers will disappear or become of less importance. Because of this constant change it is hard to know what to do about building up community institutions and the history and trends of the community should be carefully studied before any large change is attempted. It is certainly no time, however, to be indifferent to changes or to vainly mourn the good old times. The earnest consideration of all the right-minded citizens and all the outside assistance which is procurable will be needed in this difficult matter of sociological adjustment.

If some plan for the self-study of Vermont communities could be devised and some assistance provided in analyzing and adjusting conditions, it would help tremendously at this critical time.

Recommendations

Family goal. Since family life is made up of many elements, each family should have a conscious plan as to just how to weave these together to achieve the life pattern desired.

The goal of homemaking as set up for the Vermont home is to equip the next generation so that it will be better able to cope with all the problems concerned with living a well-rounded life.

This goal is to be attained only through carefully considering the elements concerned, and deciding upon a plan for family development which is understood and accepted by all members.

Family relationships. One of the elements of family life which is particularly important may be called family relationships. Under this most inclusive term, a few basic essentials are noted:

1. A clear understanding by all members of the goals and problems of family life.

2. A sharing of the responsibility for family life and a contribution by each member of time, effort or money.

3. An opportunity for each member of the family to develop individually unhampered by dominance of other member or members.

4. Sympathy, tolerance, and wise, unselfish love between all members.

5. A feeling of security—for children, no fear that divorce, illness, accident, or financial troubles will threaten the stability of their home; for adults, a certainty that the home is financially sound and will survive ordinary misfortune and assure tranquil old age. To do this, it is advised that a life insurance policy to at least the extent of indebtedness be carried, and that a serious effort be made to pay off the mortgage while the family has the labor contribution of all members.

6. A fair and just division of funds and all other privileges among all members.

Food. The provision of proper food for the family is important both from the standpoint of health and of expense. It is recommended that the family dietary be planned in accordance with accepted nutrition standards. In planning their food supply, families of limited income should consider whether by purchasing food they may not be sacrificing something which they might have if more food were supplied by the farm.

It is recommended that the maximum amount of food for family use be produced on the farm, especially in the case of small unfavorable farms or on any farm on which the time of the family is not fully employed.

Every farm should furnish milk and cream for family use, maintain a flock of hens of sufficient size to provide all the eggs and poultry meat desired and have a garden planned to meet dietary requirements of the family.

Clothing. It is recommended that the family clothing be selected with the following purposes in mind: (1) To give protection against the weather; (2) to create feeling of self-confidence; (3) to assure a consciousness of equality within the family and with outside associates; and (4) to give joy and a chance for self-expression.

With a minimum income, the protective aspects of clothing must be given major emphasis. As the income increases, more thought can be given to the æsthetics of clothing.

The home. It is recommended that farm houses be so planned that they will be efficient workshops for the homemaker, and provide space and facilities for the various activities of the family.

The farm home should be attractive and artistic, both without and within so that children may grow up surrounded by beauty, and pride in their home be instilled deeply in their characters.

Health. It is recommended that all families adopt a positive attitude toward health; that they consider the importance of disease prevention and encourage all measures to promote health within the home and the community.

Education. The family should take a very broad viewpoint of education and realize that all experiences of life are educative forces and that thought should be given to the training which a child receives in the home and with his associates as well as the more formal school experiences.

It is recommended that every boy and girl be given an opportunity to complete a high school education and receive some vocational training and that training in the fundamentals of homemaking be included in every child's education.

It should also be recognized that education is not restricted to the young people of the family, that from an economic point of view, the farm manager must continually study his profession, the homemaker must be very much alive to all new developments in nutrition, sanitation, child training and all other sides of her job; and all members of the family must never cease in their attempts to broaden their interests and information.

Special talents of any member of the family should be developed.

Reading matter of good quality adapted to all members of the family should be provided in every home.

Advantage should be taken of all community and state organizations offering educational opportunities for any members of the family.

Recreation. It is recommended that each family, through promoting community organizations, planning home and neighborhood social affairs, and providing proper atmosphere and equipment for various types of recreation in the home, attempt to make possible recreation which will serve as a real recreating force for each member.

Personal expenditure. It is recommended that in planning personal expenditures, the first consideration be given to hair cuts and similar items which develop self-esteem and that expenditures for tobacco and sweets should not be allowed to encroach upon allowances for items essential to family development.

Church and charities. It is recommended that each family take some responsibility for the support of a church and assist with worthy community welfare work.

Family contacts. It is recommended that each family clearly recognize the importance of proper contacts outside the home in the development of successful family life and well-rounded individuals.

Home selection. It is recommended that the future farm homes of Vermont be safeguarded by teaching young people to choose a farm for their family home which will provide the elements required for adequate living and which is located near a sufficient number of farms of this type so that proper community advantages may be assured.

Prepared for the Commission by its Committee on Rural Home and Community Life.

Mrs. R. C. Averill,
Chairman,
Marjorie Luce,
Executive Secretary,
Mrs. J. F. Ballard,
Mrs. J. H. Bartlett,
Mrs. J. C. Dimock,
Mrs. E. H. Jones,
Marianne Muse,
Mrs. Charles Winslow.

XII

RECREATION

Community Recreation in Orleans and Rutland Counties

The following report is a study of representative communities of Orleans and Rutland counties made for the purpose of securing information regarding the equipment, facilities and leadership of recreation.[1]

The information was secured almost entirely by interviews with leading citizens of each community—ministers, members of Ladies' Aids and other church organizations, lodge officers, librarians, club leaders, business men and store proprietors, home demonstration leaders and members, etc. In the few cases where leaders were out of town or unavailable for any reason, blanks were left for them to fill out and forward.

In Orleans county, sixteen towns, composed of twenty-eight communities were considered; in Rutland county, nine towns composed of twelve communities. This makes a total of twenty-five towns or forty communities covered in this report.

Of the communities studied, eight were villages or larger towns with a population exceeding 1,000, and thirty-two were under 1,000 in population.

Community recreation facilities and programs. A study was made of the facilities and programs for recreation in the above mentioned communities.

1. *Halls.* It was found that in the thirty-two communities under 1,000 there were forty-nine halls. It is to be remembered, however, that some of these thirty-two communities were very tiny, hardly more than crossroads, and the local schoolhouse would probably be adequate for many recreational purposes if carefully equipped with this use in mind. In the eight communities over 1,000 there were twenty-seven halls which could be used. This made an average of over three per community. In both groups, the halls were of sufficient size for their use and a goodly number of them were equipped with stages.

[1] This study was made for the Committee by Miss Alice Coutts during the summer of 1930.

2. *Outdoor recreation facilities.* Nineteen ball fields were reported in the forty-nine communities. Some of these, however, were not at all ideal, being on fair grounds or the village park. Only one playground was discovered in the communities studied and this one was not supervised except by a caretaker. Tennis courts were found in eight communities over 1,000 and in four communities under 1,000. Golf courses are maintained in four communities over 1,000 and five communities under 1,000. In this latter group three are summer resorts which probably accounts for the presence of golf courses and probably means also that they are used chiefly by non-residents. Skating rinks were reported in only four communities but doubtless there was some place to skate in many others although it might be poorly kept during very much of the possible skating weather. Five communities reported nearby lakes which were used for swimming. Two of these had beaches with caretakers or life guards during the hottest weather. Five communities reported picnic grounds which were publicly used.

3. *Game rooms.* There were thirty-four pool rooms or places to play pool in connection with lodge rooms. Seventeen of these were in the eight communities over 1,000 and seventeen in the thirty-two communities under 1,000. No figures were obtained as to the division of the patronage at these pool rooms between town and rural people but it is presumable that more town people than country people use pool rooms.

4. *Loafing places.* Sixty-nine loafing places were reported in thirty-six communities. Four of the rural communities reported no loafing places. The division between large and small communities seems to be about even, sixteen loafing places being reported in the eight communities over 1,000 and fifty-three in twenty-eight communities under 1,000.

5. *Churches.* Seventy-seven churches or missions were interviewed as to their regular programs. It seems that much of the recreation in the church is planned for the purpose of raising money rather than to provide social life for the church members. Catholic churches seem to make very little effort to include recreation in their program, there being an average of less than one social affair per year among the Catholic churches and missions. Nearly all of these were for the purpose of raising funds. Twenty-eight Protestant churches in communities over 1,000 provided 139 social affairs, the largest number of these being suppers, bazaars and socials with the commercial purpose paramount. It

was surprising to note that the churches in these larger communities averaged five recreation affairs per year while those in thirty-three churches studied in the communities under 1,000 averaged 3.5 recreation affairs per year. In the communities over 1,000 fourteen churches reported women's organizations such as Ladies' Aids or Guilds which have frequent meetings with recreation forming a part of the program. Twenty churches in the communities under 1,000 reported these women's clubs. It appears from these figures that the women in the large communities have twice as many opportunities to belong to these organizations as the women in the smaller communities.

6. *Social affairs provided by other organizations in the communities.* Organizations such as the Grange, Masons, Odd Fellows and American Legion were questioned as to their social program during the past year. The eight communities over 1,000 reported seventy affairs provided by these organizations or 8.6 per community. The thirty-two communities under 1,000 reported fifty-one social affairs offered by these organizations or 1.6 per community. It is interesting to note that the Grange provided the largest number of social affairs of any one organization both in the over 1,000 and under 1,000 group. The American Legion seemed to be unusually active, four chapters providing fifteen social affairs which is a little higher number per organization than the Granges provided. Thirteen Granges reported a total of thirty-eight affairs. In many communities other organizations were mentioned as providing a great deal of recreation for their own members but not holding many public affairs. Two that were commonly spoken of in the rural communities were the 4-H clubs for the boys and girls and the Home Demonstration clubs for women.

Local organizations which seemed to be functioning quite successfully in the territory investigated are the Glover Driving Club which conducts horse races frequently during the winter months, the Newport and Orleans Country Clubs which promote tournaments and organize bridge parties, etc., and the Horseshoe Pitchers' Association at Newport which conducts horseshoe tournaments among its members. Orleans county is most fortunate in having a series of junior bands in several communities. These were organized by a music supervisor and are self-supporting, the various members of the bands paying a small fee for each rehearsal, at which time they are given training on their instruments as well as in playing with others.

7. *Commercial amusements either in this territory or in nearby towns.* Ten theatres conducting movie shows daily or at least four times a week were reported. These eleven theatres reported 114 shows per week. An attempt was made to discover what the division of attendance was between town and rural people but the theatre managers seemed quite vague in their opinions about this. All agreed, however, that from 25 to 50 percent of their patrons were rural people, possibly 35 percent might be a fair estimate. Seven very small communities reported movies occasionally during the winter.

Chautauqua courses seemed to be very rare in these counties, summer Chautauquas being reported in only two communities and a winter Chautauqua in one. In Greensboro, several lectures are given each summer by famous people who are camping on Caspian Lake.

Of the forty communities visited, dances were held during the past year in twenty-five under 1,000 and in seven over 1,000 population. In twenty communities, lodges or organizations sponsored them. The standards in these are generally good, with the exception of seven. Two are low, with much drinking. An outside element comes in, to which people living in the communities object. The remaining five are fair. In two, the neighbors object partly for fear of fire caused by carelessness on the part of those attending the dances and partly because of the drinking and the conduct of the younger people. The majority are supervised by the groups sponsoring the dances and by the constable or sheriff. In some communities, the latter are very lax in their duties. There are six dance pavilions situated a little out of six villages. These have dances quite regularly throughout the summer months. Two are considered good, two fair, and two have much lower standards. The chief objection is to the drinking which goes on outside the dance halls.

Leadership. Sixty-three people who are taking leadership in local recreation either through church or club work were interviewed. Seven of these were ministers, seven school teachers, forty-one home-makers, five farmers and three business men. All of these leaders had elementary education and fifty-six had some high school training, fifty having graduated from a high school. Fifteen had had some normal school or teacher-training work and fifteen had college training. Only eight of these people, however, reported that they had had any training in music, athletics, story telling or in conducting recreation. They feel the need of help very keenly.

A questionnaire was answered by committees or representative citizens from forty-nine different communities[2] and in only seventeen communities was there a person reported who had training in coaching dramatics.

In teaching music, sixteen communities reported someone trained to give vocal lessons; thirteen, piano lessons; seven, violin lessons; eight, band instrument instruction.

What do the communities want? Following is a summary of the desires regarding recreation facilities which the various communities expressed:

1. *Outdoor facilities.* In the forty communities studied there was a great lack of adequately equipped and supervised playgrounds. A centrally located, attractive space for play would be a great help in keeping the children off the streets and away from dangerous loafing places. Only two communities had a safe place to swim—with life guards for protection of swimmers. A few others have swimming places, but these were unsupervised except by caretakers. Every community needs a safe and sanitary place to swim. In a northern climate such as Vermont, every community should be provided with a skating rink. Very few were found to exist. Tennis courts and ball fields are needed in many communities.

2. *Indoor facilities.* A gymnasium that can be used by school and community teams is needed in many sections. Another need most frequently mentioned was a community house.

3. *Organizations.* Practically all community leaders seem to feel the need of additional organizations that will interest boys and girls, especially of the adolescent age. Some suggest Boy and Girl Scouts; others, organizations involving constructive activities such as sewing, music, etc. One leader feels that 4-H clubs are the biggest agency in rural community recreation and should be encouraged more. Some feel that additional sports and organizations should be sponsored by the high schools. Others want recreational programs of various types which involve mass participation. Many feel the need of some organization or method of uniting Catholic and Protestant boys and girls in club work as they are in day school. In general, enough organizations are needed to keep all the young people interested, active, and at home.

[2] Survey conducted in the summer of 1930 by members of the Rural Home and Community Life Committee and the Extension Service.

4. *Leadership.* Finally the question of leadership is of importance as there is a great need for it in the forty communities visited. Twenty-nine leaders wanted more supervised activities for adults, adolescents and children. Others expressed this wish when they asked that the inhabitants be "stirred up or shaken up" because of the lack of interest shown among the parents concerning the conduct and whereabouts of the children and young people and in the improvement of community conditions. This desire fulfilled would involve more leaders who have specialized or have had a good deal of training in the various activities they are best suited to lead.

The community needs as to facilities, organizations and other wants also involve the question of leadership. For example, a safe, sanitary place to swim requires not only the beach or pool, but a life guard who has had training in life-saving methods. Playgrounds are next to use-less without a trained person on hand to teach handicraft, sports, new games or better ways of playing the old ones, and to instill into the youngsters a respect for and care of the equipment and property on the playground as well as in the community. One minister suggests some central association, official or semi-official, for the training of directors of community enterprises so that expert assistance may be given to local communities.

Recreation in Communities Selected at Random

For the purpose of learning a few general facts about community attitude toward and facilities for recreation, individuals or groups of representative citizens in forty-nine communities throughout the state were asked to fill out questionnaire blanks.[2] Of these communities, forty-one were small villages under 1,000 population, such as Berlin, Fairfield Center, Brownington, Greensboro, Williston, Waitsfield, etc., and eight were larger towns, Orleans, Barton, Springfield, Montpelier, St. Johnsbury, Waterbury, Northfield and Newport.

Of the group of smaller villages, which we shall call Group A, ten reported that they were within five miles of a larger center where the people went for some recreation or educational advantages, eighteen were between five and ten miles away and nine were more than ten miles from such a center. Twenty-eight of the forty-one reported that the boys and girls went away from that community to high school and twenty communities reported that the boys and girls boarded away

2 Loc. cit.

from home during the time or at least part of the time that they were in high school.

Organizations which offered recreation for young people. An attempt was made to discover what organizations were present in the various communities which offered recreational opportunities for the young people. Group A reported eighty-three of these, or two per community, thirty-four being 4-H clubs; twenty, Christian Endeavors; thirteen, Scout organizations; and the others were Epworth Leagues or Young People's Societies or Camp Fires. In Group B there were thirty-three of these organizations, or four per community; seven being 4-H clubs; seven, Christian Endeavors; eight, Scouts; four, Outing Groups; and the remainder, Epworth Leagues, Young People's Societies or Camp Fires.

Facilities for recreation. *Libraries.* Libraries were reported in thirty of the forty-one communities in Group A and in all of the communities in Group B. Of the thirty libraries in Group A, six were open once a week; eight, twice a week; one, three times a week; three, four times a week; four, six times a week; and the remaining seven, all the time. In the group of larger towns, three of the libraries were open four times a week and the other five, all the time or at least every day. The question was asked as to how many of the people in the various communities used the libraries. Twenty-six of the thirty communities in Group A where there were libraries answered this question. Practically two-thirds of the communities reported that more than 50 percent of the families used the library and one-third reported that between 75 and 100 percent of the families used the library. Of the seven communities in Group B where this question was answered all but one reported that the library was used by more than 75 percent of the families.

2. *Athletic fields, pools, game rooms, etc.* The forty-one communities in Group A reported sixteen athletic fields, fifteen places to swim, fourteen places to skate, twelve pool rooms of good quality or game rooms, four gymnasiums, three tennis courts and three golf courses. The eight communities in Group B reported a much higher percentage of these recreational facilities; seven athletic fields, seven places to skate, six places to swim, six gymnasiums, four game rooms, six tennis courts and five golf courses.

3. *Music.* It was thought interesting to discover how many communities offer opportunity to play in a band or orchestra or sing in community sings. In Group A, only four communities reported bands,

twelve reported orchestras and twelve commmunity sings. In many cases the report on community sings was qualified by some such word as "rarely" or "seldom" which seems to indicate that they are not common occurrences. In two of these bands and five orchestras, children could play and they are expected to take part in eight of the community sings. Communities in Group B offered many more opportunities for musical expression, there being eight bands, eight orchestras, and three communities where sings are frequent occurrences. In six of the bands and seven orchestras, the children took part and they sang with the adults in one community.

The number of radios in the various communities was questioned. In Group A, three communities reported less than 20 percent of the homes owning radios; seven communities reported 20 to 50 percent; twelve 50 to 75 percent; and nineteen 75 to 100 percent. In Group B, four communities reported 50 percent; three 70 percent; and one 75 percent.

4. *Community amusements* were reported as follows: In Group A, twenty-nine communities reported access to Chautauqua; twenty to lecture courses; twenty-four to musical programs; thirty-nine to local talent plays; eighteen to winter sport carnivals; twenty-seven to holiday celebrations; thirty-three to movies. In Group B, four communities reported access to Chautauqua; six to lecture courses; seven to musical programs; eight to local talent plays; six to winter sport carnivals; eight to community celebrations; eight to movies. In almost every case in both groups the movie reels were selected either by the syndicate or by the manager.

5. *Recreation provided by churches.* The question was asked whether the churches in the community provided recreation. In Group A, thirty communities reported that the churches did, but often qualified that statement by saying, "to a small degree" or "somewhat." The type of recreation furnished by the churches in these communities was in twenty-one cases, socials; ten, suppers or dinners; seven, picnics; six, games; and two, plays. In Group B, all the communities reported that the churches did provide some recreation: in eight cases, socials; in six, suppers or dinners; two, picnics; and in one, games.

Popularity of sports. The popularity of various sports was considered. In Group A, baseball was mentioned as first in twelve communities, swimming in eleven, basketball was first in four and second in seven, skating was first in one, second in eight and third in five. These four seem to be the most important sports in the order named. In Group B, basketball, swimming, golf and skating seem to be the most important sports. Of the forty-nine communities, five reported being within five miles of the Long Trail of the Green Mountains, five reported being within ten miles, eight within twenty miles and the remainder more than twenty miles distant.

Choice of recreation. The popularity of various types of get togethers was answered as follows: Group A reported that card parties were popular in thirty-three communities; socials were popular in thirty-three, dances in thirty, picnics in twenty-six and small neighborhood get togethers in twenty-two. Group B reported dances and card parties were popular in all communities, socials in seven, picnics in five and neighborhood get togethers in one. Twenty-seven of the forty-one communities in Group A reported that there was a growing tendency to go away from the community for recreation while only one of the larger communities of Group B reported this. As to dance supervision, sixteen communities in Group A and all of the communities that reported this question in Group B said that the dances were supervised.

Family recreation. A group of questions was asked in an attempt to discover the sort of things that families do together. In Group A, it appears that in seventeen communities more than 75 percent of the families go on auto trips and to fairs together, in thirteen communities more than 50 percent of the families attend evening entertainments together and in seventeen communities, 50 percent or more of the families have family picnics. Only seventeen communities reported that families ever go camping together. Since only two of the larger communities reported this question, no conclusions can be drawn.

Adequacy of community facilities for recreation. Questioned as to whether they felt the community facilities for recreation were adequate, only two communities in Group A and one community in Group B thought they were.

Leadership seemed to be the biggest lack in both groups, since more than twice as many asked for more leadership and more training for leadership than for any one other thing such as athletic fields, gymnasiums, tennis courts, opportunity for winter sports, etc. Better leadership would mean better use of our splendid natural facilities for recreation such as our lakes, streams, and the famous Long Trail system.

Recreational Opportunities and Their Use by Vermont Boys and Girls[3]

General characteristics and environment of the children studied.
Certain rural areas in Rutland and Orleans counties were selected for
this study. In order that any differences in the programs of village and
town children might be observed, a few large communities were included.

Children in the fifth, sixth, seventh and eighth grades in the rural
and some village schools and in as many of the seventh and eighth grades
of the town and other village schools as could be seen in the time
allotted, were interviewed as to the amount of their leisure time and the
use made of it. Twenty-three schools were visited and 424 children
were interviewed. Of these, five were large town schools where 209
children were seen; seven were village schools where 117 children were
seen; four were accessible rural schools where thirty-one children were
seen; four were remote rural schools where sixty-seven children were
seen. The ages of the children interviewed were between nine and
sixteen, the highest percentage being between eleven and fourteen.

1. *Location of homes.* Nearly one-half or 46 percent of the children interviewed lived in towns while 44 percent lived on farms and
10 percent in villages. The chief differences in these groups would be
in respect to their proximity to school; the opportunities offered by
nearby towns or villages; and last but not least, the differences in the
home life.

2. *Occupations and employment of parents.* In 303 or 83 percent
of the families the father alone was employed, while in 3 percent the
mother was the sole support. In thirty-eight or 10 percent of the
families both of the parents worked, while in eleven cases, or 3 percent,
the children reported that neither father nor mother was employed.
Of the 364 families represented in the survey, 130 or 36 percent of the
fathers were farmers; 24 percent were skilled laborers, as painters, car-
penters, salesmen, and garage mechanics; 19 percent were unskilled
laborers, such as truck drivers and road laborers; 8 percent were clerks;
6 percent were either owners or proprietors of stores. Only seven of
the fathers, or 2 percent, were professional business men. The remaining 5 percent were either unemployed or dead. Eighteen percent of the
mothers were employed in some way, either as help in other homes, or

[3] Survey conducted for the Committee by Miss Ella Gardner in fall of 1930.

as clerks or teachers. In some cases, the mother gave financial support without leaving the home, during the day, by taking boarders, or by dressmaking.

3. *Leisure time of children.* Only 2 percent of the town boys said that they had no free time whatsoever on school days, while 30 percent of the boys living on farms over ten miles from the village said that they had none. Doubtless this great difference is due, in part at least, to the added time necessary to go to and from school. Then, too, the farm boy has more chores to perform than the town or village boy. The average amount of free time that the town and village boys had was three to six hours, whereas, the farm boys had a little less, two to four hours.

Girls, on the whole, had less free time than boys, the average amount of time being from two to four hours. Also, as was found with the boys, the town and village girls had more time for play than the girls living on the farms. The average number of hours for free play in the three groups was: Village girls, four to six; town girls, three to four hours; and farm girls, two to three hours. A very few, 5 percent, of all the girls questioned said that they had less than one hour to do as they pleased, and only three had no free time at all.

On Saturdays, however, the majority of the children had much more free time than on other week days, 60 percent of the boys having at least six hours and 58 percent of the girls having the same. Some of these children had over ten hours. But here again, the village and town boys and girls seemed to have the advantage over the farm children, 75 percent of the former having six hours and over for their use on Saturday, as compared with 59 percent of the country children. Only five boys and two girls said that they had no spare time on Saturdays.

On Sundays the country boy and girl seemed to have nearly as much free time as the town and village children, 89 percent of the former and 95 percent of the latter having at least six hours or more.

4. *Work time of children.* The work done by the children was largely home chores. A few of the children worked as janitors at school, some sold newspapers, and a small number worked on neighboring farms. Very few children, 6 percent of all those interviewed, said that they had no chores or regular work to do. The largest number of village boys, 34 percent, who had chores to do, needed less than one hour daily for them, while it took 31 percent from one to two hours. Among the country boys, living on farms, 33 percent had chores which

took one to two hours daily; 23, two to three hours; while 20 percent took less than one hour. One boy reported having chores which took from eight to ten hours daily to perform. Town and village girls were kept busier than the boys; over one-half or 55 percent having daily duties which took one to two hours. This was the average amount of time needed, too, by most of the girls living on farms. However, three girls living on farms reported that they had work which took them four to six hours daily.

The amount of time spent on chores and other work daily did not average very high, the majority of farm boys and girls, 39 percent, taking one to two hours; 24 percent taking even less than one hour; 18 percent taking two to three hours. There were more boys than girls who reported having very light chores or none at all. Eight percent of the boys and 5 percent of the girls said they did no chores while 30 percent of the boys and 18 percent of the girls said they had less than one hour's work daily. However, more boys, 8 percent, than girls, 1 percent, claimed to work four hours or more daily.

5. *Brothers and sisters.* Each child was asked if he had any brothers or sisters living at home, and if so, the number and ages. Of all the children 87 percent said that they had brothers and sisters living at home. Of these, 69 percent were within two years of their own age, making them a congenial age for playing together.

6. *Playmates.* The boys and girls were questioned as to the number of playmates they had, not including their brothers and sisters or the children with whom they played at school only. Of the total number interviewed, 70 percent had one or more playmates of their own age. Usually they were of their own sex. From a social standpoint the farm boys and girls seemed to be at a disadvantage as far as playmates were concerned. Only 50 percent of the farm boys said that they had playmates other than their brothers or sisters as compared with 83 percent of the village boys and 89 percent of the town boys. The same was true of the girls, 45 percent of those on farms, 79 percent in villages, and 84 percent in towns saying that they had friends of their own age to play with. Of the town children, 7 percent and of the rural, 16 percent said they had no playmates and no brothers or sisters within two years of their own age.

7. *Frequency of meeting.* It was considered important to ascertain the frequency with which children met other playmates, outside of those seen in school, and brothers and sisters. Three-fourths of the boys, 76 percent, who had such playmates, said that they met them daily,

while slightly more, 77 percent of the girls said that they met theirs as often. Ten percent of the boys and girls saw their chums two or three times a week; 12 percent played with theirs but once a week, while the remainder met theirs less often.

Just as the town and village boys and girls had more playmates than the rural children, so also they met these playmates more frequently. Eighty-seven percent of the town and village children were able to play with their friends daily, as compared with 50 percent of the farm boys and girls.

8. *Places of meeting.* Homes were the usual and most favored places for the meeting of the girls and their playmates while the boys said that they met outdoors, which seems a natural thing. However, almost as many of the farm boys, 25 percent, said that they met indoors as compared with 28 percent who met outdoors. This is probably due to the fact that there were not enough boys in the neighborhood to play the popular outdoor games such as baseball and football while in the villages and towns there was always a gang.

9. *Activities with playmates.* The activities that boys and girls enjoyed with their companions whether brothers, sisters, neighbors or other friends were numerous. However, they may be classified under three main headings: (a) Games; (b) free play activities; (c) and social activities.

a. Outdoor games were most popular with both boys and girls, although nearly as many girls liked free play activities as well. Of the outdoor games football was most popular with the boys, though few of them played on a real team. Playing any ball games ranked second, and baseball, third. The girls liked outdoor games best, I-Spy leading the list. Cards and table games were liked by girls, too, they being the only indoor games mentioned.

b. For free play activities, roaming in the woods, playing in the leaves and going to ride in an automobile were liked most by the boys. Several mentioned hunting, fishing and trapping. Only seven boys said that they liked to ski, ride horseback, or swim. The nature of the girls' free play activities was in exact contrast to that of the boys. They liked to "fool around" outdoors, or play dolls, or house, or school. Hikes were popular, too, and more girls than boys said that they liked to ride horseback, swim, skate, and ride bicycles.

c. The last class, social activities, was much more popular with the girls than with boys, 63 percent of the former and 23 percent of the latter saying that they liked to do the things which come in this class. Talking was most popular with the girls, with cards and table games second. A surprisingly large number said that they liked to study or do housework. Sewing, knitting, making scrapbooks, dancing, going to the movies were other popular social activities mentioned by the girls. The boys liked to make things, such as shacks or electrical devices. Doing chores, selling papers, cleaning up, and reading were chosen in this order. Going to the movies or to dances were mentioned by only three boys and girls.

Home recreational facilities. 1. *Trips and other family celebrations.* A pleasure trip or outing of any kind, be it a picnic or a trip to town, has recreational value both for young folks and adult members of the family. The extent to which trips, outings, picnics, etc., are enjoyed depends largely on the home situation. It was found that fifty-four or 13 percent of the 424 children did not go anywhere. Twenty percent of the children living in remote farm areas did not go on picnics or other outings that they considered important enough to speak about. Seventeen percent of the village children reported the same, while 13 percent of those in town said that they never went on outings. The fact that the town children had more good times than the children living on farms may be partly due to the former's having more playmates and neighbors and therefore more opportunities for picnics and joint family affairs.

Of the outings mentioned by the 370 boys and girls who were fortunate to enjoy them, picnics seemed most popular, 84 percent saying that they had been on at least one during the year. Seventy-four had been on trips other than just for Sunday with their families. Going to fairs was a favorite family celebration for 70 percent of the boys and girls while 43 percent went for drives on Sundays. Thirty-one percent of the town and village children mentioned going camping with their families while doubtless it was impossible for the families living on farms to get away for so long a time, as only 16 percent of the farm boys and girls mentioned having been camping.

It was not always an outdoor trip which the children enjoyed with their families. Twenty-six percent said that they played games with their families, probably in the evening around the family circle; six boys and girls said that some one would read aloud to the rest of the family; while five mentioned going to shows with members of their family.

2. *Automobile*. The family automobile although used for business purposes should be included among the recreational assets of any home. Accordingly, each child interviewed was asked whether or not his father or any one else in the family had a car. Sixty-eight percent replied in the affirmative. Seventy-five percent of the children living on farms said that they had cars, while 69 percent of the village and 61 percent of the town children had them. Of the farm children who lived over ten miles from a village, only two said that they owned no car.

3. *Family music*. The part that music plays in the home life of boys and girls in this study was not easy to determine since time did not permit visits to the homes. Each child was asked to name the different kinds of instruments in his home and whether or not he played them himself. Included in the list of instruments named were the victrola and radio which are mechanical in type and require no skill to set in motion. However, both provide a passive form of recreation.

The most popular instrument named was the victrola, 59 percent of all the boys and girls reporting one in their homes. Nearly one-half the children, 49 percent, had radios in their homes. Pianos were nearly as popular as victrolas, 54 percent saying that they had them, while 32 percent said that they played. Stringed instruments ranked next in popularity, 29 percent owning, but only 7 percent having the ability to play. This latter defect may be due to lack of instructors in the communities surveyed. Wind instruments such as the cornet and saxophone were owned by 18 percent, nearly one-fifth of all the boys and girls, but here again, only 6 percent were able to play them.

Of the total 424 boys and girls, 8 percent said that they had no musical instruments whatever in their home. Other children said that they had brothers and sisters who played instruments. Five percent played together as a family orchestra quite frequently while 9 percent played together only occasionally.

Only 3 percent said that the family group frequently sang around the piano or to the accompaniment of some other instrument. Two percent said that their families sang together on special occasions.

4. *Reading material*. A leisure time activity frequently mentioned by the young people interviewed was reading. Hence, some of the questions asked each boy and girl were intended to show the type of literature available in their homes for them to read, and also the type they preferred to read. The majority of the children, 74 percent, had

access to some kind of a newspaper. The local newspapers were a little more popular than those from out of the state, 40 percent of the children reporting that they took the local paper, while 36 percent took out-of-state papers. In some cases, the children had access to both. Most of the children liked to read the current magazines, 64 percent reporting that they did so. Although 84 percent said that they had access to one or more in their homes, 20 percent did not read them when they had them. There was no difference in the number of village, town, and rural children who had no magazines at home to read, 16 percent in each case. Home magazines led in popularity, being named twice as many times, 459, as the farm magazine, 209, and over eight times as often as cultural, fifty-seven, and juvenile, fifty-one. Fiction magazines ranked third.

Often the reading of books, by the boys and girls interviewed, was in connection with school work, but in most cases it was a spare time occupation. Questions were asked in regard to the use of school or other libraries, and the kinds of books read during the previous year. Thirty-one percent of the children interviewed said that they did not read books. One-fifth of the boys and girls who did read, owned books themselves. Thirty-one percent used the public library and 17 percent said that they used the books from the school library. Fifty-seven percent did not use any library at all. Books belonging to the juvenile fiction class, were most popular. They were named four and one-half times as often as other fiction books which ranked second. Books of travel, nature and science were mentioned by only a few. Biographies and histories were not popular leisure time reading of these boys and girls, while poetry, drama, and essays were not mentioned at all.

5. *Trips to town.* For the rural children, a trip to town was considered a recreational activity, even though it was made principally for shopping or other business purposes. A trip to town had different meanings for children living in different localities. To some it meant a trip to a large city, while to those living in the remote farm areas it meant a trip to a rural town where the farmers' supplies could be purchased. Approximately 50 percent of the village boys and girls never went to a large town. This is not surprising when one considers that they did not need to go to do the family shopping or for commercial amusement, however, 58 percent of the farm children went to town at least once a week, probably on Saturdays. Twenty-one percent went two or three times a month. The rest, if they did not go once a month,

did go four or five times a year. Only one boy said that he went to town but once a year, and three children reported that they never had made the trip.

Of the boys and girls who went to town 70 percent gave shopping as the chief reason for the trip. Seven percent went just to visit friends or relatives, and three boys went to town to sell produce. Trips to town for shopping were often combined with other business engagements such as music lessons and appointments with barbers, dentists and doctors. Some mentioned going to church, and to the library while in town. Window shopping was a favorite pastime, especially with the girls. Very few, 10 percent, came to town for recreation only, such as the movies, but often movies added interest to a day of shopping. As many as 10 percent of the children who did have the opportunity to go to town, did not mention doing anything of interest while there. They usually just sat in the car and looked around.

Other recreational activities. This study shows that although commercial amusements did not exist in rural communities, the movies, dance halls, and pool rooms of nearby towns were frequently patronized by the older boys and girls.

1. *Motion pictures.* Thirty-one children, 7 percent, had never been to a movie. Twenty-one of these children lived on farms, although only three lived more than ten miles from a town or village where movies were shown. Six percent of the entire number had been only a few times in their lives, 18 percent went occasionally, that is several times a year. Two hundred and fifty-seven, or 61 percent, went fairly regularly, once a month or oftener. Among the country children, however, only 51 percent, as compared with 76 percent of the town and village children, went to the movies as often as once a month or more.

2. *Public dances.* A large proportion of the children interviewed 81 percent, had never attended a public dance. Six reported having been to look on. Of the seventy-eight children who did go to dances, 15 percent went as often as once a week, 13 percent once or twice a month, while the rest went only occasionally. Thirteen percent reported that they had not been to a public dance more than four times in their lives.

3. *Pool rooms.* Only 9 percent of the boys said that they visited pool rooms, and there were but three of these who said that their visits were daily.

Special interests expressed by the children. Each child was asked to name the activity that he would choose if he could do exactly what he pleased. Free play activities such as swimming, skating, etc., headed the list. Organized games such as baseball and football were second in popularity with the boys, while the girls liked to go on trips, to visit relatives or friends. Reading ranked third in the interest of the girls, but stood sixth with the boys. Mechanical interests were third with the boys, with vocational interests next. Sewing and household tasks were popular leisure time interests for the girls. Club membership was mentioned as a popular interest by both boys and girls. One hundred and thirty-nine, 63 percent of all the girls and forty-three boys, 22 percent, said that they had no choice when it came to naming their favorite sport. This indicates that these children knew no sports. Swimming, skating, and hiking were most popular with the girls, while hunting, fishing, and skating were the three sports named most often by the boys.

The church as a recreational agency. The church is an institution recognized as an important factor in organizing recreation for the people of a community. It has the opportunity to fill a large place in community social life, and its degree of success or failure can be noted in this study. In order to ascertain the extent to which the church enriched the social and recreational life of the boys and girls in this survey, each child was asked his or her affiliation with church and Sunday School, attendance and participation at church social affairs during the previous year.

1. *Attendance.* Inquiries showed that 44 percent of the children interviewed were members of some church; 92 percent had church associations and attended somewhat; 55 percent attended Sunday School. Fifty-eight percent of the boys and girls came from Protestant and 33 percent from Catholic families.

2. *Church social affairs.* Church activities of an essentially social nature, such as suppers, sales, box socials, plays and special day programs, were not participated in by the boys and girls, to the same extent as the religious meetings, 33 percent of all the children reporting attendance at any kind of church social affair during the previous year. The percentages varied somewhat according to the location of the home church, 43 percent of the town, 21 percent of the village and 24 percent of the farm children saying that they had attended such social events. These percentages are based on the total number of children inter-

viewed. Among the 390 boys and girls reached in some way by a church, 35 percent reported attendance at church social affairs.

3. *Participation in social programs.* When asked about the part they took in such affairs, only 15 percent replied that they had done anything more than attend. Recitations, acting in plays and pageants were activities mentioned by the few who did take part.

The school as a recreational agency. The school, as a factor in the recreational life of both boys and girls of this survey, was viewed from two angles. First, the physical surroundings of the school were considered, its equipment including musical instruments, literature, and the outside play facilities such as playgrounds and equipment. The second point considered was the programs carried out by the teachers and pupils. This concerned chiefly the kind of social events and entertainments which had taken place during the year and the extent to which the children participated in such. Here also, was considered how the recess period was conducted, that is, whether there was supervised play or not. The number and kinds of social events were obtained from the teacher, while attendance and participation in such events were questions asked directly of each child.

1. *Musical instruments.* Eleven of the schools had pianos, six had organs, while sixteen reported victrolas, although in only two was the selection of records rated as excellent. Three of the schools reported no instruction in music whatever; ten had singing daily; seven once a week, and three on occasions. Five town schools had a special music instructor and three boasted of an orchestra or a glee club.

2. *Libraries.* Five of the schools, three in the village and two in remote farm areas, had no libraries. Seven schools had books for reference only, while ten had both reference and fiction books. In six of the schools, books were used only in the school room, while ten allowed them to circulate. Two schools even circulated books to the parents. Six rural and two village schools borrowed books from the Free Public Library Department in Montpelier. Eight town and village schools had a town library available.

3. *Auditoriums.* Only three of the towns, and one of the village schools reported that they had auditoriums. In some cases a large class room was used for assemblies, while plays and entertainments were given in the town hall or some other building.

4. *Play-rooms and gymnasiums.* Only two schools, and they were located in towns, reported having specially equipped rooms for gym-

nasiums. Two town and one village school had the use of a room in some other building such as the community house, while in two schools, one village and one town, there were rooms in the basement which could be used for play on rainy days, but which did not have any special gymnasium equipment.

5. *Playgrounds.* Nine of the schools had adequate (three square yards per child) playground space for recess activities—none of these was a town school. Thirteen had some space, but inadequate, while one town school had none at all. Thirteen of these playgrounds were level, adaptable for organized play. Twenty-one had some equipment, such as teeters, swings, etc. Seven were used as community playgrounds during the summer months.

6. *Extra-curricular activities of school programs.* a. There was no special time given for class work in nature study, in any of the twenty-three schools. Sixty percent of the town and nearly as many of the remote rural school teachers, 57 percent, said that they had nature study occasionally, but not in the regular curriculum. Only 30 percent of the village and 25 percent of the accessible rural schools reported the same.

b. Some instruction in handicraft was reported by 40 percent of the town, 30 percent of the rural, and 14 percent of the village school teachers, although in only two cases were there regular classes for such work. Sometimes, instruction was given outside of school hours. Again, it was considered as handicraft instruction when the pupils assisted in some repair work for the school, such as mending desks, seats, etc.

c. The percentage of schools having some instruction in art was larger in all cases. Of the seven schools located in the remote rural areas, five reported having classes given to the instruction of art at least once a week, and in some cases twice, while the other two schools reported having it occasionally. Eighty percent of the town, 70 percent of the village, and 60 percent of the accessible rural schools reported having such instruction at some time.

d. Recess play is important when properly supervised. It not only gives the children a good time, but it affords an opportunity to teach them wholesome health and play habits. The noon hour, in rural schools, offers just such an opportunity too, for most of the children live too far to go home. When a teacher spends her noon hour preparing the afternoon program, she is causing her pupils to miss such bene-

fits as would result from an hour of healthful and supervised play outdoors. In nine cases the teacher organized and taught games to the
children during the recess or noon hour. Eight said that they watched
the children while they played, but left them to their own ingenuity
and devices. The rest gave no supervision whatever.

When the children themselves were questioned as to their activities
during the recess period, 27 percent replied that they had no recess.
These children were all in town schools. Forty-eight percent spent
their time in group play, tag and I-Spy being the most frequently
mentioned. These are both games of little organization. Other games
were mentioned but very few which required much organization. Playing on apparatus was named by 15 percent of the children as their
activity during the recess period while as many as 9 percent said that
they did not do anything but stand around and talk.

e. The popularity of team games such as baseball and ball games of
all kinds was much more marked in town and village schools than in
rural. Sixty percent of the town and 59 percent of the village schools
reported that they played such team games. Sixty percent of the town
and 14 percent of the village schools had teams so that they played
interclass games. The practice and playing of football and baseball
with teams is not a rural school activity, primarily because there are
too few children the same age to form a team. None of the rural
schools reported such activities.

f. Literary meetings, special programs, socials and plays given in
schools are important events in community life. Four of the village
and three of the rural schools reported that they had no kind of a social
program during the year. Six schools had parties at least once a year
and seven reported some kind of a social gathering twice a year. Only
two schools, and both were located in town, reported parties or social
programs more than three times during the year.

g. Socials and entertainments when given by the school, were
attended by a much larger percentage of the children than similar
affairs in churches or other centers such as the community club house
or town hall. After interviewing the children, it was found that the
social activities of 41 percent of them were centered in the school alone,
25 percent of the boys and girls attended social activities in the school
as well as some other center, while 10 percent said that they did not
attend any socials at school, probably because the school had none.

h. Nine of the schools in this survey had organized a Parent-Teacher Association. The largest percentage of these, 57 percent of all schools in the group, were in village schools, 50 percent in the accessible rural communities, 40 percent town and 14 percent remote rural.

i. Clubs have a great appeal to boys and girls between ten and sixteen years of age, and can be a strong influence in their lives. Such clubs should have well-rounded programs stimulating interest not only in recreational and social activities, but in vocational as well. Clubs mentioned by the boys and girls of this survey were the 4-H, Boy Scouts, Girl Scouts, and Camp Fire Girls. One-fourth of the girls, 25 percent, and slightly over one-fourth, 28 percent, of the boys were club members at the time of this survey. The majority had membership in only one club, but five girls and two boys belonged to two clubs, while one girl reported membership in three. Considerable difference was noted between the children residing in the rural sections and those living in towns and villages, 32 percent of the latter having membership in some juvenile club, as compared with 19 percent of the rural boys and girls. The proportion of town and village children, who were club members, was practically the same for both sexes (34 percent boys and 32 percent girls), but it was greater among the rural boys, 22 percent, than the rural girls, 17 percent. Of the 115 boys and girls who claimed membership in some club, 60 percent of the girls and 34 percent of the boys had been officers. When asked what particular club activities they liked best, nearly one-half, 48 percent, of the club members gave a preference for the educational side, mentioning projects as their special interest. Eighteen percent said that they liked the camping part best. Social activities were preferred by only four, while nine said that they had no choice.

The 4-H Club, fostered by the Extension Service of the United States Department of Agriculture in cooperation with State and County Extension Services, and under the direction of state and county agents and local leaders, was the only juvenile organization to which the rural children of this survey generally belonged. The chief purpose of this club is to stimulate interest among farm boys and girls, in better farming and home making, and its greatest growth has been in rural communities. Of the 115 boys and girls having membership in some juvenile organization, 63 percent were members of a 4-H Club, while three-fourths of the club children living in rural sections belonged to a 4-H Club.

The typical rural Vermont boy and his recreation. Judging by
the facts gathered in this survey, the typical Vermont boy living on a
farm belongs to a native-born American family having both a father
and mother living in congenial marital relationship. He has at least
one brother or sister within two years of his own age, who is his natural
playmate. Outside of the family, there are other playmates with
whom he has daily contact. He has chores or duties which take from
one to two hours daily, but at the same time he has two to four hours
of free time on week days. On Saturdays and Sundays he has more
free time, from six to eight hours, at least.

The family owns a car, and outings, such as picnics, are enjoyed
by the family as a group. The car may be a necessity for trips to
town. In such occasions the chief purpose of the trip is for shopping
or trading, but may be combined with some others, such as visiting
relatives, or going to the movies. In his home, the typical rural Vermont boy has access to some passive musical instrument such as radio,
or victrola. For reading facilities in the home, he has access to a local
newspaper, and to at least one magazine, both of which he reads. Although he likes to read books, he does not own them himself, but has
access to either a public or school library.

The typical rural Vermont boy has some church association and
attends Sunday School. Although he attends some of the social affairs
of the church, he never takes any active part in planning them and
seldom does more than sit and be entertained. The school is his real
social center. It is here he finds playmates and a space to play. His
school provides him with a playground of some sort. It is not ideal
in size or equipment, however. Although he admits that team games
are the second most popular activity he knows, his school makes no
provision for his playing under direction any of the simpler organized
sports that a small group, such as his, can enjoy. If he plays at all, he
usually spends his noon recess at such self-starting games as tag or
I-Spy. His school gives about two social affairs during the year. He
not only attends these programs but usually takes part. The typical
rural Vermont boy does not frequent pool rooms or dances, nor does
he go to a movie more often than once a week.

The activities that he enjoys most with his playmates are: Playing
football, roaming in the woods, and making things, such as a shack.
These are his special interests also for when he tells of the activities
he most enjoys, he mentions first of all, free play activities, such as

hunting, hiking, fishing, and camping. Next he likes organized games, of which football leads the list although he does not play on a regular team. His third interest is in working with tools.

Recreation in the Home[4]

In an attempt to discover the sort of things that individuals and family groups do for recreation in their own homes, questionnaires were sent to men and women in Parent-Teacher Associations and to women in Home Demonstration Groups representing communities in Rutland and Orleans counties. These were sorted into Group A, composed of 110 families where there were children living at home and Group B, composed of ninety-three families with no children now at home.

Recreation of individuals. The first question was as to the usual recreational activities of the various members. In both groups the mother of the family reported her recreational activities in the following order: (1) Reading; (2) autoing; (3) sewing and embroidery; and (4) an equal number reported picnics and listening to the radio. The first two recreational activities of the man of the family were fishing and reading in both groups. Where there are children, fishing was first and where there are no children, reading was first. Third in both cases was autoing and fourth was hunting. The recreational activities reported for the boy of teen age were: (1) Baseball; (2) fishing; (3) reading; and (4) athletics. For the daughter of the same age: (1) Reading; (2) swimming; (3) sewing and embroidery; and (4) dancing. The favorite activities of boys between ten and thirteen: (1) Baseball; (2) fishing; (3) swimming; and (4) reading. For his sister of the same age : (1) Reading; (2) playing in the yard; (3) skating; and (4) athletics. For the boy just starting school up to ten years old: (1) Baseball; (2) playing in the yard; (3) reading; and (4) football; and for the girl of the same age: (1) playing in the yard; (2) playing with dolls; (3) reading; and (4) skating.

It is interesting to note that reading occurs in the first four activities in all classes above six years old. Baseball is an ever present pastime with boys of all ages.

Recreation together. The things that families do together were studied chiefly in Group A. It is interesting to note that in every case

[4] Survey conducted by Home Demonstration Department of Vermont Agricultural Extension Service.

these families seem to do more things as a family unit than the children interviewed by Miss Gardner reported. This may be due to the fact that these reports were given by parents and they wish to make as good a showing as possible or that these families were somewhat selected because they were members of organizations to which the most progressive families are attracted. Twenty-three percent of the families reported singing together weekly; 28 percent playing games weekly; 22 percent reading aloud weekly; 26 percent attending the movies weekly; 34 percent attending parties occasionally; 42 percent attending socials occasionally; 40 percent attending lectures; 20 percent dances; 61 percent picnics; 36 percent auto trips; 78 percent reported attending fairs together once a year; and 30 percent reported going camping once a year.

Home recreation equipment. The attention given to equipping the home so that recreational activities may be encouraged is an index of the attitude toward recreation. Ninety-five percent of the families with children reported owning sleds; 74 percent skis; 69 percent skates; 44 percent snowshoes; 57 percent a table for games; 38 percent swings. There was other equipment in small numbers such as one trapeze, etc.

1. *Reading material in the home.* Since reading seems to be such an important recreational activity, it is interesting to discover the number and type of magazines. Group A reported a total of 557 magazines or five per family. Group B reported 441 magazines or almost five per family. These were divided as follows:

Magazines	Group A	Group B
Home	228	189
Farm	116	122
Technical	22	10
Cultural	107	103
Organization	30	14
Sport	4	3
Children's	50	..
Total	557	441

Newspapers	Group A	Group B
Local	127	127
Out-of-state	14	47
Total	141	174

It is to be noted that the amount of reading matter in these homes is far higher than that reported by the boys and girls in Miss Gardner's study.

The use of the public library was questioned from the family point of view. Two hundred and seventy-two members or 2.5 members per family of the Group A families were reported as using the library and ninety-two members or one member per family of the Group B. In both cases, the wife seems to use the library more than the husband and in Group A, the husband uses it more than any one of the children apparently.

2. *Music*. One hundred and ten homes in Group A report 280 musical instruments not including radios and victrolas. There are 195 reported by the Group B families. Eighty children were reported as having music lessons, sixty-nine on instruments and eleven for vocal culture and none of these went over ten miles for their music lessons.

3. *Use of auto for pleasure*. Whether or not the wife can drive the car has significance as to her feeling of freedom and her ability to get away from home. Ninety-two families in Group A and sixty-four in Group B report autos which are used for pleasure and about half as many women as men drive in both cases.

4. *Organizations which offer recreation*. The organizations which offer some recreation for the men and women were questioned. The women with children at home reported membership in organizations in the following order: (1) Church societies; (2) Parent-Teacher Association; (3) Home Demonstration Group; (4) Grange. The group without children reported them in this order: (1) Home Demonstration Group; (2) Church societies; (3) Grange; and (4) Women's Clubs.

The men in Group A reported: (1) Masons; (2) Grange; (3) Church organizations; (4) M. W. A. Those of Group B belonged in this order: (1) Grange; (2) Masons; with Farm Bureau and I. O. O. F. tied for third.

Vacations. In Group A forty-one women and eighty-one men were reported as having vacations, while in Group B where there are no children, forty women and thirty-three men were able to get away from home. The women's vacations seem to be mostly visits to relatives in both instances while the men report auto trips, conventions and a few visits to relatives.

Recommendations

Recreation in the home program. It is recommended to all parents that they try to arrange their children's schedule of activities so that there will be, if possible, two hours consecutive leisure time each day so that some recreational activity may be started and carried through.

It is further recommended that not more than three hours of chores on school days be expected of any child who is attending school.

Since the home seems to be the recreational center for the girls and boys (boys out of doors, girls indoors), there should be attention given to home play equipment of the sort which can be used by children alone or in groups. This should include indoor equipment such as game tables, musical instruments, books, and table games, outdoor equipment such as playing fields, skis, snowshoes, swings, teeters, etc. It is recommended also that a further study be made of types of home play equipment best adapted to children of various ages. It is also recommended that parents try to interest girls in healthful outdoor recreation.

It is strongly recommended to all parents that they preserve a proper attitude toward recreation for all members of the family. It should be clearly recognized that each child requires recreation both with members of his family and with boy and girl companions of his own age and this should be planned for in home equipment and the family time and money budgets.

School recreation programs. Since the use of leisure time determines in a large measure the fullness of a life, any educational system should give training for this. Therefore, it is recommended that all school curricula include such subjects as will provide wholesome recreational activities, such as participation in music and dramatics, the joy of creation gained through art and handicraft work, appreciation of nature through studies of birds, flowers, etc.

Since nearly all schools have pianos or victrolas and a large percentage of homes are equipped with radios or victrolas, it is recommended that music appreciation be given considerable attention in the school program.

It is recommended that recreation in high school programs be planned to include a large number of boys and girls rather than giving a great deal of attention to the perfection of selected casts of small numbers or a few athletic teams.

Since the school seems to be the social center of the small community, it is recommended that schoolhouses be equipped with movable seats, satisfactory lights, and if possible, other equipment such as a stage, etc., which would make them usable for many community gatherings.

It is recommended that each schoolhouse have a playground of at least one acre and preferably two in area. This playground space should be level so that it is well adapted to games of all sorts. Supervision of the playground activities should be provided for in the school program. If it is not possible for the teacher to take an active part in organizing games, older children should be made responsible as leaders and some training given to them for this.

Churches as recreational agencies. It is recommended that a richer social program be planned by the churches which shall provide more active recreation in which the young people may care to participate.

It is further recommended that the churches cooperate with other organizations in the community to plan a well-rounded recreation program.

A community recreation program. It is recommended that some plan be devised whereby a committee of people representing the various agencies in the community can first list all organizations and facilities available to assist with the recreational activities and then plan a well balanced and wholesome recreation program for the community.

Since there seems to be a great lack among our boys and girls of a knowledge of games and sports, it is recommended that each community provide some of the following: Game fields, tennis and volley ball courts, supervised swimming pool, safe skating rink, or recreational hall. To promote athletic tournaments, play festivals and team contests, and to provide leadership, meeting places and encourage the organizations of all clubs and other groups which will provide wholesome activity for youth and adults, should be part of the program for each community.

It is recommended that libraries in villages and towns enrich their program with exhibits and story-telling hours through using local facilities and availing themselves of the help of the Free Public Library Department.

Trained leadership in recreation. Since all of the foregoing recommendations depend to a large degree upon leadership it is recommended that there be some plan arranged for a state recreation specialist who shall assist community committees in planning their year's program of recreation, give definite training to community people so that they may direct recreation, and assist with the larger affairs, such as pageants, play festivals, athletic meets, county-wide picnics, and similar events.

––––––

Prepared for the Commission by its Committee on Recreation.

HOWARD L. HINDLEY,
Chairman,

MARJORIE E. LUCE,
Executive Secretary,

MRS. PAUL BUTTRICK,

WALLACE FAY,

E. L. INGALLS,

J. W. RUSSELL,

JAMES P. TAYLOR,

MRS. F. J. WHITCOMB.

XIII

MEDICAL FACILITIES

History

Medical history in Vermont records in several instances the beginnings of medical activities in the country at large, showing that the early settlers were not only pioneers, but also alive to the necessities of preservation of health. Even while Vermont was an independent republic, laws were made regarding the prevention of smallpox, and as early as 1784 the selectmen of towns were ordered by the Legislature to attend to cases of this disease and provide medical care for those who could not personally afford it. The selectmen were thus made the boards of health of their towns, and for one hundred years were the only recognized boards of health in the state.

Previous to 1784, physicians were scattered throughout the state without organization, but in that year the doctors of Rutland and Bennington counties applied for a charter and organized the first medical society. In 1813 a charter was granted for the organization of the State Medical Society. Whether or not the circumstances of the time had an influence on this organization is not recorded, but it is significant that during the year 1811, and particularly in the winter of 1812-13, the state passed through the greatest epidemic in its history. Dr. Joseph A. Gallup of Woodstock in a book entitled "Sketches of Epidemic Diseases in the State of Vermont From Its First Settlement to the Year 1815" describes this epidemic as "spotted fever" which seems to be the disease now known as cerebrospinal meningitis. He believed it started among soldiers quartered in Burlington, and so rapid was its spread and so fatal its results that 6,400 deaths were estimated during five winter months.

About this time also the beginnings of medical education appear in Vermont. In 1809 Dr. John Pomeroy was given an honorary degree of Doctor of Medicine by the University of Vermont, and also elected "Professor of Physic, Anatomy and Surgery." The trustees by resolution announced that any person attending two courses of lectures by this professor and delivering a dissertation upon some assigned medical subject would be eligible to the degree of "Bachelor of Physic." In

1814 Doctor Pomeroy's students had increased in number so that he required separate rooms for their accommodation. The vicissitudes of the University Medical College cannot be detailed at length in this report. Sufficient to say that it survived its troubles and discouragements and finally became the Class A college which we know today.

In 1818 the Castleton Medical College came into being and continued for twenty years. In 1827 lectures were given in Woodstock, which resulted in the incorporation of the "Vermont Medical College" in 1835. This college continued until 1856. It, therefore, appears that Vermont at one time had three reputable medical colleges, and from these were graduated hundreds of doctors who scattered to various parts of the country, carrying with them Vermont training and Vermont ideals.

Nor were the people remiss in showing their appreciation of things medical. The Legislature, for example, in 1856 passed an act providing for the registration of births, marriages and deaths, this being one of the earliest registration laws in the country. Our vital statistics are, therefore, obtainable from 1857 continuously. Hospitals date from 1836, when the Asylum for the Insane was opened at Brattleboro, and 1876 when the Mary Fletcher Hospital at Burlington was founded by private donations. In 1886 as the result of thirteen years of agitation, the State Board of Health came into existence and in 1898 the Laboratory of Hygiene.

In March, 1894, Miss Ada M. Stewart, who is now Mrs. Henry J. Markoff of West Rutland, a graduate of the Waltham Training School for Nurses, went to Proctor to do district nursing. She was the first nurse to do district nursing in the United States. Thus were the medical beginnings in Vermont set upon firm foundations of development as necessity arose or as judgment dictated, and practically without exception the wisdom of such actions has been demonstrated.

Vermont has had its trials and its problems and it has overcome them. It is, therefore, possible to view with optimism the present situation and express the belief that the state will still continue to care for its people medically as it has done since the first settlers formed their pioneer organization.

Present Status

Numerically, the medical facilities of Vermont consist of 458 physicians, 491 nurses, 39 chiropractors, 33 osteopaths and 31 hospitals.

Actually, the story is much longer and more complicated than can be shown by the mere enumeration. To obtain a complete picture, one must take into account not only numbers, but also the efficiency, loyalty, character and readiness to serve of the constituent elements of the medical service group.

TABLE I. MEDICAL FACILITIES

County	Population	Physicians	Population per doctor	Nurses	Chiro-practors	Osteo-paths	Hospitals
Addison	17,945	18	996	16	0	3	1
Bennington ...	21,647	27	801	17	2	2	3
Caledonia	27,232	37	736	20	3	2	2
Chittenden	47,376	87	544	112	4	5	5
Essex	7,144	6	1,190	1	0	0	0
Franklin	29,928	33	906	33	3	1	2
Grand Isle ...	3,940	2	1,970	1	0	0	0
Lamoille	10,945	11	995	5	0	0	0
Orange	16,690	23	725	14	0	2	1
Orleans	23,076	27	854	18	2	1	2
Rutland	48,441	58	835	84	6	4	5
Washington ..	41,732	42	993	78	9	8	5
Windham	25,985	39	665	75	4	3	4
Windsor	37,401	48	779	17	6	2	1
	359,482	458	785	491	39	33	31

Vermont has had from its beginning a spirit of independence which renders difficult a comparison with other states. It has always been noted for its characteristic of settling its own difficulties and solving its own problems. Federal aid has been accepted in some instances, but even with such assistance, Vermont has usually insisted upon working out its problems in its own way and generally been allowed to do so. Whether this independence and comparative isolation has been wise is not a subject for discussion here, but the fact remains that the medical history and the medical statistics of this state will bear comparison with any other state in the Union.

The Committee on Rural Health has been fortunate in having the cooperation and assistance of the Committee on the Costs of Medical Care whose executive committee has allotted a sufficient sum to allow a general survey of the state, and an intensive study of two counties, Franklin and Orange. The facts obtained by these studies will be used in this report, together with information collected by the Committee itself.

Physicians

Two influences have been instrumental in conserving the homogeneous nature of medical service in Vermont, *viz.*, a medical college connected with the University of Vermont, which has furnished medical graduates every year since 1853, and a State Medical Society organized in 1813 which has been an important factor in maintaining a spirit of co-operation among practicing physicians. Great changes have occurred within the experience of many of the practitioners. To go back forty years, there were listed in Vermont 693 physicians, and it was indeed a small and isolated community which did not have its local doctor. Today 34 percent of the doctors of the state are located in cities, and an additional 33 percent in towns of over 2,500 population. There are forty-three towns ranging from 500 to 1,000 without doctors, also sixty-seven towns with smaller populations. Viewing these facts alone would seem to indicate a marked reduction of medical service, together with medical hardships afflicting residents of the smaller communities. The answer, however, is not so obvious. It fails to consider the improved conditions of transportation and communication; it also fails to consider the character and service-mindedness of the doctors.

The following facts are taken from the survey of Franklin County conducted by the Committee on the Costs of Medical Care. This county was selected for study because of being typical of the entire rural section of the state, and thus furnishing a cross section of conditions as they appear in other counties:

Distribution of 138 families showed forty families less than two miles from a doctor; forty-eight from two to four miles; thirty-one from four to six miles; ten from six to eight miles; six from eight to ten miles and only one family twelve miles. The element of time was also studied in these 138 families. Under best road conditions, forty-six families were less than fifteen minutes from a doctor; sixty-two from fifteen to twenty minutes; and 131 under one hour. Only one family reported within the one- to two-hour limit. Under worst road conditions, thirteen families were within fifteen minutes of a doctor; seven from fifteen to thirty minutes; forty-two from thirty to forty-five minutes; sixty-six under one hour; forty-six between one and two hours; four between two and three hours and one over five hours.

To obtain a proper vision of what this service means to people in rural sections, one may justly compare the facilities of these people with those of equal status living in a large city and depending upon busy and often uninterested practitioners. One may also compare the distance of these families both in miles and time from a church, a grocery store, or indeed from a gasoline station, since gasoline is now one of the important factors in farm work. One must observe that an isolated family is isolated not only from medical service, but also from every public service, and their lives must be governed accordingly.

In considering medical facilities, it must always be remembered that doctors and others engaged in medical service are first of all human beings and endowed with all the varying characteristics of human nature. So far as rural practice is concerned, some one has said that, "There will always be good doctors and there will always be poor doctors," which is true of others than doctors, of course. The town or community which has a good doctor should consider its fortunate situation, while the occasional place which temporarily attracts a poor doctor must make the best of the circumstances. Medical men cannot be standardized and made to look and act alike so long as human nature runs true to form. In the same way, the prejudices of a few and local feelings towards doctors, also due to human nature, will probably continue to the end of time. Granting that a certain proportion of the rural population occasionally suffer from lack of medical service, is there some way to improve this service and bring the doctor and the patient nearer together at least in point of time?

Various methods have been tried. Some fit the community in which they start and survive for a short or longer time. Some fail from the beginning. A few may be mentioned.

Group practice. In a small town, where there is a fair sized hospital, the doctors have organized themselves into a group for the conduct of the work in their area. This group consists of three surgeons, two internists, two eye, ear, nose, and throat specialists, one obstetrician, and one roentgenologist. This group occupies common offices and all fees are billed as from the group organization and are paid into a common pool, from which distribution is then made. As the rural area covered by this group is likely to increase with the dropping out of the older local practitioners, there is particular interest in the manner in which its needs may be met by such an organization. This group is working on the plan of employing men on salary for a year or two after completing their interneship. They work from the organization offices and make daily rounds of rural offices, where the majority of cases can be handled and those requiring hospital investigation are sent to the medical center. The particular feature bearing on the problem of rural medical service is that by such organization and methods, doctors avoid duplication in travel and effort and expenses are reduced for the patients. It is too early to estimate the permanent benefits of this system, but the particular organization described has been in existence for four years.

The small rural hospital. This method has in several instances been organized by a single physician, usually a man living in a village surrounded by rural sections. The primary object of such a hospital is for the care of obstetrical cases, those requiring frequent visits by the doctor and cases of minor surgery. Unfortunately, very few institutions of this kind survive; the reasons being irregularity of patronage and consequent lack of financial support. The chief difficulty is that such a hospital must maintain one or more nurses and be prepared to care for its maximum capacity. So long as patronage continues all goes well but a period of minimum use by patients, and at times no patients at all, usually puts the venture on the rocks.

Cooperative practice. A village with about 1,700 population, with a large outside territory is served by three physicians. For several years, these doctors have divided the country practice, thus avoiding duplication of travel. On a chosen day each doctor takes a different direction from the village and sees not only his own patients, but also those who have called the other doctors, and who ·live within the specified area. On another day one of the other doctors may cover that field. The patients thus have the benefit of being attended by their own doctor, and at the same time receive medical supervision daily or oftener, as needed. This system is made feasible by the attitude of the doctors and the people. A variation of this plan is often followed by doctors practicing in adjoining towns, whereby certain limits are set by the doctors themselves. Doctor A goes as far as John Smith's on a certain road, and Doctor B makes that his limit from the other direction.

Municipal physicians. This term usually means that the town pays the doctor a certain sum on his agreement to live or maintain an office within the town limits. Generally, the doctor becomes the town health officer and agrees to treat indigent patients. The objects of the plan are two-fold, first, to secure a resident physician; and secondly, to overcome the payment of mileage rates in addition to the regular fee. The subsidy or bonus ranges from $500 to $1,000 and the arrangement is satisfactory so long as the people do not try to take advantage of the doctor. When they assume the attitude that the sum paid him by the town makes the doctor legitimate prey for all who would get something for nothing, the medical man soon gets discouraged. However, this plan has been in operation for a sufficient length of time to demonstrate its worth, when a business-like agreement is made and carried out on both sides. The laws of Vermont allow towns to appropriate money for this purpose, and towns may combine to employ a doctor or a nurse.

The "Municipal Doctor System" in Saskatchewan. This system is the subject of an investigation by the Committee on the Costs of Medical Care and its uniqueness seems to merit a mention at this time. Saskatchewan has a political subdivision known as the "rural municipality," corresponding in many respects to a county. There are 301 such political units, and within this subdivision, may be cities, towns and villages, but the service described usually relates to the rural sections not included in other units. In brief, the system consists in the employment of doctors to serve the rural families, payment being made by the municipality, either on a full-time or part-time basis and treatment being free to those families within the described limit. Under some of the contracts, additional charges may be made for obstetrical cases, surgical work and occasionally a mileage fee is allowed. The doctor also serves as health officer. The first municipality doctor system was adopted in 1921, since which time thirty-one additional rural municipalities have arranged for similar service. Salaries paid the doctors range from $2,800, with opportunity for private practice, to $5,000 on a whole-time basis. The report of the work indicates that there are many applications for positions whenever a field is vacant and that the physicians engaged are of a good type and experience. Apparently the system is generally satisfactory both to the doctors and the patients.

Use of medical students. Before the days of medical schools, doctors were trained by "riding" with a practitioner, who was called the "preceptor." In recent years an attempt has been made to revive the preceptor plan in a modified way. The University of Vermont College of Medicine has for the past few years been sending out its senior medical students to assist selected physicians throughout the state during a specified time. The objects are to furnish experience to the student, to impress him with the idea of general practice and to assist the busy doctor. No doubt several students after graduation have located in rural communities, who would not otherwise have done so. Similar reactions seem to be reported from other colleges where the plan has been in vogue.

Nurses

Reference to the tabulated statement (Table I) shows that there are 491 graduate nurses practicing in Vermont. Of these, sixty-three are rated as public health nurses and the remainder are on private duty or in institutional or industrial work. This number also includes, however, those who combine nursing with their household duties, in the case of married women as well as others who, for other reasons, are on part-time duty. The figure given does not include "domestic," "practical" or "partly trained" nurses. Allocation of these different types of nurses would be a task beyond the limits of resources allowed this committee.

Assuming that Franklin county is a fair index of conditions prevailing throughout the state, the survey conducted by the Committee on the Costs of Medical Care furnishes a picture of the nursing situation.

An effort was made to discover both the number of weeks during the year of 1929 which the nurses devoted to nursing and the number of weeks which they were not actually engaged in nursing but were available for nursing, "waiting on call." Only one graduate nurse and two practical nurses were fully occupied throughout the year (that is from forty-nine to fifty-two weeks) in actual nursing. Thirteen, practically one-half of those reporting, were engaged less than twenty-five weeks in such service. . . .

With a few minor exceptions, the private duty graduate nurses make uniform charges for all types of cases which they attend. Their charges are the following. For twenty-four hour duty, home or hospital cases, $42 a week; and for twelve-hour duty, home or hospital cases, $35 a week. For contagious diseases and mental cases the rate is $49 a week. . . .

The practical nurses charge from $10 to $30 a week, for twenty-four hour home cases. . . . For twelve-hour home duty cases, their fees range from $14 to $30.

Regarding the income of nurses, fifteen who were nursing or "on call" forty-six weeks or more during 1929 reported incomes ranging from $675 to $1,875 with a median income of $1,150. Practical nurses under similar circumstances reported incomes of $113 to $1,093, a median of $589. From these figures incomes range downward, depending upon the amount of time devoted to the work. Using Franklin county figures on incomes, one is enabled to estimate an expenditure of around $600,000 for nursing services in the state.

As with the physicians, there appears to be an adequate supply of nurses in the state, but the distribution is uneven and the concentration is in cities or larger towns. Vermont hospitals supply most of the graduate nurses and the tendency is to remain among the doctors under whom they have worked and studied. This, however, does not reduce the available service to the rural districts, provided that the nurses are willing to accept cases in the country. On this point, the Franklin county survey reports as follows:

The fact that relatively few graduate nurses are employed in rural homes does not, according to the nurses, result from the unavailability of graduate nurses for this type of service, so much as from the inability or unwillingness of country people to pay the comparatively high charges. It is true, however, that some graduate nurses, particularly the younger ones, do not like to take . . . . and a few refuse to accept . . . . cases in the country. Several of the older nurses admit that they wish to give up rural nursing. They feel that they have served their time in the country and should be relieved by the younger nurses.

Presumably this situation refers to the poorer type of country homes, since in the better class there could be no question of "serving their time" and "being relieved" other than possibly some degree of isolation in the winter.

Domestic, or practical nurses, indicate less tendency to stay in the city and more willingness to accept country practice. In fact, not a few such are the wives of farmers who, for reasons of necessity or social-mindedness, assist the local doctors in the care of patients. In view, then, of a situation which, while having the needed facilities, yet lacks the practical application, some suggestions may not be out of place.

Resident graduate registered nurses employed by the town. A Vermont law provides that a town may appropriate money for the employment of a doctor or nurse; or that towns may combine in such employment. The plan of employing (or subsidizing) a physician has been discussed under another title. The question now to be considered might be stated thus: To what extent can a trained nurse furnish medical assistance in rural districts?

It should be understood at once that no plan is being suggested whereby the nurse should take the doctor's work. To some extent, an analogy might be drawn between the work of such a nurse and one who works in a doctor's office. The latter, through training, observation and associations becomes a valuable assistant to her employer in receiving patients, taking histories, giving certain treatments, making refractions and in emergency cases furnishing preliminary attention pending the doctor's arrival.

A well-qualified registered nurse, in a section without a doctor, but associated with the doctors who practice in the town, might well be the one to receive calls in the neighborhood and decide whether the doctor is needed. She should act as assistant to the physicians, attending to the first needs of the patient, deciding as to the urgency of the cases and generally making preparations for the service of the doctor if he is needed or heading off needless calls. After the visit of the doctor she carries out his orders, reports the progress and attends to the patient in such emergencies as arise when the doctor is delayed or cannot be reached.

Somewhat similar services are performed by visiting or community nurses in large towns and cities. In a restricted territory a nurse might combine public health service with her work as a doctor's assistant. In large districts where travel is extensive or difficult, it is likely that her whole time would be occupied by service as described. Such a nurse, paid by the town, in close touch with the doctors, and in the confidence of the people, would to a great extent relieve the difficult situation in which some of the outlying districts are placed.

The training schools in the hospitals of Vermont could give their pupils some instruction for this position of "Town Nurse" by adding to their curriculum from one to three months' affiliation with a well-organized Visiting Nurse or Public Health Association.

More use of the attendant nurse. A definition is in order here. The type referred to is not the ignorant person whose only attribute is an instinctive sympathy, and whose knowledge of nursing consists in having borne children and brought more or less of them to adult life. The "practical nurse" now under consideration is a partially trained woman, active and healthy, who knows the technique of ordinary nursing service, but may lack training in surgery and the more advanced arts in which the graduate has been instructed during her hospital residence. An example of the possibilities for service by practical or attendant nurses is found in the system carried out by the Mutual Aid Association at Brattleboro.

The Committee on the Costs of Medical Care studied the Brattleboro plan of training practical or "attendant" nurses and the following description is taken from its unpublished preliminary report:

The hardships borne by families of moderate means in time of sickness was constantly brought to the attention of the Mutual Aid. The existing agencies, the hospital, the visiting nurse, the graduate nurse, did not solve the problem for the family who had to consider the cost of such services. The old spirit of neighborly assistance was disorganized and could not be depended upon for such emergencies. In long continued illnesses, the cost of a graduate nurse was prohibitive in many cases, and more often the number of trained nurses in the community was not adequate to supply the demand. The health of the workers or other members of the family, who were employed, was frequently undermined by nursing a sick member of the family. Many cases did not require the services of a trained nurse or hospital care. A realization of these situations was the impetus for the establishment in 1907 of a unique institution, the first of its kind in the country—The Thompson School for Training Attendant Nurses: This experiment to supply a new type of service in sickness has not only met a direct need in the community, but it has challenged the interest of other communities as well, and it has become the most outstanding of the many activities of the Mutual Aid Association.

The superintendent of the Mutual Aid Association, a highly trained and experienced public health nurse, is in charge of the training school. The course of training covers a period of fifteen months, divided as follows:

Two months' training at the school in demonstration and theory of nursing, personal and general hygiene, care of the home, cooking and serving of food. This preliminary course is planned to give the student a foundation for the hospital training and to prepare her for future work in the care of patients in their homes.

Six months' bedside nursing in one of two affiliated hospitals. In addition to the training in bedside nursing, the pupils are taught the general routine care of patients. They are also instructed in the routine of obstetrical work but are never allowed in the delivery room without a graduate nurse in charge. In addition they have class work and lectures by staff physicians.

Two months' practical instruction in post-natal nursing at the school.

Five months' private nursing in various types of homes under supervision.

The training staff comprises the superintendent of the school and her assistant, a registered nurse, and a graduate dietitian on the staff of the Mutual Aid. While in the training hospitals, pupils are visited by the superintendent of the Thompson Training School usually once a month, and monthly reports are sent to the superintendent by the hospitals. During the course of training, it is made clear to the pupils that they are not so fully equipped as graduate nurses, and their attention is directed to the reasons why they are not sufficiently trained to care for certain types of illness. They are also given lectures on the ethics of nursing.

Similar training for lower priced nurses has been given before; but responsible placing of the attendant nurse from an organized service office and constant help and supervision for the attendant nurse from highly trained graduate nurses adds a new and essential element in giving the service needed. The giving of the right kind of service to each case is more important than the low cost, for the insurance method hereafter described appears to make a graduate nurse practically no more expensive to the patient than an attendant nurse. Whether a graduate nurse or an attendant nurse shall be used, is thus made to depend upon the nature of the sickness and the service to be rendered, not upon whether one kind of nurse costs more than another. By this method either kind of nurse can be brought within reach of the average citizen without financial hardship whenever real need arises.

Hospital Service

The foregoing discussion of medical practice has included every form of illness and disability which comes to the attention of the physician. In the discusion of the hospital work of the State of Vermont, one must first indicate the type of work which a hospital does, both inclusive and exclusive.

Sickness and disability may be divided roughly into major and minor forms: The major forms including all those of complete disability completely confining to the bed or to the house, or of such nature that one is unable to perform one or any of his usual vocations; whereas, the minor illnesses constitute the nuisances of life, interfering with comfort, work and pleasure, yet not being of such a nature as to prevent one from indulging in those pursuits. These minor disabilities constitute the major part of medical work, and, as has been indicated, are treated not only by physicians, but by non-medical practitioners, drug stores and otherwise. These may be eliminated from hospital consideration.

The major illnesses, from the above description, may be divided into surgical cases, medical cases and obstetrical cases. This surgical group includes all the major fractures and dislocations, surgery of the neck, head and trunk, and a considerable portion of the surgery of the limbs. The medical cases constitute not only those threatening life itself, but those which involve, for the time being, complete disability. The nature of the obstetrical case is too obvious to require discussion. Another group of cases which come under hospital care are those requiring a period of observation and study in order to make a diagnosis. This observation and study involves laboratory, X-ray and other special tests which are not feasible in the home.

Various reasons govern the choice on the part of the patient, including his family, physician and attendants, in choosing between hospital and home treatment. The trend of present day life is toward small apartments as compared with the spacious home of recent years. Care of the sick in a small apartment is often inconvenient or even impossible, rendering it necessary for people in the towns to go to the hospital. In the rural districts different reasons prevail. Many farms are at a considerable distance from the physician; there is a necessary delay, a considerable interval of time, required for the physician to respond to emergencies or new developments. There is difficulty in securing trained attendants; the more remote the district, the greater the difficulty. There is too much opportunity for delay and neglect in the treatment of serious conditions so that in order to secure the treatment which the case deserves, patient and facilities for treatment must be brought into closer proximity. Obviously, the facilities cannot be brought to the patient and it becomes necessary that the patient be brought to the facilities, or, in other words, taken to the hospital. Obstetrics offers much the same problem and the above discussion applies to this group of cases. To perform good surgery the operator must work under favorable circumstances. The blacksmith would not call the watchmaker to his shop to repair his watch, nor would a jeweler require a carpenter to come to his store to build a piece of cabinet work. The members of every vocation the country over require their own shop and shop tools to do their best work, and the surgeon is no exception. Hence, an operation of any importance should be done by the surgeon in a hospital properly equipped to give him the opportunity of doing satisfactory work.

Another group requiring hospital care, even some times not of major importance, are those without homes, those who room and board, who are not surrounded by their families and must purchase outright any medical care which they may receive. This group finds it to their advantage to attend the hospital.

From the meager statistics available, we estimate that the number of patients admitted to hospitals in the State of Vermont constitute less than 10 percent of the total number of individuals who apply for medical care annually. At first sight, this appears to lessen the importance of the hospital, but of course one immediately considers that the hospital cases constitute those of major importance.

The foregoing discussion serves to introduce the question of the hospital facilities in the State of Vermont. The survey of the state shows that hospitals are located in the following towns and cities: Barre, Bellows Falls, Bennington, Brattleboro, Burlington, Hardwick, Middlebury, Montpelier, Newport, Proctor, Randolph, Rutland, St. Albans, St. Johnsbury and Springfield. These are regularly constituted hospitals organized on one or another basis and with varying facilities for the care of major cases, and, taken all in all, they constitute an organization well equipped for the handling of the hospital type of disability. The capacity of these hospitals varies from a dozen or fifteen beds in the smaller ones to over one hundred in the larger ones. Without exception, laboratory facilities are available in each to a greater or lesser extent, and a good X-ray equipment is available to the patients in each instance. A review of the past few years indicates that these hospitals have for the most part been filled to a comfortable capacity. From the very nature of their work, it is obvious that the demands vary from time to time. There have been many weeks in which the hospitals could have cared for a much greater number of patients than were in residence at that time, and there have been other instances when they were overcrowded to the limit. However, the hospital organization is quite elastic and it is doubtful if a single authentic instance can be cited where a patient has been refused medical and surgical care on account of the lack of the physical accommodations in any hospital in Vermont. Non-emergency cases have been delayed; this, though an inconvenience and disappointment to the patient and family, does not, however, result in any ultimate actual harm. One may, therefore, say that Vermont is well equipped with hospitals.

A study of the map indicates that it is doubtful if a single resident of the state lives at a distance greater than thirty-five miles from some well-organized hospital. Those who live a distance greater than twenty-

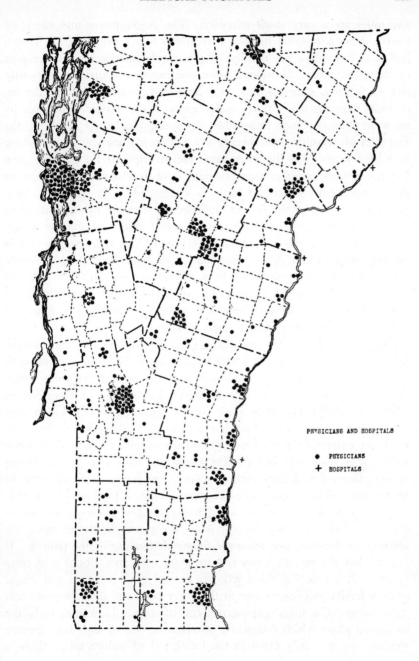

PHYSICIANS AND HOSPITALS

● PHYSICIANS

+ HOSPITALS

five miles are a very small minority. The larger towns and cities, of course, have a hospital in their own limits and a population within a radius of five miles, say nothing of ten, would include the greater part of the population. However, when one becomes acutely or seriously sick or injured, statistics have very little therapeutic value. If the individual happens to be thirty miles away, travel rendered difficult by snow or mud, or even impossible, he is not comforted at all by the fact that ninety-nine other people live within a stone's throw of where he wishes to go. On the other hand, the principle of the greatest good for the greatest number must operate here as elsewhere. So far as gross expense to society at large is concerned, it is financially economical to transport the patient the required distance by fair means or foul, rather than to develop too many hospital units. Strange as it may seem to many of the laity, transportation of the sick can be and is accomplished without harm beyond the occasional discomfort and emotional distress involved. One may, therefore, say that the hospital facilities of the State of Vermont are as available as is reasonable from the standpoint of distance, and are annually improving due to the policy of the state in regard to highways.

The costs of hospital care show great variation. One may secure hospital care at the so-called ward rates where he is in a room with other patients at a gross total cost varying from fifteen to twenty dollars per week. If operation is required, a charge of from five to ten dollars additional may be made for the operating room. Laboratory and X-ray charges may vary from two to twenty-five dollars. In the other extreme, a patient may pay in the vicinity of forty dollars per week for hospital care in a private room, may have two private nurses at, say, thirty-five dollars each per week, and board at from seven to ten dollars and fifty cents per week, thus making a total possible weekly cost to the patient of one hundred thirty dollars, exclusive of special charges. This difference in cost is by no means dependent upon the severity of the case, nor upon the financial standing of the patient. It is true that the serious cases require more care and special care costs money. It is true that those who are limited in their means and frugal in their habits will secure care at the lower cost, and the well-to-do will tend toward the more expensive type of care. However, it is the emotional phase which frequently governs the cost of the case. Severe sickness is not a daily event in the family; if of sudden onset, there is frequently pronounced mental agitation and in many instances the first impulse is to "secure the best of care no matter what it costs." The mind of the family is rightly placed on securing a favorable outcome of the illness and for the time being may not be troubled with financial matters. In other instances, there will be frank discussion with the physician or hospital superintendent as to exactly how much care is necessary and advisable. Generally speaking, we believe that a person may secure competent and adequate care in the great majority of instances at a weekly cost not to exceed thirty-five dollars, plus special charges which should average for the entire case not over twenty-five dollars. The majority of cases require hospital residence two or three weeks. It will thus be seen that with forethought and with careful consideration in advance of costs the great majority of hospital cases need not exceed at the most, a cost of over $150 for the entire case. In this, as in other matters, there are exceptions and there are cases which remain in the hospital for months. These, however, are so few as not to affect the discussion of hospital facilities. It, therefore, appears that the State of Vermont is prepared to render to its citizens hospital care at a reasonable cost.

Medical Insurance in Brattleboro

A form of medical insurance which has been carried on in Brattleboro since 1926 is, so far as known, the only system of its kind in the country. For this reason, it is here described in some detail, quoting from the unpublished preliminary report of the Committee on the Costs of Medical Care:

Safeguarding the family—Through a plan worked out with the Brattleboro Mutual Aid Association and the Brattleboro Memorial Hospital an unusual opportunity is offered to the people of Brattleboro and surrounding towns to reduce the cost of sickness by insurance. The plan known as "Safeguarding the Family" is a form of insurance benefit providing for "Nursing Service at Half Price" and "Hospital Service," either or both of which may be taken out by one person.

Nursing Service—Under the system known as the Thompson Benefit Association for Nursing Service, the Mutual Aid Association assumes the responsibility to furnish those insured, at half the usual price, with the services of a visiting nurse, an attendant nurse, or a graduate nurse, whenever requested by the physician during the period covered by the insurance. The amount of such benefits shall not exceed $200 to any one policy holder during an illness. The following are the annual premiums:

Husband and wife (a unit) $3.00
Children under ten years (each) .... .50
Children over ten years (each) 2.00
Single person 2.00

Hospital Service—The payment of an annual assessment will provide for the full costs above $30 and not to exceed $300 in case of an operation, at the Brattleboro Memorial Hospital, including the surgeon's charges for the operation and the regular nursing and hospital accommodations.

In cases not calling for an operation, it will provide half the costs in excess of $30 (and not to exceed $300) of hospital care, exclusive of physician's fees. The yearly premiums for hospital service are as follows:

Husband and wife (a unit) $7.50
Children under sixteen years (each) 1.00
Children over sixteen years (each) 5.00
Single persons 5.00

If suitable medical, hospital, or nursing service cannot for any reason be rendered to the insured, with the consent of the Mutual Aid Association and the Brattleboro Hospital, the patient may be taken elsewhere and the benefits applied on the same basis.

A schedule of fees drawn up by two local physicians (a surgeon and a physician) is used as the basis for checking the charges made by physicians for services provided beneficiaries of the hospital insurance. When aftercare of surgical cases is given by a physician other than the operating surgeon, the amount to be paid for aftercare is determined by the executive secretary of the Thompson Trust in consultation with these two physicians.

No medical examination is required for either form of insurance, but the applicant for nursing insurance is required to sign a statement that there is no existing condition that would necessitate nursing care. An applicant subscribing for the hospital insurance must sign a statement that there is no existing condition that would necessitate an operation, and that he has not had an illness which, if recurring, might require an operation. The Thompson trustees reserve the right and responsibility of accepting or rejecting applicants. Benefits under either form of insurance will not cover chronic cases or maternity cases.

If differences arise as to how much is due or whether benefits should be paid at all, they are submitted to a Board of Referees of six members appointed by the Association to hear and decide upon such cases. The decision of the Board is binding on both parties. Persons or families not making payments within thirty days after an annual assessment is due shall have their rights to such benefits terminated. Members changing their residence to other places are given the privilege of cancelling their membership and receiving a proportional part of the last annual payment.

The insurance benefits are brought to the attention of the public through newspaper publicity and by a wide distribution of pamphlets and other printed matter describing the insurance. Persons who have benefited by the insurance are depended upon for spreading a knowledge of the insurance. The Executive Secretary of the Thompson Trust and, recently, the office secretary of the Mutual Aid devote a limited amount of their spare time to selling the insurance to persons in Brattleboro.

Availability of Medical Care

This review of medical facilities of the State of Vermont as regards physicians, nurses and hospitals, indicates that the majority of the population is well supplied with medical care available within a reasonable distance. It also clearly shows that there is a small portion of our population which is located in such a way that medical service is rather inaccessible. The time necessary for the physician to reach the patient is an important factor, but is not so important to the individual as the cost of securing the physician's visit, and one can no more expect a physician to make a call fifteen miles from his office at a nominal fee than one could expect a taxi man to perform a similar service. The problem to be solved in this instance is to make available to the people who are thus unfortunately located, medical services which can be secured within a reasonable time and at a reasonable cost. We offer a solution, or at least a suggestion of a solution. We do not consider it the entire solution of the matter, neither do we assume that it will be feasible in all instances. We do believe, however, that the following suggestion contains much value and is worthy of the consideration of those groups of the public and those groups of the physicians where such a situation applies.

Adjacent to these remote districts at a greater or lesser distance are towns containing several physicians. The population of a remote district or township or village which finds itself without medical services should get together and come to an understanding concerning their needs. The physicians in the larger towns should have full knowledge of the needs of the surrounding territory.

Our suggestion is that the physicians organize themselves and decide which of them and how many of them are willing to do their share of that rural work in their surrounding vicinity. We will call this town where the physicians live A. In community B, located a certain distance from village A, are a group of families, there may be five and there may be fifty. If community B can agree that they wish to have a certain physician regularly, a financial arrangement seems possible by which certain quarters will be made available to him as an office at which on certain days of the week, say two or possibly three days, he will endeavor to be present and see patients at an office rate, and on these days will make calls charging only such mileage as would be charged if he were resident in this community. If community B cannot agree upon one man, then arrangements may be made with the group whereby one man covers the territory for a portion of the year under the above terms, and another man at another portion of the year. During such time as this agreement exists other physicians shall visit this community only on special calls and make such charge as is customary for the long mileage involved. This gives to the community the same choice in regard to physicians as though they had one resident in their midst, one who would do the work at local rates, and yet they would have the privilege of securing the services of a physician from the larger town who would charge a regular fee for the special trip. In this way the community would secure medical services at reasonable cost and the physician would be able to render these services with due conservation of time and at a reasonable and satisfactory income.

Objection is made that this does not take care of emergencies arising on the days when the physician is not in that community. Due to the fact that the physician has exclusive privileges in community B, it is only reasonable that he should make such special trips as are necessary at a price in advance of similar calls on regular days, and yet at a cost less than normal for such a special visit.

In certain instances, it might be possible and feasible for the hospital through its staff to act as the organization rendering rural medical service. In fact, in many instances the hospital staff and group of town physicians are identical. It has been suggested by an ex-president of the American Medical Association that the county medical society should assume the solution of rural practice. We have studied this question quite thoroughly in this state and do not believe this to be the proper organization. The responsibility of the care for the sick in the rural districts is one that rests upon public and profession together. This responsibility cannot be shifted. Physicians cannot handle this work without the co-operation of the rural group. The rural group cannot secure their services without the cooperation of the professional body. If this problem is approached and discussed in an atmosphere of cooperation and good-will, one local problem after another may be gradually adjusted to the satisfaction of all concerned.

The State Department of Public Health

The public health organization of Vermont began in 1886 when an act was passed providing for the appointment of a State Board of Health, consisting of three members. Previous to that time, the selectmen of the towns had constituted the local board of health, but with no central affiliations. In 1923, the Department of Public Health became one of the constituent parts of the State Government, the State Board of Health continuing as such in charge of the Department. The general duties of the board are described in Sec. 6197 of the General Laws as follows:

SEC. 6197. GENERALLY. Said board shall take cognizance of the interests of the life and health of the inhabitants of the state, shall make or cause to be made sanitary investigations and inquiries respecting causes of disease, especially of epidemics, and the means of preventing the same, the sources of mortality and sickness and the effect of localities, employments, habits and circumstances of life on the public health; and, when requested, or when, in their opinion, it is necessary, shall advise with municipal officers in regard to drainage, water supply and sewerage of towns and villages, and in regard to the erection and construction, heating, ventilation and sanitary arrangements of public buildings, and said board may compel owners of such buildings to provide them with the necessary appliances and fire escapes for the safety of individuals who may be in such buildings, and said board shall exercise the powers and authority, imposed by law upon said board. Said board may in its discretion, exercise all the powers and authority, in each town and village, which is given to a local board of health; and said secretary may likewise exercise all the power and authority of a local health officer, anywhere in the state.

The regulatory power of the Board has been confirmed on at least two occasions by the Supreme Court. The work of the Department is carried on through divisions as follows:

Administration. The secretary of the board is the administrative officer. He has general supervision of the Department, including finances, also takes the direct charge of collection of vital statistics.

Laboratory of Hygiene. A special legislative act in 1898 created the laboratory and prescribed its services. These consist of examination of specimens under the following heads: (1) Bacteriological, including diphtheria, tuberculosis, venereal diseases, malaria, typhoid fever, and various other infections; (2) pathological, examination for cancer and other tumors, and other abnormal tissues; under this head also is included the medico-legal autopsies, mention of which will be made later; (3) sanitary chemistry, including water analysis and examinations of milk specimens, also checks on water treatment and sewage disposal plants; (4) food chemistry, samples submitted for detection of adulteration or substandard articles, also collection of food and drugs for checking legal qualities; (5) serological, examination of blood for syphilis, and undulant fever, animal blood for contagious abortion and poultry specimens for white diarrhea of fowls.

The Director of the Laboratory is, by virtue of his office, also state pathologist and, as such, is at the call of the State's Attorney for performing autopsies in cases where foul play is suspected. Should the case come to trial, he is also available as an expert witness equally accessible to either the prosecution or the defense. The benefit of this plan in money saving to the state and the people has never been computed, but must run into many thousands of dollars each year.

Communicable diseases. Cooperates with health officers and physicians in the diagnosis, control and reporting of communicable diseases and devotes much time to the control of venereal diseases. Diphtheria antitoxin and toxin-antitoxin are furnished free through established stations throughout the state, silver nitrate solution is distributed directly to the physicians and anti-syphilitic treatment is furnished for indigent cases. This division cooperates with the United States Public Health Service, the director being Acting Assistant Surgeon.

Sanitary engineering. Has control of water and sewage plants, public buildings, including schoolhouses and camps, and tourists' houses. Regular inspection is made of all boys' and girls' camps, expert advice given on other matters on application, and inspection of nuisances on complaint. Special attention is given to solving the problems of health officers and town officials.

Tuberculosis. This division resulted from the transfer to the State Board of Health of activities directed toward the prevention of tuberculosis, which had previously been carried on by the Tuberculosis Commission. In 1916 it became evident that the small appropriation allowed for this work was entirely inadequate for the needs of the state and the Vermont Tuberculosis Association was organized as a constituent part of the National Tuberculosis Association. The Association took over the preventive and educational program, supplementing the state funds by private subscription. The entire work was thus co-ordinated under one head and has since been carried on with satisfaction to both parties and greatly to the benefit of the people of the state.

Maternity and infant hygiene. Conducts classes for mothers in connection with women's clubs, granges and parent-teacher associations, and instruction in child care in high schools. Sends acknowledgments of birth certificates to all mothers and furnishes literature to mothers on application, and to doctors for distribution to patients; gives instruction through lectures and motion picture reels. This division has charge of May Day activities.

Infantile paralysis. A specialized division operated under funds donated to the Department entirely outside state appropriations. Conducts clinics for examination of patients, and by two traveling nurses supervises aftercare for these crippled children, furnishes braces and other apparatus, either free or at cost, arranges for necessary operations, many of which, including hospital care, are paid for from the special fund. A subdivision of research has been conducted since 1914, at present cooperating with the Harvard Infantile Paralysis Commission. An expert is always available for assisting physicians, not only in diagnosis but also in treatment. A supply of human immune serum is ready at all times and furnished free when the case is applicable to such treatment.

Health Officers

Every city and town is required to have a health officer who, with the selectmen of the town or the aldermen of the city, constitutes the local board of health. Recommendations are made by the selectmen and a certificate of appointment is issued by the State Board of Health, the term of office being three years. Since many towns have no resident physician, health officers must necessarily be secured from various walks of life. These untrained men sometimes remain in office for many years and acquire a surprising efficiency in the control of diseases and abatement of unsanitary conditions. There is another class, however, that takes the office without enthusiasm or sometimes without interest. Such men, subject to local influences, prejudices and friendships, constitute the great problem in public health administration. Of 223 health officers in office at the beginning of 1931, ninety-three, 42 percent were physicians; sixty, or 27 percent were farmers, seven were druggists,

seven merchants, five town clerks and four were employed in stores.
Others were scattered among various occupations as shown in Table II.
According to age groups, there were sixty-six between sixty and sixty-
nine, sixty-five between fifty and fifty-nine, and forty-two between
forty and forty-nine. There were twenty-five over seventy years of age
and two over eighty.

TABLE II. HEALTH OFFICERS

Occupations	20-9	30-9	40-9	Ages 50-9	60-9	70-9	80-9	Total
Blacksmith	..	..	..	1	1	..	..	2
Buttermaker	..	1	..	..	..	..	..	1
Carpenter	..	..	..	2	1	..	..	3
Doctor	2	7	18	28	29	7	2	93
Druggist	..	..	..	5	..	2	..	7
Electrician	..	..	..	1	..	..	..	1
Expressman	..	..	1	..	..	..	..	1
Farmer	1	3	12	18	18	7	..	59
Farmer and Embalmer	..	..	1	..	..	..	..	1
Hay dealer	..	..	..	..	1	..	..	1
Health Officer	..	..	1	1	..	..	..	2
Housewife	1	..	1	1	..	..	..	3
Insurance	..	..	1	..	1	1	..	3
Laborer	..	..	..	1	..	2	..	3
Lawyer	..	..	..	..	1	..	..	1
Lumber dealer	..	..	..	1	1	..	..	2
Mail carrier	..	..	1	1	1	..	..	3
Merchant	..	1	2	1	2	1	..	7
Mill worker	..	..	..	..	1	..	..	1
Milk dealer	..	2	..	..	..	..	..	2
Quarryman	..	..	1	..	..	..	..	1
Postmaster	..	..	1	..	..	..	..	1
Postmaster and printer	..	..	..	1	..	..	..	1
Retired	..	..	..	..	..	2	..	2
Road Commissioner	..	1		..	..	..	..	1
Road Patrolman	..	..	..	1	..	..	..	1
Selectman	..	..	..	..	1	..	..	1
Sheriff	..	..	..	..	2	1	..	3
Teacher	..	..	..	..	1	..	..	1
Town Clerk	..	2	..	..	1	2	..	5
Town Manager	..	..	1	..	..	..	..	1
Undertaker	..	..	1	1	..	..	..	2
Veterinarian	..	..	..	..	2	..	..	2
Weights and Measures Sealer	..	..	..	..	1	..	..	1
Worker, store	..	2	..	1	1	..	..	4
Towns without H. O.	19	..	..	..	..	..	..	19
No information	6	..	..	..	..	..	..	6
Total	25	4	19	42	65	66	25	2	248

Sanitary Conditions

Vermont is one of the oldest settled states in the Union, and apparently from its very beginning some attention has been paid to sanitation. Early laws gave the selectmen authority to investigate "sources of filth and causes of sickness" and provide means of abating nuisances affecting the public health. Since the establishment of the Laboratory of Hygiene in 1898, more or less regular examination has been made of water supplies used by towns and cities and free analysis has been available for all individual supplies. For many years a competent sanitary engineer has been available for advice and direction in the construction and maintenance of public works. All this has resulted in making Vermont a clean state from a sanitary standpoint and this particular work is the kind that can usually be handled by a lay health officer who may know very little about the control of disease.

Water supplies are described as public and private, the former being those used by at least ten families. During the year 1930 specimens were examined as follows:

Water Samples from public water supplies (ten families or more) (Chemical and bacteriological):
Wholesome	529	
Polluted	138	
		667

Samples from treated public supplies (check on proper operation), (Bacteriological examination only):
B. coli absent	1,270	
B. coli present	49	
		1,319

Samples from private water supplies:
Wholesome	421	
Polluted	302	
		723

Samples of market milk:
Standard or above (Chemical, bacteria count, sediment)	1,352	
Below standard	592	
		1,944

Submitted samples of milk for chemical examination, only, standard	55	
Below standard	25	
		80

Submitted samples of milk for microscopical examination, normal..	25	
Abnormal	24	
		49

The growth of camping places, combined with automobile travel, has greatly increased the amount of sanitary supervision required by public health departments. Particular responsibility is felt for the boys' and girls' summer camps, of which there are about one hundred in Vermont, populated by nearly 7,000 boys and girls from practically every state in the Union. The plan of control by visitation and inspection has been followed rather than the usual method of promulgating regulations, and this has proven to be satisfactory in securing the goodwill and cooperation of camp owners. In consequence, with scarcely a single exception, any one of these camps could be highly recommended to parents. The problem of water supply, sewage disposal and general sanitation are under constant review by the sanitary engineer.

Similar service is obtainable by other camps on application but the available personnel has not been sufficient to cover all as a routine. An act was passed by the 1931 Legislature which provided for inspection of all recreation camps, tourist lodging houses, and wayside eating places.

Disease Control

The system of local health officers followed in Vermont, places the control of communicable diseases largely in the hands of men who have little or no knowledge of medical science, but as noted elsewhere, some of these health officers who continue in office for a number of years, develop a knowledge and judgment which enable them to show exceptional results. The history of public health in Vermont would include the names of many of these laymen with records equal to a trained physician. Some of these are still in office. Of the ninety-three physicians who serve as health officers for their towns, the great majority are conscientious workers with a well-developed public health viewpoint. Thus Vermont has both handicaps and advantages in disease control. The important point to consider is the matter of progress and the comparison with other states.

Problems of Public Health Service

The great problems in Vermont, as everywhere, are the local public health unit, the local board of health and health officer. Many states are solving these problems by the organization of county units, which by reason of being larger in area and population and, consequently, better supplied with funds, are able to employ trained workers. Vermont has no county organization aside from the courts, and to introduce a county health unit would necessitate a complete change from the established customs of more than a century. Town government is so

TABLE III. CASES AND DEATHS FROM CERTAIN DISEASES AND
DEATH RATE PER 100,000 OF POPULATION

	Diphtheria	Measles	Scarlet fever	T. B. lungs	Typhoid fever	Whooping cough
1900						
Deaths	50	25	16	460	112	20
Death Rate	14.5	7.2	4.6	113.9	32.5	5.8
1910						
Deaths	32	21	10	305	48	57
Death Rate	8.9	5.8	2.8	85.6	13.4	16
U. S. Death Rate ..	21.4	12.3	11.6	139.7	23.5	11.4
1920						
Cases	266	3,874	661	146	170	2,234
Deaths	21	18	15	229	37	27
Death Rate	5.9	5.1	4.2	64.9	10.4	7.6
U. S. Death Rate ..	15.5	8.9	4.7	100.5	77.7	12.6
1930						
Cases	99	1,435	438	179	24	740
Deaths	7	3	11	208	3	16
Death Rate	1.9	.83	3.0	57.1	.8	4.4

thoroughly established in New England and especially in Vermont, that
it must be recognized as practically unchangeable. Town sovereignty
is as much a principle in this state as is state sovereignty in the nation.
Such being the case, the problem to be solved is that involved in securing whole-time health officers in an area sufficiently large to support
them.

In 1919 the Vermont Legislature passed an act permitting the employment of whole-time district health officers, and appropriated the
necessary money to carry out the system. Under this plan, Vermont
became the first and only state to establish a 100 percent whole-time
rural service, ten trained physicians being employed by the Department.
This arrangement continued for four years, after which the appropriation was abolished, necessitating a return to the former local system.
The experience, however, was instructive as a demonstration and it is
within the range of possibility that something of the kind may again
be organized. The experiment was apparently launched too much
ahead of public opinion, and to reinstate it the time must be awaited
when the public and the medical profession will accept and support
such a system. It is evident that in Vermont there must be local
health officers as well as district health officers, and since both must
be paid for their services, the present financial difficulties are sufficient
to obstruct any further effort.

An alternative plan would be the cooperation of towns by mutual agreement and financial assistance to employ a whole-time district or county health officer. Such a plan is in actual operation among certain towns in Barnstable County, Massachusetts, but has not succeeded in other groups where the effort has been tried out.

There still remains the idea of continuing the present local system of local health officers, but adding some method of instructing these officers in public health work. Several years ago the State Board of Health held an annual school of instruction for health officers, continuing in regular sessions for three or four days. Attendance at this school was compulsory, so far as it could be made so, and the officers were paid their expenses and also a *per diem* allowance of $4.00. This school was carried on for eighteen consecutive years, but finally it became too much of a financial burden and was abolished. Since the return to the local system, efforts have been made to hold similar schools or conferences, with voluntary attendance, but with indifferent success. In actual practice, most of the instructing of health officers is done by correspondence with the state officer and visitation by state officials.

Recommendations

It is evident that no one system or plan of medical service is applicable in every community of the state. Towns, villages and cities have their individualities in exactly the same way as do men and women. Therefore, the kind of service acceptable in one place would meet with immediate disapproval in another. The problem is to find the type of service which fits the community which it serves. The following suggestions are accordingly presented as worthy of consideration:

1. Group practice of physicians (p. 209).
2. Subsidy of physicians by towns (p. 210).
3. Use of medical students as assistants to physicians (p. 211).
4. Organization of physicians in specified areas (p. 223).
5. Resident nurses employed by towns (p. 213).
6. Increased use of attendant nurses (p. 214).
7. Public health training of nurses as part of hospital curriculum (p. 214).
8. Some method of utilizing larger health units (p. 230).
9. Instruction of local health officers at state expense (p. 232).
10. Increased resources for inspecting and controlling camps, recreation places and tourist lodging houses (p. 229).

11. Increased efforts to secure immunizing of school children against communicable diseases.

––––––––––

Prepared for the Commission by its Committee on Rural Health.

W. G. RICKER, M. D.,
Chairman,
C. F. DALTON, M. D.,
Executive Secretary,
MRS. ARTHUR J. BLACKMER,
NELLIE BUTTERFIELD, R. N.,
A. M. CRAM, M. D.,
JOHN P. GIFFORD, M. D.,
FRANK G. SHAW,
LILLIE YOUNG, R. N.

XIV

EDUCATIONAL FACILITIES FOR RURAL PEOPLE

As a state, Vermont in 1932 proposes to spend on its roads, $2,948,000 (or 186 percent) *more* than it spent in 1924. It proposes to spend on its schools $138,000 (or 21½ percent) *more* than it spent in 1924. We have known unmistakably for some time that we were road-minded. But have we been conscious that we have come to value road development at the end of an eight-year period, more than twenty-one times (in actual dollars) as much as we value school development?

Our forefathers, as soon as the wilderness was broken, and provision was made for their own family habitations, sold lands for school support, raised taxes for school maintenance, and built schoolhouses. Adequate provision for education for *every child* is a tradition which our earliest settlers brought with them; and today it is a challenge for Vermonters to answer if anything like an equal educational opportunity is to be given to our youth the state over, and if what is given measures up fairly to what the boys and girls of other states are receiving.

The situation is tangled; self-study with a long look ahead to intelligent goals for an indefinite future, self-study, with the whole state in mind, and with our whole educational system in mind, is today our obvious procedure. The will to undertake fearless self-study, without selfish purpose on the part of a group or a town or a section, and with more thinking together by those interested in elementary and secondary schools, normal schools, and colleges, has already shown itself in the minds of many citizens. The committee asked by the Vermont Commission on Country Life to report on educational facilities for rural people has found this self-study method and state of mind the impetus for all its fact-finding and deliberations. Whatever recommendations are offered depend entirely for value on the recognition of all this, and upon the recognition that Vermont has a unique opportunity today to move forward educationally under its private citizens' own power. Experts are needed to view our schools objectively and to give us the benefit of their factual findings and reports. But the whole philosophy of the Comprehensive Survey of 1928-31—actually accomplished by Vermont citizens themselves—is a dynamic one which gives Vermont her chance for exhibition steps in educational progress over the coming years.

Financing Education in Vermont

The significant figures quoted in our opening sentence demand an examination of Vermont's system of support for its public schools, and challenge the average citizen's intelligence on the soundness of a state policy which appears to value education so cheaply. Although participation in the support of our schools by the state as a unit is not the whole of the question, it does offer a barometer; and these figures at once raise the question of our present scale of relative values and of its bearing on educational ideals at a time when changing social conditions must be met in kind. Such an examination has been attempted in a tentative way by this Committee. We quote in part from the preliminary report submitted by a recognized authority,[1] whose assistance for the purpose was granted by the United States Commissioner of Education, in response to a request from the State Board of Education of Vermont in June, 1929:

An examination of the system of financial support shows that there are inequalities in tax burdens and in educational opportunities prevalent throughout the state. Among the causes of this situation are the following: (1) Property taxation as the chief source of school support. There is general agreement of authorities on the subject that this method is unscientific, inequitable, and inefficient. (2) School support is almost wholly from local sources. This method of support usually results in two evils: (a) That local units are free to have as good or as bad schools as those responsible for local control see fit, (b) that since distribution of taxable wealth has no essential or basal relationship to geographical distribution of school units, nor to the size of the educational task measured in terms of the number of children to educate, the inevitable result is that some units have many children and little taxable wealth with which to educate them; others have wealth and few children to educate. Thus the burden of taxation and the quality of educational opportunity offered are both apt to be inequitably distributed.

A study of the wealth, the income, and the effort made to support schools by the people of Vermont indicates that as compared with the United States as a whole and certain neighboring states, Vermont is

---

[1]Katherine M. Cook, Chief, Division of Special Problems, United States Office of Education. Mrs. Cook spent considerable time in Vermont during two periods, and had the assistance of a statistician from the Washington office, who came to Vermont also.

apparently able financially to support schools measuring up to modern
ideals at least as well as the states with which it was compared. On
the whole, the people of Vermont are not making as great an effort for
the support of elementary and secondary schools as seems possible
judged by their ability or as seems necessary judged by expenditures in
other states.

Since Vermont supports its schools largely from local property taxation, certain facts concerning the results of this method are worthy of
consideration.

The state, as a unit, now assumes about 13 percent of the support
of its schools. Twenty states in the United States show a lower and
twenty-seven a higher percentage of state support. In general, the
trend in the United States during the past ten years has been toward
increasing the amount and percentage of the contributions which state
units give to school support. This trend is in the interest of promoting more nearly equalized tax burdens and educational opportunities
throughout the state.

At this point in the report, data are offered which picture the wide
disparity in Vermont towns in their ability to support schools, as measured by tax valuation, due to the fact that wealth and children are not
equally distributed around the state; and since the schools are supported by very small units, the disparities are larger.

The general truth of the principle that as units of support are increased in size and wealth, disparities of this kind are ironed out, is
demonstrated at this point also, by data which show the effect on equalizing tax burdens which would come if larger units of school support
were substituted for the present town unit—the larger units used in
the tables being the supervisory district, the county and the state. As
the size of the geographical unit is increased, potential opportunities
for education in terms of wealth per child are increased also. It is
stated that this comparison is made solely to show the effect of the
larger unit of taxation on equalization of tax burdens and school support, and not by way of recommending any one of these units for
ultimate adoption. The report continues:

Having considered the disparity among town school units to support schools, it is well to consider also the effort which they make or
must make to provide adequate educational facilities. If some communities are rich enough to support schools of high standards with
little effort while others, even with a great sacrifice in taxation, are
still unable to raise enough money to support schools of inferior
standards, it is apparent that the state school financing machinery is
discriminatory from the point of view of a state school system. The

effort which communities make to support schools can be roughly measured by the educational standards they try to maintain as evidenced by the amount of money they raise per child from local taxation, and by the rate of taxation. Vermont has not established a uniform practice in appraising property valuations for taxation. If it had done so and we then set up a minimum standard as to per capita cost of education which all districts must meet, the tax rate necessary to raise that amount could be accepted as a satisfactory measure of effort. Under existing circumstances these measures (the amount of money raised per child and the rate of taxation) have serious limitations. They do, however, *indicate* the true situation and are the best measures available at the present time.....

The very wide disparity among towns in the amount of money per child raised for school support through town taxation indicates that a variety of standards as to equality of educational facilities offered exists in Vermont.

Tables quoted show the range in amount raised per child from local taxation to be $174.89; and it follows if one town spends that much more than another per child, there must be a wide difference in the *quality* of the education furnished. Further data show that if the same educational efforts were made by all towns (*i.e.,* if the same rates were levied for schools in all towns), there would be great differences among them in the amount of money raised per educable child, also that educational standards as measured by expenditures per child do not necessarily parallel ability to support schools. The wealthy towns do not in all cases set the highest standards or raise the largest amounts of money per child for school purposes. Vermont's system of state aid, intending to equalize, to some extent, local ability to support schools adequately, and to stimulate districts to make a greater effort, has been partially successful, but the amounts so appropriated have been quite insufficient for full accomplishment of what state aid is intended to achieve. Further quoting:

Detailed data which cannot be presented in a brief report justify the following conclusions based on the premise that the people of Vermont desire to set up a school system designed to provide for the education of all the children in the state regardless of the place of their residence or the financial condition of the family or community in which they live:

1. The state, as a whole, is financially able to support schools with standards similar to generally accepted standards as compared with the United States as a whole or with the other New England States.

2. Apparently Vermont does not spend as much on elementary and secondary education as the New England States or the United States.

It spends more in proportion on higher education than on elementary and secondary education. While this should not be interpreted to mean a decrease in expenditure for higher education, it is believed that it should mean careful consideration of the possibilities of an increase in the amount appropriated for elementary and secondary education.

3. Supporting schools through property taxation wholly is no longer considered scientific and equitable. A number of authorities to this effect are cited in the complete report.

4. The present plan of supporting schools chiefly through local taxation is inequitable both in tax burdens and in educational opportunities offered, measured by available data.

5. Adoption of units of taxation larger than the town unit would reduce inequity. Full equity would not obtain through any educational or civil unit now found in the state unless a state-wide equalizing program were devised to assist in the equalization.

6. State aid as at present administered and in the amount now available does not adequately equalize among school units nor stimulate local communities sufficiently to reach standards approaching uniformity throughout the state as measured by per capita expenditures on education.

7. There is not at present sufficient data upon which to base a complete study of school financing. A thorough-going study of the whole state system of taxation and support of its institutions, civil and educational, would be advantageous and serve as a basis for intelligent conclusions on school support.

With these conclusions your Committee agrees, even suggesting that the state as a unit of entire support for public education in Vermont may be the goal to strive for. We have in Vermont a laboratory for just such a pioneer proceeding, with conditions increasingly favorable to the consideration of the idea. The progress made by Delaware in this field may be studied to advantage.

This Committee definitely recommends that steps be taken immediately for a complete study of financing education in Vermont, by an officially appointed commission with funds at its disposal to do an authoritative piece of work.

The Need for Larger Local Units

Fundamental to the above, and to all educational progress in Vermont is a comprehensive study, by a field worker, of natural community units in the state, irrespective of town lines, and with major emphasis on topography, on lines of easy communication and of trading, and on interest centers. At the same time there should be provided a planned leadership for more expression of intelligent public opinion on educational matters in Vermont. The experience of the present committee shows that there is no question as to ready contacts for this constructive move. Innumerable groups need discussion leadership to help them formulate their thinking along lines relating to future developments. The state deputies and the district superintendents frankly admit that they are too busy with the practical problems of *today* to break through, to any extent, to the goals of *tomorrow*. Besides, the breaking through is ready to come naturally and preferably from below rather than with official stimulus from above.

The recommendations for the future development of Vermont's educational facilities would be incomplete if they did not give serious attention to the question of the size of local units. Shall we look forward over a long period of years to the retention of the town as our local unit of school administration? If so, what are its weak points and inefficiencies? Can measures be recommended which will reduce these weak points to a minimum?

Though these questions are by no means purely educational problems but problems of government and social relations as well, the present study would be only a superficial one if it did not bring out into the light their bearing on the future of educational administration. The following discussion makes no pretense of being conclusive. The assembling of material from which to draw conclusions for the questions raised demands far more time and more complete organization than has as yet been available. The considerations raised, however, should be highly suggestive of the directions in which to look for facts and the use to which they can be put.

Certain inadequacies exist with the town as the local unit of school administration—instability of present unions; difficulties relative to the employment of special teachers as in music and physical education; high school tuition problems, and their inequalities; unevenness of junior high school service; difficulties in the way of economical and desirable consolidation of schools on a strictly town basis; and inequalities of taxation. These inadequacies are very apparent on the surface, and therefore should be studied without delay.

The *tentative* aim of the program here suggested will be the voluntary formation of enlarged school districts made up of several towns and portions of towns. These units should be determined by consideration of the optimum size and of geographical, trading and social factors, and by soundly guided public opinion. Each district would elect five school directors at large, who as a body would have full direction of the affairs of all the schools in the whole area. School taxation would be levied on the whole area uniformly. This aim is, as stated, purely tentative, and must probably undergo extensive revision and amplification. In its present form it at least gives an idea of the kind of local unit that seems desirable.

Among the beneficial results of the formation of such enlarged school districts would be:

1. Stable units taking the full time of the superintendent and other officials of a supervisory or service nature.

2. Uniform cost of high school education to all children within the area.

3. Better articulation of rural schools with the junior high school.

4. Foundations laid for sound school consolidation.

5. Equalization of opportunity and burden over these areas.

Precedent for this proposition can be found in the abolition of the district system in 1892. This took place after permissive legislation had been in force for twenty-two years. The mere joining of towns together to form supervisory unions is a partial precedent for the action proposed. The town of Granville has for some time been divided into two parts for purposes of supervision. An examination of the operations of welfare and service organizations, both commercial and public, would probably yield precedents in the form of operations over areas larger than towns and smaller than counties.

The difficulties of such a project must by no means be overlooked or dismissed lightly. Among them are:

1. The entrenchment of the town as the local political unit.

2. Vermont conservatism.

3. Town-country antagonism as exemplified in the setting-up of small incorporated school districts.

The program for developing an interest in larger local units is not purely an educational one. It should, therefore, be put under the general direction of a group of representative citizens of varied interests from all parts of the state.

This committee should employ a competent worker or workers to gather facts:

1. To establish the need of larger units.

2. To aid in determining the units.

As soon as a sufficient body of facts shall have been gathered, a campaign of publicity should be launched through the press and through addresses at meetings throughout the state. Particular attention should be given to discussion at such meetings, and contributions of the audiences, both favorable and unfavorable, should be carefully noted. In the last analysis, the development of any such program depends on public opinion. By making the public clearly aware of the extent to which neighboring towns are already interdependent, they may be more readily led to comprehend the value and relative simplicity of expressing this interdependence in the form of some such organization as is here suggested.

The material should be made available for debates and essays, contests in the high schools, and teachers and students in the normal schools should be kept closely in touch with the development of the idea. Some of the material can no doubt be gathered in the form of theses by university students, but no inaccuracy can be tolerated. Into the teaching of local government even in the grades should be injected the questioning attitude. The present system should not be explained as one which must necessarily last into eternity. Its weaknesses, as well as its strong points, should be frankly discussed, and questions should be raised which will need solution by the present and future citizens of the state.

All we know now is that certain situations exist which could be improved by the unified action of several towns. It is possible that state or county action is actually preferable to a grouping of towns. Further facts and opinions will have to answer this. All possible publicity should be given to established facts, but opinions as to the outcome must for several years be *admittedly fluid*.

Conceived in these terms, the work of the committee would in no sense be propaganda, but rather leadership in the exploration of the possibilities of more effective and economical local units of school (and perhaps other) administration. Even if no legislative action should be taken for ten or even twenty years, the program here suggested would start the people of Vermont thinking in terms of larger communities and wider horizons, an end which in itself is highly worthy and valuable.

Along with this study, it may be presupposed that serious consideration would be given by the committee to the future trend of school organization to a 6-4-4 basis, as now predicted by several educational authorities. It is by no means impossible to visualize the future educational system of Vermont as follows: her rural schools with grades one to six; her village schools in a central relation to these, with grades seven to ten; her city high schools developing, in addition to grades eleven and twelve, a two-year course of college work—thus making possible near home, pre-university training, semi-professional and vocational training and terminal general education. Such a reorganization might meet the needs of many rural residents more economically and effectively than a program which confined itself entirely to the modernization of the grade groupings now accepted in our system. Furthermore, it might offer a solution of certain problems in our present teacher training organization.

This Committee recommends that a group of from seven to nine representative citizens be authorized to undertake a study of the need for larger local units, as related not only to educational problems but to social and other problems as well.

Vermont's State System of School Administration

Continuous effort on the part of all citizens to keep informed on developing educational theory and successful practice in other states, and to determine to what extent Vermont's system is keeping pace with these, is absolutely essential. Publications are constantly available; educational articles are featured by the daily press and by magazines; and other sources of information are increasingly accessible. The day has long since past when the lay citizen should be content to leave with the professional educators who are his agents, all the knowledge of what the educational world is thinking and doing. The more the citizen knows of the so-called academic side of education and of progressive practice, the more willing he will be to make provision on the practical side to have his state with the procession and not lagging behind it. The latent force of intelligent public opinion on matters educational in Vermont has scarcely been tapped as yet.

Although it has been universally recognized that the state has a distinct function to perform, along with local units of administration in education, just how far it should be limited or extended is an eternal question.

On the one hand is the tendency to think of the state as all-powerful and justified in dictating educational standards and procedures to towns and individual schools, with a right of compulsion where the demanded action is not voluntarily taken. On the other hand is the attitude that the schools are solely the interest of the town, and that the state has no real right to interfere in local affairs. These widely divergent points of view are of course extreme, but they do exist, and they must be borne in mind in any attempt to arrive at a sound conception of the part the state is justified in playing in education of its people.

Approaching the question with the idea that a pupil is first of all the child of his parents, more remotely the child of the town and still more remotely a child of the state, we arrive at considerable justification for local autonomy. But when we consider further that the child may ultimately seek work and residence in some other town or even in some other state, we are aware of the necessity of certain minimum standards. Differences in the ability of communities to provide these minimum standards point to the need of carefully distributed financial aid from the state.

The state is closely interested in the education of its children in order to protect itself, not as an entity, some abstract power, but as a group of people. Complete local autonomy would result in such a wide range of educational achievement that there would be no solidarity among the people of the state. The manner in which the state protects its interest in education must be guided to the greatest possible degree by consideration for local initiative and the sense of local responsibility. Measures and agents which do not have the support and sympathy of the towns in which they work have very little effectiveness. The desirable relation of the state to the towns is very much like the desirable relation between a teacher and her pupils, promoting the greatest possible development of the resources of each individual while insuring compliance with certain inevitable requirements dictated by external conditions. The "state educational system" is then not a system of schools but an organization for promoting the best development of the schools of all local communities and for insuring in them compliance with certain minimum requirements. This distinction is an important one.

Proceeding from this idea of the function of the state in education, we turn our attention to an investigation of approved practice and theory in the set-up and function of a State Board of Education, since this is the pivot of all state educational administration. The duties of

such a Board are clearly set forth in the following paragraph, from the
U. S. Bureau of Education Bulletin, No. 18, (1926). Survey of Education in Utah:

It is generally agreed by authorities in school administration that
the functions of boards of education, appointed or elected, are largely
legislative and judicial in nature; that among the most important duties
of a State Board of Education are: (1) To determine educational
policies for the state school system; (2) to have general oversight and
control of the public schools of the state; (3) to select the chief state
school officer who becomes its executive officer, and to determine his
duties and the functions of the State Department of Education under
his direction; (4) to adopt regulations governing education in the state
concerned with such matters as school buildings, qualifications of
teachers, selection of textbooks, school records and reports, courses
of study, etc; (5) to have control of or to establish cooperative relations with teacher-training institutions conducted by the state.

A body charged with these responsibilities should represent the
state at large and be numerous enough to contribute well-rounded and
balanced opinions and outlooks. Dangers of domination from within
or from without make too small a Board undesirable. Therefore, it
is very important to inquire what practice and theory offer at this
point. According to the United States Office of Education, present
practice and widely accepted theory favor State Boards of from five to
nine members. In 1926, Boards in forty-two states varied in membership from three to thirteen. Only *six* states (and Vermont one of
them) had as few as three members. To insure continuity and to reduce possibility of political interference, the terms of office of Board
members should be at least five years and should overlap.

Comparing the composition of Vermont's Board of Education with
this standard, there is ground for an important recommendation for
improvement. Though six states in 1926 had Boards of only three
members, practice in the majority, and widely accepted theory set five
as the minimum number which is desirable. The fact that Vermont
is a small state is no argument for a small Board; that has little or
nothing to do with it. Interests and points of view are just as diverse,
as in larger states, and the dangers of domination can be just as great.
*Therefore, for the sake of providing greater possibilities for a more
representative leadership for Vermont's educational policies, this Committee recommends that steps be taken to increase the size of the State
Board of Education to at least five members.*

The staff of the State Board of Education, of course, determines to a very large degree the measure of its success in carrying out its purposes and policies with local units. For a few years previous to 1923, the staff was organized functionally, with supervisors for elementary schools, for rural school improvement, for normal training courses and for high schools. The reorganization in 1923, and the curtailment of the appropriation diminished the staff and led to what amounts to a regional organization with two deputy commissioners and two helping teachers, which arrangement is now in force.

The last biennial report of the State Board (1929-30) recommends a third deputy, "To assist our high schools in solving their difficulties, maintaining higher standards and growing in efficiency." This need is substantiated by the unofficial opinions of persons who have been aware of it for some time, by the fact that the present deputy commissioners have practically no time left for this work, and by the fact that rapid developments in the field of secondary education in recent years make a specialist necessary. *This Committee heartily endorses the recommendation of the State Board on this point.*

According to accepted educational standards, as far as ratio of staff membership to number of enrolled pupils goes, Vermont does not rank so badly, being down thirteenth on the list. But that is not the only factor to be considered. Distribution of population and spread of functions are probably more important. When compared with other states, having pupil enrollments of less than 100,000, Vermont is at the foot of the list in regard to staffing of its State Board of Education, New Mexico being its closest competitor for the last place.[2] It appears that Vermont's educational system is at a decided disadvantage, lined up with those of comparable states as to provision for staffing the State Department.

While present finances give little promise for an immediate increase of the staff beyond the possible secondary school deputy already recommended there is an even more fundamental staff need, which must be kept in mind constantly until it is met.

There is a distinct need for greater facilities for collecting and disseminating information about the schools of the state. The present survey has encountered difficulty in obtaining definite information concerning the work in high schools, the financing of education, progress

[2] Standards taken from "The Organization of State Departments of Education." Schrammel, Ohio State University Press.

of pupils in elementary and high schools, pupil mortality and other phases of school work in the state.

The service of the department of education has been described as "personal service." It is entirely fitting and natural that educational relations should be primarily personal relations, but this is by no means the same as saying that they should be solely personal relations. Though policies depend in the last analysis on judgment, each judgment should be based as far as possible on facts, and it should be possible to justify policies by presenting facts to the public.

It is, therefore, recommended that the system of records be thoroughly examined by a cooperative committee of teachers, principals, superintendents and representatives of the Department of Education with a view to determining: (1) What facts are most needed for guiding the development of administrative policies; (2) the form in which these facts will be used; (3) the form in which these facts must be obtained. Such a study would justify the continuation of many of the present records, but it would in all probability result in a wholesome revision of their form, and indicate some desirable substitutions. While less drastic than the appointment of an individual in charge of research and statistics, this procedure is much less expensive, and because of its cooperative feature could be very effective.

For the spreading of information about administrative questions and teaching procedures, special bulletins are issued by the Department of Education from time to time. These aim to make it possible for each teacher and superintendent to share the first-hand experience of all others in the state. The enlargment of this service by more generous appropriations would be of great value to the schools.

At this point it is fitting to mention the work done by Miss Sara M. Holbrook under the sub-committee on Social Agencies Affecting Education. Miss Holbrook's intensive study of the intelligence of children in the rural schools of one town suggests a real need for assistance to teachers in working with backward children. The age-grade tables turned in, in 1928-29, confirm this need. Whether a special agent of the Department of Education providing the assistance mentioned would be of greater service to the children of the state as a whole than a third helping teacher, is a question which cannot be answered from the information at hand or readily available, but it is certainly one worthy of deliberation.

This Committee definitely recommends that the above-described method of strengthening the research and statistical service of the State Department of Education be adopted.

This Committee also recommends that some provision be made to put a special agent in the field to assist rural teachers in their work with backward children.

Vermont should look forward to professional supervision of all its schools. While there is evidence of effective work by uncertified superintendents in certain cases, this effectiveness is due not to lack of professional training, but rather to the ability to gain the confidence of the people of the community. By proper selection of candidates it should be possible to secure persons of professional training who, at the same time, have this ability.

The attempt to compel professional supervision was ended by the Legislature in 1923. Since that time the Department of Education has endeavored to encourage towns to employ certified superintendents of their own accord. The progress resulting from this method is very slow but probably more sound and permanent than that secured by compulsion.

This leads to the conclusion that state rebates could well be re-adjusted so that no town could choose an uncertified superintendent on the ground that the arrangement was cheaper than one which provided for a union superintendent.

The matter of supervising principals appears to be a debatable one. It is often cheaper for the town and, therefore, an attractive way of supervising both its rural schools and its high school; but the position presupposes a person to fill it, with training and experience in both rural school and in high school problems, a combination which does not exist in every case. Then, in some towns, the supervising principal has charge of only one or two buildings. His duties are then but little heavier than those of a high school principal; yet the salary is substantially aided by the state. No strong recommendations are warranted concerning this position, but it would seem desirable to look forward to the elimination of the supervising principalship as a form of supervision for rural schools. The recommendation of the State Board in its current report, for the reduction of state aid for salaries for these positions is a step in the right direction.

Rural Elementary Schools and Normal Training Schools

Parallel in importance with the major problems of finance and administration is the status of Vermont's rural elementary schools—strategic centers of the state's whole educational system—where about 40 percent of our children are beginning their education. Inseparable from the rural schools, because their *teachers*—and not the standard or superior plates on their buildings—are their measure of achievement, is the service being given by the normal training schools. The functioning of one cannot be evaluated separately from that of the other.

Rural schools. Five or ten years ago, every discussion of the rural school problems of Vermont gravitated rightly to buildings; for adequate buildings and equipment are a primary essential, and many rural communities had grown careless of the physical provisions they were offering their school children. Very creditable progress has been made since 1921 in the improvement of rural school buildings. Public opinion has been behind the effort, individuals have stimulated progress with prizes, state deputies, district superintendents, townspeople, teachers and children have worked together with enthusiasm, and have achieved success to a praiseworthy degree. Well over half of the one-room rural schools in the state are now on the approved list; and there is evidently momentum enough in the movement to keep it going until the task is fully completed. But that momentum will have to be continually capitalized, and those who lead may well keep in mind the fact that standards are constantly improving, that eternal vigilance is the price of keeping what we have achieved, and that what has been "standardized" may soon have to be "modernized," to keep pace with educational progress. Setting our rural schoolhouses in order is no static achievement.

With the building improvement an accepted and permanent part of our educational program, we have reached the point where we may take more searching account of our manner of progress in this effort. In the interests of efficiency, we have sometimes lost sight of the influence of simple lines and pleasing proportions which some of the old buildings had, and which some of the buildings which have replaced them, have not. Architecturally indigenous buildings which our forefathers gave us have certain values which may well be preserved when we are adding the improvements of today. With all the fine possibilities which our environment offers, it is also to be hoped that the day may come when enterprising communities will see their way clear to build more schoolhouses on Vermont's countryside, which open up on one or two whole sides for free access to the out-of-doors in good weather.   Further, as regimentation methods are now passing within the schoolroom, it is evident that the technique of round table group teaching is somewhat in conflict with present building standards, especially as to lighting.   This offers a problem of adapting building standards to schoolroom procedure which is even now challenging thought.

Our present discussion of rural schools and of the training offered the teachers who are to take charge of these schools proceeds entirely from the philosophy of rural education which we accept.   This Committee has found direction for its thinking in a philosophy outlined from the "Report on Rural Education Facilities in Caledonia and Windham Counties," Section IV, by Amalia B. Conrey, as follows:

In a *democracy* the institution known as the "school" has been created by the state or government as a safeguard to its existence.   It, the school, must serve all classes, yet be dominated by no one class.   In the elementary school where supposedly *all* attend, every child should be given an opportunity to develop as far as his capabilities will carry him and, with some limitations, in the direction in which his special talents point the way.   Because the school exists for the people it is understood that the school is the one institution that must *supplement* the work done by the other institutions such as the home, the church, places of recreation, etc., so that every child, no matter where born or into what station of life he comes may be trained to use his faculties to their utmost.   The money available should be the only limiting element in putting this philosophy into practice.   Schools have changed or should have changed as other social institutions have changed in their service to society—and as the world has changed and duties and responsibilities have varied.   In these United States, because of the great variation, each school must function for its particular community.

As times have changed so has our conception of what should go on in schools, changed.   In our older conception, the school was an institution that merely trained children in the tools of learning, hence our conception of school as a place where only the three R's needed to be taught.   The home and the church did the rest.   But gradually, the home at least has changed very materially until today it functions less in the all-round training of children than it did, and the school must take up the burden laid down by the home.   That this change in schools has not kept pace with changes in the outside world is obvious and accounts for many of the extraneous organizations, such as the

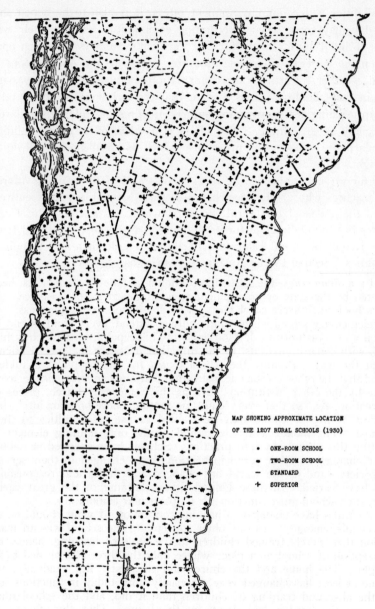

MAP SHOWING APPROXIMATE LOCATION
OF THE 1207 RURAL SCHOOLS (1930)

   •   ONE-ROOM SCHOOL

   ●   TWO-ROOM SCHOOL

   —   STANDARD

   +   SUPERIOR

FIG. 1.

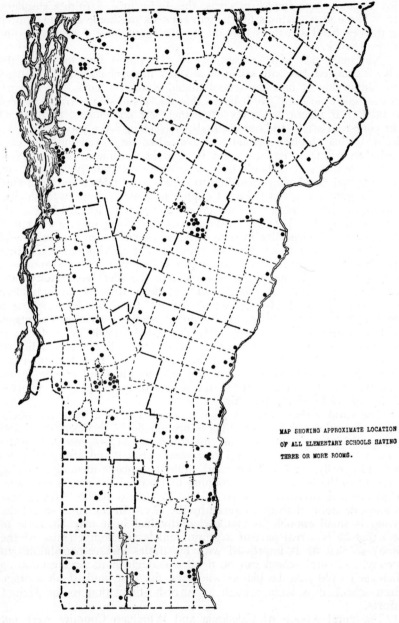

MAP SHOWING APPROXIMATE LOCATION
OF ALL ELEMENTARY SCHOOLS HAVING
THREE OR MORE ROOMS.

Fig. 2.

Boy Scouts, the Camp Fire Girls, the 4-H Clubs, Health Crusaders, etc. These organizations fill the gap between the home and the church on the one hand and the school on the other, and have done a very fine piece of work.

Not only have our conceptions of the duties imposed upon the schools changed, but with scientific advance in psychology and sociology our philosophy of how the school should attack its work has changed. In the "good old days" we believed that the school should train children to take their places in society *after* they left school, and to this end our course of study and our methods of teaching were conceived. We decided what children needed to know when they grew up, and proceeded to drill them in these often isolated facts while in school. Now we believe that school should be a place where children live day by day, growing and developing according to their special talents and aptitudes, and the guidance given them. Coupled with this is our psychological knowledge that children not only *do* what they have learned how to do but are inclined to perform in the manner in which they first learned. If, after all, children live in school and will continue to live outside of school in a social unit; then we may infer that children learn best and this knowledge functions to its fullest extent, if every schoolroom is a social unit as nearly as possible like the ideal community outside, and each child is thought of and dealt with as an individual of a social group. The elementary school, then, besides teaching a child the necessary tools of learning, reading, writing, language, arithmetic, and being a place where the tested knowledge of the past generations is given to him, must also teach him to live in a complicated society; must show him how to judge when he may have his individual rights and when these must be subjected to the good of the group known as society. The world is full of unadjusted people. How often is the school to blame for this?

The rural school offers as good a social unit as a basis for teaching as any other school unit. There are among its members older and younger children, with the adult division of society represented by the teacher. Moreover, the group represents weaker and stronger members physically, and brighter and duller members mentally, getting away from the homogeneous grouping of many of the grades—a somewhat artificial division for most of us. A close-to-nature environment is more desirable than that offered by the city. In the rural school the group is small enough so that each individual in it may be made to feel that he is a real part of a group, and large enough (most of the time) so that he is impressed with his duties and responsibilities to society. A rural school can be flexible enough in its organization so that each child may be placed where he fits best, and, if an average sized school, it is large enough to furnish stimulation to the highest efforts.

The rural schools of Caledonia and Windham Counties were *not* making the most of their opportunities—a blanket criticism for most of the rural schools of the whole country. The biggest criticism comes because of the organization, and the inflexibility of the daily routine. The schools visited were "stiff" schools, with the teacher dictating and the children following her directions. They were "teacher-centered" schools instead of "child-centered" ones. The children were docile, very obedient and pleasantly so. They did exactly as they were told to do, but they seldom used any initiative and rarely suggested a plan of action. They stood, turned and marched to the tapping of a bell; when leaders were to be chosen or monitors appointed the teacher officiated; with one or two exceptions the teacher chose the songs they sang and the subjects they discussed all through the day. When stories were chosen for dramatization they were the teacher's choice and the handling thereof was also according to the teacher's interpretation. The sand table was set up by the teacher with materials she had brought from her training school. The hand of the teacher was discernible in the drawings on the wall even when a child's name was attached. Nice looking paper cuttings served as decorations for Halloween, Thanksgiving and Christmas, but more often they were of the teacher's making at the time of her training, or—a decidedly *wrong* practice—they had been cut by some older boy or girl, *not* for the educative value to the children, but as an end in themselves, nice looking appropriate decorations. Pupil-made material is never as well made, consumes more time in the making and may be more difficult to handle, but if rightly chosen it has definite educative value. It is much harder for a teacher to merely guide pupils than it is to do things for them. It takes patience and self-control to wait while a child laboriously constructs something, which a teacher's deft hands can make in one-tenth of the time. It takes infinite patience and self-control to *lead* children to discover what they need to know about a subject, as contrasted with *telling* them what they should learn and where to find it; but think what a sense of power a boy or girl feels when he has really thought out a situation, balancing one fact against another, has formed a judgment and later tested the results. Maybe he discovers that his array of facts is too limited and eagerly, without coercion from the teacher, learns some new ones. How hard he works and what a joy his school days are!

Someone may offer as a counter-argument that children must learn *to mind,* that there is need of discipline in this world—and the school is the place to learn it. There is room for this argument and no school should be an undisciplined one, but there is such a thing as self-imposed discipline. Children *might* run wild in a school where much freedom is allowed them but somehow they do not where they are properly guided. Why do children rush pell-mell from a public meeting without regard to orderly procedure? Simply because they have been trained to march out in order *only* when a bell is tapped or a command given. Proper conduct comes from proper practice in doing the proper thing at the proper time whether told to do so or not. Ignorance of how to use freedom is one of our national problems. How can it be otherwise when the one institution which supposedly reaches all the children of the country, never guides them in learning how to use the freedom they gain after they leave school? We do not allow children to practice making decisions in school, but in life no one escapes this responsibility. Never having an opportunity to test his powers, a child may easily grow up having an "inferiority complex" which hampers his usefulness all his life. Never being allowed to display initiative and individuality, he seeks always to conform to popular opinion and has no stamina. He becomes one of a mass, easily led, a poor product for a democracy where there is always need for real leadership for the few, but *intelligent* following (not blind) for the many. Children should be taught how to be social creatures in a peopled world—where they never can do just as they please without regard to others. Only Robinson Crusoe alone on his island could do that, and as soon as Friday appeared his absolute freedom ceased and problems took on the difficulty of social ones. These are lengthy arguments for a "child-centered," or we might say a "child-and-community-centered," school rather than the present type prevalent in Vermont, a "teacher-and-curriculum-centered" one.

What is rural Vermont doing in the development of the "child-and-community-centered" school as against the too-prevalent "teacher-and-curriculum-centered" school, which we all know is passing educationally? A great many people are thinking about the changing emphasis, and a creditable number of rural schools up and down the state have teachers and superintendents, who are working at the problem "from the inside out"—in true Vermont fashion. For the doctrine of the indigenous in this state is fundamental; and the principle of making developments grow out of the actual physical and human nature of Vermont is absolutely primary in all our educational procedure.

Concretely, the recent step of the State Department of Education, in designating, under certain conditions and requirements, fifteen rural schools in the state as "model, demonstration rural schools, for the purpose of stimulating interest in improved classroom procedure, in the best modern methods, and in the training and development of the whole child" is a move of signal importance. It is the hope of those responsible for this model school plan, that it will encourage similar constructive experimentations throughout the state, show how to capitalize the distinct inherent advantages in the one-room rural school, and line up superintendents, directors, teachers, pupils and citizens for active participation in their several communities. The record of the results of the first year of this experiment is bound to be significant.

Recognizing how very important a factor is the present prescribed course of study for elementary and rural schools in Vermont, this Committee had an analysis made of this curriculum material, by a recognized expert in the field.[3] Of the seven bulletins issued by the State Department, six have been made especially for town and city schools, and although the titles state that they are for the rural school, no adaptation has been made for the peculiar organization of such schools. A seventh and special bulletin, issued in 1930, is for rural schools especially; 20 percent of its space has been given to discussion of ways and means by which the graded course of study may be made to fit the rural situation. The other 80 percent is devoted to helpful descriptions of projects carried on in country schools. The writer of the above-mentioned curriculum analysis states:

Vermont has failed to recognize the philosophy of present-day rural educators who, while they believe with Dr. Orville Brim that, "The general objectives for rural education do not differ from the objectives for urban education on the same level," also realize that the means for attaining these objectives are quite different in the two types of schools. The introduction to a new state course of study in Iowa contains the following statement, which describes this same problem in a different way: "The difficulty of making a course of study to serve both rural and graded schools arises not so much out of differences in the subject-matter which should be taught in these two types of schools as out of the differences in administrative problems involved in teaching the two types of schools. It is the belief of the executive committee that those making the course of study which succeeds this one should consider seriously the plan for issuing a separate course of study for rural school teachers and one for teachers in graded schools."

That these differences have already been recognized by Vermont is shown in the preparation of the Special Rural School Bulletin. The problem of daily program and organization of grades is considered in detail, always, though, from the standpoint of adjusting the city course of study and not with the idea of preparing a first-hand course.

The significant conclusions of this discussion offer a method of procedure which is both practical and constructive.

The rural schools of any state do not need to be the educational tragedies that the majority of people mourn over. A well organized, adequately equipped, efficiently "teachered" and properly guided rural school has within its four walls potentialities which the demonstration and experimental schools have scarcely tapped and which no graded organization can ever hope to approach.

[3] Marcia A. Everett, Research Assistant, Teachers College, New York City. Discussion of Vermont Courses of Study for Rural and Elementary Schools, 1931.

The Rural School Bulletin of Vermont is the first step this state has made toward the recognition of the full right of the country child to a satisfactory education, a step which should eventually lead to the development of the potential wealth of all phases of rural education. For work toward this end, recommendations follow:

I. Construct a new and special course of study.
   1. Appoint a curriculum committee headed by a chairman, qualified through first-hand rural experience in teaching, supervising and curriculum building, as well as professional study.
   2. This Committee should be directed to make certain detailed studies and investigations of rural conditions.
      a. Find characteristics of rural schools of Vermont from standpoint of number of months schools are in session; kinds of materials and equipment on hand or available; types of teachers and amount and kind of their training; type of children attending rural schools; etc.
      b. Make a study of work which has been done and is being done in rural demonstrations and experimental schools in other states.
      c. Make a study of ways curriculum might be constructed.
         1. Written by a few persons in short period of time, say a year.
         2. Developed as in New Jersey over a period of several years, with teachers, superintendents, etc., contributing.
      d. Study principles of curriculum construction.
         1. Decide on general plan best fitted to Vermont—(number of groups with grades to be included in groups, subjects to be taught, etc.).
         2. Begin to make the curriculum based on Vermont needs and considering basic philosophy of rural education.

II. Adapt the present course of study.
   1. Develop a rotation rather than an alternation scheme for all subjects (*see* "Four Years in a Country School" by Dunn and Everett for detailed explanation). Base on units of subject-matter in present courses of study.
   2. Combine history and geography as social science in the primary and intermediate grades.
   3. Coordinate subjects, at least those within a grade, as much as possible.
   4. Plan a more simple and workable daily program.
   5. Work out detailed techniques for:

    a. Presenting various subjects for large as well as small
        groups.
    b. Handling long study periods.
    c. Individual instruction, etc.
    d. Carrying on activities.

Carrying out the first suggestion would give Vermont the distinction of being one of the first to attack the problem of rural education on a state-wide basis with reference to the special needs of the rural child, while following either of the two would result in guidance for the rural teacher which would insure to the country child his right to an adequate education.

This Committee recommends that an entirely new and special course of study be constructed for the rural elementary schools of Vermont under the direction of a competent committee, who shall strive for a curriculum based on Vermont needs, with full consideration of the modern philosophy of rural education.

The training of teachers. Training rural teachers is a serious and complex factor in the state's educational problem. Vermont will always have a large number of one-room rural schools to challenge the *best* material the normal training courses can attract and turn out. The positions where their services are most needed require unusual resourcefulness, ability and vision, oftentimes under conditions that are difficult and without relative adequate financial remuneration. How can the *best* teachers be influenced to see the one-room rural schools in Vermont as a permanent field for the practice of their professions, rather than as stepping stones for positions in town and city graded schools? How can the citizens of the state and of the towns be convinced that the difficulties and the strategic importance of these rural schools warrant a salary basis more nearly on a level with that of the graded schools, and that too much can never be done to dignify and magnify the important place a rural school teacher occupies in Vermont's educational system?

This Committee has had neither the time nor the staff assistance at its command to go into the normal training situation exhaustively, nor into the problems of certification in relation to teaching personnel in rural schools throughout the state, So, whatever is said here is in the nature of observation rather than of conclusion. The forward step taken by the State Board of Education, whereby two years of training beyond high school will be required after this year, is commended. It would also seem very desirable to have certain requirements both as to academic standing in high school (as ranking in the highest third of the class) and as to content of high school preparatory courses for girls wishing to enter the normal training courses. The challenge of the situation justifies every possible effort to attract our best material; a considerable number of Vermont girls go every year to the normal schools of a neighboring state, where they meet higher entrance requirements. *This Committee recommends consideration of higher entrance requirements for Vermont's normal training courses.*

Inquiry into the special demands which arise from the necessity of training teachers for rural schools as distinguished from general school work, leads to the following observations:

1. *Curriculum emphasis.* The successful teacher must have an intelligent and sympathetic understanding of the problems of the community in which she serves. This is necessary not only as a background for effective teaching but also as a foundation for successful membership in the community and for the satisfaction arising therefrom. Thus far, only a very small beginning has been made toward meeting this need, through a Rural and Field Day and a course in rural sociology which has recently been instituted at one of the normal schools.

It is granted that the need is probably also met in part by less explicit measures but the studies indicate that adequate training for rural school teaching in this state demands express recognition in the form of a sociological orientation course in all the normal schools. Such a course should include study of the economic and social problems of the typical Vermont community. The conventional course in rural sociology, carried on by lectures or textbook work, cannot suffice. Even where such a course is enriched by illustrations from Vermont conditions, there is great risk of its missing its mark. Rather than being based on a textbook, illustrated by Vermont situations, it should be based on Vermont problems, clarified by frequent reference to authoritative works and to practice in the country at large. The course should be built on actual questions under discussion in newspapers and elsewhere, and other community questions which might or should be in the minds of thoughtful citizens. It might be called what it is, simply Vermont problems.

Complaints are made by some teachers that the project method is difficult to use in public schools on account of the frequency of transfer of pupils to or from some other school and the necessity of meeting standards from above. In the case of the normal schools, however, neither of these difficulties is present and the way is clear, limited only by the qualifications of the teacher, to build a course directly on the needs and interests of the students.

It is, of course, well known that the securing of a teacher for such a course is not easy. A broad background in economics and sociology would be desirable, yet most of the college courses in these subjects are too routinized to foster the attitude needed in this work. But surely it is not unreasonable to suggest that there should be on the staff of each normal school a person with sufficient intelligence, resourcefulness, informational background and love of Vermont to accept the challenge of developing a course in Vermont problems. The task would certainly not be a dull one.

This Committee recommends the establishment of an orientation course in all the normal schools based on a study of the economic and social problems in the typical Vermont community.

2. *Method.* Closely related to the course suggested above is a consideration of method, but though the suggestions here made are particularly applicable to that course, it is believed that they also have a wide bearing on the rest of the normal school work.

It is frequently stated that the rural school offers the must difficult of all teaching positions. The work places the severest demands on the initiative, resourcefulness, self-reliance and patience of the teacher. It, therefore, seems obvious that the training of teachers for such positions should be so carried on as to develop these qualities as fully as possible.

Certain steps are already being taken in this direction by the normal schools—steps away from the textbook and toward the laboratory method of study in one case, and a remarkably effective system, or rather spirit, of self-government in another, to mention only two. The Committee recommends that those in charge of the work in the normal schools give earnest thought to the incorporation in the daily procedure, in and out of class, of more measures designed to develop the spirit and practice of resourcefulness and self-reliance.

In connection with the subjects of curriculum and method, the Committee respectfully submits as worthy of consideration the following questions:

If a woman teaches for four years and is a housewife, a mother and an enlightened member of a community for thirty-four, what should be the emphasis in her training?

Are the normal schools to train teachers first and homemakers and citizens second or *vice versa?*

What elements are common in these two types of training?

What activities are common in these two types of occupations?

What desirable traits are common in the people entering these two types of occupations?

3. *Practice teaching.* The differences in the activities of teachers in rural and graded schools point to a need of differentiation in training for the two kinds of positions. Granting the truth of the statement made in one of the catalogues that "the fundamental principles of good teaching are the same in both," the Committee maintains at the same time that the conditions under which these principles are applied are so varied as to merit special attention. Both the model rural school movement in this state and the recommendations of Miss Everett pertaining to the course of study indicate that the organization and procedure in rural school work will in the future become increasingly specialized. This specialization will demand specific training and experience. In view of the large number of normal school students who enter rural teaching, the Committee suggests as a desirable aim of the schools a practice teaching program which, for each student who has not a graded position in immediate prospect, will culminate in the competent planning and unassisted execution of the work of a rural school for one week.

The organization of teacher training in Vermont has long been subject to considerable difference of opinion, personal, political, official, and to a lesser extent, professional. This Committee considers itself quite incompetent to discuss so open a question objectively and constructively. Certain factual material relative to practice teaching facilities, number and easy accessibility of elementary pupils within adjacent territory, to comparative service rendered by students from the four training schools, and to comparative costs to the state for training them in the four places, are very significant, and have been compiled from the records of the State Department of Education. These are contained in the full report of the Subcommittee on Normal Schools and Colleges.

Physical education and other special needs. In the current report of the State Board of Education, attention is called to the great need felt in the field of physical and health education. The report states that:

The teachers are doing the best that they can. But it is self-evident that the majority of them have had no training in systematic hygiene . . . in corrective gymnastics . . . and the like. The promotion of this important work calls for skilled workers, either supervisors, nurses or teachers assigned to reasonable sized districts, who will perform the sort of service such persons now render in many city systems. They should be paid by the towns and localities using their services, but the matter is of such outstanding importance to the whole state that it (the state) should assist in financing the proposition to a reasonable extent. Without such aid it seems certain that this phase of education will continue to be neglected.

When one considers that the child from the poorest home in the most congested sections of cities like New York and Chicago—the child whose heritage doesn't promise always for the future of America what the heritage of the youth of Vermont promises—has these advantages as an every day part of the public school system which educates him, Vermonters may well pause and ask why they allow this neglect to continue in our state.

Moreover, this need has more than the health and physical education factor involved; for there is also a fundamental contribution which comes from the encouragement of constructive recreation.

Physical education does not rest satisfied with the cultivation of healthy bodies. There are social values in its program which Vermont sorely needs to develop in its young people. Group games under good leadership make for cooperative effort, subordination of self for the good of the team, respect for rules and laws, self-control under strain, in short, good sportsmanship. If Vermonters learn to pull together in school there is more hope for the state.

One of the most important reasons for urging an immediate strengthening of the physical education in Vermont lies in the recreational values of the activities taught. If the young people are familiar with the many wholesome ways of "having a good time" in small communities there will be more Vermonters staying in Vermont. The schools have the responsibility for training tastes in recreation by offering the best there is at the ages when proficiency in such activities is most easily acquired, so that the coming generations, when they get beyond the age of tag, will have within themselves resources for play and recreation of a far better sort than that offered by the pool room and movie theatre. The program should be varied, including folk, square, and round dances; group games such as volley ball, baseball, kick ball, soccer, basketball and others; track and field activities; and individual sports such as tennis, swimming, skating, skiing, snowshoeing, horseshoes, ping-pong, croquet, and woodcraft. All of this last group cannot be taught directly by the school, but responsibility should be felt for encouraging allied organizations such as Boy Scouts, 4-H Clubs, and camps to develop them.

This Committee recommends a change in our present permissive law relative to teaching physical education in the schools, to one requiring a minimum of one hour a week for ALL pupils, and providing for a trained supervisor to furnish the leadership and direction so needed by the rural school teachers, and to help correlate the courses in physical education in the normal schools, with the actual work in the rural schools.

Until such a supervisor is available a temporary manual on the subject should be prepared and issued by the State Board of Education, with stated requirements as to its use. More emphasis should be given to the subject in general, conferences for teachers, and special conferences and demonstrations might well be planned, especially to assist teachers several years out of normal school who want fresh ideas. Once public opinion is aroused to the need and becomes aware of the backwardness of Vermont, in comparison with many of her sister states, in meeting this need, physical and health education will have their rightful place in our rural school program. Larger units of administration would make more easily possible the method of joint financing of such service as suggested for districts in the report of the State Board.

A similar need exists, without present ways and means of meeting it, for more music instruction in rural schools; and this committee looks forward to the day when the state Department will be in a position to assist with some state supervision in that field, or to help districts to combine for the employment of a supervisor for such service.

The Subcommittee on Social Agencies has presented a detailed evaluation of the work of the 4-H Clubs in the rural schools which shows their great importance and effectiveness. But the outstanding need revealed by the investigations of this subcommittee is that of work for exceptional children in Vermont rural schools. A study (referred

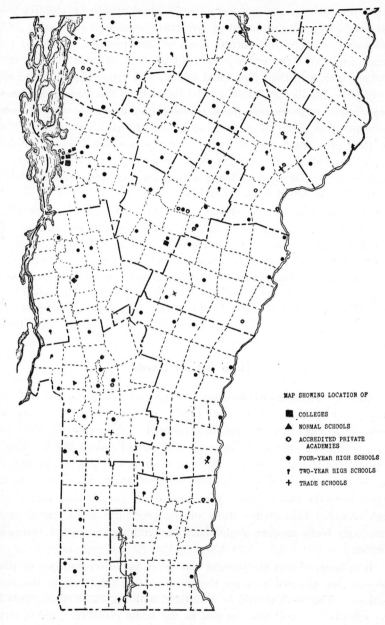

MAP SHOWING LOCATION OF

■ COLLEGES
▲ NORMAL SCHOOLS
○ ACCREDITED PRIVATE
  ACADEMIES
● FOUR-YEAR HIGH SCHOOLS
⌇ TWO-YEAR HIGH SCHOOLS
+ TRADE SCHOOLS

FIG. 3.

to previously) was made of some one hundred unselected children, representing the total enrollment of five rural schools in one town. This indicates decisively that further study of this problem should be continued, and that some provision should be made at once to assist rural teachers with it in their individual schools. A related study could well be made of the dietary habits of the children of the same given school areas, with health examinations, periodic measurements, and so forth, in cooperation with the various state Departments concerned. Until the state provides a special worker for this, a manual on the subject, giving suggestions for dealing with deficient, retarded and atypical children who offer more difficult adjustment problems in small school groups than in larger ones, should be issued.

This Committee recommends the serious and immediate consideration of ways and means to begin to meet this problem, urging especially that the Departments of Education and of Public Welfare work together to maintain a complete and continuing census of deficient children in public schools, and to establish a method of examination by clinic of those children identified as subjects for it. The position of the public schools is strategic in this realm; and the rural schools offer material for work here that will mean much to future social conditions in Vermont.

High School Needs

The investigations of the Subcommittee on Secondary Schools confirm in a very thorough and satisfactory manner, certain recommendations which have already been incorporated in this report in other sections. Especial effort is being made and should continually be made to improve the teachers and the teaching in our rural schools, so that the pupils from the rural schools may compare more favorably with the pupils from the village and city schools, at the time of their entrance to high school. This invites study of the procedure in the rural school classroom from another angle than that emphasized in the foregoing section.

It is believed that the present courses in home economics and allied subjects are planned to meet the needs of the pupils from the rural sections. The work should be continued with a greater effort made by the schools to enroll rural pupils in the home economics and agricultural courses. We also recommend that agricultural courses be established in the larger villages and cities wherever a reasonably large rural group is found in high school attendance.

We believe that the agricultural courses should be reorganized so that vocational agriculture will be offered only in those schools where alternatives make it possible to require definite vocational interest as a prerequisite for admission to the course in agriculture. We recommend that all high school courses in agriculture be developed into four-year courses, that the use of full-time itinerant instructors in agriculture be extended, that all vocational agricultural courses be developed to the Smith-Hughes standard. It is further suggested that where the above recommendations are impossible, courses in agriculture as organized today be replaced by courses in rural problems. These courses would cover the general field of agriculture through the problem method without attempting to carry on a vocational course.

Since 22 percent of the pupils in the high schools of the state are non-residents, the caring for these pupils by the school and the school town is a real problem.[4] At the present time most schools are doing little if anything in the matter of rooms and boarding places for such pupils. This is a matter calling for considerable tact and judgment on the part of the school authorities. We believe that the time is coming, if it is not already at hand, when each high school in the state must squarely face the situation and through its organizations find and approve rooming places for its non-residents.

The Physical Education work in the state is at present left to the desires of the local communities. If Vermont is to care for the young people in its schools in a proper way, provision must be made for state-wide physical education work. Far too many, even of the larger communities, are rather careless as to the type of athletics for girls. Many schools have no athletic work for girls although it is probably true that the girls need this work even more than the boys. However, unless great care is exercised in the type of games played by the girls, the rules used, and the supervision given, probably no athletics would be better than overindulgence. It must be constantly kept in mind that high school girls are in the adolescent period and that their physical education should be carefully supervised by women of experience who understand their problems. The standard of officials taking charge of girls' inter-school contests should be raised at once.

[4] Detailed and accurate data available on this and the two following points in study of "The Needs of Girls in Public High Schools in Vermont," 1930, made for the committee by Thelma Mills, Research Fellow, Teachers College, New York City.

It is evident that there is very little being done in the high schools
of Vermont along the lines of vocational and educational guidance.
This is perhaps not strange when we realize that this whole movement
is of recent origin. It is the result of the age of specialists in which
we live and the realization that we are developing in our schools too
many "square pegs for round holes." The great variety of vocations
open to both boys and girls today makes the choice of life work even
more important and for that reason more difficult.

The matter should be studied from a scientific standpoint and in
every school some member of the faculty, preferably an experienced
teacher, well acquainted with the young people and with a proper scientific background and knowledge of youth should be appointed to have
charge of this very important part of the educational work. The person so appointed should not be expected to carry a full teaching program in addition. Such a position will entail a great deal of time in
thought and planning.

The teaching load is too heavy, especially in the smaller schools.
While the number of teaching periods on paper does not seem excessive,
it must be kept in mind that when a teacher is teaching six or seven
periods a day, she is teaching four to six different subjects. The solution, of course, lies in the addition to the teaching force, which involves additional expense. It is undoubtedly true that the expenditure
of money for an additional teacher would bring about a much larger
return on the money invested because of greater efficiency.

It may be concluded that too many courses and too many different
subjects are being taught in the smaller schools.

Finances were given as the main reason for the failure of rural
pupils to enter and complete high school, and it is clearly evident from
the findings of the Committee that additional money would solve many
of the problems of the high schools. We realize that taxes are so high
at the present time that very adequate reasons must be given for any
increase. It is an established principle of economics and business that
frequently the expenditure of additional money is necessary in order
to get full returns for the money already invested. The argument that
each town should look out for its own children is no longer valid.
If we permit a poor hill town to neglect the education of its children,
these same children will, within the space of a few years, undoubtedly
become a problem for the larger villages and cities, which have cared
for the education of their own children. In these days, with present

means of transportation, distances are obliterated. Boys and girls no longer remain in the community in which they were brought up unless that community can offer something worth while. The whole state of Vermont, as well as the neighboring states, must suffer for the neglect of education by a backward town in the hills of Vermont. We must face the fact that the welfare of the children of Vermont is a problem for the whole state of Vermont.

We can never entirely equalize opportunity but at least there must be an opportunity for every boy and girl in Vermont to attend a high school without the payment of tuition by the parent. The question of transportation still remains. Transportation of pupils in elementary schools as required by law gives rise to many difficulties and can never be satisfactorily administered. We, as a committee, are not ready to make any recommendations in regard to transportation of high school pupils.

We definitely recommend that towns not maintaining high schools should pay $85 per pupil for tuition. It should be remembered that the average per capita cost in the state in 1928 was $86.52. The increase in tuition would, of course, be accomplished by corresponding increased reimbursements from the state. It is quite evident then that the towns not maintaining a high school are not assuming their fair share of the cost of educating their own children and that they are not asked to assume an unfair burden when asked to pay higher tuition. It will also be remembered that for the school years, 1929-1930, 73 percent of the schools of the state charged more than the state allowance of $60.

It is believed that high school principals, or their representatives, should make a greater effort to become acquainted with rural pupils and rural conditions. More effort should be made to interest rural pupils to attend high school. Separate curricula for rural pupils are not suggested but there should be more flexible curricula especially in the smaller schools.

We believe that there should be a director of secondary education in the State Department of Education. No school system in any state will ever reach the stage where the direction, supervision and guidance of a trained executive is unnecessary. There should be a state officer who can visualize the problem of secondary education for the whole state, and who can act as inspector, counsellor and guide to high school principals, teachers and school directors. Our field worker,

Miss Mills, clearly felt this need as expressed by the principals themselves who were pathetically anxious for help and assistance in meeting
their problems. This was, of course, more particularly true in the
smaller schools.

From our investigations it is evident that the state office does
not have the necessary force to secure and interpret data and reports
regarding the work of the high schools. The progress of high school
education in a state can only be measured by definite data on file which
show the steps of progress. We may assume and believe that we are
making progress but cannot prove it by our mere assumptions. No
business is carried on without definite reports of progress. The state
office has very little data concerning the various phases of high school
work, attendance, withdrawals, number enrolled in different courses,
percent of failures, college records of graduates and many other things
of great value in evaluating the progress of high schools in the state.
The lack of this material is, of course, due to the lack of sufficient office
force to handle the matter.

We recommend, therefore, that sufficient funds be made available to
enable the state office to secure from the high schools data of value
such as is secured by other states. This should be done so that principals and school directors may check the progress of their school with
the progress of the schools of the state, and so that the people of the
state may have definite information in regard to the work of their high
schools.

This Committee has not had opportunity to study the functioning
of the junior high school system in the state. This leaves a gap for
which *further study is recommended*. The same is true of a thorough
study of the way in which the public high schools of Vermont are fulfilling—or not fulfilling—their obligations in the preparation of students
for present-day college entrance requirements, within and without the
state. A good deal of constructive criticism is being heard on this subject. The statement of President Paul D. Moody, of Middlebury College, speaking before the Vermont Society of New York in February,
1930, comes from one who is talking on familiar ground. Said Mr.
Moody, "No one who knows the present democratically controlled
school can for a moment believe that it does the work the old academy
did. The painful truth is that the preparation of our (Vermont)
candidates for admission to college in Vermont, does not compare with
what it used to be, and with sorrow I admit that it doesn't compare

with the preparation of the student from other states." As Mr. Moody further says, "The facts, if faced, can sometimes be helped." This brings to a focus a situation which must no longer be side-stepped, and which must be met with a spirit of self-analysis, rather than of controversy on the part of those most intimately concerned.

We definitely recommend—that a serious attempt be made to begin to solve the problem of living conditions for non-resident students; that the suggested methods for strengthening interest in home economics and agricultural courses be adopted; that the special aspect of the physical education and athletic program for high school girls be no longer ignored; that the matter of vocational and educational guidance receive increasing attention and that high school principals make a greater effort to become acquainted with rural pupils and rural conditions; that high school tuition paid by the towns be adjusted to meet the actual cost; that an immediate approach be made to a thorough study of the status of college preparation facilities in the public high schools of Vermont.

College Needs

The Committee has made a detailed analysis of the utilization of Vermont colleges by students from Vermont towns, during the past fifteen years. Out of the total of 239 towns in the state, the University of Vermont has received NO students from fifty-three towns in that period; Middlebury College NO students from 120; Norwich University NO students from 144; St. Michael's College NO students from 178; and Trinity College NO students from 221. (Field work shows a slight discrepancy in some of these figures, due in most cases, to Post Office addresses.)

During the last four years there has been an appreciable falling off in attendence of Vermont students at the University of Vermont and at Middlebury College and a slight falling off at Norwich University and St. Michael's College.

This decrease in enrollment at the University of Vermont and at Norwich University is more marked from the rural than from the urban communities, but at Middlebury College the decrease has been more evenly distributed.

During the same four years there has been marked increase in the enrollment of non-Vermont students at the University of Vermont and Middlebury College, and a slight increase at Norwich University.

In the academic year 1929-1930, 32.2 percent of the enrollment at the University of Vermont were non-Vermont students, as against 75.3 percent at Middlebury College and 65.8 percent at Norwich University, and 51.3 percent for the three institutions together.

In view of the relatively small proportion of Vermont young people who are directly benefiting from the educational facilities of Middlebury College and Norwich University, it seems relevant here to ask but not to answer three questions: Why does this condition obtain? Is it desirable that it continue to obtain? If so, should the State of Vermont continue to make appropriations to these colleges? If the state policy of appropriations to institutions of higher education is to continue, namely financial aids to the non-denominational colleges and universities, the Committee respectfully inquires: Should not a wise state policy provide an annual distribution of funds between the colleges based on the number of Vermont boys and girls each year, *bona fide* residents, who complete a full year at the institutions? Financial support from the state would thus be directly proportionate to the number of students of the state served by the colleges. Appropriations to support instruction in specific fields should, of course, be allotted on an independent basis.

Although it has been impossible to make an exhaustive study of the suitability of Vermont collegiate institutions to rural needs, certain observations may be made on their standards of admission, curriculum emphasis, standards of instruction and living conditions for students. The Middlebury College plan of admission appears to be more in keeping with modern standards and practice than that of the other colleges. It is suggested that the latter adopt more optional and free choice provisions. Modification of curriculum requirements for students not mathematically or linguistically inclined, and provision of greater flexibility in requirements for degrees would bring these requirements into closer conformity with modern psychological and educational research. There seems to be little justification for forcing everyone into the same mold: higher mathematics, foreign languages, advanced composition and public speaking. The colleges should have these courses available for those who will derive greater enjoyment and benefit from them and will render larger service to their communities because of studying them, but we question whether colleges should make these courses a requirement for everyone. Living conditions in the Vermont colleges appear to be fully as good as they are in the majority of colleges.   There seems to be, however, great need of better housing facilities for freshman men at the University of Vermont, both as to dormitory and as to commons eating houses.   It is urged that steps be taken to remedy this condition.

While, strictly speaking, there is but one Agricultural College in Vermont, the State College at Burlington, the State School of Agriculture in Randolph is doing such an effective piece of work in its field that the Committee records its belief in the distinctly valuable service to rural communities being rendered by this institution.   In a résumé of the service of the State Agricultural College at Burlington, there is no claim for complete information as to the logic of the training now receiving major emphasis there—training for supervisory agricultural work, testing, county agents and so on, rather than for general farming.   The course at Randolph offers the latter preparation and sends its students back to the farms, which fact supplements the situation at the University.   The tremendous service of the Extension Department at the University of Vermont, through county agents, demonstrations, home economics work, boys' and girls' club work, has grown in the eighteen years of its activity in a remarkable way and has done an immeasurable amount to broaden horizons, to bring helpful social contacts, and to stimulate and show the way to better standards of living.   Agricultural Extension work, as practiced in Vermont has been such as to command respect and is generally considered a happy application of Federal activities.

Being impressed with the fact that many families scattered throughout the state do not know what educational facilities are available for their children, it is recommended that the State Department of Education, the Colleges, the Normal Schools, the School of Agriculture, the larger high schools, and the private academies, jointly arrange a schedule of annual visitations to every rural community of Vermont, to inform the residents of:

1. The educational facilities of the state, both secondary and advanced.

2. The opportunities for financial aid through scholarships, loans, and employment.

3. The procedure to follow in order to avail oneself of these facilities and of this aid.

Adult Education

Adult education may be classified as formal or informal. In Vermont, that of a formal nature includes the work of the Cooperative Extension Service in Agriculture and Home Economics, the Free Public Library Department and the libraries. Adult education of an informal nature includes the women's clubs, the parent-teacher associations, the Granges and other organizations which function here and there but not throughout the state as a whole. In this latter class, the Chautauqua has meant a great deal to rural Vermonters.

In a preliminary survey of the agencies working in the informal adult education field in Vermont, twelve towns were studied by the field worker,[1] and thirty-eight agencies were listed, taking account of just how organizations, individuals, libraries and other agencies were contributing to an adult education program. The following summary statement of needs and suggested remedies in the field of adult education is drawn from the report of the field worker.

The needs are summarized as follows:

1. Extension of library service to make books more available everywhere in the state without breaking down any local pride in the village library;
2. Completion of the anti-illiteracy work;
3. "Speech Readers' Clubs" for the adult deaf;
4. More attention to the public responsibility for young people leaving school before eighteen;
5. A system of vocational guidance available to all who need it, including proper laboratory facilities and a trained worker;
6. Check lists compiled carefully by some authoritative agency on the following subjects:
   (1) A list of adult educational opportunities in the state or available to people in the state;
   (2) A list of material suitable for non-professional volunteer leaders of activities;
7. Periodic conferences of all agencies and institutions of adult education in the state;
8. "A new birth of freedom" as to method and content for teachers entering the field of adult education.

[1] The Study of Adult Education in Vermont, 1929, Dorothy C. Walter, special worker.

The following improvements are suggested to meet the various needs as enumerated above:

1. Libraries.

Extend the work of the book wagon.

Demonstrate a regional library. This project is on the way.

Use the Vermont Library Association as a "commission without power" to continue studying library problems and making suggestions for improvement to the proper persons.

Work for larger appropriations for the Free Public Library Department.

Since there are many French people who are devoted to their language, add enough good French books and magazines to the library equipment of the areas where they live so that reading habits and associations with the library will be built up.

2. Illiteracy.

Anti-illiteracy programs are a part of the work of the Vermont Teachers' Association, The Joint Council on International Relations, The Vermont Federation of Women's Clubs, The Baptist Church, The Metropolitan Life Insurance Company, The American Legion and some others. Can they not all cooperate to finish the job, pooling funds or resources of interested workers or of material to reach even the bashful and the reluctant? Home class work is suggested as a means found of value in other states.

3. Work for the adult deaf.

What is needed is leadership. There is plenty of talent and education among the adult deaf of the state, and once the work was started, the proper contacts made with the national organizations working with the deaf, it would go under its own steam.

4. The Parent-Teacher Association, or some other agency, could very well concentrate some thought on the young person who leaves school at the earliest allowable age.

5. In some places "opportunity schools" or "replacement schools" are attacking the problem of vocational guidance. This work cannot be carried on well unless there is some system

of mental testing for information and capacity, so that as many misfits as possible can be avoided. That is the trouble with most correspondence courses in vocational subjects. They are generally sent out to anyone who applies, with no preliminary work to see if the student is properly prepared or endowed to be reasonably sure of success. Vocational guidance is nothing occult, nor is mental testing, but it does imply tools and somebody who knows how to use them.

6. The Department of Education or a privately endowed organization might publish check lists of adult educational activities.
7. The need for a conference of state-wide agencies of adult education should be met by a State Council for Adult Education
8. The colleges that give attention to other kinds of educational problems might well establish philosophical courses on adult education.

With this study as a point of departure, the Subcommittee on Adult Education has initiated a procedure which promises real accomplishment. The Committee asked each organization which is doing adult educational work in Vermont to prepare a brief outline showing the activities which it was sponsoring. The reports submitted by fifteen state organizations show types of activities, the organization responsible for them, numbers of people affected, results and future plans.

With a view to promoting adult education in Vermont in line with these suggestions, a round table conference was held on June 18, 1931, attended by fifty-seven people, to consider the status of adult education in Vermont and to organize for future activity. It was the sense of the meeting that a State Council for Adult Education should be organized to act as a unifying agency for all adult educational activities with a view to avoiding duplication of effort and to secure the most efficient cooperation. To this end, a provisional committee was appointed to work out a practical plan to fit this need. The functions of the proposed State Council for Adult Education are as follows:

1. To maintain a clearing house and to undertake steady and consistent publicity for the agencies now at work.
2. To "adopt" the regional library project which is now under way in twenty-five selected towns in the northwestern part of the state, watch its progress, support its purpose, and spread

its ideas, with a view to extending such service to the entire state.

3. Issue an occasional bulletin of information about adult education projects to local groups and individuals.

4. Conduct a sort of speakers' bureau to supply speakers to clubs, community groups, etc., along adult education lines.

5. Organize to get across to parents, high schools students, and others who may be interested, an understanding of the educational opportunities available in Vermont beyond the high school.

6. Promote a general program of parent education in line with the most progressive thinking and practice in this field.

7. Find a center for the Council's operations.

8. Plan for definite means of support. It has been suggested to the Subcommittee on Adult Education that there may be a possibility of getting the whole project underwritten for a period of three years as a demonstration, with a view to developing a technique which may be perfected and offered to other areas which may be interested. It will be the province of the provisional committee to make initial plans for a program sufficiently practical and definite to be presented in an appeal for substantial backing.

Library Facilities

Early in 1930, the Subcommittee on Library Facilities outlined a plan for a regional library experiment calling for intensive service to one district of the state by a regional librarian, representing the Free Public Library Department but financed from private funds. This librarian would make frequent visits to all the libraries in the district from a convenient center. He would carry in his book truck a supplementary book stock from which to freshen their collections. He would help in internal problems of book selection and cataloging, confer with trustees in administrative problems, give talks before schools, clubs, and other organizations, help tie up the libraries to adult education movements. He would help to arouse community interest in the library in isolated towns and would bring librarians in small and isolated towns into closer relationship with each other.

Because of limited funds and few helpers, the state Department, while doing most excellent work, has not been able to carry on an extensive visiting program with the small libraries, which is particularly needed in rural and mountainous states like Vermont. The idea was that the experiment in a certain area might prove of such value that this plan, or some modification of it developed by the experiment would be desired for every section of the state.

The need for such an experiment was shown:

1. By the situation in the libraries in Vermont:

a. One-fourth not open more than one day a week. Another fourth not open more than two days a week.

b. At least 125 libraries out of the 228 have a total income of less than $100. Less than thirty libraries, out of 228, have a total income of $1,000 or more per year.

c. Seven towns appropriate $15 annually or less for their libraries, about twenty-five other towns as little as $25 per year.

d. Much unselfish and courageous volunteer service linked up with this inadequate support—otherwise the small libraries could not even exist.

e. Many other libraries with moderately small incomes facing a situation where an efficient local person of passing type, who has acted as librarian for ridiculously small salary, cannot be replaced for anything like the funds available.

2. By the value of the type of state Department assistance already developed by its:

a. Traveling library service.

b. Book wagon.

c. Reference work.

d. Cooperation on school credit reading.

e. Demonstrations, exhibits, meetings, summer training courses.

3. By the fact that the state Department staff as now organized is not sufficient for much field work.

4. By the fact that the state Department is too remote to develop adequate field service without regional supervisors; a type of work quite untouched in Vermont, the need for which is irrefutable.

A precedent has already been set for just such service by the State Department of Education which has two deputy commissioners and two helping teachers stationed at strategic points over the state instead of traveling back and forth from the capital.

The region suggested for demonstration was the area centering in Lamoille county and Morrisville, and including as much of Franklin county as possible, together with some of the northern towns of Chittenden county a group of probably twenty-eight towns, accessible from this center, and among the ones in the state most needing library field service, Belvidere, Cambridge, Elmore, Hyde Park, Stowe, Waterville, Wolcott, Montgomery, Georgia, Franklin, Fletcher, Fairfax, Fairfield, Enosburg, Bakersfield, Sheldon, Colchester, Essex, Jericho, Milton, Underhill, Westford, Johnson.

If it should seem wise St. Albans and Swanton might be added to the district as the libraries in these two towns could be used as centers.

The reasons for choosing this area were: The fact that need in these towns is both acute and typical; the fact that effectiveness of library service in Morrisville and cooperative spirit of librarian there will insure regional librarian a good center from which to work; the fact that there are a number of towns with leadership and resources in area which might be factors in a permanent program for regional library service in cooperation with state Department.

As a basis of perfecting the plan, a field study was made of the libraries in the towns it was proposed to include. Conditions and interest were found without question to warrant the experiment. The proposition was laid before the Carnegie Corporation with a request for funds to carry it out. In November, 1930, a grant of $14,000 for a two-year project was received from the Carnegie Corporation, of which grant $8,000 was made available in January, 1931, and of which $6,000 will be available in January, 1932. Steps were taken at once to secure a competent librarian, with the vision and ability to undertake the experiment—a pioneer piece of work, the results of which will be awaited with great interest, for their significance in rural library practice for the whole country. A local committee was formed in the region selected, to develop the desired friendly contacts with the people of the region, to arouse greater local interest, and to stimulate all possible cooperation among the towns. The question of the rural library will be one of the educational problems brought to public notice in the near future, as the American Library Association is starting a determined movement toward obtaining Federal aid for rural libraries. Since there seems to be a fair prospect for Federal aid in the near future, it is hoped that this experiment may develop library consciousness of what this aid might do for rural libraries of the state, as well as of what the library and the state might do for themselves.

It is a real satisfaction to be able to close the report with records of plans in action, based on needs which were proved convincing enough to secure the resources with which to show how the needs may be met.

Summary of Recommendations

1. A complete study of financing education in Vermont by an officially appointed committee with funds at its disposal to do an authoritative piece of work.

2. A group of from seven to nine representative citizens appointed to undertake a study of the need for larger local units, as related not only to educational problems but to social problems and others as well.

3. Steps to have the size of the State Board of Education increased to at least five members.

4. Endorsement of the recommendation in the last report of the State Board of Education for a Deputy Commissioner for secondary schools.

5. The adoption of a definite plan for strengthening the research and statistical service of the State Department of Education.

6. Provision for a special agent in the field to assist rural teachers in work with backward children.

7. The construction of an entirely new and special course for the rural elementary schools by an especially qualified committee.

8. The consideration of definitely higher entrance requirements for the normal training courses.

9. The establishment of a sociological orientation course in all the normal schools based on the study of the economic and social problems of the typical Vermont community.

10. Change in present permissive state law regarding physical education instruction in the schools, and the provision for a trained supervisor in this field.

11. Consideration of ways and means for Departments of Education and Public Welfare to maintain a census of defective children in the rural schools, and to establish a method of examination by clinic for those children identified as subjects for it.

12. Serious consideration of the problem of living conditions for non-resident high school students; of methods for strengthening interest in the home economics and agricultural courses in the high schools;

of the special aspects in the physical education and athletic program for high school girls; of vocational and educational guidance programs; and of greater effort by high school principals to become better acquainted with rural pupils and rural conditions.

13. An increase of high school tuition to be paid by the towns to $85.

14. An immediate approach to a thorough study of the status of college preparatory facilities in the public high schools of Vermont.

15. The adoption of a definite plan to disseminate information about high school and collegiate opportunities in the state.

The Committee on Educational Facilities for Rural People offers this report, with its recommendations, not as a record of an ambitious research project, but as a human document, based on factual findings which have been interpreted as objectively as possible. It is offered as a carefully thought-out plan, which if followed will lead to desirable goals for education in Vermont, goals that shall emphasize the indigenous quality which is fundamental to all development in the state.

———————

Prepared for the Commission by its Committee on Educational Facilities for Rural People.

MARION GARY, Rutland,
Chairman,
C. H. DEMPSEY, Montpelier,
Executive Secretary,
MRS. HERBERT W. CONGDON, Arlington,
MRS. E. A. DUTTON, East Craftsbury,
FAÑNY B. FLETCHER, Proctorsville,
WALLACE H. GILPIN, Barton,
SARA M. HOLBROOK, Burlington,
R. F. JOYCE, Burlington,
ARTHUR L. MILLER, Vernon,
MRS. J. J. ROSS, Middlebury,
MARY JEAN SIMPSON, East Craftsbury,
L. JOSEPHINE WEBSTER, Burlington,
JOSEPH A. WIGGIN, Brattleboro,
THEODORE H. WILSON.

Subcommittee on Elementary Education in Rural Schools:
ARTHUR L. MILLER, Vernon,
Chairman,
BRUCE BUCHANAN, Brattleboro,
LELIA DELAPLANE, Brattleboro,
ETHEL EDDY, Brattleboro,
PAUL P. JONES, Windham.

Subcommittee on College and Normal School Facilities:
THEODORE H. WILSON, St. Johnsbury,
Chairman,
DAVID W. HOWE, Burlington,
Co-Chairman,
JOHN B. COOK, Saxtons River,
SHIRLEY FARR, Brandon,
O. K. JENNEY, Essex Junction,
JEAN W. SIMPSON, Craftsbury,
M. S. STONE, Montpelier.

Subcommittee on Library Facilities:
HELEN B. SHATTUCK, Burlington,
Chairman,
FANNY B. FLETCHER, Proctorsville,
Co-Chairman,
HAMILTON CONANT, Montpelier,
MRS. H. S. MOSES, Bennington,
ANNA MOWER, Morrisville,
GEORGE DANA SMITH, Burlington,
ELIZABETH WILLIAMS, Montpelier.

Subcommittee on Social Agencies Affecting Education:
R. F. JOYCE, Burlington,
Chairman,
SARA M. HOLBROOK, Burlington,
Co-Chairman,
ELSIE GRAY, Colchester,
PERSIS HOLDEN, Bennington,
E. L. INGALLS, Burlington,
BERTHA M. TERRILL, Burlington.

Subcommittee on the Service of Secondary Schools:
JOSEPH WIGGIN, Brattleboro,
Chairman,
A. ISABELLE BROOKS, Proctor,
MRS. MARY DEYETT, Shelburne,

A. J. Hicks, Manchester,
Mrs. J. J. Ross, Middlebury.

Subcommittee on Adult Education:
Mary Jean Simpson, East Craftsbury,
Chairman,
Mrs. Frederick Tupper, Burlington,
Co-Chairman,
Mrs. E. A. Dutton, East Craftsbury,
Mrs. Mary Lawrence, Springfield,
Mary Moody, Morrisville.
Mrs. Charlotte P. Brooks, Burlington,
J. E. Carrigan, Burlington,
Mrs. Dorothy C. Fisher, Arlington.

Subcommittee on Financing Education:
Wallace H. Gilpin, Barton,
Chairman,
G. L. Adams, West Brattleboro,
Waldo F. Clark, Addison.

Research Material on Which Committees' Findings Are Based

Preliminary Report on the Support of Public Education in Vermont, 1930, Katherine M. Cook, Chief, Division of Special Problems United States Office of Education.
General Characteristics of Vermont's School System and *The Need for Larger Local Units,* A. John Holden, Jr., Special Field Worker.
Field Study and Report on Rural Educational Facilities in Caledonia and Windham Counties, 1930, Amalia B. Conrey, Formerly District Superintendent in Minnesota.
Discussion of Vermont State Courses of Study for Elementary and Rural Schools, Marcia A. Everett, Research Assistant, Teachers College, New York City.
Report on Physical Education in Vermont, Helen W. Congdon.
Report of Subcommittee on Rural Elementary Schools.
Report of Subcommittee on Social Agencies Affecting Rural Schools.
Special Study Relative to Needs of Exceptional Children in Rural Schools, Sara M. Holbrook.
Report of Subcommittee on Secondary Education.
Study of the Needs of Girls in Public High Schools, Vermont, 1930, Thelma Mills, Felix Warburg Fellow, Teachers College, New York City.
Report of the Subcommittee on Normal Schools and Colleges.
Educational Outlook of Certain Vermont Towns—A Study of the Utilization of Vermont Colleges, 1930, Dorothy C. Walter, Special Field Worker.
Tabulation of Enrollment by Towns in Vermont Colleges, 1916-1930, Orlo K. Jenney.
Report of Committee on Adult Education.
Adult Education in Vermont, A Field Study, 1929, Dorothy C. Walter, Special Worker.
Report of Committee on Library Facilities.
Preliminary Study of a Group of Libraries in Northwestern Vermont, 1930, Frances Hobart.

XV

THE CARE OF THE HANDICAPPED

Introduction

This Committee was organized to give consideration to those groups in Vermont in need of special care—the blind, the deaf, the crippled, the pauper, the feeble-minded, the insane, neglected and dependent children, as well as juvenile delinquents and adult offenders against the law.

Present method of care. Vermont's method of caring for its handicapped centers around the town overseers of the poor, the Department of Public Welfare and certain private institutions and agencies. Below is given a brief statement of the situation as it exists today.

The overseers of the poor in the two hundred and forty-eight towns and cities of the state are charged with the duty of relieving poor and indigent persons within their borders "either in the poor house provided by the town or in such other manner as the town directs." Where it is ascertained that a pauper has a legal residence in some other town, the expense for his support may be charged to that town.

The state provides institutions for the care and treatment of the insane, feeble-minded, incipient cases of tuberculosis, criminals and juvenile delinquents. The Department of Public Welfare is in charge of all of the state institutions and of probation and parole. It designates indigent tuberculous persons for institutional care at state expense, pre-tubercular children for Preventorium care, and also deaf and blind children to educational institutions. It is empowered with the licensing and inspection of all private institutions caring for dependent and neglected children and of all foster homes boarding children under two years of age. Town overseers of the poor and private child-caring institutions and agencies are required by law to report to the Department of Public Welfare, and the placement of children by overseers is subject to the approval of the Department. The Department receives dependent and neglected children committed to it by courts and cares for them temporarily in its receiving home and then in foster boarding and free homes. It also administers mothers' aid to dependent children kept with their own mothers.

The public care of the handicapped is supplemented in Vermont by the work of various private institutions and agencies, both sectarian and non-sectarian. Thus the expense of caring for the needy is met from two sources, public taxes and private contributions from benevolently-minded individuals.

Method and scope of work. It was obviously impossible because of the limited time and money available for the Committee to attempt anything approaching a thorough study of all the handicapped of the state. As the problems of the handicapped first come to light in the various towns and are usually brought to the attention of the overseers of the poor, it was decided that the first undertaking of the Committee would be to study as intensively as possible the work of the town overseers. Forty-two towns in four counties were chosen as a representative cross section of Vermont; in these were included an industrial city, a prosperous dairy region, a back hill section and a mining district. A worker was employed who spent over four months in gaining first-hand information as to the nature and scope of the problem and the overseers' methods of meeting it.

The next undertaking of the Committee was a study of the aid rendered to these forty-two towns by public and private institutions and agencies of the state in the care and training of its handicapped children. This study led directly to the child-caring resources of the state, and while it was by no means an exhaustive or critical study of the individual institutions, it did give a complete picture of the provision Vermont has for the care of its dependent, delinquent, feebleminded and physically handicapped children.

The Committee was fortunate in including in its membership men and women in direct touch with the social problems of the state. A pooling of the knowledge of its individual members and a statement of the goals set by each in his own field was the third phase of the Committee's activity. Individual reports dealing with each one's specialty were prepared by the committee members which, after discussion and some revision by the Committee as a whole, became a part of its program. An effort was made in all of the Committee's thinking to keep "the long view" and to set up goals many of which are obviously not within reach at present. It is hoped that the Committee's objectives may contain some recommendations which may be utilized

at an early date and others which may act as a guide and incentive
for years to come.

Poor Relief

The work of the overseers of the poor in the two hundred and
forty-eight towns and cities of Vermont is the foundation of the
state's care of its handicapped. "The fact that Vermont is a rural
state makes the problem of poor relief none the less serious. In the
hamlets of Vermont there are forces at work which are even more
menacing than those which attract the attention of social workers in
areas densely populated and many of these insidious agencies are
closely interwoven with the administration of public charity."[1]

Outdoor relief. The giving of relief in families, or "outdoor
relief" as it is called, is the most difficult problem confronting the overseer. The handling of this problem necessitates the giving of considerable time and thought for investigation of the facts and available resources; time and thought for making a constructive plan by means of
which to develop the self-respect and economic and social potentialities
of the family; and time, energy, money and an understanding and love
of one's fellows to work out an effective plan. Few of the overseers
are in a position to give the time, even though they possessed all the
other qualifications. They are necessarily busy about their own affairs,
as in most cases the payment they receive is a mere pittance. In the
forty-two towns studied twenty-seven overseers were being paid twenty-
five dollars or less per year. Great credit is due many overseers for a
gift of time and effort in behalf of the poor of their communities out of
all proportion to their financial reimbursement.

In some instances gratifying results are achieved but it is inevitable
that in many cases there is inadequate handling of complex social
problems. Investigations are all too frequently incomplete. The
amount granted occasionally seems to depend upon the persistency of
the applicants and the amount of aid demanded more than upon the
actual need. A mother struggling to bring up her children is sometimes given such meager help that she endangers her health by over-
work and the children stray into delinquency while she is working outside of the home. If the mother is inclined to be morally weak, she
may even resort to questionable ways of living in order to keep her

[1] Poor Relief in Vermont, K. R. B. Flint, 1916, p. 7.

family together. The law allows an overseer to break up a home and place the children if the family is supported in whole or in part at the expense of the town. The threat of an overseer to take her children from her has been known to prevent a mother from asking for sorely needed help.

Strictly interpreted, the job of the overseer is concerned only with families or individuals applying for public relief. Almost every community in Vermont has its "sore spot" where neglected children and neglectful and discouraged or demoralized adults live in such a manner as to jeopardize the health and morals of other members of the community. Often such families are wise enough not to ask for public assistance or to show evidence of violation of the law. Under the existing law such cases are the concern neither of the overseer nor of the prosecuting officer of the town or county. What is needed is family case work administered by an organization closely identified with the community and near enough to the trouble to do constructive and effective work.

Welfare units. For situations like the above, which come without the strict limits of the duties of the overseer of the poor, and in order to provide assistance to the overseer for all of his problems, the Committee would recommend a long time program involving the establishment throughout Vermont of welfare districts. These districts could consist of a combination of towns in which an experienced case worker would work in connection with a board of representative citizens of both men and women. In Vermont it is possible that a district larger than a county might be a practical working unit. It is suggested that topographical features should be the controlling factors in making up such districts. The Committee is not at present prepared to recommend what unit shall be chosen but suggests that the matter be studied in connection with other committees facing the same problem. The work of such local units could do much to prevent the break up of family homes and resulting dependency and delinquency of children.

Psychiatric clinic. Another need which is felt by many agencies working in the field of health, education and social service is for a traveling psychiatric clinic. Such a clinic, composed of a psychiatrist, a physician, a psychologist, a social worker and clerical assistance might well be established under the combined auspices of the State Board of Health, Department of Public Welfare and Board of Education with private organizations cooperating. It would have as its aim: (1) To diagnose and recommend treatment for physical and mental defect and disease; (2) to diagnose and outline treatment for behavior problems; (3) to provide expert consultation for state institutions, judges, teachers, ministers, overseers of the poor and other welfare and health workers. A clinic of this kind should be a powerful agency for the prevention of insanity, delinquency and other maladjustments.

This committee joins with the Committee on Educational Facilities in recommending the immediate consideration of ways and means of establishing a psychiatric clinic. Even though Vermont may have to begin in a small way with part-time service, it is believed that a clinic would soon demonstrate its worth and grow as its services were understood and utilized.

The value of a psychiatric clinic depends to a large extent upon the availability of good case work facilities to carry out its recommendations. Without such follow up, diagnosis and recommendations have a very limited value. The suggestion made in the preceding section for welfare districts with capable case workers would supplement the work of the clinic and should be kept in mind in connection with any clinic program. The use of psychiatric clinic in relation to work with various classes of the handicapped will be discussed in subsequent sections of this report.

Aged poor. Many aged poor are no longer cared for in Vermont in almshouses but are being supported in their own homes or boarded with relatives or neighbors. The plan of caring for the so-called normal aged poor in families results in greater comfort, happiness and self-respect for this class of dependents *provided adequate support and adequate supervision are given.* Without such supervision it is subject to great abuse. Several states have already provided for the aged poor by the establishment of old-age pensions, thus removing the fear of pauperism which hovers about old age.

The Committee recommends for the aged poor who are not problems of physical or mental health or defect:

1. The ultimate establishment of old-age pensions.

2. Adequate support in their own homes or in boarding homes at the expense of the town.

Effective results from either of the above plans depend upon skillful case work which should be administered either publicly or under public supervision. The district welfare worker previously recommended could be used for investigation and supervision of the aged within the district.

Institutional relief. *Minute classification* is the corner stone upon which a poor relief system should be erected. Such classification is beyond the realm of possibility in the town poorhouse where the sick, the normal aged, the crippled and the mentally unsound live together in confusion. The money now spent in maintaining inadequate not to say deplorable town and city poor farms would go a long way toward the building of a state infirmary for the chronic sick for whom there is now no room in the regular hospitals of the state. Towns or cities should bear a considerable part if not the whole of the expense involved in the care of patients. Such a system of institutional relief should not stand in the way of town or city homes for the aged in communities where funds or other resources are available for this purpose. Such homes, however, should not receive other unfortunate individuals and should not be connected with a farm. There is no relationship between successful farming and wise treatment of the derelicts of society.

Recommendations for poor relief.

1. *Abolition of town poor farms.*
2. *Old-age pensions or the relief of the aged poor in their own homes or in carefully selected and supervised boarding homes.*
3. *Establishment of a state infirmary for the indigent chronic sick, the expense of whose care should be met in whole or in part by the towns.*
4. *Establishment of welfare districts with skilled agents for case work with families and individuals.*
5. *Establishment of a traveling psychiatric clinic, available to state institutions, courts, schools, health and welfare agencies.*

Dependent Children

For every child a home and that love and security which a home provides; and for that child who must receive foster care, the nearest substitute for his own home. (The Children's Charter, White House Conference, 1930.)

Cared for in own homes. Vermont is one of forty-five states of the Union which make public provision to keep children of good mothers in their own homes. On July 1, 1930, aid was being granted through the Department of Public Welfare to ninety-four mothers representing 252 children. In addition the Department had a long waiting list of applications from other mothers eligible under the law but for whom no money was available.

To keep children with their mothers by means of pensions is not only the humane but the economical way of providing for them, but as yet this is not thoroughly understood or appreciated. In the forty-two towns which the committee studied intensively, there were only eight families receiving mothers' aid and twenty-four overseers had no knowledge of the law. All too frequently the home is needlessly broken up and the children placed in institutions or foster homes. To quote from Commissioner Dyer's last report:

There is a practice among some overseers when a good and worthy mother asks for temporary aid from the town to threaten to remove her children from her and place her in the poorhouse separated from the children. The consequence is naturally that the mother gets on the best she can and the children are undernourished and become broken in health, and are sent at state expense to the Preventorium for treatment. Adequate provision for mothers' aid will remedy this, but public sentiment in the towns where this may be the practice should be aroused to the extent that such methods be stopped for they are barbarous and relics of slavery days that have no place in our beloved State of Vermont.[4]

The law provides for the payment of $2.00 a week per child, the expense to be divided between the town and state. This is obviously in many instances an inadequate allowance and defeats its own purpose of providing suitable care for children in their own homes. A mother forced to do hard work to supplement her pension, often away from home for many hours of the day, cannot do justice to her children. In place of the $2.00 a week allowance now in force, the Committee recommends that the Legislature empower the Department to make elastic grants based upon the budget needs and resources of the family and that the appropriation be large enough to care for all eligible mothers and children.

Mothers' aid should be accompanied by careful supervision by case workers. The Department is at present so understaffed that adequate supervision is impossible. The Committee recommends either larger appropriation to increase the Department's staff or a system of cooperation with the welfare districts previously recommended.

[4] Biennial Report of the Department of Public Welfare, June 30, 1930.

Cared for away from own home. Approximately 1,300 dependent children are cared for in Vermont outside of their own homes. The number of dependent children cared for away from their homes per 10,000 of the total population of the state is about thirty-six. This is a high proportion as compared with other states, except for the other New England states whose rate is about the same. It is significant that the number of Vermont children receiving mothers' aid per 10,000 of the total state population is seven, a very low rate compared with other states. In states in which mothers' aid is fairly adequate the number of children receiving assistance in their own homes is at least as large as the number under care of institutions and agencies.

The above facts would indicate that Vermont is not providing the most humane and economical care for many children whose homes might be preserved. Another reason which undoubtedly increases the number of children cared for away from home is the lack of family welfare work in local communities. Case work applied in time by a skilled worker can often overcome the dangers which threaten a home. To meet this urgent need, the Committee again recommends welfare districts with experienced case workers.

With every effort made to preserve to children all family homes worthy of the name of home, there will still be many children who because of the death, illness or unfitness of their mothers must be cared for elsewhere. For them the state should provide the best substitute possible, which means the study of each individual child to determine where and how he can best develop. Institution or foster home should be chosen not because there is a vacancy or because of financial considerations but because it is fitted to the child's particular need.

As a general rule young normal dependents should be cared for in foster homes, and institutions should develop their resources to give specialized types of care to older children with vocational or trade training emphasized. For both institutions and foster homes the character of the persons intrusted with the care and training of the children is of the utmost importance. Except in unusual cases where a child would be handicapped by his family, he should be kept in his own community as far as possible. The welfare unit previously mentioned could well undertake the placement and supervision of many of these children.

A careful intake policy based on adequate case work should be a part of the equipment of every child-caring institution and agency and is essential if they are to serve the children who need them most. All private institutions and agencies caring for dependent children should be inspected and licensed annually by the Department of Public Welfare.

No study was made by the Committee of illegitimacy or adoptions though it realizes that these are subjects which need very careful consideration.

Recommendations for Dependent Children

1. *The establishment of welfare districts with competent case workers to salvage threatened homes and place and supervise homeless children who are kept in their own communities.*

2. *A large enough appropriation for mothers' aid to give adequate relief to all eligible mothers.*

3. *An amendment of the mothers' aid law enabling the Department of Public Welfare to make elastic grants based on a budgeting of income and need.*

4. *Increased appropriation to the Department of Public Welfare so that it may be adequately staffed for its work of direct care of children and supervision of private child-caring agencies and institutions.*

Delinquency

For every child who is in conflict with society, the right to be dealt with intelligently as society's charge, not society's outcast; with the home, the school, the church, the court and the institution when needed, shaped to return him whenever possible to the normal stream of life. (Children's Charter.)

This report concerns itself almost entirely with the *juvenile* delinquent. Vermont is noted for its prison system and handling of adult offenders. Comparatively little preventive work can, however, be done with the adult offender. Prevention and study must begin with the juvenile delinquent, or better, with all children that show signs of maladjustment.

No accurate statement of the delinquency problem is possible. Delinquency is so closely related and interwoven with the problem of the feeble-minded, dependent and neglected child that one is unable to draw a close line between them. Vermont in common with all sections has the problem and must face it constructively. The state has excellent physical equipment for caring for delinquents in the training school at Vergennes.

The problem of understanding the underlying difficulties of which the delinquency is but a symptom is complex. The state lacks facilities for solving it. The clinic already proposed would be a great help in working with the delinquent and pre-delinquent child. It would also do much toward making specific recommendations as to the type of training which would most benefit the child, once he had been committed to the State Industrial School.

Increase of probation and parole facilities would reduce the number of delinquents committed to the institution and would insure greater success of the individuals leaving the institution. It would mean also that delinquents could be discharged after a shorter stay in the institution, because of more effective supervision available. It would protect the investment already made by the state in these persons. At the present time one parole officer from the State Industrial School is attempting to supervise 122 cases. This is obviously too great a load to secure the best results.

Another activity in which the state can well afford to engage is that of parent education. Juvenile delinquency is largely due to failure on the part of parents. Eventually, parent education should materially decrease delinquency by bringing to parents a better understanding of their children and of the best methods of training them.

At present Vermont is unable to handle defective delinquents satisfactorily. Separate provision, preferably in a special institution, will sometime be necessary. For the adequately studied and classified delinquent, special classes and types of training must be provided. These include specially trained personnel and more facilities for hand training.

Recommendations for the Prevention and Treatment of Delinquency

1. *Increase in the number of probation and parole officers.*
2. *Adequate case records for use of juvenile court judges.*
3. *Provision for separate care of defective delinquents.*
4. *The establishment of a traveling psychiatric clinic.*

5. *A program of parent education under the auspices of the state.*
6. *Family case work in welfare districts to prevent neglect and consequent delinquency of children.*

The Physically Handicapped

For every child who is blind, deaf, crippled or otherwise physically handicapped, and for the child who is mentally handicapped, such measures as will early discover and diagnose his handicap, provide care and treatment, and so train him that he may become an asset to society rather than a liability. Expenses of these services should be borne publicly where they cannot be privately met. (Children's Charter, White House Conference, 1930.)

No complete figures of the number of persons involved under this head are available. A survey should be made for the purpose of ascertaining how many blind, deaf, crippled and otherwise physically handicapped individuals exist in the state. Vermont's program for the care of the physically handicapped children is in accord with the recommendations of the White House Conference. So far as is known, all blind and deaf children eligible for training in special educational institutions are receiving such education. It is possible, however, for the state to do much more toward early discovery and diagnosis. Welfare districts as mentioned previously in this report would undoubtedly lead to the finding of cases of physical handicap at a much earlier date. They would also contribute to the prevention of physical handicaps through elimination of their causes.

In all cases of blindness and deafness early detection is noted as the chief instrument in successful treatment and cure. The use of the audiometer for detection of deafness, for example, is advantageously used in many school systems. All the New England states except Vermont use this device for measuring the hearing of school children. Pre-school clinics and medical inspection in schools aid greatly in early discovery and treatment of eye troubles. Such clinics must be accompanied by adequate follow-up work. Babies are still discovered in Vermont, blind from ophthalmia neonatorum, showing that there is still room for better preventive measures at birth.

There exists a federal statute which assists states in the vocational rehabilitation of adults crippled in industry. This Committee believes that Vermont should study this statute with a view of the possibility of taking advantage of its provisions and assistance in reeducating crippled adults.

Those afflicted with tuberculosis in the various stages constitute a large group whose problem is being effectively met. Here again prevention is greatly needed. Physical examinations for school children and education of all adults as to prevention and cure are most important. Health colonies for bridging over the time between discharge from the sanatorium and the taking up of everyday life have been suggested by the Vermont Tuberculosis Association. The Committee recommends study of its plan. The need of case histories in the proper diagnosis and prevention of tuberculosis once more brings out the usefulness of the welfare district. A worker in such a district would be able to help with such histories and might even have much of the material already on file.

With no desire to minimize the very fine program of treatment and aid now in effect in Vermont, the Committee makes the following recommendations which it feels will greatly strengthen and further the program of early diagnosis and *prevention* of physical handicaps.

Recommendations for the care of the physically handicapped.

A. For the blind and deaf.

1. *A survey of all blind and deaf in the state.*
2. *Early detection of blind and deaf in schools with preventive measures and special classes where practical.*
3. *Enforcement of Section 6206, Chapter 267, of the Laws of Vermont dealing with prevention of blindness.*
4. *Adequate follow-up of blind and deaf children after discharge from special schools.*
5. *Provision for adequate instruction of adult blind and deaf at state expense.*
6. *Larger local responsibility for blind and deaf.*

B. For the crippled.

1. *Greater local interest and responsibility to the end that crippled children may be found and brought to already available resources of training and treatment at the outset of trouble.*
2. *Provision for continuance and permanence of the poliomyelitis clinics and for after-care of Vermont poliomyelitis patients when needed.*
3. *Study of the desirability of the state's taking advantage of the federal act for vocational rehabilitation.*

4. *Study of ways and means of providing education and training for crippled children unable to attend public schools.*

C. For the tubercular.

1. *Health education and physical examinations in the public schools as important preventive measures.*
2. *Study of the plan for health camps to bridge the gap from sanitarium to private life.*
3. *Improvement of facilities for obtaining case histories through establishment of welfare districts.*

The Feeble-minded

The exact number of the feeble-minded in Vermont is not known but it is estimated that there are about 5,000 such persons in the state.[2] On June 30, 1930, 272 pupils were enrolled in the Brandon State School. Of these, 232 were cared for at the school, sixteen girls were at the Rutland Colony and nine boys at the Farm Colony. The remaining fifteen boys and girls were on parole. There is no question but that there are in the whole state a great many more mental defectives who need special help to enable them to become assets to society and not liabilities. Early identification of the feeble-minded child is paramount. This can be accomplished by routine reporting of retarded school children who should then be given special tests by qualified examiners. Here again is found an urgent need for the psychiatric clinic. It is generally accepted that the public school is responsible for working out a program to fit the need of the great majority of mentally defective children. This is a matter which pertains more directly to the Committee on Educational Facilities. Special classes are doubtless the solution of the problem for numbers of defective children living in centers large enough to make such classes practical. In other cases a special agent to assist rural teachers in their work with backward children, as recommended by the Committee on Educational Facilities, is here approved.

Community supervision and responsibility for the feeble-minded are important planks in a state's program for the care of its defectives. Social service in the local communities is needed for the feeble-minded as for the other maladjusted classes of the community. For this purpose welfare districts are again recommended. In a state program

[2] First Annual Report, Eugenics Survey of Vermont, 1927, p. 15.

for the control and training of the feeble-minded, the state institution is the pivot about which should revolve all other machinery. The present tendency is to receive the teachable young child at the Brandon State School and after a period of intensive training to return him to the community. Studies made of the after-school careers of such children indicate definitely that the large majority are able to take their places in community life as ordinary, decent, working citizens who mind their own business and make their own way in such a manner as to be in no sense a social burden.

Vermont this year adopted a program of voluntary sterilization of certain defectives. Its marriage laws also take cognizance of the danger to the state of the marriage of defectives by forbidding a clerk to issue a marriage license to certain enumerated classes.[3]

Two problems connected with the care of the feeble-minded have been noted by the Committee but it is not yet ready to make recommendations in regard to them. The first is the care of the low grade feeble-minded. Many such are now being cared for in poor farms. If poor farms are abolished as recommended on page 287, some other provision would have to be made for the care of this class as it is doubtful if they could be satisfactorily boarded in family homes. Some of the low grade feeble-minded are now in the Brandon State School and at Waterbury State Hospital but are neither trainable at Brandon nor proper subjects for a hospital for the insane.

The other problem is that of the defective delinquent, both adult and juvenile. There are many pupils at the Industrial School who are feeble-minded but who because of their delinquency do not fit into the program of the training school at Brandon. The delinquent feeble-minded woman is even a worse social problem. While in the Reformatory at Rutland she is easily managed and happy; when discharged at the expiration of her sentence she returns to the community quite unable to meet its requirements because mentally she is only a little girl. Usually she becomes a sex offender and her neglected children either legitimate or illegitimate further tax the social resources of the state.

Recommendations for the care of feeble-minded.

1. *Early identification by means of reporting of retarded school children, followed by psychometric and psychiatric examinations as the need is indicated.*

[3] Public Acts of the 1929 General Assembly, State of Vermont. Permanent No. 51.

2. *Special classes in larger centers and special aid to the rural school teacher in meeting the educational need of defective pupils.*

3. *Community supervision and responsibility by means of case work in the welfare districts previously recommended.*

4. *Selection of suitable defective children for intensive training in the State School with the expectation of returning them as assets to the community.*

5. *Further study to determine the best program for the low grade feeble-minded and the adult and juvenile defective delinquent.*

6. *A traveling psychiatric clinic, available to state institutions, courts, schools, health and welfare agencies.*

The Insane

The Committee did not attempt to make an extensive study of the problem of the insane in Vermont. On June 30, 1930, there were in the State Hospital at Waterbury 879 patients and 608 patients at Brattleboro Retreat, making a total of 1,487 mental patients receiving hospital care. Undoubtedly there are many other Vermont patients cared for in private sanitariums both in and out of the state. The extent of the problem is evidenced by the fact that there are in Vermont more patients in hospitals for the insane than there are hospital beds in the entire state for the physically sick.

Science is discovering what a large place there is for prevention in the field of mental disease. Mental breakdown can in a large measure be prevented if the trouble is detected and treated in its early stages. Better yet, mental hygiene programs for the inculcation, especially in early childhood, of right attitudes and wholesome habits of thought and behavior are doing much in some communities to build up a balance of personality that can withstand the strain of our modern life. Vermont has no organized activity which has for its object the promotion of mental hygiene or the prevention of mental disease. The Committee for lack of time did not make definite study or recommendations along this line but points out the need for further study.

The work of the State Hospital at Waterbury could be greatly helped by the introduction of trained social service as a part of the hospital resources. The psychiatric social worker, trained in social service has in addition special training in psychiatry. She makes the contact between the State Hospital and the community, visiting the homes of the patients and collecting information in regard to the patient's home environment and the factors that led up to the mental breakdown.   She also takes charge of the patient when he leaves the hospital and is thereby able to determine whether or not he is making a good readjustment at home.   If the patient is not getting along satisfactorily she reports to the hospital any untoward symptoms that are developing.

The psychiatric clinic suggested above is urgently needed for preventive and remedial work with the insane.   Instability which results in mental breakdown in adult life is often apparent in childhood, showing itself in such symptoms as so-called "nervousness," excessive shyness, temper tantrums, and other behavior difficulties.   If such children can be understood and properly handled, there is reason to believe that much insanity can be prevented.   A psychiatric clinic would be an invaluable help to parents or guardians of such children; could detect and diagnose mental disease in its early stages and help the state hospital in follow-up work with paroled and discharged persons.

Recommendations for the care of the insane.

1. *The inclusion of psychiatric social service with the work of the state hospital.*
2. *The establishment of a traveling psychiatric clinic.*
3. *The establishment of welfare districts with competent case work with which the hospital and clinic can cooperate.*
4. *Dissemination of information regarding generally accepted principles of mental hygiene.*

Conclusion

The Committee's program for the care of Vermont's handicapped rests upon the following foundations:

1. *The establishment of district welfare units.   This is in accord with a statement in section 19 of the Children's Charter which reads: "Full-time public welfare service for the relief, aid, and guidance of children in special need due to poverty, misfortune, or behavior difficulties, and for the protection of children from abuse, neglect, exploitation or moral hazard."*

2. *Care of the normal aged poor in their own homes or boarding homes under adequate supervision and the establishment of a state hospital for the indigent chronic sick.*
3. *The establishment of a traveling psychiatric clinic.*
4. *A strengthening of the resources of the Department of Public Welfare, especially in the way of personnel, so that it may assure adequate care and protection to all of the state's handicapped by:*
   (a) *Development of its own program of direct care by the state.*
   (b) *Standardization of the work of private organizations.*
   (c) *Help to enable local communities to give suitable care near home to as many as possible of their unfortunates.*
5. *A coordination of the work of all public and private agencies, each supplementing and enforcing the work of the others.*

All of the recommendations of this report are made with a view to a long-time program and with the thought of prevention always in mind. The Committee presents this proposed program with the hope of having it tested by the thinking and experience of men and women from many walks of life in all parts of Vermont. Only when the program has met this test of public opinion and been revised thereby can it hope to become a real program for Vermont's care of its handicapped.

———————

Prepared for the Commission by its Committee on the Care of the Handicapped.

W. I. MAYO, JR.,
  Chairman,
L. JOSEPHINE WEBSTER,
  Executive Secretary,
T. J. ALLEN, M. D., Brandon,
K. R. B. FLINT, Northfield,
HOWARD N. HANSON, Vergennes,
C. RUSSELL LITTLE, Fair Haven,
MARY E. MCKEOUGH, Rutland,
ANNA R. MCMAHON, Montpelier,
LENA C. ROSS, Rutland,
FANNY G. SHAW, Burlington,

HAROLD W. SLOCUM, Burlington,
E. A. STANLEY, M. D., Waterbury,
WM. H. DYER, Montpelier,
(Consulting Member).

Source Material on Which Committee's Findings are Based

Report on Mental Deficiency, T. J. ALLEN, M. D.
An Ideal Poor-Relief System for Vermont, K. R. B. FLINT.
Report on Juvenile Delinquency, HOWARD N. HANSON.
Report on Institutions for Children, W. I. MAYO, JR.
Report on Mothers' Aid, ANNA R. MCMAHON.
Report on Certain Physically Handicapped Persons in Vermont, FANNY G. SHAW.
Special Report on the Tuberculosis Situation in Vermont, HAROLD W. SLOCUM.
Report on the Waterbury State Hospital, E. A. STANLEY, M. D.
Report on Child-Placing, L. JOSEPHINE WEBSTER.
A Study of Relief by Overseers in Forty-two Towns, MARY V. BOLTON.
A Study of Aid Rendered to Forty-two Towns by Certain Public and Private Institutions, MARY V. BOLTON.
Possible Objectives in Social Endeavor for Vermont, SARAH H. SPENCER.
Addresses and Abstracts of Committee Reports—White House Conference on Child Health and Protection, 1930.
Annual Reports, 1927-1930, Eugenics Survey of Vermont.

The Eugenic Aspects

There are two problems that call for our very best attention when we think of those among us who are crippled, blind, deaf, insane or endowed with less than enough brains to make their way in the world, or of those who through these or other causes are incapable of earning their own living—the aged and those who have been or still are chronically sick. The first of these problems, that of the treatment of the handicapped by social agencies and methods, having been discussed, it remains to consider the prevention of further defectiveness. The immediate need that confronts us is to lessen distress of body or of mind in those about us. Common humanity calls for that. It is not a simple task. It demands the best efforts of keen minds, a long and careful study of conditions, needs, resources and approved methods. No hamlet is so small as to be exempt and every state and town has problems of its own concerning its unfortunate, its underprivileged, its handicapped.

The second of these problems, that of prevention, can be stated in the form of questions. How can a community, after caring to the best of its abilities for those who suffer from devastating ills, proceed to govern itself in such a way as to better its chances for the future? Are there any known and tried methods of lessening the danger of an increase or a continuance at present rates of mental and physical damage in our population? If my neighbor breaks his leg in a hole in my dooryard I first get a doctor, later send in some flowers and then I proceed to fill up the hole. We have been getting doctors—better and better ones as time has gone on. We have sent lots of flowers. But it has escaped us that there are ways of preventing future mishaps and that it is our job to use them. We are just beginning to wake up to such things. Eugenics is finding out what to do and has already much sound advice to offer us. If we will listen to that advice and follow it, there will be fewer defectives and delinquents among the population of coming Vermont than in the past or the present. There will be a larger proportion of the people who will enjoy the richer life that is made possible by sound minds in healthy bodies, and our children's children will be less hampered by the social and economic drag of avoidable low grade Vermonters.

The Eugenics Survey of Vermont has been engaged since the autumn of 1925 in a study of heredity in Vermont families and gratifying progress has been made in the gathering of useful facts. It has attempted to deduce conclusions leading toward the adoption of remedies and has been given not a few opportunities to place its findings and its recommendations before the people of this and other states.

Because more information had been previously gathered by social agencies than was elsewhere available, the records which were at hand to use as a starting point when the Survey began were those of families or persons who had at least come into contact with social agencies, and these were naturally dependent, deficient or delinquent. More than fifty families of these sorts were studied and catalogued, numbering in their five or six latest generations some six thousand persons. They

TABLE 1. CHART OF DEFECTS FOUND AMONG FIFTY-FIVE DEGENERATE FAMILIES STUDIED [1]

Pedigree number	Number of generations	Number of individuals	Main defects	Other important defects
1a	7	407	Huntington's chorea	Pauperism
1b	5	215	Low mentality	....
1c	5	147	Insanity	....
2	6	244	Feeblemindedness, cripples	Criminals, pauperism, sex offenders
3	5	104	Feeblemindedness, thievery	....
4	6	471	Feeblemindedness	Nomadic habits, dependency, criminality
5	6	211	Pauperism, tuberculosis	Low mentality, immorality
6	7	262	Pauperism, feeblemindedness	....
7	5	44	Feeblemindedness, pauperism	Tuberculosis
8a	4	27	Insanity	
8b	2	9	Insanity	....
8c	4	12	Insanity	....
9	6	117	Feeblemindedness	Sex offenders, pauperism
10	3	36	Feeblemindedness	Sex offenders
11	3	35	Friedreich's ataxia	Feeblemindedness
12	4	22	Feeblemindedness	Epilepsy
13	6	297	Insanity, immorality	Feeblemindedness, dependency
14	6	454	Criminality	Alcoholism, sex offenders
15	3	7	Insanity	Feeblemindedness
16	3	8	Insanity	....
17	8	597	Insanity	Feeblemindedness
18	3	29	Insanity	Feeblemindedness
19	3	25	Feeblemindedness	Sex offenders
20	3	30	Feeblemindedness	....
21	4	34	Huntington's chorea	....
22	5	81	Criminality	Feeblemindedness
23	4	34	Alcoholism, insanity, feeblemindedness	Hare lip, cleft palate
24	4	19	Feeblemindedness	....
25a	4	55	Pauperism, feeblemindedness	....
25b	5	47	Pauperism	....
26	5	233	Criminalism	....
27a	4	21	Pauperism	....
27b	3	6	Feeblemindedness, epilepsy	....
28	4	18	Feeblemindedness	Venereal disease, insanity, delinquency
29	3	17	Insanity	....
30	3	21	Criminality	Degeneracy, feeblemindedness
31	4	16	Feeblemindedness	Epilepsy, goiter
32	4	27	Feeblemindedness, immorality	Venereal disease
33	4	29	Feeblemindedness, tuberculosis	....
34	6	105	Feeblemindedness	Sex offenders
35	4	30	Pauperism	Feeblemindedness, epilepsy, sex offenders
36	3	19	Pauperism	Feeblemindedness
37	4	34	Feeblemindedness	Pauperism
38	4	48	Sex offenders	Feeblemindedness, insanity
39	2	7	Feeblemindedness, pauperism	....
40	6	383	Feeblemindedness	Sex offenders
41	2	5	Feeblemindedness	Cretinism
42	5	36	Insanity	Sex offenders, alcoholism
43	3	18	Insanity	Feeblemindedness
44	5	40	Huntington's chorea	....
45	4	60	Tuberculosis	Arthritis, feeblemindedness
46	3	16	Insanity	....
47	3	31	Feeblemindedness	Pauperism
48	3	41	Delinquency	Sex offenders, feeblemindedness
49	5	25	Sex offenders	Feeblemindedness
50	4	14	Feeblemindedness, insanity	Epilepsy, blindness
51	6	98	Huntington's chorea	....
52	3	10	Insanity	....
53	4	10	Insanity	....
54	5	105	Criminalism	Pauperism, tuberculosis, insanity
55	5	101	Feeblemindedness	Sex offenders
Totals		5,704		

[1] Reprinted from the Fourth Annual Report, Eugenics Survey of Vermont, 1930, page 36. A limited number of the four reports is available for persons desiring copies on request to the Eugenics Survey, 138 Church Street, Burlington, Vt.

TABLE 2. SHOWING TOTAL EXPENSE OF TEN PEDIGREES TO VERMONT, NEW YORK AND MASSACHUSETTS[2]

Pedigree number	Number of individuals	No. at public expense					No. of feebleminded and insane					Expense		
		State		Town	Total[3]	Percent of family dependent	Institutions in		Not in institutions	Total[4]	Percent of family affected	Vermont	Other states	Total
		Vermont	Other states				Vermont	Other states						
2	244	22	2	30	42	17	3	0	15	18	7	$ 33,745.49	$ 745.74	$ 34,491.23
3	104	16	6	13	27	26	5	2	2	9	9	19,563.48	3,368.33	22,931.81
4	471	37	10	45	72	15	5	2	18	25	5	43,807.41	11,391.15	55,198.56
5	211	6	0	66	71	34	3	0	4	7	3	9,675.38	......	9,675.38
6	262	16	2	37	40	15	3	1	8	11	4	15,241.26	629.36	15,870.62
7	44	2	0	7	8	18	2	0	2	4	9	4,452.73	......	4,452.73
13	297	29	6	14	39	13	8	0	11	19	6	49,928.69	9,680.05	59,608.74
17	274	6	4	1	9	3	4	4	7	14	5	3,108.50	13,249.76	16,358.26
40	383	12	1	11	15	3	2	0	27	29	8	21,262.83	60.00	21,322.83
54	96	17	0	7	22	23	4	0	0	4	4	17,884.28	......	17,884.28
Total......	2,386	163	31	231	345	..	39	9	94	140	..	$218,670.05	$39,124.39	$257,794.44
Duplication[5]	130	21	2	13	25	..	7	0	6	13	..	31,398.65	745.74	32,144.39
Net total..	2,256	142	29	218	320	14.2	32	9	88	127	5.6	$187,271.40	$38,378.65	$225,650.05

The statistics for the feebleminded are undoubtedly much lower than they should be, because only those have been called feebleminded and insane who have been tested or who have been so manifestly feebleminded or insane that there seemed to be no question about it. There were very many other incompetents who are "not able to manage their affairs with ordinary prudence" and are undoubtedly feebleminded.

[2] Eugenics Survey of Vermont Second Annual Report, 1928, page 19.
[3] Total after deducting for individuals that are an expense to both state and town.
[4] Total after deducting for individuals that are both in Vermont institutions and in institutions in other states.
[5] Duplication of individuals belonging to more than one pedigree.

came from many different parts of the state and every institution and social agency was drawn upon for reliable information about them, besides which, personal interviews were the principal source of data.

The types of defects found in the families studied and the prominence of two particular types—namely, pauperism, and feeble-mindedness—are represented in Table 1.

The betterment of the race is a far more important matter than can be measured in dollars, but a pretty forcible argument—especially to certain types of mind—for the eugenical program can be read in the hard facts of costs to the taxpayer. Social wrongs are wont to take on a greater significance to most of us if and when we discover that they are costly in our money as well as in manhood. Accurate figures showing the total costs cannot be secured, principally because of the absence of complete and reliable records for the earlier periods. We have given in Table 2 only such figures as have been verified, well knowing that they show far less than actual total expenditures and we have avoided even a conservative estimate of what the additions ought to be.

It is startling to discover that more than seventeen cents on the dollar of state and town taxes goes for the costs of dependency and delinquency in Vermont. This was computed by students under the direction of one of the members of the Committee and the figures were checked by him. They include not only direct costs for maintenance of poor, defective and inmates of penal institutions but of police, criminal court officers and costs of commitments, arrests, etc.

But the financial argument is sordid and cheap in comparison with all the other reasons for striving to raise the levels of our population. We are not meeting our responsibility as loyal Vermonters if we neglect any reasonable measure for making this state the best possible home for its future citizens.

Recommendation

In addition to the articles included in the report of the Committee on the People of Vermont (chapter III of this volume), the Eugenics Survey makes the following recommendation:

Through the quickened public conscience aroused by the methods of education outlined in chapter III, we recommend the strict enforce-

ment of our laws governing marriage of defectives and such other measures as are calculated to check the multiplication of the unfit.

Prepared for the Commission by the Eugenics Survey.

H. F. PERKINS,

Director.

XVI

THE VERMONT FOUNDATION

General Scope and Purposes

The Vermont Foundation is a community trust. The first community trust was created in Cleveland, Ohio, in 1914. The plan has spread rapidly. At present, there are over seventy similar organizations throughout the country, entrusted with many millions of dollars. Donors and testators are finding the community trust an approved, convenient and effective channel for the administration of funds devoted to public charities.

Persons interested in the welfare of Vermont, its people or any of its communities, may now utilize this new philanthropic enterprise.

The plan. In the Vermont Foundation, the funds are held and invested by banking institutions. This ensures safety of principal and a good income.

Any trust company or bank possessing the power of acting as trustee may be chosen by the donor or testator to act as trustee of his gift or bequest. The trustee adopts the Resolution and Declaration of Trust as hereinafter set forth.

The income is distributed under the direction of a Committee carefully chosen and well informed concerning the State of Vermont and its various communities. This ensures wise disposition of the funds. The members of the Committee serve gratuitously.

Appointment of committee. The administrative Committee of the Foundation is selected by a Board of Appointment consisting of the Chief Justice of the Vermont Supreme Court, the Governor of the State of Vermont, the Commissioner of Finance (or State Treasurer), the President of the Vermont Bankers' Association, and the Chairman of the Committee.

Gifts for special charities. The donor may designate some particular purpose or organization to receive his bounty. The Committee will respect and carry out the donor's expressed wishes, until, in the good judgment of four-fifths of the Committee, conditions are such that the donor's purposes have become illegal, impracticable, or contrary to public interest. The spirit of the donor's gift will be carried out when it would be impracticable to carry it out literally. This prevents the beneficent intent of a gift for a specific purpose becoming nullified by unforeseen changing conditions.

Life uses. Gifts may be accepted subject to annuities or life uses provided by the donor. Upon the termination of the annuity or life use, the gift will be used as directed.

Principal safeguarded. The principal of the donation will be held and invested by a banking institution. This secures the benefit of a permanent trustee, with officers having skill and good judgment in investing money and managing trust funds. Donors may thus be assured that their funds will be conservatively invested and wisely safeguarded.

Publicity and inspection. The plan provides for proper inspection and audit of the books and records of the trustees and Committee, and the making and publication of reports.

Public charities. Within the term "public charities" are included educational, moral, civic, scientific, recreational and other philanthropic purposes.

Small gifts. The plan provides for perpetuating small gifts by combined investment management, while retaining the name and individuality of each fund as fixed by the donor.

The plan provides a convenient and responsible agency by which the man of moderate means, as well as one of larger wealth, may make permanent gifts for the benefit of any community or public cause in which he is interested.

Secretary. When sufficient funds have accumulated in the Foundation to warrant the expense, an Executive Secretary may be appointed by the Committee to assist in the administration of the Foundation.

Advisory committees. The Committee may appoint local committees in various communities to advise and assist in the disbursement of funds destined for distribution in such communities.

General purposes. The Vermont Foundation is primarily intended for the creation of trusts for the benefit of charitable organizations within the State of Vermont whose perpetuity or facilities for holding trust funds are open to question, for the promotion of public causes not served by institutions of permanence and character having trust powers, and particularly for the help of small communities.

The Vermont Foundation may be used, among other purposes, to foster creative literature, art or music, to assist young people to obtain higher education, to encourage village improvements, to conserve public health, to provide wholesome recreation, and to promote good citizenship and patriotism.

The purposes served by gifts to the Foundation may be state-wide in scope, or limited to particular groups, causes or communities.

The Vermont Foundation is available when there is uncertainty as to the wise method of giving to any secular philanthropic cause within the State of Vermont.

Resolution and Declaration of Trust

The form of Resolution and Declaration of Trust for the Vermont Foundation follows:

THE VERMONT FOUNDATION

W H E R E A S, it has been made apparent to this Trust Company that there is need of the establishment and maintenance of a state-wide community trust in the State of Vermont, for the purpose of encouraging and assisting charities and charitable enterprises, and especially by affording opportunity to donors and testators to make their several gifts, grants, bequests and devises to different trustees of their own selection, providing methods for safeguarding the permanent security of such gifts, ensuring wise and efficient distribution of the available funds, meeting changing needs of future years with flexibility in the power of distribution, promoting economical and efficient administration by union of available funds, and generally securing to the State of Vermont and its various communities the benefits of a community charitable trust; and

W H E R E A S, this Trust Company is desirous of acting as a trustee under such trust, named and designated "The Vermont Foundation,"

N O W, T H E R E F O R E, on this   day of   , A. D., 19   , the   , a banking corporation with power to act as trustee, organized and existing under the laws of the State of   , and located at   , in the County of   , State of   , hereinafter called the "Trustee," by its Board of Directors, does hereby adopt the following

RESOLUTION AND DECLARATION:

§ 1. **Acceptance by Trustee.** The Trustee aforesaid declares that it will accept, hold, and distribute gifts, grants, devises or bequests made to it as Trustee hereunder for the charitable uses and purposes and subject to the powers and duties hereinafter set forth.

§ 2. **Name.** The trust hereby provided for and all property accepted and held hereunder shall be designated as "THE VERMONT FOUNDATION."

§ 3. **Other trustees.** It is understood that other banking or financial institutions may accept, hold and administer trust funds for "The Vermont Foundation," but nothing herein contained shall be deemed to make such institutions or any of them co-trustees, joint tenants or tenants in common of any estate or property accepted or held hereunder or deemed to make this Trustee a co-Trustee, joint tenant or tenant in common of any estate or property accepted or held by any other such institution.

No trustee shall be answerable for the acts, receipts, neglects or defaults of any of the other trustees.

§ 4. **Wishes of donors.** The wishes of donors or testators, as expressed in the instruments making their gifts, grants, bequests or devises to the Foundation, as to the time when and the charitable purposes for which the income or principal of their gifts, grants, bequests or devises shall be used, either for a definite or indefinite period of time, shall be respected by and shall govern the Committee hereinafter provided for; provided, however, that if and whenever the Committee shall by resolution adopted by vote of four-fifths of its entire membership determine that for the period named in the resolution, or until further action of the Committee, it is illegal, unnecessary, impracticable or contrary to public interest under conditions as they may at any time or from time to time exist, to apply the available funds or income thereof to the purpose or purposes indicated by the donor or testator, or to comply literally with the terms of the instrument creating the gift, grant, bequest or devise, said Committee may at any such time direct the application of such gift, grant, bequest or devise, when proper, or the income thereof, to such charitable purpose or purposes within the scope and purposes of this Foundation as the Committee may deem will most nearly fulfil the wishes of the donor or testator.

Any donation shall bear the particular name or designation, if any, provided by the donor.

§ 5. **Charitable purposes.** Except as herein otherwise provided, the income of the invested portion of trust funds hereunder, together with any and all amounts received for present distribution and not for investment, less proper charges, expenses and deductions, shall each year be applied to such public charitable uses and purposes within the State of Vermont, excepting sectarian and denominational religious uses or purposes, as the Committee hereinafter provided for shall in its discretion, from time to time select as most deserving and beneficial to inhabitants of the State of Vermont, and without in any way enlarging or limiting the generality of the foregoing but rather in illustration and explanation thereof, for the following uses and purposes among others:

(a) For assisting charitable institutions (including educational institutions not operated for private profit), whether supported wholly or in part by private donations or by public taxation;

(b) For promoting scientific research for the advancement of human knowledge and the alleviation of human suffering;

(c) For the care of the sick, aged, homeless and helpless;

(d) For the care of needy men, women and children;

(e) For aiding in the reformation of: (1) victims of narcotics, drugs and intoxicating liquors, (2) released inmates of penal and reformatory institutions, and (3) wayward or delinquent persons;

(f) For the improvement of living and working conditions;

(g) For providing facilities for public recreation;

(h) For the encouragement of social and domestic hygiene;

(i) For the encouragement of sanitation and measures for the prevention or healing of disease;

(j) For investigating or promoting the investigation of or research into the causes of ignorance, poverty and vice, preventing the operation of such causes, and remedying or ameliorating the conditions resulting therefrom;

(k) For erecting and maintaining public buildings or works, or otherwise lessening the burdens of government;

(l) For promotion of science, art, literature, patriotism, good citizenship and education;

(m) For the preservation of places or objects of natural beauty or historic interest and of monuments and works of art;

(n) For the study of the work of charitable foundations, trusts and institutions within the state, and for the coordinating of their work and efforts.

§ 6. **Gifts subject to life estates.** The Trustee may accept gifts subject to directions of the donor to pay the income to individuals for life or for term of years, and if such gifts are accepted, such directions shall be binding until the expiration of such lives or terms of years, and thereafter such gifts shall be held, subject to the provisions hereof, for the charitable objects and purposes within the State of Vermont designated by the donor or in the absence of such designation, for the charitable objects and purposes herein set forth.

§ 7. **The Committee.** The Committee to select or determine, when proper, the objects and purposes to which the income or gifts for distribution in the hands of the trustee shall be applied and to determine the amounts to be distributed to such objects or purposes, respectively, hereinafter called the "Committee," shall consist of five citizens of the United States, not less than four of whom shall be residents of the State of Vermont, men or women interested in charities, and possessing a knowledge of the educational, charitable, recreational, physical, civic and moral needs of the State and its various communities, each member preferably having special knowledge of one of such needs. Any banking or financial institution adopting this Declaration of Trust after the first appointments shall have been made hereunder, shall be deemed to have accepted the Committee as then and thereafter constituted.

§ 8. **Board of appointment.** The Committee shall be constituted and appointed by a Board of Appointment consisting of the Governor of the State of Vermont; the Chief Justice of the Supreme Court of Vermont; the Commissioner of Finance of the State of Vermont, or the State Treasurer if at any time there is no Commissioner of Finance; the President of the Vermont Bankers' Association; and after the appointment of the first members of said Committee, the chairman of said Committee shall be a member of said Board of Appointment.

In making appointment of the members of the Committee, the persons upon whom such power of appointment is conferred, shall be the incumbents for the time being of the several offices specified and act solely in their individual capacity and by virtue of the power and authority herein conferred.

§ 9. **Term of office.** All members of the Committee shall hold office during a term of five years, ensuing the first day of January succeeding their respective appointments, except those first appointed, whose terms shall begin with the date of their appointment and end with the expiration of the respective periods for which they are appointed ensuing the first day of January succeeding their appointment, the first appointments to be made for terms of one, two, three, four and five years, respectively.

Each member shall hold office for the term appointed and until his successor is appointed.

§ 10. **Vacancies, how filled.** Vacancies in the Committee caused by expiration of term, death, resignation, refusal or inability to serve, or otherwise, shall be filled by the Board aforesaid. Any such appointments made upon the expiration of terms shall be for the full term of five years, and any made to fill other vacancies shall be for the unexpired term. In the event of failure of said Board to make such appointment within sixty days after written notice of the vacancy is mailed to the then Governor of the State of Vermont by the Chairman of the Committee, or the Executive Secretary, under registered mail, such appointment shall be made by the remaining members of the Committee, such appointee to serve until said Board shall have made appointment.

§ 11. **Disqualifications.** If any resident member of the Committee removes from the State of Vermont, or if any member fails without reason satisfactory to the remaining members of the Committee for three successive meetings to attend committee meetings, such member shall thereby be disqualified and be deemed to have resigned from the Committee, and upon written notice from the Chairman of the Committee, or the Executive Secretary, authorized and directed to be given by the remaining members of the Committee and mailed under registered mail to the then Governor of the State of Vermont, which notice shall be conclusive as to fact of such disqualification and resignation, a vacancy shall be created which shall be filled as hereinabove provided.

§ 12. **Organization of Committee.** The Committee shall annually organize by the election of a Chairman and such other officers as it desires, and shall provide for such other meetings and adopt such rules governing its proceedings as it deems necessary or desirable. It shall keep complete records of its proceedings, which shall be open at all reasonable times to the inspection of any duly authorized agent of the Trustee.

§ 13. **The secretary.** An Executive Secretary of the Foundation, who shall not be a member of the Committee, may be appointed by and hold office subject to the will of the Committee.

§ 14. **Salaries and expenses.** The proper expenses of the Committee, and of its members and the Secretary, including such compensation to the Secretary as shall be fixed by the Committee, shall be paid out of the income of trust funds, or funds for immediate disbursement. Members of the Committee shall serve without compensation.

§ 15. **Disbursements of funds.** Disbursements of income, or of principal when proper, shall be authorized by, and made pursuant to, vote or written order of a majority of the Committee, and certified to the Trustee, stating beneficiaries and amounts, by the Executive Secretary or Chairman and one member of the Committee from time to time designated by the Committee for that purpose.

Failure of the Committee to take action for eighteen months after written notice from the Trustee to the Chairman or Secretary that there are funds available for the purposes of the Foundation, shall empower the Board of Directors of the Trustee to apply such funds to such purposes of the trust as may be proper until such time as the Committee shall direct the application thereof, to the end that there shall be no failure to carry out the charitable purposes hereof. A vote of the Committee to postpone disbursement of such funds shall be deemed action by the Committee.

In the distribution and application of funds available for distribution hereunder, payments may be made: (a) to individuals, (b) to corporations or associations maintaining institutions for public charitable uses or purposes, (c) to corporations, committees or associations formed to distribute and apply such funds to such charitable purposes, or (d) to corporations, committees, associations or agents formed or appointed for such charitable purposes by the Committee.

The Trustee shall be fully protected in acting upon any such certificate or direction of the Committee and shall not be responsible for any act or omission of the Committee, and or of the payee of any certificate issued hereunder by the Committee.

The Committee shall not be held liable for any neglect or wrongdoing of any officer, agent or agency appointed or used by it hereunder provided reasonable care shall have been exercised in their selection.

§ 16. **Advisory committees.** The Committee may by resolution appoint Advisory Committees in such communities within the State of

Vermont as shall to it seem necessary or beneficial to advise it respecting the disbursement of funds destined for distribution in such communities, and may authorize such disbursement to be made through such local committees.

§ 17. **Annual audit.** The Trustee's receipts and disbursements on account of the Foundation shall be audited annually by an independent auditor; but an audit made under the authority of the Bank Commissioner of Vermont, or by a national bank examiner, or other public official having like powers of examination, shall be deemed a compliance with this requirement.

§ 18. **Inspection of investments and books.** The Committee shall have the right at all reasonable times, by its members or duly appointed committee or auditor, to inspect the books, vouchers, records, securities and investments of the Trustee pertaining to the Foundation; and the Trustee shall at least once each year submit to the Committee accounts of the funds of the Foundation in its trust, designating such as are available for distribution.

§ 19. **Publication of statements.** The amount of the income of the Foundation and a detailed list of the purposes for which payments have been made with the amount paid for each, and a classified statement of expenses, shall be furnished by the Committee once a year to the Governor of the State of Vermont for public inspection, and to the two newspapers published in the State of Vermont reputed to have the largest circulation, and to such other newspapers as the Committee may deem wise and proper.

§ 20. **Apportionment of expenses.** The expense of such inspections and audits, expenses of the Committee and its members and the Secretary and the compensation of the Secretary, shall be apportioned among the Trustees by the Committee as it shall deem just and equitable, having in mind the amount of trust funds held by, and income thereon received by each trustee.

§ 21. **Payments from principal.** Where there is nothing in the will or instrument of gift which makes it improper so to do, payments may be made from the principal of the Foundation for any purpose within the scope of the Foundation with the approval of four-fifths of the entire Committee as then constituted; provided that not exceeding 20 percent of the entire amount held as principal shall without consent of the donor be so used during any period of five consecutive years.

§ 22. **Public supervision.** The Committee, as well as the Attorney General of the State, shall have the right to institute proceedings in any court of competent jurisdiction to restrain, correct or recover for maladministration of the Foundation by the Trustee or its abuse of powers. The Trustee shall also have the right to apply to any such court for instructions as to its powers and duties.

§ 23. **Construction.** In so far as shall be consistent with the decision or direction of a court of competent jurisdiction, each and every provision hereof is to be regarded and construed as so far independent of every other provision that if it shall be determined that any provision is invalid, such determination shall not affect the validity of any of the remaining provisions, and the trusts hereby created shall be administered to carry out as far as possible the purposes of the Foundation in accordance with the remaining valid provisions.

The word "gift" or "donation" as used herein shall be deemed to include grant, devise or bequest, and the word "donor" to include testator.

§ 24. **Successor Trustees.** Should a successor Trustee or Trustees be for any reason appointed during the continuance of the trust hereby created, such Trustee or Trustees shall have all the powers and duties, discretionary or otherwise, herein given the Trustee, and upon the appointment and acceptance of such successor Trustee or Trustees, the trust fund shall vest in it, him or them without any further act of conveyance as if it, he or they had been the original Trustee.

§ 25. **Powers conferred upon Trustee.** In administering the funds and property of the Foundation, unless it is otherwise specifically provided in the instrument of gift, the Trustee acting through its Board of Directors shall have power in addition to any power or authority conferred by statute or other law:

(a) To take by purchase or otherwise and to hold any real estate which may be necessary or proper for the execution of the trust; to sell from time to time at public or private sale any real estate forming a part of the trust property, and to bid for and become the purchaser of any real estate sold at any public sale, and to again sell the same without being liable for any resulting loss; to make partition of any such real estate, either through legal proceedings or otherwise, and that although the Trustee may hold in some other capacity another interest in the same real estate, and to give or receive money of equality of partition; and to plot, lay out, and dedicate streets and ways;

(b) To lease any real estate at any time constituting any portion of said trust property for such terms and rentals, and with such conditions and provisions, including such agreements for renewals and for the purchase or disposal of buildings upon, or to be placed upon, any such real estate, as it may deem proper;

(c) To keep all real estate from time to time a part of said trust estate properly repaired, and insured against loss by fire and other casualties, and generally to manage any such real estate and disburse moneys for the benefit of such real estate as a prudent owner would do;

(d) To change and vary from time to time any investment of personal property, and for this or any other purpose of the trust to sell any investment at public or private sale or broker's board, with the same right to purchase at public sale and to resell without liability for loss as in the case of real estate;

(e) To execute and deliver any proxies, powers of attorney, contracts, assignments, deeds and other instruments as it shall deem necessary or proper in the administration of the trust property;

(f) To determine whether money or other property coming into its possession shall be treated as principal or income, or partly one and partly the other, and to charge and apportion expenses and losses to principal or income as it may deem just and equitable; and to make good any losses of principal or premiums paid for securities out of the income over such periods of time as it may deem advisable;

(g) To take and retain from the gross income received or derived from the trust property, a reasonable compensation for its services as Trustee;

(h) To use its discretion in all matters relating to taxation, and to protect the trust and all property of the trust and the Trustee's interest thereto from attack of any kind, and to uphold the validity of all gifts to it, testamentary or otherwise, intended for the Vermont Foundation;

(i) To consent to the extension, refunding or renewal of any securities held hereunder, and to the extension or renewal of any mortgage or lien securing the same;

(j) To make or join in any plan or plans of reorganization or of readjustment in respect of any corporation of which any of the shares of stock, bonds or other securities or obligations at any time constitute part of the principal of the fund, and to accept and hold any property or new securities in exchange for or in place of any securities surrendered in accordance with any such plan in the place of the securities so surrendered;

(k) To refrain, in its discretion, from setting aside any part of the income received by it from securities taken or purchased as part of said fund at a premium as a sinking fund to retire or amortize such premium;

(l) To vote upon all stocks held by it, to unite with other owners of the securities of any corporation in carrying out any plan for the reorganization thereof, to exchange the securities of any corporation for others issued by the same or by any other corporation upon such terms as said Trustee shall deem proper; to assent to the consolidation or merger of any corporation whose securities are held by it with any other corporation, to the lease by such corporation of its property or any portion thereof to any other corporation, or to the lease by any other corporation of its property to such corporation, and upon any such consolidation, merger, lease or similar arrangement to exchange the securities held by the Trustee for other securities issued in substitution therefor; to pay all such assessments, expenses and sums of money as it may deem expedient for the protection of the interest of the fund as holder of the stocks, bonds, or other securities of any corporation or company;

(m) The Trustee, unless otherwise provided by the donor, may retain as an investment any stock, bond or other property given or bequeathed to it hereunder as long as it deems advisable without being liable for such retention;

(n) The Trustee may at any time resign and surrender property held by it to such of the other Trustees as the resigning Trustee may, with the consent of the Trustee thus desig-

nated, designate and the Committee approve and shall there-
upon be discharged and released from its obligations under
any gift, grant, devise or bequest of such property and hereunder;

(o) The Trustee at its option may hold and manage any gift as a
separate fund or may commingle it with any other fund or
funds hereunder for purposes of investment and management, and if commingled with any other fund or funds, the
principal or income of such gift shall thereafter be considered to be that proportion of the principal or income of the
combined fund as the amount of such gift shall bear to the
amount of such combined fund.

(p) The Trustee shall exercise any of the foregoing powers respecting the management of the property and investments
of the Foundation in the same manner and through such
officers and committees as its by-laws shall from time to
time provide for the management of other trust estates;

(q) Any corporation which shall be the successor to or shall acquire the property and assets of the Trustee, whether by
merger, consolidation or otherwise, shall forthwith be and
become Trustee hereunder with all the rights, power and
duties vested in the predecessor Trustee by the terms hereof.
In no event shall any person purchasing property from or
making any payment to the Trustee be obligated to make
inquiry into the propriety of the action of the Trustee, or be
concerned with the application of payments made to the
Trustee.

§ 26. **Amendment.** By resolution adopted by affirmative vote
of four-fifths of the Committee and with the written approval of the
then Chief Justice of the Supreme Court of Vermont, the methods of
distributing income and other details of administration may from time
to time be changed, the number of the members of the Committee may
be increased or reduced and the method of appointment of its members
may be changed, or any defect or omission herein be supplied or amendment made which said Committee may, with the approval of the Chief
Justice, then deem advisable to carry out the purposes of this trust
properly and effectively; but no such change shall in any way alter or
abridge the public charitable objects and purposes of the trust.

Phraseology Employed in Wills Using the Vermont Foundation

"I give, devise and bequeath to .... (here name any Bank or Trust Company which is a Trustee of The Vermont Foundation), IN TRUST, for the uses and purposes and upon the terms contained in the Resolution and Declaration of Trust creating The Vermont Foundation, heretofore adopted by the Board of Directors of said .... (repeat the name of the Trustee), all of which Resolution and Declaration is hereby incorporated herein; (if the donor wishes to indicate the precise charitable purposes for which he wishes his gift employed, the following clause may be added), providing, however, that I desire that the net income thereof be devoted to the support of ...."

In cases of trust deeds, the first line of the above form should read: "I give, assign and set over," etc.

Funds may be set up in The Vermont Foundation at once (by living trusts), or at the death of the donor (by will), or after the termination of "life uses."

Professional legal advice, of course, should be utilized in the drafting of any will or deed of trust.

————

Prepared for the Commission by its Committee on Vermont Community Trusts.

CLARENCE P. COWLES,
Chairman,
WILLIAM F. FRAZIER,
A. J. HOLDEN,
HAROLD MASON,
EDMUND C. MOWER,
JOHN G. SARGENT,
LEVI P. SMITH.

XVII

RURAL GOVERNMENT

For the purposes of local government, the State of Vermont is divided into fourteen counties, eight cities, and two hundred and forty-three towns, three of which—Averill, Ferdinand and Lewis—are unorganized and have no representation in the Legislature. The cities in Vermont are Vergennes, Burlington, Rutland, Montpelier, Barre, St. Albans, Newport and Winooski. Cities in Vermont operate under special charters but the general form of government is similar except in the case of St. Albans which operates under the City Manager plan. In each instance there is a mayor and a council, the council varying in size from two in St. Albans to twelve in Burlington. In addition to these municipal units which are recognized in the statute law, there are in the state sixty-seven villages and several fire districts which have been created for the purpose of providing those municipal services which were not demanded by the residents of the countryside.

To understand the extent to which local government in Vermont is a rural problem one has only to consider that of the two hundred and fifty-one cities and towns in the state, one hundred and ninety-one have less than 1,500 inhabitants.

The County

Although historically the Vermont county has had other functions to perform, today it is a unit of little importance other than for the administration of justice. Practically all county activities rotate about the court house and the jail.

The most important elective officers are the side judges, who are charged with the care of county property, the state's attorney who prosecutes all offenses committed within his jurisdiction and the sheriff who is the custodian of the jail and who has the right to appoint deputies. The high bailiff is an unimportant elective officer who may serve writs when the sheriff is incompetent to serve. The county clerk, the county treasurer, and the county auditor are appointed by the judges of the court.

In eight of the counties, there is a single probate district which bears the name of the county while six of the counties are divided into two districts each. The judges of probate are elected by the free men of their respective districts.

The county is the unit for electing to the senate and in the case of Washington County it has been made a unit for the establishment of a tuberculosis hospital. The assistant judges and the county clerk form a board of jury commissioners to prepare lists of names for jury service within the county. The justices of the peace who are chosen in towns at the general election have jurisdiction throughout their respective counties.

The Town

Whereas the county is an unimportant unit in the field of local government in Vermont, the town is an exceedingly important one. Historically, the maintenance of roads and bridges, the relief of the poor, the establishment of schools, and the assessing and collecting of taxes to carry out these activities, have been delegated to the town by the state and, although with the passing of the years, many responsibilities have been transferred to the state, the town is still the corner stone of local government.

The town meeting, which may be termed the local legislature, is held annually on the first Tuesday of March and all persons have the right to vote who are twenty-one years of age, who have taken the freeman's oath and whose lists, including polls, have been taken in the town at the annual assessment preceding a town meeting and whose taxes were paid prior to the 15th day of February preceding such town meeting. Those who have attained the age of twenty-one years subsequent to the last annual assessment or who are exempt from taxation for any cause are also entitled to vote.

The principal officers in a town are the moderator, clerk, selectmen, treasurer, listers, and auditors, all of of whom are elected. Other elective officers are the overseer of the poor, road commissioner, collector of taxes, trustee of public money, constable, an agent to prosecute and defend suits and one or more grand jurors. Fenceviewers, poundkeepers, inspectors of lumber, shingles and wood, and weighers of coal are appointed by the selectmen. In thirty-one Vermont towns the selectmen act as overseers of the poor.

The selectmen are, in fact, the permanent governing board who are responsible for the general supervision of the affairs of the town, and must cause the duties required of towns and town school districts and not committed to the care of any particular officer, to be duly executed.

The listers are charged with the important responsibility of appraising the real and personal property in the towns of Vermont. The grand list is based upon these appraisals and is thus defined: "One percent of the appraised value of the real estate taxable to a person shall be added to the list of his personal estate; and the sum so obtained, with the amount of his taxable poll, if any, shall constitute his grand list."[1]

The board of civil authority consists of the town clerk, the selectmen and the justices of the peace. Their duties consist in preparing the check list and counting the ballots after the polls are closed. With the listers, they form a board for the abatement of town, and town school district taxes.

Besides functioning as a local government area, the town plays an important part in state affairs as a result of the fact that it is the election unit for freemen's meeting which is held biennially on the first Tuesday following the first Monday of November.[2] It is in this November meeting that justices of the peace, representatives to the General Assembly, county and state officers, representatives to Congress, and United States senators and presidential electors are chosen.

The Village

It is provided by law that upon petition of a majority of the voters in town meeting residing in a village containing thirty or more houses, the selectmen shall establish the bounds of such village which shall become thereby a municipal corporation.[3]

Generally speaking the time of holding regular meetings and the officers to be elected are fixed by charter, but in the absence of such legislation the officers consist of five trustees, a clerk, a treasurer and a collector of taxes.

An incorporated village may enact such by-laws as are expedient, not inconsistent with law, particularly such as relate to streets, sidewalks, public lighting, erection and regulation of buildings and public

[1] General Laws of Vermont, Sec. 779.
[2] Beginning in A. D., 1914 (Constitution of Vermont, Sec. 35).
[3] General Laws of Vermont, Sec. 4104.

safety generally. The trustees of a village, incorporated under general or special law, are charged with the responsibility of seeing that the by-laws are executed, and they must perform the duties legally enjoined upon them by such corporation.

Villages may, at a meeting legally warned for that purpose, vote a tax upon the polls and taxable estate therein, for the lawful purposes of the corporation. In such an event the trustees make out and deliver to the collector a tax bill, with a warrant for its collection and the collector is clothed with the same powers to collect such tax bill as is a collector of town taxes.

Fire Districts

Fire districts may be established for the purpose of promoting public safety upon the application in writing of twenty or more free-holders of a town who are residents in the proposed district. The area of such a unit must not exceed two square miles and the bound-aries of it are to be determined by the selectmen. Although intended primarily as a unit for fire protection, the fire district is clothed with the power of eminent domain and may be authorized to construct sewers and sidewalks and to sprinkle and oil streets.[4]

Manager Form of Government

Springfield, St. Johnsbury, Windsor and Rockingham (including Bellows Falls) are now operating under the Enabling Act which author-izes towns and villages to employ managers who are charged with the administrative work of the municipal corporation. The city of St. Albans employes a manager under authority of its charter. In a town the manager is chosen by the selectmen and in an incorporated village, by the trustees, and for cause he may be removed from office by the same officers who appointed him. He is responsible for the maintenance of parks and playgrounds, for the sprinkling of streets and highways, has charge of the system of sewers and drainage and performs the duties now conferred by law on the road commissioners.

He has charge of the fire and police departments, performs all duties now conferred by law upon the overseer of the poor, is the general purchasing agent for the town or village, has charge of all the public buildings and all the repairs thereon and supervises all building

4 General Laws of Vermont, Chapter 180.

done by the town or town school district unless otherwise specially voted. He has to furnish a bond and his pay is fixed by the selectmen of the town or the trustees of the incorporated village unless otherwise specifically voted by the municipality.

The manager is not, however, permitted to call special or annual town meetings, prepare tax bills, draw orders, lay out highways, establish and lay out parks, make assessments nor award damages. He cannot act as a member of the Board of Civil Authority nor make appointments to fill vacancies which the selectmen are now authorized by law to fill. The schools and the library are in no way under the control of the manager.

A town or incorporated village that has adopted the Municipal Manager form of government may reject the same by a majority vote of the legal voters present and voting at an annual meeting provided, however, that a proper article is inserted in the warning for such meeting. Ludlow adopted the manager plan in 1926, but abandoned it after a short trial. Brattleboro, the last Vermont community to try this form of government, rejected it in the 1931 March meeting.

Finance

Taxes are levied on the taxable polls of an incorporated village, an incorporated school district, a city, town or county, according to varying needs. In incorporated towns and villages, the tax is determined and levied by the voters. In cities the tax is laid by the Board of Aldermen or City Council according to the charter. If the county tax is less than 2 percent, the assistant judges lay it; if more than 2 percent the General Asembly lays it Such a tax is collected as are other taxes and is paid to the county treasurer on the order of the selectmen of towns and the mayors of cities. The state may, of course, impose a tax upon polls and property within its limits and it also taxes, through the office of the State Commissioner, transportation companies, public utilities, and various other types of corporations.

It is provided by statute that "A municipal corporation shall not incur an indebtedness for public improvement which, with the previously contracted indebtedness, shall in the aggregate exceed ten times the amount of the last grand list of such municipal corporation."[5]

[5] General Laws of Vermont, Sec. 4082.

In 1915, the General Assembly passed an act providing for the establishment of a uniform system of accounting in towns and villages and stipulated that the warning for each town and village meeting in towns and villages that have not adopted the system shall on petition of ten legal voters contain an article to see if the town or village will vote to install the uniform system of public accounting. All blanks, schedules and books of account, necessary to install the system may be had at cost from the State Purchasing Agent.[6]

On January 1, 1927, out of 203 cities and towns which reported, sixty-one stated that their respective towns had adopted the system recommended and ninety-seven reported the adoption of the system as a whole or in some modified form. Only two town clerks reported that the system had not worked satisfactorily.[7] The question is agitated in many town meetings each year and gradually the number is being increased.

Defects and Remedies

In the scheme of local government, as it now exists in rural Vermont there are several shortcomings some of which are truly serious. One defect lies in the grotesque distribution of county areas. Perhaps the most notorious example of this is to be found in Addison County, most of which lies in the watershed of the Champlain Valley, while one town, Granville, lies on the east side of the mountain range and ought, by any rule of logic, to belong to Orange or to Windsor County. This means that litigants in the White River Valley have to go to court in Middle-bury to settle their differences. It is significant that in economic and social considerations which would call ordinarily for a districting of the state along county lines this unit is almost always disregarded—a fact in itself which ought to show the need of new alignments. A constitutional amendment would be necessary, however, in order to correct the situation.

A second defect lies in the field of taxation. One of the worst situations comes from the inequalities of property appraisals. The law states that property shall be placed in the tax list at its true money value. This, however, is rarely done as the local listers are prone to appraise property below its true value in order to evade a state tax when such a levy is made, an important item when, as in 1930, there

---

[6] General Laws of Vermont, Sec. 3996.
[7] Proceedings of the Second Institute of Municipal Affairs, pp. 8-13.

was a state tax of 22½ cents on a dollar of the grand list. In the absence of an equalizing board it would seem that all direct state taxes should if possible be abolished. This would leave the taxing of real estate and personal property exclusively to the counties, towns and school districts for the support of these governmental areas. Once the state tax is done way with, inequalities in listing, as between the towns in the state, become of no importance.[8]

Not only is there a lack of justice in appraisals as between different communities in the state, but inequity exists as between individuals in a particular community. Every quadrennial appraisal results in the penalizing of many who have been prompted by civic pride to make improvements upon their premises and it is common knowledge that a new house usually goes into the list at a figure entirely out of proportion to the appraisal of one which may have been listed for a quarter of a century with no regard to changing realty values. This situation can be corrected only by mobilizing public opinion against such rank violation of the basic principle that *a just tax system presupposes an equal distribution of the financial burden over the various properties located in each taxing unit* and a demand as well for listers who are better trained in the difficult task of appraising. It is entirely possible that it will be found necessary to enlarge the taxing unit in order to secure the trained officials.

To the farmer the whole tax question is a matter of tremendous import. Naturally he is interested in the amount of the gasoline tax and the size of the capitation tax; he cannot disregard such matters as exemption, the tax rate upon the savings deposits and public utilities. His great concern, however, is regarding the taxation of securities. The farmer cannot pass the tax burden to the consumer of his products as is done by the middlemen who distribute those products. In other words, he sells his produce and buys his own necessities at prices entirely beyond his control. This situation is due of course to the fact that overemphasis is placed upon tangible property as an indication of ability to pay taxes, and there are many students of the question who are convinced that intangibles should be taxed by income rather than by appraisal and that the system should be administered through the office of the Commissioner of Taxes.

A third shortcoming is to be found in the law of municipal indebtedness in Vermont. As has been pointed out, any municipal cor-

[8] See report of the Vermont State Tax Commission, pp. 43-45.

poration can issue bonds for a period of twenty years for a public improvement, but there is no distinction made between a water system which would last for forty years and a tar sidewalk which might have to be replaced within a ten-year period. Such disregard for the basic principle in public finance that *bonds should not be issued for a period longer than the life of the improvement* cannot be justified.

A municipality should not be permitted to borrow money for current expenses for minor capital outlays or for the purpose of meeting any charge that is intended to be met out of revenues. Of course, this does not apply to borrowings which are often necessary in anticipation of taxes. The only real exception would come in the case of an emergency in which the health or safety of the people might be involved necessitating such large sums of money as to justify long-term borrowing. Refunding has been all too common and scores of rural communities are staggering under old debts which ought to have been retired on the serial plan.

To be truly effective a municipal debt statute must be based upon the existence of strict and unequivocal budgetary provisions and practices. It should not be limited to bonds, not even to borrowing, but should cover all forms and descriptions of debt. It is debt in general that needs to be dealt with, not merely certain kinds of debt, and no avenue of escape should be provided whereby the obligations of a municipal debt statute can be evaded.

Municipal reports do not reflect, in many instances, a true financial picture and it is to be regretted that municipal accounts are not more frequently audited by certified public accountants. One can hardly imagine an up-to-date business corporation being content with an audit made by citizens picked at random from the community and it is difficult to defend such practice in the case of municipal corporations.

It should be remembered also that any departure from proper practice on the part of one municipality not only affects unfavorably its own credit, but it has a depressing effect on the credit standing of other municipal corporations, not infrequently involving the state itself. Consequently one of the greatest needs is provision in the Statutes for some centralized agency clothed with power to supervise and regulate certain features and to advise on others in connection with municipal debt.

Perhaps the most serious need in Vermont is the consolidation of municipal units. The setting up of villages within towns, while ac-

companied by many advantages, has also been attended by some very
unfortunate developments. All too frequently village and town have
been jealous of each other with the result that a geographical area
which should have a social and economic solidarity has been divided
against itself. An example of this is where in one town meeting the
farming population voted down a proposal to purchase fire fighting
apparatus with the slogan "Let the village buy it, a village fire means
nothing to us." Apparently, there was no appreciation of the fact
that when a fire destroyed property to the extent of $100,000 the cost
of government, remaining stable, would have to be distributed over the
remaining property in the town.

In 1927, Brattleboro made a sweeping consolidation which did away
with the village of Brattleboro, the Brattleboro School District, and
the West Brattleboro Fire District and left a single municipal corporation, the town of Brattleboro, in which the administrative work was
placed in the hands of a municipal manager until the 1931 March meeting when the manager system was abandoned. This experiment in
consolidation is being watched with interest by other Vermont communities and it is not unlikely that the next few years will see the
unification of many areas.

There is need, however, of another type of consolidation, or at
least a grouping of political units, which will make for efficiency and
satisfaction in rural living. Present-day civilizaton demands for farm
families not only physical and moral safeguards, but reasonable cultural opportunities as well and the size of the local government unit
in Vermont today makes this atmosphere impossible. There are two
ways in which the situation can be corrected.

One lies through the establishment of what may be termed "rural
municipalities" in which the government of a town like Waterbury, for
instance, would be so extended as to include the governmental functions
in several of the outlying towns, including a minimum population of
5,000 people with, perhaps, the manager form of government. As a
single family which cannot support a school can with forty-nine other
families maintain an excellent institution, so fifty families which find
it impossible to maintain a hospital or fire department can with 950
other units maintain adequate facilities for public health and safety.

An alternative would be to authorize by law the grouping of small
towns so that they might avail themselves of the advantages of a
municipal manager or in some other way eliminate the duplication of

effort and the crushing expense which characterize the attempt of too few people to support the institutions which are essential to modern standards of living. Such a plan would mean simply the extension of the "Union superintendent" idea in education so as to include the other activities of local government.

The suggestion in the preceding paragraph raises a question regarding size as a prerequisite to the successful operation of the manager form of government.

There is probably no doubt that most of the cities in Vermont could, if they desired, operate very successfully under the municipal manager plan. There is but little question that its adoption would be feasible in the larger towns of the state, although it must be remembered that the size of the grand list is a more important factor than population. It is exceedingly doubtful whether the many places having from 1,500 to 2,000 inhabitants would find it to their advantage to employ the type of man with whom they would be satisfied; and to argue the municipal manager form of government in the 191 towns in Vermont which have less than 1,500 inhabitants, would be akin to installing a large scale production machine in a one-man shop.

Prepared for the Commission by K. R. B. Flint, Professor of Political Science and Director of the Bureau of Municipal Affairs, Norwich University.

XVIII

CITIZENSHIP

It seems apparent that any satisfactory plan for the future citizenship of this state must aim to secure for this and succeeding generations a body-politic which is capable and willing to work intelligently and cooperatively to promote civic well-being and which exists under conditions suitable for the attainment of that end.

Survey in Lincoln and Charlotte

The citizens of today will, in general, be the parents of the citizens of tomorrow and will in considerable measure determine the characteristics of succeeding generations. Hence, any acceptable plan, if it is to have serious value, must have its foundations resting firmly upon facts definitely established, or readily demonstrable, pertaining to the lives of this generation.

In an effort to establish a factual basis for such a plan, the citizenship characteristics of the people living in the towns of Lincoln and Charlotte have been carefully studied. These two towns were selected because it was obviously impracticable with the limited means available to cover all of the towns in the state and because these towns seemed to be a fair sample of rural Vermont.

Lincoln is distant from the main highways of travel and from any large urban influence; her home-builders are, in general, old Vermont stock; the average wealth of her people is relatively low. Charlotte is on main highways of travel and is relatively near the largest urban community in the state; she has a backbone of old Vermont stock, but a considerable number of her homes are occupied by people who have recently come into the state from other states of the Union or from foreign states; the average wealth of her people is relatively high.

Procedure. Investigators were sent into these towns, who, by use of all available records and by personal interview, collected the necessary data. The characteristics considered included age, wealth, sex, marriage, parenthood, type of citizenship, size of family, national stock,

education, religion, occupation, taxes, and income. These characteristics were studied objectively in their relation to the public record of
each individual in an effort to determine what effect, if any, they had
had upon party regularity, the percentage of eligible voters who voted,
the inclination of the people to seek or hold public office, and the
amount of other public service rendered. The records used were the
available check lists for the direct primaries and the general elections of
1924, 1926, and 1928; the grand lists for the years, 1924-1929; and the
records of surveys made in Lincoln and Charlotte by the Department
of Agricultural Economics of the Agricultural Experiment Station.

Voting and Office-holding. The results obtained which deal with
voting and office-holding are significant (see table on page 331). They
show that men are 26 percent more likely to vote and 62 percent more
likely to hold office than women; that married persons are 3 percent
more likely to vote and 6 percent more likely to hold office than persons
who have not been married; that persons forty-six years of age or
older are 11 percent more likely to vote and 181 percent more likely
to hold office than persons thirty-one to forty-five years of age; that
persons forty-six years of age or older are 57 percent more likely to
vote and 4,688 percent more likely to hold office than persons twenty-
one to thirty years of age; that persons thirty-one to forty-five years of
age are 42 percent more likely to vote and 1,606 percent more likely to
hold office than persons twenty-one to thirty years of age; that persons
with children are 7 percent more likely to vote and 136 percent more
likely to hold office than persons without children; that natural-born
citizens of the United States vote 26 percent more frequently than
foreign-born citizens; that foreign born citizens do not hold any public
offices; that persons who have 0-2 brothers and sisters are 16 percent
more likely to vote and 38 percent more likely to hold office than
persons who have a greater number of brothers and sisters; that persons of pure English or Irish stock are 10 percent more likely to vote
and 245 percent more likely to hold office than persons of other stocks;
that persons of pure English stock are 38 percent more likely to vote
and 2,932 percent more likely to hold office than French-Canadians;
that persons of pure English stock are 0.17 percent less likely to vote
and 107 percent more likely to hold office than persons of pure Irish
stock; that persons of pure Irish stock are 38 percent more likely to
vote and 1,364 percent more likely to hold office than French-Canadians;

VOTING AND OFFICE-HOLDING BY GROUPS

Group	No. of persons	Percentage voting	Percentage of available time in public office
Male	730	64.0	8.29
Female	638	50.9	1.15
Married	1,123	59.2	8.23
Unmarried	244	57.3	1.12
21-30 Years of Age	259	40.4	0.17
31-45 Years of Age	443	57.3	2.90
46 Years of Age or More	663	63.5	8.14
With Children	962	59.2	9.69
Without Children	403	55.1	4.11
Natural Born Citizens	1,281	58.4	6.84
Foreign Born Citizens	47	46.3	0.00
0-2 Brothers and Sisters	544	63.8	8.54
3 or More Brothers and Sisters	809	54.8	6.19
Pure English or Irish Stock	556	60.0	12.34
Other Stocks	804	54.4	3.58
0-8 Grade Education	927	55.3	5.16
More than 8 Grade Education	438	63.4	10.73
Protestant	912	62.5	8.38
Catholic	331	48.1	0.97
No Religion	118	46.7	7.65
Farmer	408	68.9	8.53
Housewife	524	51.8	0.05
Laborer	163	49.1	2.30
Other Occupations	273	58.3	10.26
Individual Wealth Above Average	452	66.9	11.18
Individual Wealth Below Average	910	52.8	2.82
Individual Taxes Above Average	493	68.2	11.08
Individual Taxes Below Average	865	51.4	2.37
Individual Income Above Average	611	61.5	8.69
Individual Income Below Average	749	54.8	4.66

that persons who have more than an eighth-grade education are 15 percent more likely to vote and 108 percent more likely to hold office than persons who have a smaller amount of formal education; that Protestants are 30 percent more likely to vote and 764 percent more likely to hold office than Catholics; that Protestants are 34 percent more likely to vote and 10 percent more likely to hold office than persons who profess to have no religion and who insist that they have no preference as between Protestantism and Catholicism; that Catholics are 3 percent more likely to vote than persons who have no religion, but the latter are 689 percent more likely to hold office than Catholics; that farmers are 33 percent more likely to vote and 16,960 percent more likely to hold office than housewives; that housewives are 5 percent more likely to vote and 98 percent less likely to hold office than laborers; that laborers are 16 percent less likely to vote and 78 percent less likely to hold office than those included in all remaining occupations; that merchants are 9 percent more likely to vote and 631 percent more likely to hold office than farmers; that persons whose individual wealth is above the average ($1,770) are 27 percent more likely to vote and 293 percent more likely to hold office than those whose individual wealth is below the average; that persons whose individual taxes are above the average ($15.55) are 33 percent more likely to vote and 368 percent more likely to hold office than those whose individual taxes are below the average; and that persons whose individual income is above the average ($444) are 12 percent more likely to vote and 86 percent more likely to hold office than those whose individual income is below the average.

By referring to the chart on page 333, it will be observed that those groups whose voting percentages are above 60 are: (1) men, (2) persons forty-six years of age or older, (3) persons having less than three brothers and sisters, (4) persons having more than an eighth-grade education, (5) Protestants, (6) farmers, and (7) those above the averages in wealth, taxes, and income. Those groups whose voting percentages are below 50 are: (1) persons 21-30 years of age, (2) foreign-born citizens, (3) Catholics, (4) those having no religion, and (5) laborers. It should be added, perhaps, that some groups which are not shown separately as such on this chart, because their numbers are too small, have voting percentages above 60. Included in these groups are: (1) those of pure Irish stock, (2) merchants, (3) nursery men, and (4) mill owners or manufacturers.

It is somewhat difficult to explain why those 21-30 years of age should have such an exceedingly low voting percentage. One might expect them to be fighting for principles—voting for ideals. Instead, they appear to be indifferent. Possibly, this situation is due to a tendency on the part of their elders to monopolize control of public offices and public affairs generally. Possibly, the greater experience of those who are older in the control of public affairs has developed in them an interest in voting which the younger generation has not had an opportunity to attain. It may be that the average level of intelligence of the younger generation is lower than that of the older groups due to the rearing of larger families among those of lower intelligence. It is undoubtedly true that government has become more complex than it was thirty years ago and it may be, and probably is, true that we have not given those who are included in this younger generation an

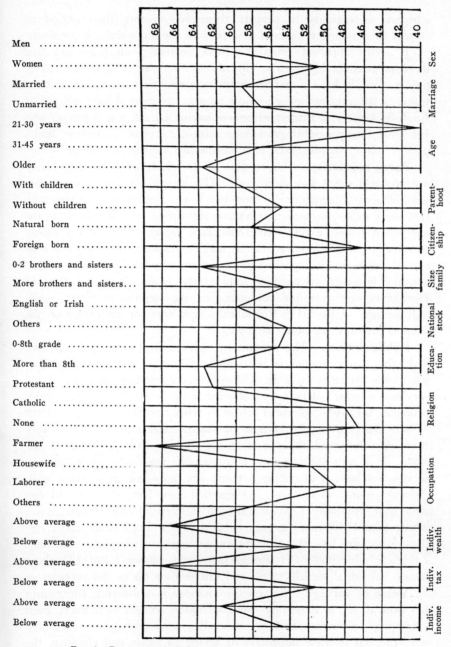

Fig. 1. Percentage of eligible voters in two towns who voted, 1924-6-8

adequate opportunity to prepare themselves during their period of formal education development to cope with the more difficult problem.

It seems apparent from the facts presented on page 331 that there is considerably greater probability that one will be elected to public office, if he is a married man forty-six years of age or older, a father, a natural-born citizen whose parents are natural-born citizens of English ancestry, a Protestant or one having no religion, a person who has more than an eighth-grade education, a merchant or farmer, and a person whose wealth, taxes, and income are above the average.

Party regularity. The results of the study of party regularity are probably much less significant. The Republican party is so overwhelmingly in the majority in these two towns and in the state generally that there exists no particular motive for voting for candidates on the opposition ticket, except that Democrats, being otherwise, in effect, practically disfranchised so far as state or national elections are concerned, might find it expedient to vote in the Republican primary. This appears, however, to be done only rarely. Only eleven of the 155 Democrats ever vote for candidates on the Republican ticket, while only seventy of the 1,135 Republicans ever vote for candidates on the Democratic ticket in these two towns.

Public service. The amount of data collected on jury service and other public service is relatively small and, for that reason, they may not be seriously valuable. Moreover, some of those who performed service for which data were collected were selected for that service primarily because of physical fitness to render army service during the World War rather than because of any peculiar knowledge or ability they may have had to cope with the normal civic problems of the state. It is interesting to note, however, that practically all of the jury service has been rendered by persons who now fall into certain well-defined groups. They are: (1) married men forty-six years of age who have children; (2) natural-born citizens of the United States whose parents are natural-born citizens of the English ancestry; (3) those who have less than six brothers and sisters; (4) those who have 7-8-grade education; (5) Protestants; (6) farmers, and (7) those whose individual wealth, taxes, and incomes are above the average.

Value of survey. The specific purpose in collecting these data has been to try to determine what attributes seemed to promote good citizenship and what attributes seemed to accompany poor citizenship with the end in view ultimately of trying to locate and eliminate the evils which tend to hamper development of good citizenship. In this process, it has seemed necessary to measure good citizenship in terms of the civic activities of the people. It has been assumed that citizenship of high quality will normally find expression in civic activities.

On the whole, the means employed seem to be amply justified by the results obtained. It must be pointed out, however, that these results cannot be taken as final without further analysis. For instance, it would be ridiculous to class women as undesirable citizens simply because they do not vote, hold office, or render service with a high degree of frequency. Indeed, it may be that our civic activities will have to be carried on without a great deal of direct control by women, but they will, nevertheless, continue to be considered a highly desirable portion of the population. On the other hand, it is probable that the comparisons here drawn are, in some considerable measure, unfair to women because it was only recently that they acquired the privilege to vote and hold office and it may be that they do not yet adequately understand the problems involved. Moreover, their indirect influence for good is, doubtless, highly important.

Likewise, those who are between the ages of twenty-one and thirty-one years are a highly important part of the population in spite of the fact that they do not seem to be shouldering their civic responsibilities as they should. The next problem is to find out what the causes of the deficiency are and to apply the necessary corrective. Is it low intelligence? Is it lack of proper education? Is it lack of opportunity? There may be any number of causes, but it is probable that not all of them apply in any one given case. Further research will be necessary to locate specific causes of deficiency. In the meantime, remedies which can do no harm and which may do a great deal of good can and should be applied to correct deficiencies wherever they occur.

Probably the most serious defect of our survey is that intelligence test ratings have not been secured and made part of the record for each individual. It has seemed unwise even to attempt to secure such ratings for the adult population and, although the data that would be thus secured are vital, it has seemed expedient to wait until some later time to attempt to make use of intelligence tests.

Plans for Future Citizenship of the State

Surveys to be made. As a preparation for future surveys, certain preliminary records, dealing with the children in all elementary

and secondary schools in the state, should be systematically collected,
tabulated, and kept in a central office to be created by law or in some
existing office which shall be authorized by law to render this service.
These should include intelligence ratings and final standing in school
for each child.   In order to insure greater accuracy and uniformity in
the administration of intelligence testing, this work should be done by
persons of recognized ability operating from the central office.   There
should be at least three intelligence test ratings made for each child.
The interval between tests should be prescribed in law.   It is important
that there be at least two tests made for each child before he reaches
the end of his compulsory education period.

Education—in elementary schools.   In the meantime, there
should be much greater emphasis placed on instruction in the schools
which prepares directly for the solution of social problems.   In the
lower grades, the children are adapting themselves to meet the basic requirements of social existence, but not later than the eighth grade, they
should be required to take a course in which they are taught by highly
skilled teachers the basic principles of social conduct.   To some extent, this problem has been met by courses in social civics, but it is
probably true that the vast majority of those who are now teaching
eighth-grade work in the schools of the state have had little or no formal
training in the underlying principles governing social problems.   It is
undoubtedly true that a considerably smaller percentage of them have
had formal training in presenting this subject-matter to eighth-grade
minds.   It is sometimes assumed that, if one knows Latin or history,
he is capable of teaching civics or government or economics or other
social sciences.   We would not think it wise to allow a man to drive
an automobile simply because he knew how to drive a horse or a motor-
cycle and we should certainly not allow our children to be taught
the nature of civic problems by teachers who have not at some time
given tangible evidence that they have a definite amount of knowledge
of the institutions and underlying principles involved.   No attempt is
being made to belittle training in other fields of knowledge.   They undoubtedly are important, but the political problems of the future are
much more likely to be met wisely and efficiently, if the children of
today are given specific training which will prepare them to solve those
problems when the need arises.   It may be contended that this is mere
fancy—that such a need does not exist.   It need only be pointed out to
the skeptic that there is serious evidence in the world today that popular

government is breaking down. Training of our people in the problems of government is probably the best insurance we can get that they will guide the ship of state wisely through any crises which may arise.

Education—in secondary schools. In the high schools, preferably in the senior year, each child should be required to take a course in civics lasting throughout the year, taught by teachers of recognized ability and specialized training, dealing with the problems of American government. The institutions should be studied, of course, but it is tremendously more important, for instance, that the child know why we have justices of the peace than it is that he know the number of such justices or the salaries which they are paid. It is more important that the child know why we have separation of powers than it is that he know that there are three branches of government organized in certain ways. It is more important that he know why we have a governor than that he know the legal qualifications for the office of governor or the specific routine of that office. Civics teaching, as it now exists, is in a great many cases, and probably in the great majority of cases, simply a process of shoveling out facts which are forgotten as soon as the required examinations have been passed. Facts must, of course, be taught, but, if their relation to social existence be definitely fixed in the mind of the child, there is a considerably greater probability that they will be retained for future use. Interest in government is probably not going to be created by compelling a child to memorize the facts contained in a civics textbook. It must be made a vital part of the life which the child is living and is going to live.

Adult education. Adult education, dealing with the problems of citizenship, is also exceedingly important, though probably somewhat more difficult to administer in a comprehensive way. Either the Commissioner of Education should be authorized by law to organize classes in various communities in the state to receive instruction from teachers drawn from the various colleges in the state and paid at state expense or some other method of accomplishing this purpose should be provided.

Citizenship training school. The state has no more important problem than that of providing specialized education for the possible future leaders in its civic activities. There is serious evidence throughout the country that the importance of this problem is being realized. Syracuse University has established its School of Citizenship; Yale has its Institute of Human Relations; Princeton is providing specialized training for candidates for the foreign service. At the recent (December 29-31, 1930) meeting of the American Political Science Association at Cleveland, the need for specially-trained men and women in public office was repeatedly emphasized as one of the most important in America today.

To accomplish this end, some new institution should be created either entirely separate from all collegiate institutions in the state or as an integral part of some existing college or university. It would be preferable to have it separate from all existing institutions, as it would thus be more free to mold its own course and as it would be more nearly possible in this way to develop a high degree of community of interest among those selected to carry on its work, either as teachers or as students. However, it is probably impracticable and it might even be inexpedient to embark on such an experiment at this time, as new machinery will have to be developed and new traditions established.

The alternative method would require the erection of new dormitories and a new class-room building together with the necessary appurtenances for carrying on effectively the work of this unit of instruction, including offices, a library, a dining room, a gymnasium with a swimming pool, tennis courts, etc., on the grounds of some existing institution. The instructional staff should be the best that can be obtained. It should include only persons of high intellectual standards who are good teachers and who insist upon a high standard of acccomplishment by the pupils whom they teach. The instruction methods must be such as to allow a high development of individual initiative. The students must be encouraged to think for themselves. The field of instruction should include the social sciences, *i.e.,* economics, history, philosophy, political science, psychology, sociology, and eugenics, and physical education. There should be opportunity for election in the parent institution of courses in agriculture, home economics, natural science, and teaching methods. The students should be selected in definite numbers, approximately twenty-five of each sex, from the best in the secondary schools in the state each year by a board created by law for this purpose. The standards used in this selection should include educational accomplishment, intelligence test rating, personality, leadership, character, and physical fitness. Educational accomplishment should be determined on the basis of uniform examinations given to the members of the senior classes in all secondary schools in the state. These examinations should be similar to the Regents' Examinations given each year in the state of New York. Intelligence testing should be done only by a trained psychologist. The tests could be given while the students are still in high school or at the time they appear before the board as candidates for admission to this new school. Physical fitness should be determined by physicians who are members of the board or who have been designated by the board for this purpose. All-round fitness, not athletic ability must be the test.

Only citizens of the United States who are residents of Vermont should be eligible for admission.[1] Participation in intercollegiate athletics should be prohibited, but, otherwise, athletic sports should be encouraged so as to insure the development of strong healthy bodies. The men and women should be housed in separate dormitories, but these should be relatively near to each other so as to encourage the development of a community of interest. Admission should be free and there should be no charge for either board or room.

The advantages of such a scheme are numerous. It would be far cheaper and wiser to have leaders picked and trained in this organized way than it would to have them picked at random or in accordance with individual desire, as frequently happens, and trust that they will be trained in office after they have been selected. The people would then know that there are certain people in each of the various communities who were trained for public service and who secured that training because of fitness for leadership. The training would be secured in Vermont, thus increasing the likelihood that those receiving that training would remain in the state after graduation. They would be associating with people of the opposite sex who had equally high intelligence, thus increasing the probability that they would intermarry and reproduce children of high intelligence who might serve as leaders in succeeding generations. Higher education is now to some serious extent the privilege of those who have wealth. Under this new scheme, ambition in the highly capable would be encouraged whether or not they possessed funds sufficiently adequate to permit them to obtain a college education. Merit alone would be the basis of selection. The scope of knowledge is so broad that it is impossible for any individual to know more than a small portion of it. This new school would provide intensive training in preparation for civic leadership in Vermont. Fields of knowledge which have no direct bearing on the goal to be attained would not be covered. A reward for merit would be provided

[1] If students who reside outside the state are permitted to enter this school, they should be required to meet the same entrance requirements as students residing within the state and they should be charged a tuition fee sufficient to pay cost of their instruction.

which should stimulate greater effort among children in the elementary and secondary schools of the state.

Suffrage Regulation

It is well known that one of the most serious problems of popular government today is that of the non-voter. In every election the problem of getting out the voters is a serious one. Studies that have already been made indicate that ignorance is one of the main underlying causes of failure to vote. There are two important ways of attacking this problem effectively: (1) restrict the suffrage to the more intelligent and (2) simplify the problem of the voter by reducing the number of elective offices which he has to fill and by eliminating or seriously modifying those institutions which needlessly complicate the problem for him. The use of either or both of these methods would be decidedly helpful. It is to be hoped that both of them will soon be accepted as fundamental to our scheme of government.

Suffrage restriction. In restricting the privilege of voting to the more intelligent, education rather than intelligence tests will have to be used until intelligence tests are more widely accepted as bases for determining ability. It seems entirely fair to use education tests in an age of compulsory public education. The basic requirement must, of course, be arbitrarily fixed by law, but it does not seem unreasonable to require that no new name shall be added to any check list in this state, except upon presentation of a certificate showing that the individual concerned has satisfactorily completed the work of the sixth grade or some higher grade in some elementary or higher school in this state in which the standard of instruction is at least as high as that required by our state course of study at any given time, or upon presentation of a similar certificate showing satisfactory completion of equivalent work in some school (or schools) in some other state (or states), such certificate to be countersigned by the Commissioner of Education or by his authority, or by passing an examination administered in and by the public schools in this state under the direction of the Commissioner of Education, which would require an equivalent education. This requirement would not operate as a bar against any one who had previously had his name on any check list in this state.

The short ballot. In order to simplify the problem for the voter through the reduction of the number of elective offices, a plan similar to that shown in Fig. 2, covering all offices to be filled by popular election and arranging their distribution by years, should be provided by constitutional amendment.

Elections	1932	1933	1934	1935
National	President Vice-President Senator Representative		Senator Representative	
State		Governor Treasurer Legislator		
County		(Co. Board)		
Town		Selectmen Treasurer		Selectmen Treasurer
City				Mayor Treasurer Alderman

FIG. 2.   Proposed plan of elections.

Under this plan, the election of state and local officers is so arranged as not to conflict with the election of national officers, the election of national officers being left unchanged. The number of state and local officers to be elected is seriously reduced and the term of those officers is, in general, increased. For instance, the number of state officers to be elected is reduced to three and the term increased from two to four years. This conforms to the trend in the development of state government in the United States today. For example, New York, by constitutional amendment approved by popular vote in November, 1925, reduced the number of executive offices in its state government to be filled by popular election to four (including the lieutenant governor) and Virginia, by constitutional amendment approved by popular vote in June, 1928, reduced the number of such offices to three (including the lieutenant governor).

It will be observed that the plan here proposed does not provide for the election of a lieutenant governor. Thirteen of the states of the Union do not now have lieutenant governors, so that we cannot be accused of trying to set a new precedent by abolishing this office. Moreover, it seems unwise and unnecessary that we be required to fill an office by popular election when the only significant function of that office is to wait for the governor to retire from office, by death or otherwise. It is true that the lieutenant governor presides over the state senate, but that body could, doubtless, pick one of its own members who could preside over its deliberations at least equally well. So far as succession to the office of governor is concerned, there seems to be no logical reason to believe that the interests of the state would not be as well served if the presiding officer of the upper (or only) chamber were in the line of succession instead of the lieutenant governor.

The county board is placed in parenthesis in this plan, because it is not clear that there need be any such board. However, if there need be such a body, to look after county property, then it should be elected as indicated above. It does not make any particular difference whether the board thus provided is known as "the side judges" or the county board or by some other name.

The elections should all occur on the same date and, since the national elections are held on the first Tuesday after the first Monday in November, it seems desirable that all other elections be held on that date. But the idea of the March meeting has become so firmly fixed as a part of our Vermont tradition that it may be difficult to secure this change. It may seem wise, therefore, to continue to elect town and city officials at that time and this presumably would not make a great deal of difference, provided the general plan, as herein presented, were otherwise adhered to. In fact, some advantage might be secured in this way, since the ballot would be shortened for the November elections in which state officers were chosen.

The plan calls for the acceptance of a one-chambered legislative body. The use of the unicameral system is not new in Vermont. There was but one chamber in our legislative body from 1777 to 1836. This was one of the most glorious periods of Vermont history. It is true that we decided to change to the bicameral system in 1836 after serious consideration of the problem, but it is also true that there is not a single one of the arguments advanced in favor of the change at that time which appears, after serious study, to have had any validity.

except the contention that the legislative bodies of the national and other state governments were organized on a bicameral basis. Even that argument has little importance at a time when there are (or recently have been) movements on foot in a number of states, including Alabama, Arizona, California, Kansas, Nebraska, Ohio, Oklahoma, Oregon, South Dakota, Washington, and Wisconsin, to secure the adoption of the unicameral system. Vermont has a much greater claim to the unicameral scheme than any other state and should not be behind other states in securing its adoption. The old Vermont scheme, imperfect as it was, was superior to the one which replaced it. The new scheme should provide for a single chamber of approximately fifty members apportioned on the basis of population and elected from compact single-member districts made up of contiguous towns or parts thereof. It is to be hoped that it will not ordinarily be necessary to cut across town lines in districting the state for this purpose.

All other offices now elective should be made appointive by state authority for state and county governments and by town and city authority for town and city governments, respectively. For instance, those judges who are now selected by popular vote should be appointed during good behavior by the governor with the approval of the legislative body. Other judges might well be made appointive, but there is good reason for believing that the present system, so far as these judges are concerned, is working well and the problem of the voter would not be seriously simplified by making them appointive. Prosecuting attorneys in the various counties in the state should be appointed by the governor on recommendation of the attorney-general and on approval of the legislative body for terms exceeding that of the governor. They should be subject to removal for cause by the governor on recommendation of the attorney-general. Sheriffs should be appointed either by the county boards or by the governor, but they should be subject to removal for cause by the governor on recommendation of the attorney-general. Similar rules should be followed in determining the method of appointing other officials whose offices are now elective.

There are numerous advantages to be derived from the adoption of such a short-ballot plan. State and national elections would be separated and the voter would be required to vote on only one set of candidates and issues at a given time. Candidates for state office would be compelled to develop and stand on platforms made of planks dealing with Vermont issues. The cost of government would be reduced by the elimination of useless offices and by setting up a system which would be less complicated and which should be much more efficient. Responsibility for failure to perform the duties of office would be much more easily placed as the voters could more easily understand the system. More voters would be able to comprehend the problems involved in the exercise of the suffrage and, consequently, a much higher percentage of the voters would probably participate in elections.

The direct primary. In order to complete the task of simplifying the problem of the voter, it will be necessary to abolish or seriously modify the direct primary. Multiplicity of elections tends to confuse the voter. Besides, there are inherent defects in the direct primary system which make it an undesirable institution of government. There can be no official selection of candidates in the primary. Except in so far as it may be manipulated under cover by wholly irresponsible political bosses, it gives the voter an opportunity to select only from among those who, because of personal ambition, have been able to get their names placed on the ballot. No attempt is being made to deprecate such personal ambition. In fact, it should be lauded. The point is that the man seeks the office and not that the office seeks the man. The only thing that the voter can do is to pick the least of the evils presented, if he votes at all.

This defect is much more serious in Vermont than in most of the other states, because we have what amounts to a one-party system in this state. To all intents and purposes, candidates for public office are, with rare exceptions, elected in the direct primary. The two-party system is considered one of the basic foundations of popular government in the United States. We have considered it desirable to have one party in power and another party out of power sufficiently strong to hold the party in power responsible for its official acts. So long as we retain the direct primary there will be no party in opposition of any consequence and there will be no party responsibility. As it is now, if a Democrat desires to have any share in determining who shall hold public offices, his only opportunity is to vote the Republican ticket in the direct primary. It may be contended that this is of no consequence, that the Republican party is superior to the Democratic party, and that there is, therefore, no important reason for changing the system. But that is not the point. The goal must be to secure a system of government which is responsible and efficient. There is not one chance in a thousand that the Democratic party will ever get control of the government of Vermont, but there is a possibility that it might get sufficiently strong so that its leaders would have a hearing before the public on public questions, if the direct primary system were modified. Competition will tend to give energy and enthusiasm.

A native Vermonter, Prof. P. Orman Ray of the University of California, has outlined what he believes to be a desirable method of reforming the direct primary system.[2] It is a combination of the direct primary and the caucus-convention system which retains what is desirable and eliminates what seems to be undesirable in both systems. The essential features of this plan are included in the diagram shown in Fig. 3.

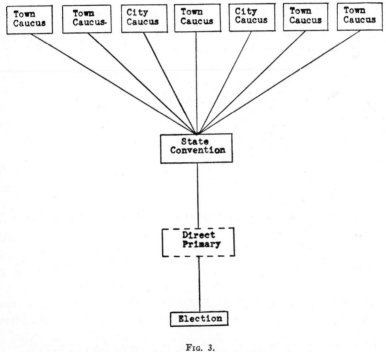

FIG. 3.

Under the system proposed, the town or city caucus, the state convention, the direct primary, and the election would be held on dates

[2] This or some other modification of the plan proposed by Charles Evans Hughes should be adopted.

and under conditions prescribed by state law. The statutory regulations would be no less rigid than those which now apply to the direct primary. The state convention would nominate candidates, formulate a party platform, and, in the years of presidential elections, select delegates to the national convention and nominate presidential electors. The direct primary would not be held unless a petition signed by at least 20 percent of the qualified voters of the party in the state, requesting the substitution of certain names for others which the state convention decided should be placed on the election ballot, were filed with the secretary of state on or before a specified date prior to the date fixed for the direct primary. In the direct primary, if held, the voters of the party would decide between the candidates proposed by the convention and those proposed by petition. No one should be permitted to vote in the primary of a party unless previously registered, in accordance with law to be enacted, as a member of that party. The direct primary would presumably not be held unless the convention had been obviously corrupt or unwise in its decisions.

Under this system, party leadership would be brought out into the open and forced to shoulder responsibility for its decisions before the members of its own party and the party in opposition. The party organization, developed through the caucus-convention system, would be forced to put up its candidates and have them run on platforms which the voters within and without the party would have an opportunity to criticize. Candidates which the party did not want would have very little opportunity to get their names on the election ballot and those elected could thus be definitely held responsible for their official acts by the party. Evasion of issues or of official duty would be much more difficult. The office would seek the man and not the man the office. Candidates without wealth could afford to run and the cost to the state would be much less than under the present system, since the direct primary would, in all probability, rarely be held.

———

Prepared for the Commission by its Committee on Citizenship.

CHARLES A. PLUMLEY,
Chairman,

FRED C. MARTIN,
Vice-Chairman,

D. B. CARROLL,
> *Executive Secretary,*

WALTER H. CLEARY,

MRS. CHARLES H. GREER,

A. W. LAWRENCE,

R. L. PATRICK,

B. L. STAFFORD,

MRS. MARTIN VILAS.

XIX

RELIGIOUS FORCES

Early Background

The founding of New England coincided with the birth and growth to influence and power of the nonconformist movement in England. The first half century of its history found most of the larger Protestant sects then in existence in sharp conflict upon questions of doctrine, the sacraments and church government. Baptists, Separatists (Congregationalists), Friends and Presbyterians were positive, profoundly in earnest and inclined to magnify their differences rather than their unities. Each of them fought for a place among the colonies along the northern Atlantic seaboard and they quietly made themselves secure in their position. When during the last half of the eighteenth century the rising waters of immigration began to wash the highlands of Northern New England these religious divisions were still deep and emotionally intense. If not mutually intolerant to the point of violence, they were at least convinced of the essential truth of their respective positions and the unfortunate error of all others.

When Vermont, however, was being settled, there was a new intellectual and religious stir abroad. Protestantism was seeking to adapt itself to Newton's discovery of the magnitude and unity of nature and to the literary mood of the French enlightenment. A century which possessed few books and therefore read them the more seriously had numbered among its writers, Locke, Newton, Berkeley, Hume, Voltaire, Rousseau and Swift. Rationalism and naturalism were in the ascendancy. The brilliant preacher Tillotson was ready to declare unhesitatingly that "nothing ought to be received as a divine doctrine or revelation without good proof that it is so." It was increasingly hard to identify the God of abstract reason or the God of nature with the God of the Christian tradition. Consequently the very weapons forged to make religion seem more reasonable were used to attack the whole Christian tradition.

Deism, the English counterpart of the French enlightenment, noisy, verbose and intellectually unrespectable, gained ground everywhere in the colonies as well as in the mother country. When authority was invoked to suppress the advancing wave of apparent infidelity, the deists were led to attack all claims to authority other than those residing "in the axioms common to all men." Religion, they affirmed, consists of those simple truths whose very familiarity causes us to overlook them. Men search for them "as the butcher did after his knife when he had it in his mouth." Let every man act according to nature and do all the good he can and he will posses religion enough. There is no difference between morality and religion except that one is "acting according to the reason of things considered in themselves; the other is acting according to the same reason of things as the rule of God."

It was a mood admirably suited to the independent, self-reliant, adventurous life of pioneers in this new and mountain country. Where every man must of necessity be self-sustaining and every community looked to itself for its own defence, what could be more natural than to believe in utter intellectual democracy and self-reliance as well? Every man carried with him his own chart and compass and was dependent upon his own wits whereby to keep himself alive. Was it not to be expected that a "few simple axioms common to all men" should likewise be found in his kit and that they would prove quite sufficient to guide his soul aright?

The manner of argument in vogue among the English and colonial deists was as acceptable to a self-reliant frontiersman as was the subject-matter. Their opponents were "dull fools," "knaves," "pneumatical madmen," "learned lunatics," "heathen philosophers" and "Platonizing Christians." Leibnitz was one of the "vainest and most chimerical men that ever got a name in philosophy"; Plato, the "great corruptor of Christianity," "sinks down, and lower no writer can sink, into a certain Socratic irony, into certain flimsy and hypothetical reasonings that prove nothing and into allusions that are mere vulgarisms." Paul is often "absurd or profane or trifling" with the style of a writer "the least precise and clear that ever writ"; while Moses' account of creation "cannot be read without feeling contempt for him as a philosopher and a divine." "Observe the inconsistencies," they cried, "between the different accounts of the creation! Does not the creator of the universe, the fountain of all wisdom, the origin of all science, the author of all wisdom, the God of all order and harmony, know how to write? Thomas Paine can write a book without forgetting in one page what he had written on another; cannot God Almighty?"

That such extravagant language and judgments were bound to make their appeal to the early settlers among the Green Mountains is abundantly witnessed both by the style of Ethan Allen's writings in particular and the fulminations which the settlers of the New Hampshire grants hurled repeatedly at their foes.

It must not be assumed that the majority, or even a large minority of the early settlers of Vermont were avowed deists. In a number of communities, such as Bennington and Newbury, churches were established by the first comers, almost immediately upon their arrival. These were earnest people whose religious faith would bear transplanting. Not infrequently the town government founded a church as a civic duty and often to this day the light and airy basement of the white church will be found to be owned and used by the town for its public meetings. There were, moreover, communities so divided in belief and practice as not to be able to unite in a single religious fellowship, which early constructed a union church building where several sects in turn were privileged to conduct their worship.

The vast majority, however, of the Protestant churches of Vermont, were not established without great effort, sacrifice and privation by missionaries and itinerant preachers, notably from Connecticut. These men remarked often and with good reason upon the hardness of the human soil with which they were working. It was almost impossible to secure resident clergymen to shepherd the little groups of the faithful, and these young churches maintained a discouragingly tenuous hold upon life. There are great drifts of intellectual weather, whose shadow gives character to each age. Countless persons, too indifferent to formulate their own philosophy, reflected the mood of their day. When Vermont was settled this mood was the morally earnest undigested rationalistic realism we have described. Even those who would most repel its conclusions unwittingly shared the common life. What other meaning can the stark, stoical words from Richard the Third have, which adorn the marker at the grave of Jedediah Dewey, that able, gracious, high-minded man, who was the first pastor of the First Church of Bennington, and the first church permanently organized in Vermont:

"..............Of comfort no man speak,
Let's talk of graves, of worms, and epitaphs:
Make dust our paper and with rainy eyes
Write sorrow on the bosom of the earth."

The Reaction

It was inevitable that the deistic movement should provoke a swift reaction. Not all people found that "the few axioms common to all men" were sufficient to satisfy their life's dilemmas. Nor could they bring themselves to exchange the tender beauty of a more personal faith for the worship of nature or reason though the cause be urged with genuine moral insight and conscience as well as violent popular passion. Fanny Allen, a daughter of Ethan Allen, became a devout Roman Catholic and was the first New England woman to become a nun. Both the energies and the persuasiveness of the Methodist movement which at just this time found its way into the colonies were greatly augmented. To the left and to the right genuinely religious persons were seeking some satisfactory ground in the face of these new and vehement popularizations of old ideas.

On the one side there rose a group of earnest people shocked by the war of creeds and the harshness of sectarian rivalries; and these were organized into a movement by Abner Jones, a Baptist of Lyndon, Vt., in 1800. They acknowledged no other creed than the Bible and desired to be called simply Christians. At one time they came to number some sixty congregations in Vermont and exercised considerable influence. Their humble pietism was not sufficiently vigorous, however, to withstand the more aggressive sects and they have at last been reduced to two small churches. On the other side, the Universalists who were first organized in Gloucester, Mass., in 1779, made large headway in Vermont especially under the leadership of Hosea Ballou who became pastor of the Barnard congregation in 1803. Ballou, a man of genuine religious qualities and quite out of sympathy with the destructive aspects of deism, nevertheless put the whole emphasis of his eloquent preaching on God's Fatherhood of the whole human race. The Calvinistic theology was abhorrent to him and the moral insight of the deists became an integral part of his religion.

It is impossible to understand the religion of Vermonters or intelligently to forecast its future without a clear conception of this early history. The ferment which was active in the life of the state at its birth has not ceased to work. It is perhaps not altogether an accident that the greatest naturalistic rationalist in America, if not in the world, is a son of Vermont and at one time an attendant if not an adherent of one of its leading Protestant churches. Nor is it remarkable that there should still be found among its choicest people in this generation some who have turned from the nonconformist churches to those bodies which magnify authority, the sacraments and tradition.

Protestant Episcopal Growth

Taking the state as a whole, few of the settlers who entered Vermont prior to 1800 had been trained in the Episcopal Church. Among these, however, were some of staunch religious faith; and a missionary from Connecticut reported in 1767 that prayers had been publicly read in Arlington by a layman since its first settlement. The fines and exactions imposed upon them in the older New England states for non-attendance upon Puritan worship and for the use of the prayer book, together with the inducement of the glebe lands made by Governor Wentworth were among the reasons leading to the establishment of some twenty small unorganized parishes in the southeastern and south-western portions of the state during those earliest days.

Until 1832 these scattered groups received encouragement and Episcopal oversight through their association with all the other New England states save Connecticut in the Eastern Diocese. Since that time the Diocese of Vermont has been coterminous with the boundaries of the state and its membership has grown from 1,100 to nearly 10,000 communicants, more than two-fifths of whom live in rural communities.

Roman Catholic Development

Long before the people of Massachusetts and Connecticut began to pour into the southern part of Vermont, there were small stations of French colonists established for military reasons in Isle La Motte and at other more southern points along the eastern shore of Lake Champlain. While these earliest days are shadowed in obscurity there can be little doubt that the first Christian religious cult practiced within the borders of Vermont was that of the Roman Catholic Church. These earliest encampments were not, however, permanent. The drift of immigration which actually laid the foundations of the state was from southern New England and contained few if any adherents of this church.

Both the French and Irish immigration came at a later date. Not until 1822 is there any authentic record of a Catholic priest connected with a congregation in Vermont. The Rev. James McQuaide at that

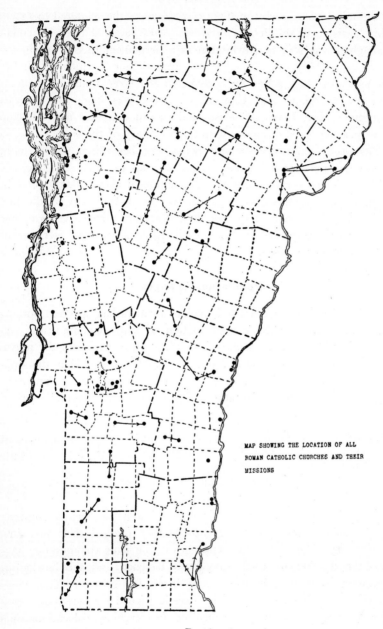

MAP SHOWING THE LOCATION OF ALL
ROMAN CATHOLIC CHURCHES AND THEIR
MISSIONS

Fig. 1.

time did missionary work for about a year among the scattered members
of his parish at Middlebury. Seven years later, Father Jeremiah
O'Callaghan was sent to Burlington as a permanent missionary in the
then diocese of Boston. Under this jurisdiction Vermont Catholics
remained until 1853, when on account of the large number of immigrants from Ireland and Canada, the state was made the See of
Burlington. Rev. Louis de Goesbriand was in that year made Bishop
with a jurisdiction coterminous with the boundary of the state.

This organization whose first permanent beginnings in Vermont
are only a little over a hundred years old, has now over 100 priests,
112 churches and serves a Catholic population of about 90,000 persons.
The significance of this growth can be seen in another way by the fact
that in 1926, 23 percent of the people in Vermont thirteen years of age
and older were members of this church, while 25 percent were members of all other churches.

Population Changes

The immigration of French Canadian farmers has operated both as
a cause and effect in the transformation of many communities. As
buyers of land they made a market which greatly facilitated the movement of many old Protestant families from the soil. That the drift
away from the farm would have taken place in any event cannot be
doubted since in spite of the taking of so much land in certain parts of
the state by Canadian immigrants, there are plenty of examples of
land being allowed through disuse to return to nature. Moreover, the
willingness of these older Protestant families to sell must constitute
a chief inducement to the buyers.

No such transpositions of population can occur, however, without
difficulty and at least temporary loss of social momentum. One of the
serious problems of the Roman Catholic Church has been to minister
to these isolated families and groups as they pressed their way into
new territory. The Protestant churches in the same communities have
found the number of their supporters lessened and the burden of
maintaining their church life one of increasing gravity. The whole
transition, though characterized by excellent good temper and friend-
liness, has resulted in many serious and far-reaching dislocations during its progress.

The Catholics have answered the problems involved with characteristic vigor. Bishop de Goesbriand made repeated trips to the Old World to bring back men to work in the mission field here. Mission churches established under humble circumstances and holding their services amid many difficulties, have been growing into strong parishes. A program of building involving beautiful church edifices, schools, hospitals and other charitable institutions, is being continuously pressed by Bishop Joseph John Rice. No one can doubt but that the Catholic Church is bending its best efforts to minister effectively to its most remote and scattered communicants and is earnest in its desire to make good American citizens as well as good Catholics of these newcomers.

Church Membership

In the State of Vermont 51.9 percent of the adult population are church members compared with 55.4 percent for the country as a whole. The weight of this discrepancy seems definitely to be with the Protestants, for about 36 percent of the non-Catholic population above thirteen years of age are members of the churches in Vermont, while the average for the nation as a whole is 46.5 percent. Many causes of religious indifference in Vermont are the same as in other states. The reason for Vermont's smaller church membership must be located, however, in those conditions which are peculiar to Vermont or particularly accentuated here.

Probably no section of America has maintained so essentially the blood and spirit of eighteenth century England as has Vermont. A certain amount of persistent realistic, though no longer boisterous, rationalism exists everywhere. One of the reasons may be the not too remote influence of the earlier deism which tended so strongly to identify God with nature and true religion with morality. This is ventured as a first peculiarity.

In the second place, Vermonters will not pretend to a wisdom or an experience they do not enjoy. The frugal and often laconic character of conversation in rural Vermont is an evidence and the natural consequence of this refusal to embellish or embroider reality. The feverish type of religious appeal and a periodic evangelism running counter to this folkway, though persisting in other parts of the country, early lost their hold in Vermont, and now for the best part of a generation have altogether disappeared. They evoked a certain sentimentality

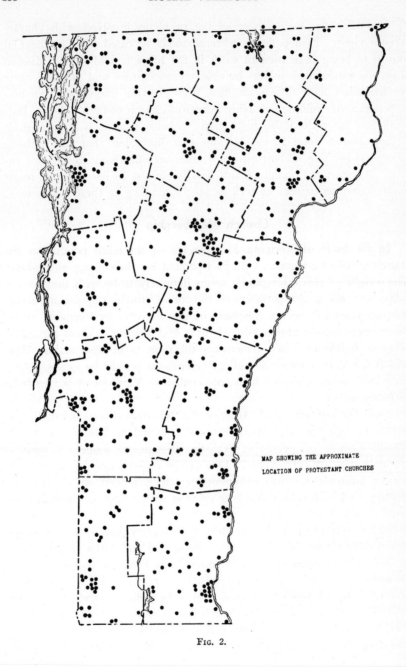

MAP SHOWING THE APPROXIMATE
LOCATION OF PROTESTANT CHURCHES

Fig. 2.

and heightening of emotion which the average northern Yankee instinctively felt to be strained and alien to him. He knew that they did not conform to his private experience and whatever others might do he would not simulate a warmth of enthusiasm which he did not feel.

Not infrequently, however, he did accept the statements of zealous proponents of conversion that only those who possessed a witness within of this definite transformation of their lives were prepared for church membership. A large number of people past middle age can still be found who live with the utmost rectitude, attend and support the church both by personal service and with generous gifts of money and yet who quietly decline to receive its sacraments or unite with it. When questioned they may even speak of the institution with honest affection but add that they do not think themselves qualified for full membership.

In the third place, sectarianism and the drive produced by sectarian fanaticism has long been at a minimum both among the laity and the clergy of Vermont. The swift rise of the Christian movement at an early date with its renunciation of all creeds and its emphasis upon the unity of all who follow Christ is a witness to this. The equally swift disappearance of the movement, when it was apparent that it was only destined to add one more to the number of sects, is perhaps a further evidence.

Today there may be ministers and laymen among the nonconformists who prefer that their own church shall remain unmerged with any other Protestant body in their community; but this preference is seldom based upon any sectarian conceit that their church is intrinsically superior to its neighbor in origin, creed, government or the type of Christian character fostered. Certainly there is no sectarian impulse tending at this time to further duplication of organization among these bodies. Nearly all of their ministers prefer to work in communities where there is only one church and many are frankly intrigued by federated churches representing two or more denominations in spite of such difficulties as may arise from more complicated organizations.

When sectarian interest is so slight, it is quite possible that in communities where there is more than one Protestant Church, there will be found persons, with whom the excuse that they do not care to unite with one of these bodies but would be interested if there were only one church serving the community, is something more than subterfuge. The nonconformist churches of Vermont began nearly forty years ago to sense this situation and to develop their work as denominations along non-sectarian and community lines.

Interdenominational Comity

With the passage of the years, the breaking down of sectarian barriers and the promotion of a sense of their essential unity have been the object of consistent thought and endeavor on the part of several of the larger denominations.

The total drift of population away from certain Vermont communities and the substitution of a Roman Catholic for a formerly Protestant population, to which movements reference has already been made, have provided throughout one of the strongest factors in promoting this spirit of unity. It may almost be said to be the chief strategy in meeting the most serious problems in which the nonconformist churches find themselves involved throughout the state.

The history of this interdenominational cooperation is so unique in character and so pregnant with future possibilities that it demands a brief statement here. In the early spring of 1899 the Protestant churches of Williston entered into an informal agreement "to try cooperation." This agreement has persisted without definitely formulated articles of federation to the present time. In the spring of 1901 Prof. Walter Howard read a paper at Rutland entitled "Some Lessons From the Trusts for the Churches." This was in the heyday of corporate mergers under the famous trust plan and before the rise of the progressive movement with its fears of such great combinations. A member of the Castleton Church who was present went home with his mind full of the subject and resolved to bring into a single organization the Baptist, Methodist and Congregational churches of that place. Within a year the thing was accomplished. Friends Meetings and Christian, Universalist, Presbyterian and Unitarian churches have likewise participated in such unions.

Slowly the number of federations grew until the outbreak of the World War brought its increased economic pressure, a heightened sense of community solidarity, and a scarcity of ministerial leadership. The time was ripe and with hearty encouragement on the part of denominational leaders, there was a withdrawal by mutual consent from many over-churched communities and united enterprises were organized by federation in a great many others.

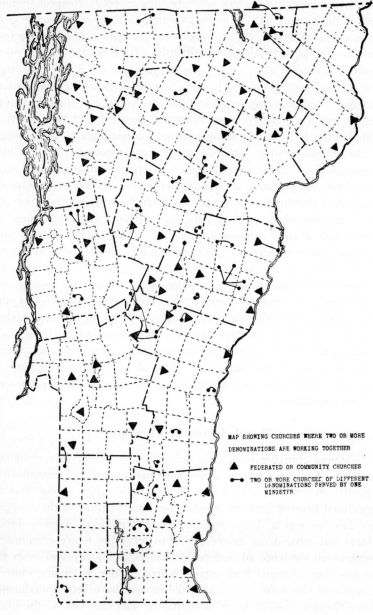

MAP SHOWING CHURCHES WHERE TWO OR MORE
DENOMINATIONS ARE WORKING TOGETHER

▲   FEDERATED OR COMMUNITY CHURCHES

●—● TWO OR MORE CHURCHES OF DIFFERENT
      DENOMINATIONS SERVED BY ONE
      MINISTER

FIG. 3.

With the further progress of time, the impetus towards unions waned on the part of local communities though there was a quite general agreement that the religious needs of the state could best be met by further developments in the elimination of competition. The postwar disillusionment may have been responsible or it may be that unions were already perfected in those communities where the greatest solidarity existed. In any event in 1926 after some consultation it was agreed to call a meeting of representative ministers and laymen from the Methodist, Baptist and Congregational denominations at Burlington. An evening and a forenoon were spent together. An analysis was presented of the progress made during the previous ten years and of the existing status of union enterprises. Every community of less than five thousand population, in which there was more than one church, was described as to population, number and membership of churches and a clear statement made of all missionary funds still used in competing endeavors. At the same time those towns were considered which enjoyed the services of no resident minister. Finally the relations of these three denominations to each other and to the total problem of religion in Vermont was thoroughly discussed. Quite directly from this meeting there issued a new group of united churches and the movement has continued steadily since that time. The average year sees some half-dozen new unions launched. There are only forty-two communities of less than five thousand population remaining in Vermont in which there is now competition between the churches of these denominations.

Church Union in Vermont

The united church arising as a federation of two or more religious groups has not always proven to be a permanent form of organization. Frequently the weaker churches have disbanded after a time and all have entered heartily into the membership and program of the stronger which has become a denominational church working upon a broad platform and recognizing its obligation to serve the whole community. Sometimes all evidence of federation has passed away and even the name has been changed back again to that of the continuing church. But, however the form of the united life may have been transformed to meet changed conditions, it is a striking fact that out of the great number of such unions only one has completely failed.

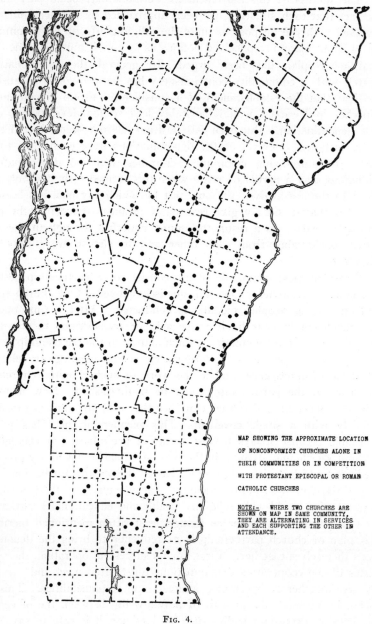

MAP SHOWING THE APPROXIMATE LOCATION
OF NONCONFORMIST CHURCHES ALONE IN
THEIR COMMUNITIES OR IN COMPETITION
WITH PROTESTANT EPISCOPAL OR ROMAN
CATHOLIC CHURCHES

NOTE:- WHERE TWO CHURCHES ARE
SHOWN ON MAP IN SAME COMMUNITY,
THEY ARE ALTERNATING IN SERVICES
AND EACH SUPPORTING THE OTHER IN
ATTENDANCE.

Fig. 4.

The success of this movement in Vermont may be in part due to the fact that each situation has been approached by the denominations involved with the purpose to unite the religious life of the community and without many preconceived notions as to how it must be done. No ready-made plan has been urged. In general the denominational church with a community consciousness has been favored because of the fear that the establishment of a considerable group of community churches in Vermont would inevitably lead to the development of a new denomination. But even this position has not been adhered to in every instance. Several of the denominations have even gone to the length of subsidizing community churches with no denominational affiliations over a period of years when this seemed to be the only way out. In the last analysis the only test by which any plan has been rejected is that it did not give reasonable promise of meeting the community's needs. As a result the united churches throughout the state differ considerably from each other and in almost every important respect.

The plan most commonly in use consists of a partnership between two or more churches. One minister is employed. One church school and one young people's meeting is conducted. After a time one set of church buildings is likely to be sold or transformed to suit some special need of the community. Each church in the partnership is represented by the minister in its larger ecclesiastical meetings or relations. To outward appearances and in the work of such a united church the members of the partnership cannot be distinguished. New members join whichever of the partner churches they will and they are received publicly with a single covenant. This partnership plan has proved workable because it lays to rest sectarian prejudices and competition without sacrificing anything in the way of valuable, not to say precious, traditions and loyalties. It keeps alive all the worthy forthgoing interests of the churches; and the members continue unabated their intelligent support of a world-wide religious, health and educational program.

One of the most valuable though least often mentioned merits of this plan of church partnership is its tendency to bring the denominations themselves together. First, for its successful operation, the secretaries of the cooperating denominations must often meet and carefully go over together their common interests and responsibilities. This has meant in Vermont the growth of a fellowship between the officers of the various Protestant bodies such as does not, it is safe to say, exist elsewhere in the nation. In the second place, when the Vermont Congregational Conference meets there is a good leaven of Methodist, Universalist, Baptist and Presbyterian ministers sitting with full right of participation as members of the body. In fact, approximately one-fourth of the ministers at such a meeting are members of these other churches. Under conditions suited to the nature of their organization the same thing holds true in the state meetings of each of these other bodies. Likewise the members of the local churches are being educated by the interchange of church school literature, the ministry of the clergy of other denominations, and even through personal acquaintance with the executive officers of other denominations to value the essential unity of the Christian tradition. Obviously, the plan operates as a vigorous force calculated actually to bring the denominations themselves into the closest understanding if not eventual unity.

The ultimate goal of these interdenominational relationships in Vermont has never been publicly formulated. It would appear, however, that most of those engaged in guiding the activities of these nonconformist bodies not only heartily approve of such progress as has been made, but look forward with some wistfulness to the time when this phase of the work shall have been completed and there shall be only one representative Protestant Church in each community. Certainly they are working with considerable consistency to bring this condition to pass.

From the first it has been believed that a unified religious approach to each community was calculated to make the church to an increasing degree a rallying point of community life and more truly representative of the religious conviction of the state. It seemed to make possible a higher type of ministry, and better support. Parishes in even comparatively small communities might in this way become large enough and interesting enough to command all the energies of high-grade leadership. There has also grown increasingly the conviction that this is a natural and Christian development suited to the mood and faith of Vermont Protestants. No creeds, ecclesiastical forms, or endowments have so far prevented the growing consciousness of unity and its concrete expression.

The Utilization of Church Buildings

The merging of religious societies has produced a problem with respect to the care and use of unnecessary church buildings. Increasingly, united churches find it in the interests of economy to use one edifice. In some places the population has so declined that it is impracticable to continue public religious services. What shall be done with respect to the care and use of these buildings is a matter of public importance. Left to decay, uncared for in the weather, they may become a most depressing sight. Used as a parish or community house, a public library or to supplement the ordinary auditorium, they may be a real addition to the life of the parish. In one or two instances they have had associations which make it possible for them to become historic shrines. *If, however, they can no longer serve any public purpose, these old church buildings should be reverently dismantled and removed.*

Religious Education

The conviction on the part of all of the larger religious bodies at work in Vermont that the most hopeful method of enlisting new members is by a program of year-round education is well founded. The precise nature of such a program has varied widely with the different religious bodies. The Roman Catholics, being convinced that the teaching of religion cannot be divorced from other teaching, are building up their parochial schools, boarding schools, and academies. Among these institutions with a state-wide significance are St. Mary's in Burlington; Villa Barlow at St. Albans; and St. Joseph's and St. Ann's Academy at Rutland. It is not to be understood that this development reflects any antagonism toward the public school system, but simply the deep conviction that religion is so inextricably associated with every part of life that both the other disciplines and religion suffer through a divorce in their teaching. The growth in the parochial schools, which now number 23, is naturally attended by a decline in Sunday Schools and here is to be found a partial explanation of the fact that, while in 1906 the number enrolled in Sunday Schools in Vermont was almost 8 percent larger than the average for the country as a whole, by 1926 this ratio had been reversed and the percentage for Vermont was almost 9 percent below the 44.1 percent shown by the nation.

Many intelligent Protestants share the conviction of the Catholics as to the unwisdom of the divorce of so-called secular education and religion. They are, however, so certain of the importance of the public school system that they are attempting to provide a rich and diversified program of religious training to supply the want. Sunday Schools to the number of 585 are regularly functioning and the great majority of these are in the open country or small villages. The average enrollment is less than eighty and only fifty have an enrollment of over 100. So far as the Protestant population is concerned these small church schools are the most important formal agency in the moral and religious training of our people. The distinctly rural schools of Vermont enroll more than two-thirds of the 45,872 Sunday School scholars in the state.

The Daily Vacation School during the last eight years has been developed as an excellent supplement to the Sunday School. In 151 communities with an enrollment of 5,006 it has been held for from two to four weeks daily in the summer. The schedule of instruction continues from nine until noon. It is an institution of much promise and capable of further development. Thirteen Protestant communities moreover have launched after-school or school-time sessions for religious education. Special communicant classes are on the increase and a large number of village churches have character-building classes or service clubs for their youth.

Among other essentially educational organizations under the auspices of the churches tending to develop character along recreational, devotional, service or missionary lines, there are deserving of special mention the following: The 4-H Clubs, the Boy Scouts, the Rangers, the Girl Scouts, the Campfire Girls, the Girl Reserves, the Y. M. C. A., and Y. W. C.A., the Christian Endeavor, the Baptist Young People's Union, the Epworth League and the Junior Knights of Columbus.

Functioning sometimes through these organizations and sometimes as independent institutions there are operated either within the state or accessible to the youth of Vermont, a large number of camps and conferences. Over 7,500 campers come into the state each year to enroll in camps among our mountains and lakes. Most of these camps provide a good mental, physical and moral atmosphere for those who enjoy their privileges. In addition, in an average year almost a thousand Vermont young people attend camps conducted under church or semi-religious auspices (407 at Camp Abnaki, 208 at Hochelaga, 200 at Billings, 65 divided between Plymouth, Sunrise and Winnepesaukee, 17 at Merrowvista, 97 at St. Ann's and Ziptekana). Each year about 700 youths and leaders from the churches of Vermont attend distinctly religious training camps of a week or more.

The normal training school established at Concord, Vt., in 1822-23 by Rev. Samuel A. Hall, D. D., for the improvement of church school teachers, is believed to be the first in America. Since then the program for teacher training in both public and church school fields has been consistently emphasized in Vermont. Each year over 1,200 religious workers are studying in these schools or conferences.

In 1817 the first Sunday School Convention in the world of which we have any record, convened in Greensboro, Vt. It was called a "Sunday School Exhibit" and aimed to create better methods in religious education as each convention delegate studied the "exhibit" of work done by other schools than his own. This "Convention" idea has grown and been adopted by many other religious groups. In Vermont there are over 7,500 delegates each year for one to five days' conference on the work of their own particular phase of religious activity. Last year sixteen state and county Sunday School Conventions were attended by nearly 2,500 delegates. State and county Christian Endeavor Conventions enrolled approximately 1,000 representatives. The State Y. M. C. A. and Y. W. C. A. registered 436 delegates in their Older Boys' and Older Girls' Conferences. Protestant state and district meetings and Church Conferences were held during 1930 with a total registered attendance of over 3,000. State and County Youth Councils enlisted the activity of over 1,000 young people.

We recommend that the Protestant organizations concerned make a careful study of their very valuable but greatly diversified program of religious education to the end that it may be made more effective through wise integration.

A religious education implies a wealth of life-enriching truth, a discriminating judgment in moral situations, a purposeful habit of mind, an understanding love for great music and art, a happier disposition, a nobler character, generosity to the point of sacrifice, and an appreciation of the world's choicest personalities.

These things are the birthright of the child and the glory of a mature person. It is the privilege and duty of the religious forces of Vermont to provide such a training for every child of its constituency. The minimum responsibility of each religious community is to assure the necessary building, the curriculum, and the leadership. This provision is more or less adequately made in many of our larger communities but sometimes in the rural field there is an inferiority complex that says "this may be possible for the city but it would never work here in the country." We believe that there is no greater need in the religious educational world today than the wise standardization of the program of the church school for all communities. A workable plan for small schools is imperative for the little Sunday School holds a strategic place in the education of the youth of Vermont. Youth in the country deserves and should be given opportunities equal to those of the larger communities.

The matter of morals is a community concern. The modern church school no longer teaches sectarianism. Today its acknowledged task is to build the spiritual character of those committed to its classes. Hence, our work is a common one, which no one church can do alone. Only as each shares its part can the whole be accomplished. The church and vacation schools must feel their responsibility as educational institutions. They must realize that their importance is not one whit less than that of the public schools. They must do their part of the work of education with as much definiteness of aim, soundness of method, and efficiency of organization as the public school.

We, therefore, urge the people to lend their earnest support both financially and, where needed, by personal service to the end that every Vermont child may receive a sound religious training.

We recommend that there be provided a trained leadership skilled in making effective the principles of religion in the lives of boys and girls.

We are convinced that the future of our state and the very question of a livable social order depend upon the development of inner controls of conduct and the adequate preparation of youth for life in this changing world.

Without attempting to indicate to any communion how these things shall be achieved or what other desirable features shall be added to their curriculum, we do feel that here at least is a minimum to which both our tradition and public interests compel us.

The Ministry

It is a signficant fact that only 57.8 percent of the 602 ministers of Vermont serve a single church, while 28.6 percent serve two, 11.5 percent serve three, 1.3 percent serve four and .8 percent serve five churches. It may be true that certain of these scattered parishes owe their existence to an unfortunate measure of sectarian competition tending to diffuse unreasonably the efforts of their ministers. In general, however, as other facts and maps we have exhibited here tend to show, the great majority of these men are exercising a wide ministry in the interests of economy and the efficient care of the smaller communities.

It has been generally believed that small scattered communities adjacent to cities are less adequately served by the religious forces than either the cities or the more distant rural areas. The survey of the Montpelier area carried through during the past winter by the local communities with the cooperation of the Vermont Commission, indicates that here, at least, this presupposition does not hold. These smaller adjacent communities do not compare unfavorably with the state as a whole. The reason for this good showing immediately apparent is that the ministers and churches of the larger centers and stronger rural communities such as Plainfield, Waterbury, Worcester and Montpelier have been aware of their responsibility and have saved the situation through their cooperative ministry. This leads us to recommend that each larger center carefully study its outskirts and rural environment to discover how the needs of nearby communities which are now neglected may be met.

The greatly improved means of transportation which are available today may make it wise to draw people from a larger area to worship at a central place. Or it may enable one minister to serve effectively two or more yoked churches lying some distance apart. Under either condition it becomes possible to provide a larger and more interesting field of labor. This is of prime importance in securing the ablest and most desirable type of ministry. The average minister in thinking of a relocation is certain to desire a parish large and interesting enough to demand all his energies. No monetary or social rewards can quite atone for the growing impatience a conscientious man feels with what seems to him really but a part-time work.

We, therefore, recommend that the Protestant churches study in the interests of a better paid and more effective ministry the possibility of yoking neighboring communities either of their own or kindred denominations wherever this can be done with reasonable prospect of improving the service rendered to each community.

Other states have used to a greater extent than Vermont what is known as the larger parish plan. This provides for the yoking of a number of churches in a section with natural geographical limitations into a single parish unit. A staff of several workers, laymen and ordained ministers possessing diverse gifts and functions are employed. We are not certain why this plan has not made greater progress in Vermont since there are sections which seem admirably suited to it. *We, therefore, commend the larger parish plan for study and experi-*

ment as possessing many apparently excellent features adapted to our needs.

During past years an astonishing number of men and women born and reared in Vermont have given themselves to Christian service. The story of Joseph Dutton deserves to be one of the hero tales of history. Born at Stowe, Vt., a veteran of the Civil War, he became a Roman Catholic, a brother of the Trappist Order and a missionary to the lepers of Molokai. For more than a half century he led his devoted life, dying at last in Hawaii during the past winter.

Again such a town as Cornwall has given at least twenty-four of its sons to the ordained ministry or to the missionary service of one denomination and many other communities have only a little less enviable record. Protestants and Catholics, not only throughout the nation, but the whole world round, have felt the impact of the vigorous young life which Vermont has thus given with sacrificial abandon to share its noblest aspirations and to render its Christian service.

Today, however, every religious group in the state covets for itself a greater proportion of ministers and priests born and reared in the state, men who can understand with the sure touch of a native how to quicken the heart strings of our people. There is certainly a Vermont quality of life which is among our most priceless possessions. Seldom can one unacquainted from childhood with such manners and customs serve with the highest facility and wisdom as pastor of a Vermont community. *To secure such natural leadership and to carry forward to a larger degree in the next generation the traditions of Christian life enlistment which have characterized the last is a major concern of our churches.*

Prepared for the Commission by its Committee on Religious Forces.

JOHN E. WEEKS,
        Chairman,
EVAN THOMAS,
        Vice-Chairman,
SAMUEL B. BOOTH,
        Executive Secretary,
A. RITCHIE LOW,
        Assistant Executive Secretary,
W. P. CROSBY,
ERNEST DUNKLEE,

W. F. Frazier,
Arthur W. Hewitt,
H. I. O'Brien,
M. J. Paulsen,
G. E. Robbins,
H. H. White.

XX

THE CONSERVATION OF VERMONT TRADITIONS AND IDEALS

"If the spirit of liberty should vanish in other parts of the Union, and support of our institutions should languish, it could all be replenished from the generous store held by the people of the brave little State of Vermont." This sentence from ex-President Coolidge's "Bennington Address," now widely known, might well be taken as the keynote of a wide range of literature of varied kinds and types, including letters, journals, diaries, historical and social documents, novels, essays, poems, orations and speeches, in which the authors have praised various attributes and characteristics of the state and its people. The amount of such material, merely suggested here, is decidedly impressive; and much of it was written and spoken by men and women with no ties of allegiance to the state—in many cases by those who were in actual intent and purpose hostile, or, at least, unsympathetic toward Vermont.

The student of the subject might begin with the yellowing pages of a magazine published in Philadelphia in 1792, in which an unknown writer wrote of the state's people as those "who enjoy a liberty as pure as the air they breathe, which is not excelled on the globe. Health reigns and cheerfulness and vigor, those greatest of earthly treasures." Pondering a hundred references and more on his journey toward the present, the interested student might linger a moment on this statement by George Washington: "The country is very mountainous, full of defiles, and very strong. The inhabitants a hardy race, composed of that kind of people who are best calculated for soldiers; in truth who *are* soldiers," and close his study after covering a century and a half with the words of Sinclair Lewis, famous for his unhesitating directness and frankness of utterance: "I have never spent more than eight months in any one place, have traveled through thirty-six states and lived in eight or ten in addition to visiting eighteen foreign countries, but Vermont is the first place I have seen where I really wanted to have my home—a place to spend the rest of my life."

Though the emphasis on the characteristics of the people of the state be directly or indirectly phrased, the total evidence, briefly indicated here, of appreciations of the state is significant, and must be accepted by the unbiased student as indicating values in *Green Mountain life and ways that merit consideration in any study of the problems of the state's future well-being.* The reasons for the existence to this day of pronounced traditional and idealistic qualities of mind and heart that give Vermont and Vermont folk their particular significance can be stated with some assurance of accuracy, but not, surely, within the confines of a limited report which this discussion purports to be. In any statement of the reasons, we may add in passing, the following factors would probably have their place : Factors of environment with elements of isolation, factors of association and heredity involving the "will-to-do" of a hardy, independent, liberty-loving, brave and individualistic people, still as stubborn as were their fathers in opposition to what they consider to be against their rights or whatever fails to appeal to their judgment and common sense.

The particular problem which the Committee on Traditions and Ideals faced was to find ways and means of preserving the distinctive values, repeatedly emphasized in the state's past and present, which have to do largely with immaterial rather than material possessions of any kind, and which are easily recognized in the history, literature, and the general life of the people. At the outset, the difficulty of dealing with such intangible elements was apparent, even though the committee included members whose working days have been spent with just such problems in the field of imaginative literature. The problem, of course, has been recognized by thinkers of the state whose vision and thought, transcending the mere economic and social, have taken into consideration those intangible elements of the inner life of a people whose outward manifestations are readily recognized by many who do not grasp their deeper significance. One able recognition of this problem might be mentioned in passing: The baccalaureate sermon preached by President John M. Thomas of Middlebury College, June 15, 1913—*The Idealization of the Near—a Plea for the Small Town of Vermont.*[1]

A further difficulty arose from the fact that no technique of investigation and study, already developed by investigators of similar problems elsewhere, was at hand, nor could any be discovered, probably because no such studies seem to have been made. Able discussions of a limited

[1] Middlebury College Bulletin, Vol. VII, No. 6. July, 1913.

type, however, were found useful, particularly a chapter, "The Town's Possibilities: Ideals," in Douglass' *"The Little Town—Especially in Its Rural Relationships."*[2] Since the inception of this study, however, by the committee, evidences of a growing realization in the country of the value and necessity of preserving and fostering regional literature and culture have become increasingly apparent.

Early in the process of analyzing the general problem and later in the endeavor to synthesize findings of many variant types, it became clear that the traditions and ideals which had formed from the past into the present a unifying principle in Vermont life had been most advantageously preserved and emphasized in: (1) The lives of notable Vermonters whose records of achievement in the state and outside were proof of the existence of those very elements of individualism, self-sufficiency, independence, courage, integrity, loyalty, and faith in the value of "doing little tasks in the light of great principles" to which we were seeking to give a definite meaning. (2) Further, it became apparent that in historical documents, written by men closely in touch with vital events in the state's past, who were many times a part of the event they chronicled, in letters and journals by the lowly and the great, in orations and addresses by native sons gifted with eloquence who had spoken of and for Vermont, in essays and sketches by competent observers of Vermont scenes, incidents, people, other valuable material was present that would serve the committee's purpose. (3) In addition, it was discovered that in Vermont villages, and in rural sections particularly, ballad and folk-song material of a rich type, unknown even to professional students and investigators of ballad lore, had been preserved—in some cases through generations in one family. This material with its folk flavor, its close relation to those phases of Vermont life associated intimately with work and play, with the inner relationships of everyday life, was particularly valuable. In another sense it revealed significant values in its indication of connections dating back to English ballads of ancient lineage. (4) Finally, still another aspect of a distinct type emerged in the effort to reach at the idealistic elements in the problem; and the poetry of the state—surprisingly rich even in early periods—yielded the values sought, for it is in poetry that some of the most intangible and precious aspirations and faiths of a people are found most adequately expressed—in dreams

[2] Douglass, Harlan Paul. "The Little Town." The Macmillan Co., New York, 1921.

they have dreamed, scenes they have loved, causes for which they have died, beliefs they have maintained when all else had failed.

The general conceptions, as outlined, were reduced to four specific projects, and members of the committee were assigned to each project. Fortunately, the committee was able to make use of the results of research begun years ago by certain members of the committee who unselfishly in true Vermont traditional fashion, turned over to the committee material that would have been costly if purchased on a fee basis. Fortunately also, the personnel of the committee included members competent to edit such material. As a result of the cooperation thus made possible, four books were prepared, based on extended research and careful editing; and, as a whole, it is believed that they serve to give a "habitation and a name," within reasonable limits, to the traditions and ideals that have motivated Vermont life for over a century.

The series of books include a book of biographies, a miscellany of prose, a compilation of folk-songs and ballads with tunes, and an anthology of verse. The first, under the title *Vermonters: a Book of Biographies,* was prepared under the editorship of Mr. Walter H. Crockett, whose familiarity with the past history of the state and knowledge of men and events of the present qualified him for a difficult assignment. A list, carefully compiled, of Vermonters whose lives revealed special achievement in diverse activities was approved by the committee; and the sketches were written by scholars, students, and critics, known to be conversant with sources of material concerning the subjects assigned them. In addition to serving specific ends the committee had in mind, it was felt that the book would meet a definite need for a popular, compact history of the lives of eminent Vermonters. The volume of prose, under the title of *Vermont Prose: A Miscellany,* was prepared under the editorship of the chairman and Harold G. Rugg, associate librarian of Dartmouth College. In this volume, the effort was made to gather, so far as was humanly possible, memorable prose, drawn from many sources, that reflected significant and pertinent phases of Vermont life, character, and feeling. The compilation of folk-songs and ballads, under the title *Vermont Folk-Songs and Ballads,* was prepared by Mrs. Helen Hartness Flanders and Mr. George Brown. The book is the result of devoted labor by Mrs. Flanders in an unexplored country where she was forced to do pioneer work against many obstacles of a difficult type. The tunes were gathered by Mr. Brown; and the story of Mrs. Flanders' search for ballads and Mr.

Brown's adventuring for tunes is a fascinating human phase of the work of the committee which cannot be told here. The preparation of the anthology under the title *Vermont Verse: an Anthology* was entrusted to Mr. Walter J. Coates, editor of *Driftwind,* and Professor Frederick Tupper. Mr. Coates had already completed an exhaustive study of Vermont verse with the intention of publishing a definitive volume of Vermont poetry; and his willing sacrifice of much of his material for the committee's book was again in keeping with the traditional Vermont attitude of self-sacrifice for the good of a state interest.

If these books with their distinct Vermont presentation of Vermont traditions and ideals are to serve their purpose, they should be widely distributed in the state. What the extent of this distribution will be is, however, problematical. The close relation between the material in the books and certain vital aspects of rural Vermont life is evident to any one who can recognize traditional values of even a simple type; and the committee hopes that the books may be made available for all rural schools, granges, clubs, libraries and homes generally. That the books will be of value to the libraries of the state may be assumed, for there are no books extant that parallel these in material. Their use in schools may be expected as they will be of distinct service to superintendents, principals, and teachers who believe in teaching Vermont boys and girls something of Vermont history, literature, and biography. They will be purchased to some extent, without doubt, for the home libraries of Vermonters with a personal interest in the subjects of the books. Distribution beyond these classifications will be sought by publicity and so far as funds permit by advertising. The limitation, however, to distribution by such means is definite. The books must prove their value first; thereafter, granting that they do, it is hoped that Vermonters generally will be glad to aid in furthering by every means possible a wide use of the books. At this point, it should be made clear, perhaps, that except for payments made to secure competent technical assistance and to insure the editors against financial loss, no editors have been remunerated for the exacting labor and sacrifice of time and energy that have gone into the books. The preparation of the volumes represents an altruistic enterprise of an unusual type. Done as a commercial project, the cost would have been prohibitive. Finally, credit for the actual publication of the books must go to a group of loyal Vermonters who advanced the funds necessary to meet the cost of manufacture.

At the same time that the project having to do with the publication of the *Green Mountain Series* was being studied and, finally, adopted, Miss Sarah N. Cleghorn of Manchester, Vt., was entrusted with the writing of a pageant that would reflect in imaginative form the essential scope of the entire work of the Commission in so far as it related to the future of the state. This pageant, entitled "Coming Vermont," was presented at the June conference of the Commission in Burlington.

A second phase of the committee's work has had to do with the problem of finding other ways and means of carrying out in the future the general design outlined earlier. While the attention of the committee has been concentrated on the specific project now accomplished, preliminary studies have been made of other possible lines of investigation. Some of these are listed below for brief discussion. No attempt is made to classify the projects, but the intention is to suggest the possible angles from which work can be done. Some of the projects may suggest a slight encroachment into the fields of study already occupied, but in any case where such invasion occurs, it will be undertaken only with the full approval and willing cooperation of the organization involved.

The Preservation of a Characteristic Vermont Architecture

Such a project will seem new and novel to those who have not pondered this particular phase of Vermont life. The town hall, the church, the houses of the hamlet and the village, the homesteads of the farms—all have distinct characteristics, such as are not found, as a rule, in larger centers. These characteristics, indicating an adaptation to home and community uses, are vital and important features of Vermont's individualism and should be preserved. Architecture has a definite bearing on the life of a people; moreover, it has significance for others. When visitors come to Vermont from the Middle West, or for that matter from any section of the country other than New England, they cherish the idea of a Vermont in which there are old-time meeting houses with steeples, colonial houses, painted white with green blinds, and other characteristic features associated with New England villages and farms. It is good business and a patriotic duty to preserve a distinctive New England type. We ought to preach this doctrine extensively. It is entirely compatible with the idea of modern progress to preserve all that is good in the early Vermont or New England Period.

The Function and Value of Music

Community music has immense social power. "It harmonizes men as well as voices. Men work together better for singing together. Nothing more inevitably tends to carry over incidental neighborhood into conscious brotherhood. It is the art which most directly realizes unity through harmonious cooperation."[3]

The day of the singing school and the rural music festival may have passed, but any student of the general subject knows that music has a valuable place in rural and community life. Unquestionably, in Vermont an opportunity exists for revivifying and fostering that latent interest and love of music still to be found in rural communities. The value of music as a cultural agent in the lives of men is beyond question. As a means to the end suggested, one member of the committee favors a project looking forward to the creation of the office of a state supervisor of music whose field of work would be the public schools. This supervision would apply particularly to the rural schools. Nine of the states have found such a system to be successful.

Art in the Rural Community

Some fragmentary love of beauty is evident to the trained and seeking eye in every rural group, hamlet, or village of Vermont, more in some, less in others. Vermont villages and homesteads where men and women dwell who have inherited from their forefathers a sense of civic beauty, a liking for gardens, for fitness of surroundings and settings, are beautiful as more than one visiting artist has attested again and again. The energizing of this innate love of beauty, the offering of practical plans and assistance, the encouragement of the isolated believer in the value of beauty to the individual and the community—all should be attempted after wise and patient study of the problem. In addition, here and there, in the rural districts, the committee has discovered individuals, struggling alone as a rule, to paint or draw some of the beauty about them in their Vermont environment. That means should be found to aid them goes without saying. Only the ignorant or the obtuse would declare that such individuals are few and far between. Vermont is one of the most beautiful states in the Union, yet it has developed few artists; and the reasons why cannot be found in any popular explanation.

[3] Douglass, H. P. "The Little Town," p. 178.

Further Study of Folk-Song and Ballad Material

Funds should be made available for the continuation of the search for folk-songs and ballads so successfully begun by Mrs. Flanders. The value of her work has been made abundantly evident in the introduction and content of *Vermont Folk-Songs and Ballads*. Mrs. Flanders will gladly give her best energies to collecting and editing such material and making it available for the usual singer, historian and literary scholar.

The value of her work has been recognized by well-known and influential organizations interested in the study and collection of ballad and folk-song material; she is now the Vermont representative of the United States Section of the International Commission on Folk Arts and is vice-president of the Folk-Song Society of the Northeast.

The Collection and Preservation of Historical Material

There is no question that valuable historical material exists uncollected and unclassified in various sections of the state. Members of the committee have crossed the trail of correspondence, journals, and other materials reposing in attics and trunks. Town and village records and documents, dating back to early days, are often carelessly filed and stored. A determined search for all such material should be made, and, where found, arrangements should be agreed upon for transferring the originals to the Vermont Historical Society, or permission to make copies should be secured. Any project of this type should be undertaken under the supervision of the Vermont Historical Society. It should be carried out and without undue delay.

Interest in Drama

The success of the Vermont State Grange Dramatic Contest under the able leadership of Mr. Guy B. Horton, lecturer of the Vermont State Grange, is an index to the fact, startling to some myopic Vermonters, that among our rural people there is a wide range of dramatic ability and interest. Fortunately, the Agricultural Extension Service of the University of Vermont has found it possible to include dramatic contests as a part of its recreational program. Not only adult rural groups are eligible to these extension contests, but in the present year the system of contests has been extended to include the 4-H club groups. The interest taken in the contests mentioned and the success of scattered local community dramatic clubs suggest the possibility of organizing a state federation of amateur players' groups somewhat on the lines of the Federated Community Players' Clubs which have been an effective force in Maine in creating common interests and understanding between the smaller communities in the state. The benefits of a community interest in drama are far-reaching and important in their reactions on community and individual life. Social, cultural, and æsthetic forces are released that make for a finer community feeling and interest; and any system that brings separate communities or rural sections together in the developing and witnessing of home talent plays serves not only ends worth while in themselves but ends that yield lasting results of a favorable type in many other relations and activities. A sense of the dramatic and an interest in drama are traditional in Vermont rural communities, as any student of the subject knows, and ready support should be given those leading the movement.

The Preservation and Enrichment of Vermont Village Life

At one time, the villages of Vermont were among its chief glories. Such factors as the shifting of population to larger centers, and, worse still, attempts to imitate the cities or large towns, have been destructive forces. The village and small town have their place in the sun, their own individual and characteristic life; and it may not be an egregious error to vision the day when Vermont villages once more will come to their own and develop an existence highly distinctive and thoroughly enviable.

The Teaching of Vermont History, Literature, and Biography

Without in any sense extolling the virtues of Vermont above those of any other state or section of the country, it is possible to give Vermont boys and girls an understanding of the forces and influences that have created the state. This may be done, not only through the study of Vermont history, but through poem and essay that speak of ideals and faiths, through fiction that pictures character, scene, and incident with a Vermont background, through biography that tells the story of Vermont lives richly, fully, and splendidly lived, some afar, some within Vermont's own hills and valleys. Such lines of study, even if only a

minor element in a school curriculum, bring benefits that seem obvious
and beyond contradiction—the kind of results needed if Vermont is to
maintain its individuality against forces threatening the life of the state,
largely destructive of individualism, and, in many instances, heralding
false gods.

Creating Local Centers for Preserving Relics and Records of Community History

In deepening and enriching the background of local life, in fostering
a sense of traditional heritage—and traditions cannot be bought or
hired—the existence of a group in a community interested in gathering
relics, records, implements, tales, legends, of the locality, is most valuable—particularly if a room or building is available for the storing of
material of this kind. Beginnings have been made in a number of
Vermont communities to attain such ends, but the movement should be
widespread and more effectively organized. As the earlier days recede,
they carry into oblivion memories and records that can never be re-
covered in a later day, no matter how great may be the interest of a
later generation.

Residents and Visitors Appreciative of Vermont

It is apparent that the state offers a pleasant environment for
authors, artists, college teachers, and others in the same general classification; and the reasons lie largely in those phases of Vermont's traditional and idealistic aspects to which reference has already been made.
It would be fortunate for the state and its people if more and more
men and women of this desirable type sought Vermont for summer or
permanent homes. They are far more valuable to Vermont as summer
residents or as habitual dwellers in the state than other classes that
might be mentioned. Two comparatively large colonies have been established, but there still is room for many others. The state will do
well to provide every opportunity for the writer, the artist, and teacher
to find in lovely valley and peaceful hamlet the type of home he prefers.
The testimony of resident writers, artists, and others of the same group
makes it clear that they find the Vermonter in the rural community
and the village congenial.

Preparation of Bibliographies of Literary and Historical Materials

As time goes on and memories fade and data go unrecorded, it is growing more and more imperative that bibliographies of materials available for literary and historical study be prepared. This is a special area of study primarily of interest to scholars and students, but its importance should not be overlooked if any adequate conception of the state's inner life is to be created. The results of such study will outlast many lines of work that seem at present more important and more permanent.

Publication of Special Books

Books of a special type, intimate and personal treatments of Vermont themes that do not lend themselves to successful commercialization, should be aided toward publication. Such books are often written in an altruistic spirit, often with the devotion of years of sincere labor, with affection for the subject studied; and while never widely popular, they usually have long life and are treasured and used by gifted minds whose influence widens out in community and state thought in subtle ways not easily charted but always evident to the discerning. Such books, fortunately finding publication, often preserve traditional aspects of state life that otherwise would perish.

Conservation of the Beauty of the State

Various agencies in the state are doing excellent work in impressing upon the Vermont consciousness the necessity of protecting and emphasizing the beauty which is one of the major assets of Vermont. The entire problem of achieving wide and permanent results seems to need careful analysis and restatement, and then concerted action by all organizations in state and community, looking forward to the creation of a definite and authoritative policy. As has been suggested already in nearly every community there are groups who are aware of the part that beauty plays in the life of individual and community; village improvement societies and special committees of various clubs already exist, and they, with other like organizations, welded together with a clear philosophy to teach, a sound policy on which to act, could maintain an unbroken front against the forces which more and more will be destructive of Vermont's peace and beauty unless held at bay.

An Exhaustive Study of Vermont Poets and Vermont Poetry

This work which has been undertaken by Walter John Coates, editor of *Driftwind,* has involved persistent and careful investigation in a field never before cultivated to any extent. It aims at a reconstruction of those factors—many of them long since forgotten or unknown by contemporary Vermonters—that have built up bit by bit, segment by segment, a body of poetical literature in connection with our state and its history. The study has demonstrated that our Green Mountain folk, while developing a distinct culture along other lines, have also developed a poetical technique and idealism of their own.

For over six years Mr. Coates has devoted himself persistently and intensively to a study of this particular field of native expression— the achievements of our home folk in poetical literature. The result is an immense mass of manuscripts, including poems, biographies, and bibliographical data, which he has collected, collated, and organized for future use and which it is hoped some day may be published for the benefit of all who may wish to know more about the achievements of the state in this particular field. *Poetic Vermont* is a general title under which may be included the threefold results of this work: First, an *Anthology,* or representative collection of Green Mountain poetry from colonial times to our own day; second, a *Biographical Gazetteer,* consisting of detailed sketches of those Vermonters who have achieved worthily in verse; third, and still more important from the standpoint of scholars and research workers, a *Bibliography*—the most complete ever yet attempted, in fact, the *only* one yet attempted— listing the titles and descriptions of books, pamphlets and broadsides in verse that have been published from time to time by Vermont poets. That this particular form of Vermont literature is extensive and variegated may be adduced from the fact that Mr. Coates has already listed about one thousand Vermonters who have produced printed verse of consequence, half of whom, or thereabouts, have published such verse in the three forms above cited. The remaining five hundred or more are classified as newspaper or magazine poets. The field is a large one, with a wealth of material in it, and offers great possibilities both to the student and to the reader who is looking for cultural values.

Publication of Historical Readers and Source Books

The Legislature of New Jersey appropriated $40,000 to cover the expense of preparing and publishing a complete, fully documented history of the state. Such a project, no matter how it appears to the casual eye, has sound reasons for its establishment, and the same tendency is seen in other states to support with ample funds the work of its historians. A single Vermont historical reader and source book, authoritatively edited, would serve to bring the past vividly before the eyes of teachers and students and would supplement effectively the general histories used to some extent in the state.

Turning aside from a review of a series of projects which have their focus in the inner rather than the outer life of a people, one faces the challenge of the possibility, inherent in all, of defeat—the question of ever combating successfully the ceaseless change that in many of its aspects in this day and generation seems to be destroying so much of the life of the state that is traditional and idealistic. One of the problems lies in the very nature of the work to be done. Home, one of our Vermont poets has suggested, was never really *home* to the pioneer woman until she had her flower garden by the homestead door. Surely, one could not easily chart by any known technique the value of such flower gardens through the years to Vermont and Vermont people, yet only the thoughtless would argue that such gardens have had and do have no real value in creating something fine, even if intangible, in the lives of those touched by the gardens. Vermont was never a homeland, one of our essayists suggests, until on some pine-topped knoll or in some lot by road or lane, the pioneer laid his loved ones in their last sleep. This deep attachment, powerful as it is, escapes the analyst who would reduce it to a working formula and list it side by side with the findings of economic research. The values are there, nevertheless, and the problem.

Interesting and suggestive as a statement of the whole question are the words of the late Senator Frank L. Greene:[4]

You and I as toilers in the treadmill of publicity, used to the drab and shabby and seamy side of human nature as well as to the brilliant spectacle now and then, know full well how far short of its ideals our race and its civilization fall. Sometimes, I have no doubt you feel as I do, that perhaps the present-day generation is not quite as keenly alive to the sentimental influence of the old traditions about some things

[4] Written to E. E. Whiting of the *Springfield* (Mass.) *Republican*.

as its fathers and mothers used to be, and that, too, making all allowance for the customary distrust of the rising generation in every period that is so characteristic of men in a generation that is no longer "rising."

Sometimes, we are moved to wonder whether our people are actually losing something of their ancient attachment to institutional life and forms and rituals (I mean the healthy part of them that makes for steadfastness and loyalty to something definite and worthy) and are drifting carelessly and flippantly along with the current, and nothing more. Sometimes we are moved to wonder whether the ancient Green Mountain Boys' tradition and all that it meant to their day and down to the present time is in this period a living, inspiring influence in the minds of most men and women we meet on the streets.

Mr. Whiting adds this comment:

There was Frank Greene, a man we like to remember; of New England's best. We quote his letter also, for another reason: Because one sees in it, within the devotion to New England idealism, the constant love of Vermont—"the ancient Green Mountain Boys' tradition and all that it meant in their day and down to the present time." He feels that could that great, stout, clean tradition guide or influence us, our world would be the better for it.

The challenge with all its implications seems evident, but the answer does not rest on one issue alone; if it did, defeat might be certain. The effort to recreate, to vivify, to clarify, and then to conserve by means of such projects as have been outlined and others not mentioned the traditions and ideals of the state must be only a part in a program that gathers strength from every fibre of its texture. Such a program, the present writer assumes, should emerge from the work of the committees under the Vermont Commission; and the program involves, in the last analysis, the question of leadership. To quote from the baccalaureate sermon, already mentioned, by President Thomas:

It is not beyond reason to hope that the tide of population may be turned back again to the fields, that the old towns of the State, which have been losing ground for half a century, may regain their prestige, and that the State as a whole, instead of being saved from actual loss only by the commercial centers and the quarrying towns, may take her place again as one of the most healthfully vigorous and progressive of the American nation. The task is not more difficult than that which confronted the first leaders of Vermont, when a State on either side of us lusted for our territory, when a dallying Congress parried over our claims, when the army of England hung on our northern border— that glorious day of the independent republic of Vermont.

"When thy young flag was suddenly unfurled,
And thy lone eagle left his stormy nest,
Soaring above grim Mansfield's darkening crest,
And screamed defiance to the whole armed world."

The old stock is here still, in greater proportion to the total population than in any other commonwealth of the north. The old spirit is by no means dead. All we need is organization, the power and habit of working together for a fixed and determined purpose. And all we need for organization is leadership—leaders who see the goal plain, and who will consecrate themselves to its attaining in high patriotic devotion.

———

Prepared for the Commission by its Committee on Vermont Traditions and Ideals.

ARTHUR W. PEACH,
Chairman,
SARAH CLEGHORN,
WALTER J. COATES,
WALTER H. CROCKETT,
ZEPHINE HUMPHREY FAHNESTOCK,
DOROTHY CANFIELD FISHER,
HELEN HARTNESS FLANDERS,
BERTHA OPPENHEIM,
J. D. SHANNON,
MARY SPARGO,
FREDERICK TUPPER.